Literatures and Cultures of the Islamic World

Series Editor
Hamid Dabashi
Columbia University
New York, NY, USA

The LITERATURES AND CULTURES OF THE ISLAMIC WORLD series will put forward a critical body of first rate scholarship on the literary and cultural production of the Islamic world from the vantage point of contemporary theoretical and hermeneutic perspectives, effectively bringing the study of Islamic literatures and cultures to the wider attention of scholars and students of world literatures and cultures without the prejudices and drawbacks of outmoded perspectives.

Kamran Talattof

Nezami Ganjavi and Classical Persian Literature

Demystifying the Mystic

Kamran Talattof
School of Middle Eastern & North Africa
Studies and Founding Chair of
the Roshan Graduate Interdisciplinary
Program in Persian and Iranian Studies
University of Arizona
Tucson, AZ, USA

ISSN 2945-705X   ISSN 2945-7068   (electronic)
Literatures and Cultures of the Islamic World
ISBN 978-3-030-97989-8   ISBN 978-3-030-97990-4   (eBook)
https://doi.org/10.1007/978-3-030-97990-4

Cover illustration: Jean-Philippe Tournut / Getty Images

This Palgrave Macmillan imprint is published by the registered company Springer Nature Switzerland AG.
The registered company address is: Gewerbestrasse 11, 6330 Cham, Switzerland

In praise of reason

PREFACE

Research and publication on the influential Nezami Ganjavi (1140–1202) and his enduring five books of narrative poetry, collectively known as *Panj Ganj* (Five Treasures) or *Khamseh* (Quintet), have grown in the last four decades. However, an overwhelming majority of these works, if not all, interpret Nezami's poetry as the product or advocacy of Islamic mysticism or Islam and pay little attention to his literary techniques and his profound and complex perception of poetry, rhetoric, and eloquence. In this book, I offer five explications and arguments about Nezami's poetry, often in comparison with the works of other major poets to clarify the nature of his artistic approach to poetry:

1. Nezami's understanding of rhetoric as Sakhon.
2. The constitutive role of genre in Nezami's narrative.
3. Diversity of themes in his *Five Treasures*.
4. Sources of Nezami's inspiration, information, and creativity.
5. Nezami's literary techniques in creating what I conceptualize as Nezamian pictorial allegory.

Through these theorizations and comparative analyses, I design a structuralist and allegorical reading of Nezami's poetry to challenge the dominant and grossly reductive mystic, religious reading of the poet's work. This literary reading of Nezami's poetry will cast serious doubt on the poet's alleged mystic or religious advocacy.

Why is it important to challenge the notion that Nezami advocated Sufism or Islamic faith? As a reader, you might have experienced the difficulty of rendering Nezami's verses in another language or even into fluent Persian prose. On such occasions, many of us try to benefit from the valuable and arduous work of the commentators who have edited Nezami's poetry or the numerous scholars who tried to facilitate reading. At that moment we might take the easy road and explain the difficulty in terms of mystic secrets or try to realize the unique inventive mind of the poet. It is the latter alternative that brings us closer not only to the poet's meaning, but also to a state in which we can appreciate the poet's remarkable and profound rhetoric and technique.

Thus, the book begins with one of its primary arguments. What connects Nezami's thematically various poems is his passion for words, literary creativity, and polymathic fluency with the art of rhetoric or Sakhon, which he enriches with themes and subjects such as love, religion, science, wine, philosophy, which are all rendered in an exclusive style and with intricate technique. The book studies these issues in the context of genre and discourse by contrasting the works of Nezami to the pertinent poetry of several masters of Persian poetry such as Ferdowsi, Jami, Rudaki, and others.

Furthermore, this book's conceptualization of Nezami's notion of Sakhon and the *Nezamian pictorial allegory* will help to prove that his main concern was to weave poetry and not promote religiosity. In his poetry, he renders space and cosmic constellations, but it does not mean he was an astronomer; he writes on philosophy, but it does not mean he was a philosopher; he ponders justice, but it does not mean he was a scholar of law; he incorporates veganism in his romance, but it does not mean he was a vegan; he speaks of music, but it does not mean he was a musician. He regularly mentions gems such as ruby, emerald, diamond, garnet, and pearl as physical objects, adjectives, or metaphors, and that does not make him a gemologist either. When Nezami refers to and uses religious and mystic concepts, it does not mean he was a religious zealot or Sufi activist. An analysis of his poetry reveals that he was familiar with many subjects and sciences. Still, he used such materials as themes rather than including them in his verse to market any ideology. It means he was a remarkably knowledgeable and creative poet. The book will illustrate Nezami's use of his historical and conceptual knowledge paradigmatically and of his language and literary skills syntagmatically in his allegories. Any poet with any worldview would have done the same to write such allegories.

He evokes and refers to Koranic verses, but he refers to Greek philosophy and Christianity, and like Ferdowsi, he also reflects on and refers as well to Zoroastrian concepts and ethics, particularly those expressed in the book of *Minuye Kherad*, written in Pahlavi (Middle Persian), directly or indirectly.[1] In it, a character named Dana (the Sage) poses 62 questions, and another character named *Minuye Khered* (the Spirit of Reason or Heavenly Wisdom) answers them.[2] By apprehending Nezami's frequent praise of *kherad* (reason) we might be able to rethink the modern convention that the medieval mindset understood that human reason alone could not imagine a redemption. Many of these poets' characters escape their predicaments independently without the intervention of the divine or a Sufi wise man. This mindset changed for many poets much later and only within Sufi discourse, and we cannot implicate Nezami in what came after him.

To substantiate these arguments and understanding and those more peculiar to individual chapters, I have provided textual, philosophical, and historical analysis of texts and genres. In doing so, I have relied on a several editions of *Panj Ganj*. When I first began focusing on Nezami, Hasan Vahid Dastgerdi's edition was considered the most authoritative version. I also believed that considering philology was more important and useful than ideology in an editorial rendition of Nezami's poetry. As such, I found Dastgerdi's editorial methodology closer to my approach, notwithstanding its numerous errors. Using several manuscripts, including an old copy dated as far back as 718/1318, Vahid Dastgerdi produced a critical edition of 3657 lines, omitting 1007 couplets or interpolations by Nezami and others after him. Later, in addition to that of Dastgerdi and the Moscow edition, more accurate editions of *Panj Ganj* by Behruz Sarvatian and Barat Zanjani (partially) became available (with more than 4500 lines). I occasionally consulted and benefited from them as I did from the digital versions that came about much later.

The English prose and poetic of translations Nezami's poetry include G. E. Wilson's *The Haft Paykar*—The Seven Beauties; James Atkinson's *Laili and Majnun*; and Reynold A. Nicholson's rendition of some stories.[3] I have provided a literal translation of some verses because my main concern is to be as close to the original meaning as possible. In addition, I have benefited from Seven Beauties by Julie Scott Meisami and *Layli and Majnun* by Dick Davis.[4]

The transliteration of Persian words and names is mainly based on how they sound in the Persian language close to a modified *Iranian Studies* system.[5]

I am thankful to Asghar Seyed Gohrab for commenting on an early version of the manuscript. I am also grateful to the admirers of Nezami's work in India, Iran, and the Republic of Azerbaijan, who invited me to talk about Nezami. Small parts of this book are based on those speeches as well as previously published materials.

NOTES

1. Some believe that a few books of *kherad* (which survived Alexander's burning) were translated into Greek, and some were retranslated from Greek to Arabic, as stated by Ibn Nadim who quotes Abu Sahl Nobakhti on this matter. However, he also uses materials from Greek philosophical meanings in many of its 2260 verses.

2. *Minu-ye Kharad*, translate from Pahlavi/Middle Persian to Persian by Ahmad Tafazoli (Tehran: Bonyad-e Farhang, 1975). The title is often translated into English as The Spirit of Wisdom, but I will discuss later this rendition might not be precise. As explained in The *Encyclopædia Iranica*, the book is "a Zoroastrian Pahlavi book, in which a symbolic character called Danag ('knowing, wise') poses questions to the personified Spirit of Wisdom (Menog i xrad), who is extolled in the preamble and identified in two places (2.95, 57.4) with innate wisdom (asn xrad)." Tafazzoli, *Encyclopædia Iranica*, Vol. VI, Fasc. 5, pp. 554–555.

3. See G. E. Wilson's translation of *The Haft Paykar* (The Seven Beauties), (London: Late Probsthain and Company, 1924) and Nizami Ganjavi, *Laili and Majnun*: A Poem translated by James Atkinson (Allahabad: Panini, 1915).

4. Nizami Ganjavi, *The Haft Paykar: A Medieval Persian Romance*, translated by Julie Scott Meisami (Oxford: Oxford UP, 1995). Also see, *Layli and Majnun* by Nezami Ganjavi, Dick Davis, trans. (Odenton, MD: Mage Publishers, 2020).

5. Transliterated words and titles are based on how they sound, except for quoted texts and titles. And here are the exceptions to the *Iranian Studies* transliteration scheme.

| آ and ا | a |
| ع and ء | ٰ |

CONTENTS

CHAPTER 1

Nezami Ganjavi and Classical Persian Literature

Nezami (Nizami) Ganjavi (533/1139–599/1203), one of the greatest Persian poets and thinkers, lived in the city of Ganja in a region, which until 1918 was called Arran and Shirvan and is now located in the Republic of Azerbaijan.[1] Ganja and Shirvan (about 145 miles apart) in the twelfth century played a somewhat similar role in the Persian literary productivity to Samarqand and Bukhara (159 miles from each other) on the eastern side of the Caspian Sea played in the ninth century.[2] Based on Nezami's poetry and the writings in a few Tazkereh books, his mother was Kurdish and his father was possibly from Qom.[3] He was a prolific poet who wrote five masterful books of narrative poetry (masnavi epics in rhymed couplets). The five long poems in his five books, known collectively as the *Khamsa* (Quintet) or *Panj Ganj* (Five Treasures), composed by Nezami in the late twelfth century, set new standards in his time for elegance of expression, sophisticated characterization, and richness of narrative. They were widely imitated for centuries by poets writing in Persian and languages influenced by Persians, such as Urdu and Ottoman Turkish.[4] No detailed estimate has ever been made of the Persian, Turkish, Pashto, Kurdish, and Urdu (and other languages of the Persianate tradition) who emulated Nezami's example. Still, by all indications, the figure certainly exceeds 60. The extraordinary dissemination of Nezami's Five Treasures throughout Persianate literature is a remarkable and largely unexplored

© The Author(s), under exclusive license to Springer Nature
Switzerland AG 2022
K. Talattof, *Nezami Ganjavi and Classical Persian Literature*,
Literatures and Cultures of the Islamic World,
https://doi.org/10.1007/978-3-030-97990-4_1

phenomenon. Even though the poets who were inspired by him wrote on similar themes and versified identical stories and sometimes even surpassed him in terms of quantity, none could achieve the poetic beauty or the thoughtfulness with which Nezami wrote. Based on this widespread popularity, one might think of the Five Treasures as a bonding literary string throughout the four corners of the Persianate world and beyond.

The reasons for Nezami's unique place in Persian poetry are related to his deep and broad knowledge, the diversity of his subjects and themes, his humanistic approach to life, and his systematic understanding of literature.

His first book, *Makhzan al-Asrar* (*The Treasure House of Mysteries*, 1163) contains passages and tales on ethics, morality, philosophy, and religion expressed in more than 2200 couplets. To understand many of its complex and extraordinary verses, which readers might interpret in diverse ways, one needs to concentrate deeply and sometimes consult other sources, but most importantly to know his approach to poetry.

In 1180, Nezami wrote the eloquent, thoughtful composition of his first romantic epic, *Khosrow o Shirin* (*Khosrow and Shirin*), which features the romance between the Sasanian king Khosrow II (590–628) and his lover Shirin, focusing on the romantic and behavioral aspects of the relationship and numerous related stories such as Farhad's love for Shirin. Ferdowsi fully versified this epic in his *Book of Kings* and Nezami wrote his own version in 6500 verses about two centuries later. It features more pre-Islamic Iranian cultural and personal characteristics than his first work mostly because the story is specifically about a Sasanian king.

He composed his profound, complex, vivid story of Layli and Majnun in September 1188. It became highly popular in the Persianate world and beyond. The story consists of the star-crossed, tragic love between a poet native of the Najd region named Qays (who becomes known as Majnun, which means "crazy.") and Layli. The date of this 4720-verse work is somewhat uncertain, but, according to the poet, he wrote it in four months at the age of 50 and during a sad period of his life, when he had just lost his wife and parents.

Then, in 593/1197, he completed his sophisticated *Haft Paykar* (Seven Beauties), portraying the love affairs of the pleasure-seeking Sasanian prince, Bahram Gur, in seven episodes featuring his encounters with seven princesses of seven regions over seven days in seven palaces, painted in seven distinct colors. This 5136-verse book also features a pre-Islamic Persian king and bases the logic and rationale expressed by many of its characters on a Zoroastrian, Pahlavi mentality. Countless shorter tales adorn the frame story.

Finally, around 1197, he composed his two-volume *Iskandarnameh* (The Book of Alexander). It consists of two separate volumes titled *Sharafnameh* (in 6800 verses) and *Kheradnameh* (in 6800 verses). The book consists of the story of Alexander and his invasions, his transformation, and his search for a utopia. Like the other books, this one is not a historiography and should not be read as such.[5]

The dates of four of his poems have been determined only indirectly from allusions to historical names and events in the manuscripts themselves, and there are significant variations among such details, even in the earliest of these works.[6] Scholars, including Safa, agree with the medieval biographer Dolatshahi who wrote that Nezami had 20,000 other lines of poems in lyric and ode forms constituting a divan of its own; however, only some of them have survived to this time.[7]

Scholars of classical Persian literature are clear regarding the significance of these books. All agree that he was a pioneer in romance writing, narrative poetry, and even in the subgenre of wine poetry (*khamriyat*). No one expresses doubt about the influence he had on the later poets who came after him to the extent that some adopted Nezami's stories and formats to write their work. Some scholars even believe that Nezami is on par with both Abolqasem Ferdowsi (ca. 940–1020), the poet of Iran's heroic tradition, and the author of *Shahnameh* (*Book of Kings*) as the most cherished book in terms of literature and most consequential in terms of culture, and with Jalaluddin Rumi (1207–1273), whose *Divan-e Shams or Divan-e Kabir* (Great Divan) and *Masnavi Ma'navi* (Spiritual Couplets) effectively define the forms of mystical lyric and mystical narrative poetry, respectively.[8] Many also believe that Nezami's narrative poetry is more comprehensive than that of either Ferdowsi or Rumi in that it includes a deep and insightful romantic portrayal of human relations and the heroic. No one can argue against the fact that Nezami brought about a comparable expansion of the language of poetry. He was among the first poets in Iran to combine the lyric style of court poetry, with its rhetorical intricacy and metaphoric density, to narrative form. Moreover, his genius grasp of the language is as much a presence on the narrative stage as are the characters and events it depicts.

However, these pioneering scholars also always tend to draw on Islam or Sufism in the explanation of Nezami's worldview and his poetry, a tendency that is hermeneutically applied to other classical Persian literary texts to explain the alleged Sufi meaning of the text and the ideology of the author. If not mysticism, they see Persian literary works as the product of Islam. Such notions have been dominant in over a hundred years of scholarship on Nezami's work. The scholarly analysis and publications on Nezami have increased in recent decades, but so has the Islamization of his poetry. Every year, new articles and books are published in Iran to ascribe jurisprudence and theology to his poetry.[9] In recent decades, scholars in Europe and the United States have shown more interest in close reading of Nezami's work, which sheds light on the complexity and uniqueness of his work.[10] However, the dominant approach to his poetry remains hermetic. It portrays him as a Sufi thinker, making no distinction between Sufism and spirituality or between religiosity and wisdom while ignoring the rhetorical, semiotics, and performative aspects of the genre. They have not paid close attention to the fact that Nezami uses the word "Sufi" and some of its derivatives negatively in several of his poems.[11] He does not favor them, and he does not mention any Sufi trends.

Most if not all, scholars believe in Nezami's religiosity and piety when they write about him or his poetry. Early on, the pioneer scholar and literary historian E. G. Browne writes, "He [Nezami] was genuinely pious, yet singularly devoid of fanaticism and intolerance…he may justly be described as combining lofty genius and blameless character in a degree unequaled by any other Persian poet."[12] He was not the first. This characterization began with the medieval *Tazkareh* texts. Others followed by exaggerating Nezami's piety and religiosity and continue to read his poetry in those terms.

I want to point out that a profound intellectual consciousness or rather a jouissance informs his poetry; however, unlike the Sufi or pious poets, his work does not focus on the evocation and articulation of the transcendent dimension of existence or the invocation of religion and Sufism. Neither does he use literary activities as a means of religious affinity.

Thus, challenging the Islamization (Sufi or otherwise) of Nezami is another running theme in this book which provides the textual analysis of what is perceived to be the most religious and mystical verses and stories. Therefore, in the context of the discussions of the literary aspects of Nezami's narratives, this book clarifies that an expression of spirituality is part of the post-literary construct and is not necessarily synonymous with Sufism and Islam.

For Nezami, discourse, or eloquent speech (*Sakhon* as it was pronounced in that era), or more particularly, the poet's colorful and signifying language was his main preoccupation or his raison d'être of the art of poetry. For him, poets have nearly divine status and a highly sacrilegious attitude. He repeatedly draws attention to the aesthetic function of Sakhon and as a source of clear moral or ethical guidance, he compares it to the *Koran*: a bold assertion for his time.[13] In *Makhzan al-Asrar*, he writes, "The first manifestation of existence was speech....Without speech, the world has no voice."[14] That pretty much set the tone and the attitude for *Makhzan al-Asrar* and his forthcoming works, which are all similar in this emphasis on aesthetics. He even developed a literary technique for creating the units of his masterpieces, which I will conceptualize and discuss (in two different chapters). For me, the conceptualization of his allegorical strategy answers the question: What then is Nezami's literary mission, source of creativity, and explanation for his prolific career?

Another reason for the dominant misconceptualization of Nezami's preoccupation is that despite his immense importance, we know little about the events of his life. We do not know to what extent he possessed a "blameless character" and whether it is relevant. As is so often true of Iran's pre-modern poets, there are virtually no contemporary sources about his life, and the occasional biographical notices that appeared in subsequent centuries are all too often pleasant anecdotes. Only his poems contain reliable biographical information for our purpose and analysis.[15] From there, we learn that he was born in AD 1140 in the trans-Caucasian city of Ganja or Ganjeh (Elizavetpol, Kirovabad), a prosperous orthodox (Sunni) Muslim community on the border of Byzantium.[16] He appears to have spent his entire life in the same region and died there approximately 75 years later.[17] He was married and widowed a few times but mentioned in his work only his first wife, Afaq, whose family was Kurdish. He had one son, Mohammed. His father, Yusuf, and mother, Ra'iseh, died while he was still relatively young, but his maternal uncle, Omar, assumed responsibility. As mentioned, it has been surmised that his father migrated to Ganja from the Tafresh area. On the other hand, he displays in his poetry an impressive familiarity with all the branches of learning of his day, which suggests that his family was urban and had sufficient means to provide him with a good education.[18]

Western fascination with his romances and *Panj Ganj* also goes back to the eighteenth century, starting with French, British, and German scholars and translators who translated parts of his work adapted to their poetry or plays or wrote the poet's biography.[19] In the nineteenth century, we have W. Bacher's excellent monograph on Nezami's life and work, previously mentioned, that provided the basis for the articles on Nezami in subsequent European literary histories.[20] Later, the discussion of Nezami's works was mainly confined with the discussion of literary histories.[21] Helmut Ritter, in his excellent monograph published in 1927,[22] broke new ground by focusing on the construction of metaphor in Nezami and attempting to explain how Nezami's treatment of various broad categories, such as nature, man, and man in nature, differs from that of western poets like Goethe, on the one hand, and Arab poets like Ibn Mu'taz and Abu Tamam, on the other. Beyond that, we have a useful monograph on the poet by Bertel, which refines and extends the research of Bacher.[23]

Ritter, in collaboration with Rypka, also prepared the first scholarly edition of Nezami's poems.[24] Soviet Azeri scholars publishing in Baku, and more Persian scholars working in Iran have prepared crucial critical editions of the *Panj Ganj*.[25]

The publication of Julie Meisami's *Medieval Persian Court Poetry* in the late 1980s substantially advanced the interpretive study of Nezami's poetry.[26] The central chapters are devoted to a long and insightful study of *Khusraw and Shirin, Layli and Majnun*, and the *Haft Paykar*. Meisami's study focuses on the moral seriousness of romance and the extraordinary integration of theme and metaphor in Nezami's poetry. Meisami also sees *Layli o Majnun* as an example of the genre (narrative) romance encouraged and flourished in Fakhruddin As'ad Gurgani's *Vis o Ramin* to replace (narrative) epic genre, the remarkable example of which is the *Shahnameh*.[27] In the last two decades, as well, Christoph Bürgel has devoted a sizable portion of his scholarly efforts to Nezami and has published several studies that illuminate important thematic questions.[28] He has also published poetic translations of *Khusraw and Shirin*, the *Iskandarnamah*, and the *Haft Paykar* into German.[29]

More recently, Asghar Gohrab, Christine van Ruembeke, Mathew Hotham, and others have shown creative interest in a close reading of Nezami's work which sheds light on the complexity and uniqueness of his work. They have paid close attention to the text, which might include traces of mysticism which, as I argue, is simply another subject in Nezami's basket of topics. They do acknowledge that such characterization of the poet can be debated.[30] In an excellent edited volume titled *A Key to the Treasure of the Hakīm: Artistic and Humanistic Aspects of Nizami Ganjavi's Khamsa*, editors Christine van Ruymbeke and Johann-Christoph Bürgel have included a considerable number of chapters that cover numerous aspects of Nezami's work. One of the many strengths of the volume is that the editors have open-mindedly incorporated various approaches to Nezami's poetry.[31] Another recent event is the skillful translation of *Layli o Majnun* into English by Dick Davis in the same tradition of the 1915 beautiful rendition by James Atkinson.

In Persian two studies that departed from Iranian scholarship's biographical emphasis on Nezami appeared in the late 1980s: Jalal Sattari's study of *Layli and Majnun* and A. A. Sa'idi-Sirjani's comparison of Layli and Shirin.[32] Sattari's monograph examines the tale of the two unhappy lovers stage by stage as a kind of metatext, moving freely between Arabic materials that preceded Nezami, Nezami's poem, and imitations of his work by subsequent poets, especially those of Amir Khosrow and Maktabi Shirazi. The late Sa'idi-Sirjani, famous for his polemic interpretations of classical literature, read Shirin and Layli against each other as embodiments of the two societies in which their stories are set.

The 850th anniversary of Nezami's birth was marked by several conferences in Iran (Tabriz) and the United States (Washington, DC; Los Angeles). These produced a spate of new scholarship.[33] The Nezami International Center and other institutes in the Republic of Azerbaijan have also organized conferences.

The rise of Islam to state ideology after the Islamic Revolution of 1979 has affected cultural production in Iran, lending new prominence to religious readings of classical literary texts. A considerable number of ideologically inspired by interpreters such as Ja'fari, Muvahhid, Zanjani, Hakimi, Rashid, and Sarvatiyan have since focused on Islamic and Sufi elements in Nezami's stories, subjecting their topological and allegorical levels to reductivism and predictable Islamic exegesis. Ja'fari, for example, states that Nezami does not write to demonstrate his art but to express himself 'at the moment of prayer.' He has dedicated an entire book to topic of prayers, invocations, and benediction in Nezami's work: a book which also mostly covers general writing about those topics.[34] According to Zanjani, Nezami's strength in art lies not in storytelling but in the ability to incorporate moral teachings and advice as a means of strengthening Islamic principles and faith. Rashid insists that Nezami's work has Sufi tenets, as does Sarvatiyan, who states that Nezami thinks of only the world of brotherhood and religious equality.[35] He writes, "The philosopher's treasure [Nezami's book] is a book that begins with 'in the name of God the merciful,' and the readers have to say 'in the name of God' in order to understand the mysterious secrets and to understand its meaning."[36] As mentioned, the pioneering literary historian and scholar, E. G. Browne, as early as he wrote about Nezami, gets close to describing the poet's characteristics, but at the same time, he too attributes to the poet piety, spirituality, religiosity, and abstinence to the extent that he claims Nezami did not even consume wine.[37] His evaluation of Nezami was influential on later literary criticism. Even A. H. Zarkub, with somewhat more secular tendency, concludes in his book on Nezami that the poet is in search of a mystic utopia in his poetry.[38] These readings seem to hinge on the works of medieval biographers Samarqandi (d. 1491), Awfi (d. 1242), Bigdili (d. 1780), and the poet Jami (1414–1492), who were convinced of Nezami's membership in one or another Sufi school but provided no reliable evidence of this.[39] Ever since, every book or article that discusses Nezami attaches the ossified adjectives mystic, Sufi, or pious (or a combination of them) to his name. Nezami's spirituality is present in his writings, and it would be hard to deny traces of Sufi learning. However, such learning was relatively commonplace, and its presence is hardly sufficient to establish his membership in a Sufi brotherhood.

NEZAMI'S SECULARISM

Reductionism in reading Nezami's poetry (and classical Persian poetry in general) is exacerbated when the reader has a foot in religious experience or a fascination for mysticism resulting in the diminution of the role of literary language. While this book does not strive to prove that Nezami was not a Muslim, it seeks to prove that he used Islamic and mystical materials and concepts in his poetry but not necessarily to preach them. Moreover, and generally, we should not assume that all Nezami's verses and fictional figures necessarily reflect his own beliefs. Similarly, his use of religious sources, Koranic verses, and the hadith, mostly by the voice in the prefatory parts of his romances, does not necessarily indicate advocacy of a particular ideology, the same way that his use of the pre-Islamic sources does not make him a Zoroastrian. His clear references to Greek sources such as Plato's *Republic* where he portrays his own utopian city, "Shahr-e Nikan," some versions of which have paradoxically appeared in some Islamic sources as well, does not reflect any profound change in his religious beliefs. As we will see, Islamic materials and pre-Islamic thinking and myths are only some of the numerous concepts, subjects, philosophy, and sciences he uses to construct his allegories and so his long poems. It also seems that earlier in his career and in his *Makhzan al-Asrar* (which consists of shorter stories and anecdotes), he depended more on Islamic sources and then less so in his romances. In western literature, a plethora of poetic texts, some highly secular, employ Biblical references and materials that a wide readership would understand. A reference to holy books simply signaled knowledge of religious (elite) languages in both traditions.

Ignoring those realities even affects the laborious editorial work on Nezami's manuscripts. Pezhman Bakhtiyari, in his editorial work on Nezami's manuscript, eliminates verses that undermine his rather rare interpretation.[40] Furthermore, Sarvatian diligently sifts through many manuscripts of Nezami's work to develop a rendition that suits his religious interpretation. Even Vahid Dastgerdi, who, in his editorial work, is faithful to Nezami's language and logic, is occasionally disappointed when he does not find a corresponding religious verse to explain an otherwise unexplainable complex line. Considering the differences between the older manuscripts, it seems that over the years, perhaps it is possible that the scribes also replaced problematic words with what they thought would be more accessible.[41]

If we assume there was no such a concept as secularism in the medieval or Islam period because the kings and the caliphs, the philosophers and the poets, the judges and clerics all were out there to promote the dictum that "There is no God but Allah, Muhammad is the Messenger of Allah," then it seems natural to read Nezami's poems as manifestation religious observance. However, with all the qualities and knowledge that have been attributed to Nezami by scholars of classical Persian literature, he could have then been as secular (if not laic) as possible in twelfth-century Persia.

Each of the remaining chapters of this book includes evidence for this contention as well. And each chapter provides a comparative analysis of a specific theme.

In Chap. 2, Nezami, the Persian Wordsmith: Sakhon in Classical Persian Poetry, I explain that Nezami works with various themes and motives in his poetry to produce Sakhon (discourse or eloquent speech), which I eventually content to mean literature. Comparing to other poets, I will illustrate how Nezami holds a high opinion of Sakhon, particularly in its poetic forms, and considers poets creative artists with nearly divine status.

Chapter 3, Women and Love in the Works of Nezami, Ferdowsi, and Jami covers the seminal topic of gender and love. To provide a comparative context for the analysis of the characterization of women, I study the works of Nezami Ganjavi (1140–1202), Abul Qasim Ferdowsi (932–1020), and Abd al-Rahman Jami (1414–1492), three major classical Persian poets, in whose work female characters figure prominently, albeit to differing degrees. Specific love stories are familiar to at least two of these authors. Moreover, their stories include familiar characters often based on historical figures. Finally, Nezami was inspired by Ferdowsi significantly and referred to his work, while Jami was inspired by Nezami and referred to him. Perhaps for these reasons, prominent scholars of classical Persian literature, including Meisami, Bürgel, and Moayyad, have compared some of these female characters. However, the existing literature on the topic does not provide reasons for such diverse characterizations but merely offers engaging descriptive analyses.

Chapter 4, Faith, Facts, and Fantasy: Stories of Ascension and Nezamian Allegory discusses Nezami's portrayal of Me'raj or story of ascension in which he speaks of stars, astrology, and horoscope (tale') like in the rest of his poetry with an intense focus. The chapter explains that the iterations of the story alone can disqualify Nezami as a Muslim or at least a pious Muslim poet because Islam technically forbids astrology and horoscope as harmful. However, through comparative literary analysis, the chapter explains the literary reason of his five portrayals. In fact, the relationship between the poets and the court was most of the time complex.

Chapter 5, Wine and Identity in the Works of Nezami and Rudaki covers the literary representation of wine, a dominant theme in Persian poetry giving rise to endless debates about the nature of wine and its metaphorical implications. Nezami, like other poets, renders wine and wine drinking throughout his works, which again could be an indication that he was not a devout Muslim. However, through contextual and historical analyses and drawing on the Bakhtinian concept of chronotope, this chapter argues that his wine is often literal and much needed for storytelling. After all, he is a pioneer in the *Saqinameh* genre, which is a type of poetry about wine and wine drinking. These points become clearer when Nezami's portrayal of wine is compared to a long poem by Rudaki entitled "The Mother of Wine."

Chapter 6, Nezamian Pictorial Allegory in *Layli o Majnun*, focuses on the love story of Layli and Majnun because it includes countless examples of Nezamian pictorial allegory. I further support the arguments about the sophisticated aspect of Nezami's allegorical poetry to show how Nezami's narrative poems include a series of allegorical constructs that together cement the structure of his romances. I have conceptualized it as a Nezamian pictorial allegory because of its unique characteristics as a short, structured, and interconnected passage, often referencing extra-textual images.

Chapter 7, Medieval Masters of Metaphors: In Search of Religion and Dantean Moments in "The Story of Mahan" further challenges the religious reading of Nezami's poetry by responding to a growing trend which strives to find evidence of Nezami's religiosity by comparing him to other religious authors of other literary traditions. The chapter examines more Nezamian allegories with brief references to Dante's *Divine Comedy*.[42] Even though they lived in different eras and distinct cultural settings, Nezami Ganjavi (1141–1209) and Dante Alighieri (1265–1321) share creative imaginations and eloquence. Their literary works have a few thematic similarities, which include their interest in religious symbolism and love poetry, and allegory. However, beyond these surface similarities, the chapter shows these authors' distinct positions in their literary message and allegorical meanings. The comparison sheds light on the nature of Nezami's poetry.

Chapter 8, Sublime Métier, Literary Techniques, and Allegory is the conclusion of the book, clarifying Nezami's overall literary endeavor and his literary techniques. By elucidating Nezami's system of ethics in terms of the situation he sets up in his highly allegorical works, I contend that Nezami's ethics and, indeed, his morality are not derived from any meta-ethical notion. I also explain how and why in his portrayal of characters and concepts, he relies overwhelmingly on allegories (tamsil) that are short, on comparison techniques (tashbih), and metonymy (badi', degargui) and sometimes he redesignates them as well. Finally, I illustrate Nezami's literary mechanization within a textual and discursive analysis of the themes that might deceptively seem to critics as Nezami's source of ethics or religious advocacy. I believe his métier as a Sakhon writer and romancer explains not only his style of creativity but also his ethics.

In a sense, I am raising issues of ontology and teleology, which help connect these various literary constructs in Nezami's vast amount of poetry, to show an enduring problem in interpreting Nezami's work. Most analyses have tried to minimize the effects of ontology (poetry as a creative aesthetic process) and teleology (creativity outcomes as aesthetic elements rather than decided philosophical conclusions), ignoring the relative autonomy and dialectics of Persian classical literary paradigms. Being aware of these issues will help locate and appreciate the preternatural, the symbolic, panegyric, prolix, anthropomorphic, zoomorphic, elliptic, macaronic lexical, and (of all sorts) thematic presentations in Five Treasures. The conceptualization of Nezamian Sakhon and the Nezamian pictorial allegory and identifying his various subjects and themes will hopefully rest the case and increase interest in literary interpretation and a cultural, contextual investigation of his poetry.

NOTES

1. His full name is Jamal al-Din Abu Muḥammad Ilyas Nezami Ganjavi. Some biographers have different dates of his birth and death. Early on, I relied on Nezami Ganjavi, *Kolliyat-e Hakim Nezami Ganjavi*, edited by Vahid Dastgerdi (Tehran: Behzad, 1999), which has since been reprinted in various forms several times without any significant changes except for the location of commentaries and explanations (one version published Amir Kabir in 1987 even eliminated the commentaries). I refer to this book as simply *Kolliayt*. This edition also includes an introduction by Sa'id Qaemi, which offers useful information about Nezami, but also reinforces the perception of Nezami as an isolated, clean language, mystic. I have consulted the editions by Sarvatiyan and Zanjani. Dastgerdi's earlier edition had the commentaries at the end of the page, and in the newer version, the comments are published in a separate volume. Amir Kabir publishers also once printed the same exact book without commentaries.

2. Ganja or Ganjeh was at a crossroad that connected many cities and regions, hosting travelers of all sorts. Nezami's poetry reflects the resulting multiculturalism, tolerance, and open mindedness. In the Saljuqid dynasty, Nezami found patrons for his poetry; however he did not become a regular part of their courts.

3. For the debate over the nationality and the occasional misrepresentation of the native language of Nezami, see Siavash Lornejad and Ali Doostzadeh, *On the Modern Politicization of the Persian Poet Nezami Ganjavi* (Yerevan: Caucasian Centre for Iranian Studies, 2012) and the informed review of the book by Paola Orsatti (2015) "Nationalistic Distortions and Modern Nationalisms," *Iranian Studies*, 48:4, 611–627. Nezami lived when Iranian regions under the Seljuk Empire and other areas between the Mediterranean and Central Asia enjoyed a period of cultural efflorescence.

4. See Jalal Sattari's work in note below, page 18. Meisami examines the impact of Nezami's poetry on the Iranian historian Ravandi. Nezami's work and, his *Layli o Majnun*, have been imitated by numerous (allegedly up to 86) other authors. Radfar has mentioned 31 imitators by name (of these works, ten are published, and 21 are available in manuscript form). Twenty-six have been mentioned in the books of *Tazkareh*. The rest are not in Persian. See Abol Qasem Radfar, *Ketab Shenasi Nezami Ganjavi*

(Tehran: Motale'at va Tahqiqat-e Farhangi, 1992). These do not include countless translations and retellings and rewritings of Nezami's various romances in south Asian dialects.

5. For detailed information see the earlier sources such as A. H. Zarrinkub, Pir-e Ganjeh (Tehran: Sokhan, 2001); Z. Safa, *Tarikh-e Adabiyat dar Iran* (Tehran: Ferdowsi, 1984); and E. G. Browne, *Literary History of Persia* (Cambridge: The UP, 1951–1956).

6. François de Blois, *Persian Literature: A Bio-bibliographical Survey Begun by the Late C. A. Storey*, (London: Royal Asiatic Society, 1994–1997). De Blois includes a bibliography of editions and translations of Nezami's work in his article.

7. Z. Safa, *Tarikh-e Adabiyat dar Iran* (Tehran: Ferdows, 1990).

8. Dabashi studies Nezami alongside Ferdowsi, Sa'di, and Hafez as masters of Persian literature, whose works are part of Persian literary humanism. In terms of romance writing, he compares Nezami with Manouchehri, Onsori, and Asjadi, whose "fragmentation of the authorial subject moves from lyrical and epic into panegyric (chief among its medieval master practitioners Manouchehri, Onsori, and Asjadi) romance (Nezami Ganjavi in particular), and finally comes to a crescendo, in terms of its varied narrative dispositions, in the abundance of the karamat literature dealing with saintly miracles (with Sanai, Attar, Rumi, and Jami as the main beacons)." See, Dabashi, Hamid. *The World of Persian Literary Humanism* (Cambridge: Harvard UP, 2012), 30. He also writes, "Nezami's achievement in *Khamseh* brought the Persian romance tradition to a height comparable to that of Ferdowsi's achievement in epic poetry. In a masterful construction of a dramatic narrative, Nezami, always personally present in his tales, constructs a literary humanism resting on nothing but the dramatic movement of his own power of storytelling," 126. I should add that for Nezami, the concept of Sakhon also conveyed all those traits.

9. In addition to the other names, see, Hadi Khadivar and Fatemeh Sharifi, "Eshterakate *Layli o Majnun*-e Jami va Nezami va Amir Khosrow Dehlavi" in *Majaleh-e Zaban va Adabiyat, Daneshgah-e Azad-e Fasa*, 1, 2, 2010, 37–56.

10. See Christine van Rymebe "Nizami's Poetry Versus Scientific Knowledge: The Case of the Pomegranate"; Asghar Abu Gohrab, "Majnun's Image as a Serpent"; J. Christoph Burgel "Occult Sciences in The Shahnameh"; and others in *The Poetry of Nizami Ganjavi: Knowledge, Love, and Rhetoric*, edited, ed. K. Talattof and J. Clinton (New York: Palgrave Macmillan, 2000).

11. Even in the tale of "Haji and Sufi" from *Makhzan al-Asrar*, the Shaykh, Darvish, and Sufi are all used negatively. *Kolliyat*, 59–60.

12. E. G. Browne, *A Literary History of Persia* (Cambridge, 1964) vol. 2, p. 403.

13. About the importance of this concept in Nezami's work, see Hamid Dabashi, "Harf-e nakhostin: mafhum-e sokhan dar nazd-e hakim Nezami Ganjavi," *Iranshenasi*, volume 3, number 4 (Winter 1992), pp. 723–740.

14. *Kolliyat*, 16.

15. In addition to Dastgerdi, Wilhelm Bacher's *Nezami's Leben und Werke und der zweite Theil des Nezamishcen Alexanderbuches, mit persischen Texten als Anhang* (Leipzig, 1871) provides textual references.

16. The belief that Nezami was born in Taad, a village near Tafresh city, and that his family migrated to Ganjeh when he was a child persists among some scholars, particularly in Iran. The belief is rooted in lines of poetry written about Nezami in a later period. And there is no dispute that Nezami only wrote Persian poetry.

17. In a verse, he expresses a desire to move away from that city. *Kolliyat*, 97.

18. van Ruymbeke illuminates a point on which Nezami gave preference to poetic metaphor over scientific knowledge in her essay in this volume entitled, "Nezami's Poetry versus Scientific Knowledge."

19. See, Amir Azar and Najafi "An Investigation of Nezami's Works Translated in the West," in *European Online Journal of Natural and Social Sciences*, 2015; www.european-science.com, vol.4, no.2 pp. 260–272.

20. Wilhelm Bacher, *Nezami's Leben und Werke und der zweite Theil des Nezamishcen Alexanderbuches, mit persischen Texten als Anhang*, (Leipzig 1871).

21. Principal among the Western literary histories are those of Browne, *A Literary History of Persia*, volume II (London 1906; reprinted Cambridge, 1964), Rypka et al., *History of Iranian Literature* revised and expanded English edition (Holland, 1968), and Yarshater et al., *Persian Literature* (Albany: Bibliotheca Persica, 1988). In Persian, the standard history is that of Zabihollah Safa, *Tarikh-e adabiyat dar Iran* (Tehran 1362/1988).

22. Helmut Ritter, Über *die Bildersprache Nezamis* (Berlin: De Gruyter; Reprint 2013).

23. Bertel's, Evgenii. *Nizami: Tvorcheskii put' poeta* (Nizami: The Creative Path of the Poet). Moscow: Izd-vo Akademii nauk SSR, 1956.

24. *Heft Peyker, ein romatisches Epos*. Ed. H. Ritter und J. Rypka (Prague 1934).

25. For details on editions and translations, see de Blois, *op. cit.*, pp. 448–95.

26. Meisami examines Nezami's works in several essays as well, all published in *Edebiyat: A Journal of Middle Eastern and Comparative Literature*.

27. Julie Scott Meisami, "Kings and Lovers: Ethical Dimensions of Medieval Persian Romance," in *Edebiyat*. 1, 1, 1987, 1–27.

28. For example see, J. Christoph Bürgel, "Nezami" in *Die Grossen der Weltgeschichte* Band III (Zurich 1973); "Nezami über Sprache und Dichtung"; "Die Frau als Person in der Epic Nezamis," *Asiatische Studien* (1988) 42:137–55; "The Romance" *Persian Literature*, ed. E. Yarshater (New York, 1988) 161–78.

29. *Nezami: Chosrou und Schirin* (Zurich, 1980), *Nezami: Das Alexanderbuch* (Zurich, 1991), *Nezami: Die Abenteuer des Königs Bahrām und seiner Sieben Prinzessinenen* (München, 1997). Bürgel's essay, "Nezami über Sprache und Dichtung," (see previous note) also contains verse translations of excerpts from the *Makhzan ol-Asrar*.
30. See the valuable contributions by Christine van Ruymbeke "Nizami's Poetry Versus Scientific Knowledge: The Case of the Pomegranate"; Asghar Abu Gohrab, "Majnun's Image as a Serpent"; and others in *The Poetry of Nizami Ganjavi*.
31. Johan Christoph Bürgel and Christine van Ruymbeke (ed.), *A Key to the Treasure of Hakim Nizami*, (Leiden: Leiden UP, 2011).
32. Jalal Sattari, *Halat-e 'Ishq-e Majnun* (Tehran 1366/1988); Sa'idi-Sirjani, *Sima-ye do zan* (Tehran, 1367/1989).
33. Mansur Sarvat, ed., *Majmu'ah-e Maqalat-e Kungreh Hakim Nizami* (Tabriz: 1993). Those from the conferences in Washington, DC, and Los Angeles appeared as a special issue of *Iranshenasi*, edited by Jalal Matini (volume III, no. 4, Winter 1992).
34. M.T. Ja'fari, Hikmat, *'Irfan, va Akhlaq dar She'r-e Nezami*. (Tehran: Kayhan, 1991).
35. Ja'fari, *Hikmat*, Ibid. Barat Zanjani, *Laili va Majnun-e Nezami Ganjavi* (Tehran: Danishga-e Tehran, 1990), 5. Muhammad Rashid, "Eshq va Etiqad dar Makhzan al-Asrar," in *Majalih-e Danishkadih-e Adabiyat-e Ferdowsi*, no. 88–9, Spring 1990, 87. Behruz Sarvatiyan, *Sharafnamah-e Ganjah'i* (Tehran: Tus, 1989), 23.
36. Behruz Sarvatiyan, *Ainih-e Ghayb-e Nezami Ganja-e dar Masnavi Makhzan al-Asrar* (Tehran: Nash-e Kalamih, 1990), 129.
37. E. G. Browne, *A Literary History of Persia*, vol 2 (Cambridge: CU Press, 1969).
38. A. H. Zarkub, Pir-e Ganjeh (Tehran: Sokhan, 2010).
39. Cf. Safa, op. cit., volume 2, p. 798.
40. See Pizhman Bakhtiyar (ed.), *Makhzan al-Asrar-e Nezami*, (Tehran: Peygah, 1988).
41. See the note below on this subject of editing.
42. The chapter on Nezami's Layli and Majnun mentions the relevance of this romance and *Khosrow and Shirin* to Shakespeare's *Romeo and Juliet*.

CHAPTER 2

Nezami, the Persian Wordsmith: Sakhon in Classical Persian Poetry

So long as Sakhon exists –may it exalt eminence, may Nezami's fame be enlivened for his eloquence.	تا سخن است از سخن آوازه باد نام نظامی به سخن تازه باد[1]

The single verse above can support many of the points I am trying to make in this book. That of all the things he can wish, hope, or pray for, Nezami wishes for a legacy based on his literary works. This proves my argument about Nezami's motive and love of his literary profession above all.[2] The line is from a segment of *Makhzan al-Asrar* called "Goftar dar Fazilat-e Sakhon" [Discourse on the Superiority of Sakhon], which is also followed by a segment titled "Bartari-ye Sakhon-e Manzum az Sakhon-e Mansur" [On the Superiority of Poetry Over Prose].[3] The first segment indicates that the work meant something more substantial as he goes beyond the comparison of prose and poetry and covers the process of poetry writing: all the knowledge that a poet needs to learn; a version of "The four virtues," that is, philosophy, courage, continence, and the required knowledge of religions and skies; and the expectations he has from his readers. One line, however, is not enough to counter the ongoing Islamization of Nezami's poetry. In this chapter, I will conceptualize what the word "sakhon" meant to Nezami by analyzing the concepts presented in both of those segments and several other verses from his different books. It is a

© The Author(s), under exclusive license to Springer Nature Switzerland AG 2022
K. Talattof, *Nezami Ganjavi and Classical Persian Literature*,
Literatures and Cultures of the Islamic World,
https://doi.org/10.1007/978-3-030-97990-4_2

necessary step for understanding his view of his métier, his art, his Sakhon writing and romancing, and his real advocacy.

The word Sakhon (سخن), as it was pronounced at his time, abounds in Nezami's poetry. The variation of the word Sakhon over the years includes *sokhon*, or contemporarily pronounced *sokhan*. The word means "parole," "speech," "words," or "harf." Today, *sokhan goftan* means "to speak" and a *sokhanrani kardan* means "to lecture."[4] There is hardly any other word that runs so significantly through all of Nezami's poems, connecting them as tightly as this word in the *Five Treasures*. The words might be rendered a collection of poetic words, profound aesthetic word (s), or logos in literature. I argue that for Nezami, the term "Sakhon" refers to a much deeper concept beyond its literal meaning; it has a somewhat broader sense that might be understood in terms of eloquent rhetoric, a quality he has demonstrated in his poetry, and that became synonymous with poetry and literature itself.[5] He clarifies in the same verse when he has other meanings (such as oral statements) in mind for the word. For example, unlike other Persian poets, he occasionally portrays sokut or khamushi (silence) as a negative quality, and in such a case, he juxtaposes it with Sakhon. However, using Sakhon seems to be speaking about written speech, and he provides theories and advice on writing poetry. Because of this centrality of Sakhon, and because Nezami uses numerous subjects and concepts, including science, love, religions, in the construction of his Sakhon poetic narratives, this chapter elucidates the concept.[6]

For Nezami, Sakhon, I maintain, is synonymous with "literature," "literary work," and "poetry." Comparing Nezamian's Sakhon with the use of the word in the works of Rumi (d. 1273), Sa'di (d. 1291), and Hafez (d. 1389/ 90), who have also used the word frequently, I maintain that for these latter poets, Sakhon is closer to its common, contemporary usage. For them, it means parole, speech or talk, or simply "harf." I will explain why Nezami holds high esteem for Sakhon, particularly its poetic forms, to the extent that it becomes an independent, discernable theme in his work and a connecting motif that holds his poetry together. Realizing the centrality of the role of Sakhon in Nezami's work enables a better understanding of his use of various themes, including scientific, philosophical, romantic, and religious motifs, and thereby his literary representation.

The significance of words in human intellectual activities is often connected to the act of articulation in the realm of religious signification.[7] Hamid Dabashi notices the importance of Sakhon in the works of Nezami as a more essential and broader concept. He stresses that language and the concept of Sakhon provided Nezami with a unique identity. He states that, for Nezami, "being" is conceived by Sakhon, and it is used "not only to convey meaning but also create,"[8] as they did in Genesis. Shahrokh Meskub makes a similar attempt as he explains the role of sokhan in the *Shahnameh*. He starts his analysis by citing the creation story of Genesis and the first verse of the Book of John that reads, "In the beginning was the Word, and the Word was with God, and the Word was God," and finding similar concepts in the Koran and in the words of Zoroaster in the Avesta. The latter, he believes, created a tradition that Ferdowsi adopted. Meskub believes that sokhan for Ferdowsi is similar to the concept of the spoken word presented in the religious books, and it is the embodiment of ideas and, above all, the idea of creation, man, and the truth of his transcendental world.[9] However, the author sheds a more pertinent light on the topic when he states that Ferdowsi, like other poets such as Hafiz, perceived sokhan as a structure, a design that resulted in the writing of the *Shahnameh*. I should first mention that the *Shahnameh* presents epic and love stories based on material from mythical, heroic, and historical periods of Iranian history versified in lucid language that uses nearly exclusively Persian vocabulary. Ferdowsi remains relatively faithful to his historical sources and to the logic of the epic stories he versifies. It is the genre, rather than the utter beauty of the words, that carries out the labor.

In addition to religious exegeses, we have to consider other factors in explaining this concept of Sakhon. Indeed, a comparative study of classical Persian poetry reveals that each of these poets takes a different position in the realm of language philosophy that may go beyond the biblical notion, the Platonic doxa (opinion), the Augustan concept of "fleshly" speech (words produced by the mouth for the ears), the Aristotelian concept of the mimetic nature of language, and the Aristotelian logos-like discourse. For example, while the opposition between living speech and writing does not play out in the works of these classical Persian poets to any significant extent, Nezami seems to prefer the written form. In addition, unlike Augustine, who advanced writing over speech because of its visual and stable qualities and its similarity to the divine logos, Nezami prefers the written form because it provides more opportunities for embellishment.[10] Furthermore, references to fauna and flora in the works of some Persian poets, often acknowledged as part of Sakhon, have been influenced by mystical schools of thought where the believer is encouraged to come to peace with all creatures. At times, these references serve as a reminder to man that he should keep his priorities straight by behaving more peace-fully. All these, of course, may create the opportunity to speak of God. However, as the findings on the use of Sakhon in Persian poetry show, poets have different, multiple, and even contradictory understandings of the word.

In applying the concept of the divine logos to Persian poets, one must also pay attention that such a concept is more in line with the ideology of scholasticism, in which a sweeping distinction between medieval Christian philosophers and theologians and their philosophical exposé and theologi-cal writings did not exist. Unlike the scholastic authors, most Persian poets did not all use their entire rhetoric to justify and elaborate on faith. The closest ideological influence one might detect in Persian poetry is mystical elocutions (more accurately, Sufi poetry by which virtue, familiarity with Islamic ideology was no doubt a prerequisite) for the expression of which the poet's language demonstrates a significant difference from the author of a theological exposé. In mystic poetry, the poet feels much freer in his inward expression, imagination, and depiction. For example, even in a highly imaginative, surrealist description of the ascension (معراج me'raj), and after fantastic portrayals of the angelic boundaries, Nezami refuses to nar-rate the words that the prophet hears from the One. Without such free-dom and imaginative aspiration, the poet would produce a more established and structured form of work, such as a prayer or a مناجات *monajat*, as did Ansari.[11]

Therefore, it might be more productive to look for the actual meanings covered by the term Sakhon in the Persian poets' verses. The works of Rumi, Sa'di, and Hafez combined contain hundreds of occurrences of the word Sakhon; Nezami's *masnavi* alone contains more than 700 occur-rences. While the works of Rumi, Sa'di, and Hafez together contain 100 *misras* that start with the term, there are 210 such half verses in the work of Nezami. Moreover, there are a few occurrences of the plural or deriva-tive forms of Sakhon in the works of Rumi, Sa'di, and Hafez; whereas Nezami's works are replete with these including many creative derivatives combined with a suffix, a prefix, or another word.[12]

Beyond these approximate statistics, it is crucial to illustrate the way these poets have used the term. What does each poet mean by the word? How does each poet vary in his use of the term? The similarities of the works of Rumi, Hafez, and Sa'di in their use of the word, notwithstand-ing, all creatively use Sakhon.

SAKHON IN RUMI'S WORK[13]

In both *Mathnavī-yi Ma'navī* (spiritual couplets) and *Dīvān-i Shams*, Rumi's best-known works, the term occurs as Sokhan and in hundreds of verses, occasionally more than once in the same verse:

Sakhon is exalted for the Sakhon-knower It descended from the sky, it is not inferior.	سخن به نزد سخن دان بزرگوار بود ز آسمان سخن آمد سخن نه خوار بود[14]

The use of the word is a way of expressing ideas and feelings. Knowing Rumi's approach, the word often refers to the expressions of the amorous, the drunken, and the unusual, those who often speak best. In his estimation, drink improves speech:

Give me that stoic wine to advance happily, Oh Cupbearer! Once drunk as they say, I will speak of you frankly.	بده آن می رواق هله ای کیم ساق چو چنان شوم بگویم سخن تو بی محابا[15]

Moreover, Sakhon can be the subject of unusual verbs and the theme of strange circumstances. For example, it can have a taste, either bitter or sweet, or even a fatal consequence (which causes the death of a parrot upon hearing unwelcome news):

If you want to talk sweet as sugar Be patient, avoid greed, and do not eat this sweet yet.	گر سخن خواهی که گویی چون شکر صبر کن از حرص و این حلوا مخور[16]

It may be eaten, function like an arrow, and may even represent the sound of a fly's wing.

When the old master heard this from the stone He swiftly then decided to sojourn.	چون شنید از سنگها پیر این سخن پس عصا انداخت آن پیر کهن[17]

Nevertheless, Sakhon must be pronounced by one and heard by another:

For one soul's sake how should anyone plead with thee? Before thee the soul is hourly decaying and growing.[18]	جان پیش تو هر ساعت می ریزد و می روید از هر یکی جان کس چون با تو سخن گوید

It can be endless, as expressed in more than 45 verses starting with (این سخن پایان ندارد). For example, this sokhan has no end.

There is no end to this talk, however we shall recite the entire story.	این سخن پایان ندارد لیک ما باز گویم آن تمامی قصه را[19]

Thus, Rumi displays tremendous ability, creativity, and philosophical effort in the use of the term. At times, his repetition of the word is used as a rhetorical device. The term refers to nothing more than a mode of expression that is often subject or even victim of its circumstances, for example, in the verses where he decrees silence.

SAKHON IN SA'DI'S POETRY[20]

Sa'di uses the term more than 300 times. His use of the term as "talk" is more formal than Rumi's Sakhon (or Hafez's, as we shall see). In the *Gulistan*, he writes:

He spoke, and expanded his skirt of jewels- of speech With such a grace, that the king extended his sleeve-in rapture.[21]	سخن گفت و دامان گوهر فشاند به نطقی که هاش آستین بر فشاند

In this couplet, Sakhon is equated with (نطق), meaning "speech"; it is official, and it will be rewarded if it is good. While there is vagueness in the verse about the content of that rewarding speech, the following verse that stands among the contemporary sayings and proverbs reveals more about the nature of Sa'di's Sakhon:

Until a man hath spoken, His defects and his skills are concealed.[22]	تا مرد سخن نگفته باشد عیب و هنرش نهفته باشد

In the section entitled "On Being Silent," Sa'di's prose indicates that the term also means "parole," "talk," "discussion," and "harf." Both anecdotes preach the avoidance of unnecessary speech. Sa'di also advises thoughtful speech:

When unsure, one cannot quickly speak	به پندار نتوان سخن گفت زود
So long as I was uncertain, I spoke not, (…)	... نگفتم تو را تا بقیم نبود
One should not speak when unprepared	نباید سخن گفت نا ساخته
What's not spread out cannot be cut,	نشاید بریدن نیناخته
Words you've not said are still within your hand	سخن تا نگویی برو دست هست
But what's been said may get the upper-hand of you.[23]	چو گفته شود باید او بر تو دست

In opposition to Rumi and Hafez, for whom Sakhon comes from all possible sources and most often the heart, Sa'di's Sakhon often comes from the head:

I've heard that once by the Tigris stream	شنیدم که یکبار در حله ای
A head addressed a devotee. (…)	... سخن گفت با عابدی که ای
Of propriety I speak, good management and character	سخن در صلاحست و تدبیر و خوی
Not of horses and playing-fields or polo-sticks and balls![24]	به در اسب و میدان و چوگان و گوی

The qualities of good management and character are attainable and will enhance the speaking ability, which, according to the first verse of the Bustan, was given to man by God:

In the name of the God who created life!	به نام خدایی که جان آفرید
The One who created speech-creating for the tongue.[25]	سخن گفتن اندر زبان آفرید

Sa'di stresses that Sakhon is a good quality to posses; it fosters admiration and respect, however, possessing this ability does not entitle one to talk in front of a superior:

They would say: 'Henceforth behave not so disgracefully/ It is not mannerly to speak before the great![26]	که من بعد بی آبرویی مکن
	ادب نیست پیش بزرگان سخن

Indeed, gender and class play a role in Sa'di's conceptualization of Sakhon. Like any other utterance or conversation, Sa'di's Sakhon can be negative:

Shaytan of overturned fortune heard this speech	شنید این سخن بخت بر گشته دیو
In lament, he raised a shout and cry.[27]	... به زاری بر آورد بانگ و غریو

He concludes that the evil-fated backbiter in one breath/ creates hostility between two people.[28] Sa'di effectively uses the term سخنچین (today *sokhanchin*). It is not present in Nezami's poetry as a prominent concept. In any case, whether it is positive or negative, whether it is valuable advice or a source of antagonism, Sakhon can only be heard through the ears. A number of verses convey this.

No sooner had the traveler heard these words	همان کاین سخن مرد رهرو شنید
Than, going out, he was never seen again within that place (..)	... برون رفت و بازش کس آنجا ندید
The man of many words has stuffed-up ears	فراوان سخن باشد آکنده گوش
counsel will not take except in silence.[29]	نصیحت نگیرد مگر در خموش

To be sure, the term is often juxtaposed with or accompanied by the word دهان or دهن (*dihān, dihan* which means mouth). For example,

The words once spoken do not come back to the mouth	سخن گفته دگر باز ناید به دهن
Man would think first if he wishes to be wise.[30]	اول اندیشه کند مرد که عاقل باشد

Sa'di begins many of his anecdotes with the phrase "I heard," as exemplified above. Then of course his Sakhon also requires an audience.

Although a discourse be captivating and sweet	سخن گر چه دلبند و شیرین بود
commanding belief and admiration.	سزاوار تصدیق و تحسین بود
When the hearer does not understand the discourse	فهم سخن چون نکد مستمع
expect not any effect of genius from the orator.[31]	قوت طبع از متکلم مجوی

Sakhon ceases when two people in argument choose to stop all communication.

What crime have I committed that you speak no more	چه جرم رفت که با ما سخن نمی گویی
What acts have I done that I deserve your separation?	چه کرده ام که به هجران تو سزاوارم[32]

The speaker of Sakhon should not be interrupted.

I heard a sage say, that no one confesses his own ignorance, excepting he who begins speaking, whilst another is talking; and before the discourse is ended.[33]

یکی را از حکما شنیدم که می گفت: هرگز کسی به جهل خویش اقرار نکرده است مگر آنکس که چون دیگری در سخن باشد همچنان نا تمام گفته، سخن آغاز کند.

Like many other classical poets, Sa'di also uses Sakhon to describe his own orating ability where he also follows this up with the mother of self-compliments.

I will write no more poetry because the flies/ trouble me for the sweetness of my words![34]

من دگر شعر نخواهم که بنویسم که مگس زحمتم می دهد از بس که سخن شیرینست

In all these compliments, the term refers to his wise sayings rather than to his poetic craft. In the final analysis, Sakhon may be the oral expression of an idea or a feeling. It is most often praise for a beloved or for himself. However, in all of those cases, Sakhon has a didactic mission: Sa'di maintains that he is conveying useful Sakhon and asks his readers to listen carefully. As a final point, I should add that in chapters one, two, and seven of Bustan, Sa'di writes on the advantages of silence (sokut). The fact that he writes rather profusely on the praise of silence also attests to his view of Sakhon more as oral speech rather than a conceptualized form of written expression.

SAKHON IN HAFEZ'S POETRY[35]

In the *Divan of Hafez*, portraying the life and historical events in his birth town Shiraz, I have come across the word Sakhon more than 80 times. Given the relative small size of Hafez's work compared to that of the other poets analyzed here, this is a high incidence of the term. For Hafez, too, the term often means simply "harf," even when used in an allegorical sense. For him, *Sakhon guftan* means *harf zadan* (to speak). For example:

The rose laughed and said: "I don't mind hearing the truth, but/ no lover speaks harshly to his beloved."[36]

گل بخندید که از راست نرنجیم ولی هیچ عاشق سخن سخت به معشوق نگفت

Tale-bearers caused a lot of vexation. However/ If any abuse happened among the companions, let it be.[37]

از سخن چینان ملالتها پدید آمد ولی گر میان هم نشینان نا سزایی رفت رفت

Do not try to argue. A fortunate slave [of love]/
accepts with all his heart whatever his beloved says.[38]

مزن ز چون و چرا دم که بنده مقبل قبول کرد به جان هر سخن
که جانان گفت

In the first half verse of the first line, *rāst* (راست) is an adjective for the
word Sakhon, even though this latter term itself is missing. It implies that
Sakhon can be true or false and straightforward or vague. The truth or
straightforward Sakhon is harsh and that is why in the second misra, Hafez
advises lovers not to say anything harsh to their beloved. Sakhon, therefore, becomes the subject of human conditions and circumstances. This
concept is creatively portrayed in the verses that follow. The word has the
same meaning in the following verse, part of which has become a saying:

Do not boast of miraculous powers with tavern-
dwellers/ Every word has a time and every remark a
place.[39]

با خرابات نشینان ز کرامات ملاف هر سخن وقتی و هر نکته
مکانی دارد

Furthermore, Hafez's Sakhon comes from the heart,

When you hear the speech of men of heart, don't say it is
wrong
The problem is, my dear, you are not an expert in
speech.[40]

چو بشنوی سخن اهل دل مگو که خطاست
سخن شناس نئی جان من خطا اینجاست

What need is there to express yearning? For the quality of
the heart's fire
can be known from the blaze of words.[41]

بیان شوق چه حاجت که سوز آتش دل
توان شناخت ز سوزی که در سخن باشد

The term also appears in contexts referring to discussion and conversation, making a single conceptualization of Hafez's use difficult. Occasionally
he refers to his poetry and to the fact that it is written in Persian. However,
we can conclude that for Hafez, it seems that Sakhon is a complex issue
belonging to the realm of human relations. His speech is often critical of
the established social norms.

Thus far, I may conclude that there are similarities in Rumi's, Sa'di's,
and Hafez's use of the term Sakhon. They understand it to mean "uttered
words," "parole," or "harf," which may occasionally be expressed in a

poetic form. They also use it to refer to wise sayings that come from one's soul, mind, or heart when they strive to explain the content of their Sakhon. They distinguish between good Sakhon and bad Sakhon. Finally, they all use it to refer to their own didactical sayings as an example of good Sakhon. Other poets, besides the three above, have dealt with the Sakhon in an extensive manner, not only quantitatively but also in terms of the significant place they have given the term in their works. For example, in the poetry of Nasīr Khosrow (1004–ca. 1088), especially in his *qasa'id*, the term frequently occurs to conceptualize a variety of philosophical, didactic, and religious statements.[42] He is among those who have been influenced in his metaphysics by Aristotle through the works of *Avicenna* and *al-Farabi*.[43] All these philosophers consider a similar origin and nature for the soul from a metaphysical point of view. Examples are numerous, and a separate study would be needed to cover all the nuances in his work.[44] Nasīr Khosrow praises good speech/discourse (sokhan) frequently, but in the same segment, he mentions the topic of silence, albeit somewhat different from Sa'di's notion[45] means that for him, too, speech is about speaking. However, the word Sakhon is mostly used in the ways discussed above.[46]

SAKHON IN NEZAMI'S WORK

The term Sakhon appears more often in his work than in those discussed above. This might be related to the fact that for him, Sakhon is an art, his chosen art. Often, and contrary to other poets discussed, Nezami uses the term to present the particularities of this art. He determines its boundaries and its different shapes. Poetry is a form of Sakhon art and he of course considers poets to be creative artists with an almost divine status. Makhzan al-Asrār starts with a section titled "The Beginning of Sakhon" (آغاز سخن) followed by another subsection titled "Discourse on the Superiority of Sakhon" (گفتار در فضیلت سخن). These indicate the relation between his book of poetry and the word Sakhon, leaving the possibility that to him they are synonyms. Indeed, he continues to equate the two in many other places. In the "Discourse on the Virtue of Sakhon," the term appears 32 times. He is not referring to the act of speech, or the act of conversation between two individuals, nor is he making a mystical reference to the holy text. Here, he talks about Sakhon as the most essential element in existence:

The first movement of the Pen	جنبش اول که قلم بر گرفت
produced the first letter of the Word.	حرف نخستین ز سخن در گرفت
When they drew back the curtain of non-existence,	پرده خلوت چو بر انداختند
the first manifestation was the word.	جلوت اول به سخن ساختند
Until the voice of the Heart spoke,	تا سخن آوازه دل در نداد
the soul did not submit its free self to the clay.	جان تن آزاد به گل در نداد
When the Pen began to move,	چون قلم آمد شدن آغاز کرد
it opened the eyes of the world by means of the Word.	چشم جهان را به سخن باز کرد
Without speech, the world has no voice;	بی سخن آوازه عالم نبود
much has been spoken, but	این همه گفتند و سخن کم نبود
Word has not diminished.	در لغت عشق سخن جان ماست
In the language of love, speech is our soul.	ما سخنیم این طلل ایوان ماست
We are speech; these ruins are our palaces.	خط هر اندیشه که پیوسته اند
The line of every thought which is written,	بر پر مرغان سخن بسته اند
is bound to the wings of the birds of speech.	نیست درین کهنه نو خیزتر
In this ever changing old world,	موی شکافی ز سخن تیزتر
there is no subtlety finer than speech.	اول اندیشه پسین بر شمار
The beginning of thought and the final reckoning	هم سخنست این سخن اینجا بدار
is speech; remember this word.	...
...	گر چه سخن خود نماید جمال
Though speech does not show its beauty	پیش پرستنده مشتی خیال
to the worshippers of imagination,	ما که نظر بر سخن افکنده ایم
We have looked upon speech, are its lovers,	مرده اویم و بدو زنده ایم
and by it we live. (...)	با سخن آنجا که بر آرد علم
To such a degree that where the Word raises its banner,	...
language and voice are both silent. (...)	حرف زبادست و زبان نیز هم
Saying: "Tell me, which is better,	که سخن تازه و زر کهن
the new speech, or the old gold?	...
He answered: "The new speech." (...)	گوی چه به گفت سخن به سخن
So long as the Word exists,	تا سخنست از سخن آوازه باد
may its fame continue; may the name of	نام نظامی بسخن تازه باد48
Nizami be kept fresh by his words.47	

In these verses selected from a section titled "On the Virtue of Sakhon," the poet asserts that the world begins and ends with Sakhon (which could have been translated as "discourse," "speech," "poetry," or "book," in addition to "word"). Moreover, words have not only created the world but also the soul. The passage also indicates that the poet wants to establish a relationship between himself, his art, his world, his philosophy, and his career. He asserts that the world begins and ends with words. Words, indeed, have created not only the world but the soul, too. Meisami aptly acknowledges the importance of sokhan in Nezami's work. She refers to the poet's description of sokhan discourse as "flawless soul," one that holds "the key to unseen treasure."[49] Of course, as pointed out, this statement also mystifies the verses. Otherwise, at the beginning of his first book, he refers to the phrase "In the Name of God" as the key to his treasure. If that is the key that numerous analyses mention, then there is no mystery about it. However, *Sakhon* might be the key that appears in other verses of Nezami. In his Sakhon, there is plenty of room for the creative and subtle use of Koranic verses to show how he can combine different concepts from high culture to popular beliefs, from the ancient period and his own time, from his homeland and beyond; a form of colossal osmosis.[50]

In the following subsection, titled "The Superiority of Poetic Sakhon over Prose [dispersed] Sakhon" (برتری سخن منظوم از منثور), Nezami provides a short comparison of the two forms while elaborating on specifications of Sakhon:

Since the ordinary unrhymed speech	چونکه نسخته سخن سرسری
is as a gem to the jewelers,	هست بر گوهریان گوهری
Remember this subtle point, see what a weighed	نکته نگهدار بین چون بود
subtlety would be when it is measured.	نکته که سنجیده و موزون بود
Poets who raise their voices,	قافیه سنجان که سخن بر کشند
gain the treasure of both worlds by their poetry.	گنج دو عالم به سخن در کشند
Especially as the key of the treasury	خاصه کلیدی که در گنج راست
lies under the tongue of the poet (as we will in his poetry).	زیر زبان مرد سخن سنج راست
He, who made [weighs] the balance [scale] of speech,	آنکه ترازوی سخن سخته کرد
educated the fortunate ones by his words.	بخوران را به سخن بخته کرد
The poets are the nightingales of heaven;	بلبل عرشند سخن پروران
how do they resemble others?[51]	باز چه ماند به آن دیگران[52]

Thus, Sakhon is an art that can be expressed in poetic or prose form. Can, then, Sakhon mean literature? If Sakhon with *qafiyeh* or "rhyme" means "poetry,", and *qafiyeh-sanjan* "the appraisers of rhythm means" "poets" (he uses the term شعر (she'r "poetry") several times in the same passage almost as a synonym for Sakhon), and if *Sakhon-I manthur* means "prose," then what can Sakhon mean but "literature," which can be written in the form of poetry as well as prose? Is this then the word that has been missing from the Persian language to mean literature? When did the word *adabiyat* or *adab* become prevalent?[53] Was it when improvisation, such as the recitation of literature by authors or rhapsodists, became less

practiced? At such a time, prose and poetry should have possessed approximately the same written value.

Along with his high regards for Sakhon/literature, Nezami assigns the
poet a high status in *Layli o Majnun* where he once again elaborates on his
Sakhon or literary discourse. He ranks his own verses with the Koran, an
ambitious aspiration for his time, not to mention that such a claim stands
against the religious belief that the Koran could not and cannot be written
or imitated by a human being. On the other hand, he praises the book as
a high form of literature or Sakhon. Finally, he correctly portrays Sakhon
as an immortal art.

Look round: of all that God has made	بنگر از هر چه آفرید خدای
what else, save discourse, does not fade?	تا از او جز سخن چه ماند بجای؟
The sole memorial of mankind	یادگاری که آدمیزاد است
is discourse; all the rest is wind.[54]	سخن است آن دگر همه باد است[55]

When words had followed words, speech passed	چون سخن در سخن مسلسل گشت
to one most eloquent.[56]	بر زبان سخنوری بگذشت[57]

Through his Sakhon, he hopes or plans to become immortal, just like
prophets or kings. In a more worldly sense, he compares himself with
kings in the *Sharafnameh* (The Book of Honor), considering himself a
great poet who is imitated by others. In the *Makhzan al-Asrar*, he makes
the wish:

So long as Sakhon exists –may it exalt eminence,	تا سخن است از سخن آوازه باد
may Nezami's fame be enliven for his eloquence.	نام نظامی به سخن تازه باد[58]

He uses the term in varied contexts, often presenting criteria against
which the art of Sakhon may be appraised:

If thou acquires a pearl, do not wear it immediately	سینه مکن گر گهر آری بدست
seek a better one than thou hast (…)	بهتر از آن جوی که در سینه هست
	…
It is better to accept words slowly –	به که سخن دیر بدست آوری
so that thou mayest receive them from a sublime hand.[59]	تا سخن از دست بلند آوری

In *Khosrow o Shirin*, he writes:

Shorten your work if you have plenty to say, and don't make a hundred words out of one, reduce a hundred to one.	سخن بسیار داری اندک گی یکی را صد مکن صد را یکی گی ^{60}

Here the poet is talking about the difficulty of creating original works, expressing ideas in succinct ways, knowing the old stories, being able to give the work some epigrammatic quality, and finally, of acquiring fame. In this verse, he has used a relevant literary device/technique which is a word play with repetition (here numbers rather than nouns or verbs), conveying a sense of urgency and trepidation as well. In the same book, Nezami continues his deliberations on his art.

Words must be written based on criteria without which, they are loads for donkeys.	سخن باید که با معیار باشد که هر گفتن خران را بار باشد ^{61}

He returns to this topic in the *Iqbalnameh*.

Peaceful speech indicates wisdom, rough speech emanates from madness.	سخن گفتن نرم فرزانگیست درشتی نمودن ز دیوانگیست ^{62}

He also embodies the art in the story of Shirin.

He poured sugar generously as he began to narrate the story of Khosrow and Shirin With the story, constructing a jewel foundation, and in that art, he provided his words with justice.	شکر ریزان همی کرد از عنایت حدیث خسرو و شیرین حکایت که گوهربندی بنیادی نهادی در آن صنعت سخن را داد دادی ^{63}

In this section, Nezami praises Shirin, his favorite character, for her power of speech. Clearly, the poet is not merely speaking of a word or a number of words every time he mentions Sakhon. In fact, the more we read the adjectives, attributions of the words Sakhon, and the contexts in which it is being used, we realize that the word signifies field, a matière, an art.

Nezami's women are portrayed favorably, and similar qualities are attributed to Layli. However, one of their admirable qualities is often related to writing and reciting Sakhon.

Layli, with matchless elegance	لیلی که چنان ملاحتی داشت
was also blessed with equal eloquence.	در نظم سخن فصاحتی داشت
With her fluency and savor refined	با سفته دری و در هی سفت
she composed her fondest original verse.[64]	چون خود همه بیت بکر می گفت [65]

As this passage continues, Nezami states that the two lovers exchange their feelings through poetry, for which he uses the word Sakhon. He expresses similar ideas in the same *masnavi*, in the section on the occasion of the compilation of the book, saying that Sakhon reigns high and art is scripted in the jewel box. He continues to refer to himself as the one capable of magic speech.[66]

In his description of Layli, he writes that a message from the court requested that he compose a poem in memory of Majnun; the composition had to be as unique as the character of Layli. The king also mentioned in his message that he was a connoisseur of skillful writing. This is the section in which Nezami expresses his hesitation about composing the poem since the story did not provide much material for creativity.[67]

The word *bekr* translated as "virgin" or "original" (بکر), not only refers to Layli's body, but also to the creativeness of her poems. To achieve this, one should be a literary expert and a savant of Sakhon, like Nezami who claims to be able to distinguish between old and new poetry and between repetitive and genuine poetry. Nevertheless, he continues to compose the poem, and, in a section on the complaints of those who are jealous of him, he writes that he is so perfect in the magic art of Sakhon that he is nicknamed the Invisible or Mysterious Mirror. He claims that his speech, because of the way it shines, is like fire. If you were to lay a critical finger on it, your finger would burn.[68]

There is no doubt that Nezami mostly talks about the written word. For example he writes:

Friends created Sakhon out of locution/language	یاران سخن از لغت سرشتند
They often wrote a different locution.	ایشان لغتی دگر نوشتند [69]

Chastise to educate, literate that which is generosity	گوش سخا را ادب آموز کن
Thus, illuminate, vivify the candle of Sakhon.	شمع سخن را نفس افروز کن [70]

The first passage distinguishes *Sakhon* from *Loghat*; the former being made by the latter. The second passage differentiates between Sakhon and *Adab*. Such juxtapositions should also encourage us again to seek a deeper meaning for the concept of Sakhon.

The usual "Humble or Prostrator's Address" in *Makhzan al-Asrar* from which the lines above are rendered is a complex pictorial allegory.[71] It starts with praise, description, and metaphorical use of such natural elements as the moon, the sun, the light, fish, lion, butterfly, pearls, water springs, rivers, prairies, and mythical heroes and moves to praising the addressee who is the God but can also be the king. Usually, support and promotion of poetry are not what one would ask God to do; however, if Nezami is addressing God, it might be for conforming to norms or even pleasing the authorities who will certainly read his work either way. He prays for or requests support for the importance of Sakhon and wishes for the addressee to acknowledge his work. Moreover, and regardless of the allegory itself, the word *qalam* or "pen" (قلم) and the verb *nivishtan* which means to write (نوشتن) indicate the nature of the Sakhon genre. Sakhon might be read aloud or recited, but it is always created by the might of the pen. The juxtaposition of *adab* and Sakhon in the second verse is also revealing, as *adab* here does not mean "literature." Indeed, the word *adab* appears in the *Makhzan al-Asrar* more than 25 times and hardly ever does it refer to literature per se.

In the *Sharafnameh*, he presents and reemphasizes some of the principles, ideas, and theories that, in his opinion, shape the art of Sakhon.

When I was preparing this work (*Sharafnameh*)	چو می کردم این داستان را بسیج
speech was straight-moving (fluent) but the road (of information) ambient. (...)	سخن راست رو بود و راه پیچ پیچ ...
To circulate much about a wonderful matter	بسی در شگفتی نمودن طواف
Draws the rein of speech into foolish talking.	عنان سخن را کشد در گزاف
And if thou should utter speech without some wonder (the subtlety of verse)	و گر بی شگفتی گزاری سخن
the old books (void of the imagery of verse) would have no freshness.	ندارد نوی نامه های کهن
Of speech, keep watch to this extent	سخن را به اندازه ای دار پاس
that in imagination one can believe it.	که باور توان کردنش در قیاس
Although speech (verse) produces (in the orator's opinion) the splendor of the jewel	سخن گر چه بر آرد فروغ
When it is not believed it seems the lie.[72]	چو نا باور افتد نماید دروغ[73]

Here, he believes that the art of Sakhon requires a certain element of surprise by saying that the existence of a certain level of *shigifti*, "wonder" or "surprise," makes the work original. Judging by his writing, his portrayal of his characters, and the intricate stories of the *Haft Paykar*, one

may conclude that *shigifti* is something similar to the notion of the sublime. This makes sense, considering his advice that one should not remain
in a sublime mode too long because that will give Sakhon an element of
exaggeration. He delves, at times stoically, into this topic again in the
Iqbāl Nāma, saying that it is not easy to be creative all the time and that
one needs to be versed in knowledge and prosody in order to be at ease in
the creation of Sakhon.[74]

These passages, which represent a small portion of Nezami's writing on
the theories of Sakhon, indicate his importance of literary creativity. There
is no limit to the themes and topics of Nezamian Sakhon, which covers
such diverse subjects as logic, philosophy, Islam and Islamic jurisprudence,
Ash'ari doctrine, Zoroastrianism, culture, nation, love, women's portrayals, *kalam* (speculative theology), geometry, astronomy, geography, history, music, and architecture.[75] In his own words, in the *Iqbalnameh*,
Sakhon should indeed have different themes ranging from the divine to
nature.[76]

This allegorical passage illustrates a few significant points of this book.
Even though it is not directly about his own poetry and Sakhon, it indicates Nezami's awareness and preoccupation with subjects, themes, and
fields of knowledge as the sources of his allegories. The words he puts in
the mouths of his characters refer to such diverse fields/themes/subjects
as nature, theology, mathematics, geometry, culture, and morality. It also
exemplifies his pictorial allegory. The first four lines use the metaphors of
colors, birds, and music to set the tone for expressing the mood of the
next scene, the state of Alexander's mind, and the minds of the characters
featured in the second part of the allegory.

Knowing several languages and familiarity with ancient literary traditions (as he mentions) enabled him to enrich his ideas and knowledge with
borrowings from foreign sources. In addition, he often points out that to
be knowledgeable in these fields is helpful in the creation of Sakhon by
being open to the enrichment of one's rhetoric. This makes him a wordsmith. And in a passage entitled *Saqinameh* (the Book of the Cupbearer),
he explains the process of his matière in general and the process of the
composition of his *Iskandarnameh* in particular. The passage is available in
the notes but the most telling verse reads,

Having collected a grain of information from various sources	پراکنده از هر دری دانه ای
I adorned them (the Sharaf-Nameh) like an idol-house.[77]	بر آراستم چون صنم خانه ای[78]

In the broader passage about authoring this book, Nezami says that he began the book in a visionary state (*khiyali*, a word that could have also meant imaginative and illusory). Then, he decided to write imaginative scenes (*pardeh*, which also has other connotations) by expressing his imaginations, the charm of his mind, into magical Sakhon. Thus, he can create this book on this world, starting with what he wrote on Dara.[79] Therefore, of all the incredible Sakhon of the history I had read, I selected the clearest ones to versify. I believe if we need to analyze the prefatory and postscript segments that bookend Nezami's narratives to hear him more directly, we might find the most specific meanings, and information about him in those segments are written about the "reason for writing the book," "about the ending of the book." In those segments, he talks about the nature of his poetry and his expected compensation.

The passage also answers an important question or criticism of Nezami's *Iskandarnameh*. In numerous commentaries, critics and readers point out that the scenes and episodes that bring together Alexander, Plato, Aristotle, and a few other philosophers and scientists from various times and places are erroneous. As if Nezami had predicted this question, he says that if the chronology of Alexander's events is not correct, it would be a minor point, and there will not be a need to be concerned.[80] For writing poetry, such minor deficiencies or such liberties are necessary. Just pay attention to how "I have constructed the poetry like Arjang," the drawing book of Prophet Mani.[81]

The couplet above thus means that Sakhon should contain ideas, innovative ideas, and that it is about form and content, another evidence that to him it meant literature. The verse emphasizes that the resulting temple was built with straight walls. Nevertheless, because of the significance of form, which he also discusses extensively, he offers another theory about the translation of Sakhon. He treats Sakhon as a literary art again when he mentions the question of translation. As a literary critic, he argues that poetry is hardly translatable at all.[82]

Speaking of form, Nezami believes that in the art of Sakhon, as a genre, there is a distinction between form and content, a notion with which present-day literary critics would agree. By including all the above branches of knowledge, he has supposedly taken care of the content, but he also acknowledges the effort and work it takes to write good poetry by pointing out the issues of editing and proofreading.[83] In the *Makhzan al-Asrar*, he writes:

Revise the words that lack courtesy and eloquence
because doing so is a custom and perquisite.
I say cross out the writings that
does not promote knowledge.

هر سخنی کز ادبش دوریست
دست بر او مال که دستوریست
و آنچه به از علم بر آرد علم
گر مم آن حرف درو کش قلم ⁸⁴

He repeats this point in the *Sharafnameh.* But the fact is that Nezami manifests this idea about literary form and content as he creates his works. Regarding the issue of form in the *Haft Paykar,* Meisami writes that both the story's character Bahram, and Nezami's reader learns about the nature of the human design through the medium of "discourse – specifically, structured discourse." She refers to Nezami's verses where he "calls attention to the importance of his poem's design," observing that "design is a recurrent motif throughout the poem, reiterated in the references to buildings (the palace of Khavarnaq and of the Seven Domes, ultimately transformed into fire-temples (51, 17–52: 10), exemplifying building of this world and building for the next and to astrology and astronomy, and expressed in terms of number and geometry. Design and number are, indeed, the principles upon which the poem is based."⁸⁵ Khaleghi-Motlagh also emphasizes the importance of form in Nezami's work, noting that his art is not limited to discursive and conceptual design. It includes the creation of the desired structure for his stories.⁸⁶ A prime example of such artistic effort, as Ghanoonparvar points out, is the "Story of the Black Dome" in *Haft Paykar,* where Nezami presents an overly complex design for his poem.⁸⁷ His aesthetic games are not limited to his preoccupation with form but are demonstrated in verses as well. In numerous parts of his work, some of which mentioned already, he emphasizes his artistic ability in that regard.

Let us revisit one of the lines quoted above, which reads, "An ke trazuye Sakhon sakhtah kard /sakhtvarn ra be Sakhon bakhteh kard." Here, Nezami conveys several meanings with only one word as he says, that he, who made/created the balance of Sakhon, educated/awarded the fortunate ones/hardworking ones by/with his word. In the early printings of some editions, there were no dots on the first letters of *[-]akhtvarān* and *[]akhta,* but were altered in more recent printings.⁸⁸ I wonder if the poet left the dots out deliberately. Without the dots, the verse can be read in diverse ways, and all are meaningful. The construction of the multiple and, at times, contradictory meanings is itself meaningful. It implies that a man of speech can characterize someone as good or bad by changing a dot. That a scriptural error can result in such a meaningful construct is rare. The multilayer meanings are also in accordance with Nezami's frequent uses of words with more than one possible meaning to create multiple readings. Naderpur aptly states, "Nezami throws his arrows to the neighboring meanings of words instead of targeting the most direct meaning."[89] I believe this is not aphasia or a shortcoming in the poet's work. It is a deliberate and creative aspect of his work. Nezami does all of this in the name of Sakhon. This passion for Sakhon, for words, this adroitness in rhetoric runs through his diverse poetic utterances like an ornamental chain, connecting them all together intertextually and stylistically.

Such an understanding of the word Sakhon is consistent with Nezami's many compound and derivative forms of the word. In addition to the plural Sakhon-ha, such forms include Sakhondan or Sakhonvar (سخنور، سخندان), meaning a person who demonstrates an oratorical, eloquent, and poetic manner when writing or speaking. Other compound words with similar meanings also appear, such as:

سخن آفرین، سخن پرور، سخنران روان، سخن شناس، سخن گستر، سخن سنج

This creativity points to an eloquent rhetorician who knows the value of words, an excellent writer, or orator who has made a career of this art. Can we translate some of these words into contemporary Persian terminology as follows?

Man of letters	ادیب	سخندان
Poet	شاعر	سخنور
Writer, orator	ادب پرور	سخن پرور
A literary master	ادب شناس، ادب سنج	سخن شناس
Eloquent poet	شاعر خوش بیان	سخن گستر
Ungifted poet	شاعر بی استعداد	سخندان بی توشه

If so, then each of these words could not have referred to any other concepts but the terms, "poet" and "writer," "creative writer," or related terms. In addition, there are a considerable number of verbs compounded with Sakhon, from the simple *Sakhon goftan* (سخن گفتن) to the complex *maghz-i sokhan sakhtan* (مغز سخن ساختن). The following cases are from the *Makhzan al-Asrar* alone, and they all refer to the act and ability in the métier of creative speech or creative writing.

سخن آفریدن، سخن آغاز کردن، سخن آرایی کردن، سخن آمیختن، سخن دانستن، سخن افکندن، سخن دارا بودن، سخن داشتن، سخن باز کردن، سخن پخته کردن، سخن
افشاندن، سخن بر کشیدن، سخن بستن، سخن پروراندن، سخن پیش بردن، سخن پیش داشتن، سخن تازه کردن، سخن خواندن، سخن خوردن، سخن دادن، سخن دانستن،
سخن در کشیدن، سخن بر آمدن، سخن در گرفتن، سخن آرایی کردن، سخن آوازه کردن، سخن راندن، سخن رستن، سخن زدن، سخن ساختن، سخن سفتن، سخن کردن،
سخن واگشادن، سخن بدست آوردن

Can we translate these verbs to contemporary Persian as well? If so, the
renditions make sense if we take Sakhon as poetry or literature.

To recite poetry	شعر خواندن	سخن خواندن
To develop prosody	قافیه پردازی کردن	سخن آرایی کردن
To create literature, creative writing	نوآور ادبی	سخن آفریدن
To write poetry	شعر سرودن	سخن آرایی

If so, their meanings do not refer to any concept except creative and
poetic writing and reading. In any case, by virtue of the above verbs, we
have ascertained that Sakhon is certainly not simply harf or "parole." If it
were, there would be no need for so many compound verbs. I must add
that Nezami's genius in coining compound verbs and nouns in Ferdowsi's
style is not limited to his creations around Sakhon; his books are replete
with such stable and appropriate outcomes.

Finally, like many other poets, Nezami mentions the word Sakhon
when he praises his own work. Contrary to the belief that for Nezami the
art is a purely religious matter,[90] these flattering references show that he
looks at his art of Sakhon as a means of achieving prosperity, a means of
living, a life challenge, and legacy. In his *Dīvān*, he states:

Through words gain the treasure of felicity because they are alchemy able to turn rocks to gold.	به سخن گنج سعادت به کف آر که سخن کیمیاست که بر سنگ نهی زر گردد[91]

In *Khosrow o Shirin* he writes:

Make your words as strong as steel just like Alexander I did so, and through such coinage, I gained coins.	سخن پولادین کن چون سکندر بدین سکه درم را سکه می بر[92]

In addition, he advocates valuing one's work. He writes,

Since thy poetry is as sweet as honey, do not demean it do not let flies contaminate the sweetness of thy poetry.	چون سخنت شهد شد ارزان مکن شهد سخن را مگس افشان مکن[93]

This emphasis on the material value of one's literary work is a highly relevant topic to the discussions of Nezami's profession as a poet and we will return to it in the later chapters. He repeats these notions in *Sharafnameh* frequently, where he ends by writing:

Here, I bring my discourse to an end	سخن (سر آمد) مرا تا بدینجا سر آید
You know what to do, do what you want.	تو دانی دگر هر چه خواهی بکن...
... If the king bestows upon me his beneficence	گر اقبال شه باشدم دستگیر
My poems will be ready faster to report	سخن زود گردد گزارش پذیر...
Nezami who made himself your servant	نظامی که خود را غلام تو کرد
Penned his poems in your name.	سخن را گزارش بنام تو کرد[94]

Without these references in the context of his career, his Sakhon discourse would have not been complete. Through them, he further emphasizes and theorizes the art of book writing, the question of publishing, the challenges of creating a long-lasting work, and the sublime. The passage also indicates how far Nezami is willing to prove his loyalty to the ruler, perhaps mainly to secure compensation. He is ready to portray himself as a slave and servant to the king, a notion that would not often apply to a pious Muslim poet or a Sufi poet.

It should also be mentioned that while Nezami in his conceptualization of Sakhon might be considered as an anomaly, the proximity of the meanings of Sakhon and literature is not foreign to the Persian literary tradition. This notion used by Nezami is only unique in the sense that it becomes a constitutive element in his work. Others have occasionally come close to such an understanding of the word. Ferdowsi, for example, as discussed earlier, writes at the beginning of the *Shahnameh* that whatever he is about to write has already been uttered by others who have entered the garden of knowledge.[95]

Classical authors of literary criticism also discussed this notion of Sakhon. For example, the eleventh-century author Muhammad ibn Umar al-Radūyānī talks about the interpretation of eloquence, and he offers a notion of the proper structure of Sakhon, which to him, too, means poetry and literary prose.[96] For some of these authors, the issue has additional significance as they relate it to the Islamic tradition of knowledge. In the Qur'an, for example, on many occasions both knowledge and speech are revered.

To be sure, Nezami's description of Sakhon complies with the description of Nezami Aruzi's definition of the art of poetry in which the poet arranges "imaginary propositions, and adapts the deductions" and the artist "must be of tender temperament, profound in thought, sound in genius, clear of vision, and quick of insight. He must be well versed in many diverse sciences and quick to extract what is best from his environment, for poetry is of advantage in every science, so is every science of advantage in poetry."[97] About the notion of the social qualities of a poet, Aruzi continues: "And the poet must be of pleasing conversation in social gatherings, of cheerful countenance on festive occasions; and his verse must have attained to such a level that it is written on the page of time and celebrated on the lips and tongues of the noble, and be such that they transcribe it in books and recite it in cities."[98] On these classical notions, Landau writes that "Defined as a part of logic, poetry is distinguished from all other possible schemes of rational discourse—be they demonstrative, dialectical, rhetorical or sophistical—by the fact that it cannot claim to affect the audience by winning its assent (تصدیق). Poetry works, rather, by stirring the audience's imagination (تخیل)."[99]

Nezami Ganjavi's description of Sakhon also later arises in Amir Khusrow Dehlavi's four conditions for the art of poetry:

> Now it should be kept in mind that a poet who fulfills four conditions will be regarded as an absolute master by the far-sighted. First, he should implant the banner of poetry in such a manner that its magnificence impresses others. Second, having the essence of what is important, the style of his verse should be sweet and simple like the (ancient) poets and not like the preachers and Sufis. Third, the components of his writing should be free of errors. Fourth, like the stitcher of leather, he should not prepare a gown of a thousand patches with the rags of (different) people."[100]

All this explains why, of Nezami's approximately 30,000 verses, more than 2500 deal with issues of language, aesthetics, and rhetoric, representing his effort to explain and elaborate on the concept of Sakhon. Furthermore, these dealings are expressed in passages and not in sporadic single verses. Contrary to examples from other poets where references to Sakhon are limited to a verse or two, in Nezami, the deliberations on the topic can span a dozen consecutive verses. Now, one has to ask this question. If Nezami is so professionally preoccupied with artistic production and readership, why should he not use popular and pleasing subjects as the themes of his creativity? Readers such as the "noble" were surely interested in wine, spirituality, love, and religion just to name a few, and the poet paid attention.

Various Subjects and These as Sakhon's Ingredients

Thus far I have listed subjects and themes which Nezami uses in the construction of his Sakhon and allegories. A few of the next chapters focus on more specific subjects and themes. Here, I would like to briefly point out a few subjects that might sporadically appear in different Nezami's books to point out that Sufism or Islam is not the only content in his work.

Health and Medicine

Immediately after this jurisprudential musing which includes a couple of lines on eating and health, in the same segment about the death of Layli's husband, Nezami draws on a medical topic. In *Layli o Majnun*, he illustrates the deterioration of the health of Ibn Salam, Layli's husband, in these profound verses.[101] He first foreshadows his work with the health and diet-related terminologies using the word "salt" (*namak*) in two different meanings and then explains how and why Layli's husband became ill and died.[102]

Her life seemed tasteless, saltless, but then heaven	این بیُنکی فلک همی‌کرد
Rubbed salt into the wounds she had been given	وان خوش نک این جگر همی‌خورد
Until the skies' relentless turning made her	تا گردش دور می‌مدارا
Show outwardly how heaven had betrayed her	کردش عمل خود آشکارا
They stayed apart and banished from her side	شد شوی وی از دریغ و تیار
Her husband longed to see his absent bride,	دور از رخ آن عروس بهار
Till Ebn Salam grew weak, then weaker still	افتاد مزاج از استقامت
And it was clear that he had fallen ill.[103]	رفت این سلام را سلامت [104]

And the allegory goes on to portray how different factors contributed to the decline of his health and ultimate demise. Nezami has other passages that are even more directly related to medicine. Christine van Ruymbeke explains Nezami's knowledge of pharmaceutical and medical properties and uses by examining his remarks on certain plants.[105] Nezami has also written on medicine in combination with statesmanship. The knowledge used for such allegories was part of the three major branches of the so-called occult sciences.[106]

Nezami also writes on the body, including women's body, and this distinguishes him from the lyric writers for whom the beloved is genderless and bodyless. The descriptive, realistic, romantic portrayal of the body

refutes mysticism as Nezami's motivation as well as gives nuance to the
theory that Nezami was a link between two different eras and
perspectives.

PEACE AND JUSTICE

Peace and justice are two concepts that can constitute elements of a virtuous, ethical, or moral system. Nezami's works are replete with praise for
these concepts. His story of the old woman and King Sanjar (Dastan-e
Pirzan va Sultan Sanjar) from Makhzan al-Asrar has been explored frequently. In *Haft Paykar* he makes it clear that in addition to writing beautiful poetry, he wanted to promote justice. His utopian city (*armanshar*)
in *Iskandarnameh* is characterized by the practice of justice and peace. His
reference to the God or Angel Soroush is often connected to the concept
of Justice. Sometimes he criticizes Muslim rulers for practicing injustice,
showing them examples from the Zoroastrian eras. Here are some examples of how masterfully he plays with words to express these concepts in
Layli o Majnun.[107]

If you are not acting righteously	چون راست نمی‌کنید کاری
What purpose has your sword fighting?	شمشیر زدن چراست باری
As they heard each other's accord	چون خواهش یکدگر شنیدند
They terminated their rancor.	از کینه کشی عنان کشیدند

Perhaps because this is part of a storyline, the verses are not allegorized.
Nevertheless, the wording still draws attention to outside images. Making
such a connection is particularly obvious in the last line, which resists a
literal translation. Yet, in other places, such as in *Makhzan al-Asrar*, he
ponders the concept of justice in a highly allegorical way.[108]

Justice is a messenger of happiness and wisdom	عدل بشریست خرد شاد کی
It is a labor to develop nations	کارگری ملکت آباد کی
A nation will survive because of justice	ملکت از عدل شود پایدار
Your affairs will be ordered because of justice	کار تو از عدل تو گیرد قرار

Nevertheless, searching the poet's work for similar expressions does not
support these themes as overarching or vital organizing elements in his
works except that the same trend in assigning specific meanings through
allegory continues in this thematic area.[109]

Peace arrived holding a trident	صلح آمد دور باش در چنگ
So war between the groups was forsaken	تا از دو گروه دور شد جنگ

In this couplet from *Layli o Majnun*, stretching out imaginations, peace is compared to a soldier holding a trident. This comparison seems to have had no ground except the necessity of coming up with an allegory or a simile. Here, it is tough to argue that the poem's purpose is to praise peace instead of creating a new image. The same thinking applies to his imagery regarding justice in the other verse above where he writes, "Justice is a messenger of happiness and wisdom/It is a labor to develop nations." In fact, in some verses, justice is the main ingredient for collective happiness and prosperity, a theme that did not have to be expressed in such a picturesque writing if the purpose was just to promote justice for all. This, though, is Nezami; he selects a suitable subject to construct a becoming of a pictorial allegory in a proper spot in his plots. On this topic, stories such as the encounter between Iskandar and Queen Nushabeh in the *Book of Alexander* and "The Story of Sultan Sanjar and the Old Woman," and the "Story of Khayr va Shar" have been discussed by others on multiple occasions.

WAYS OF CONDUCT

Nezami has countless verses where his broader and various notions regarding social and cultural behavior, including moderation, sensitivity, and aggression, come together as the basis of proper behavior and conduct. These themes are naturally a good space to express principles of ethics. Here are some examples from *Khosrow o Shirin*.[110]

Once the water level rises beyond moderation	چو آب از اعتدال افزون نهد گام
It will result only in submersion	ز سیرابی به غرق آرد سرانجام
Look at people, how senseless and mindless	تو مردم بین! که چون بی رای و هوشند
They give up life for a price, a piece of bread	که جانی را به نانی میفروشند
Whether conscious or drunken	اگر هشیار اگر مخمور باشی
Live to stay away from aggression	چنان زی کز تعرض دور باشی

Of course, like other topics, this theme appears in several other places. Poets after Nezami have written different versions of the same expressions. Here, behavior and conduct stem from a more profound preoccupation with life and engagement with one's surroundings, all of which are uttered in allegorical ways.[111] In fact, without the allegories, these concepts about proper conduct or the descriptions of life events would be too rudimentary or didactic to be the subject of a writer aiming for high-quality poetry. To add to the creative aspects of such expressions, he uses and demonstrates several types of *tashbih*.[112] Consequently, all these preoccupations serve the purpose of his writing Sakhon. In *Sharafnameh*, he expresses this point clearly.

| Sealing the lips with a needle is better | دهن را به مسمار بر دوختن |
| Than wasting, burning, blustering words. | به از گفتن و گفته را سوختن[113] |

KINGS AND RULERS

He also writes in praise of the kings, with the sheer beauty, knowledge, and profound interest he writes about other subjects, using the same technique of allegorizing. The love story of Layli and Majnun, for example, ends with verses about the king.[114] Using appropriate, albeit exaggerated, adjectives he compares Shervanshah, who requested the verification of the tale, with such kings as Jamshid, Kayqobad, Khaqan, Kaykhosrow the Second, and many others. However, without any expectation, he praises Jamshid, who is, by the way, reported to have authored a text of *khered*, in all his books. He also offers advice to the kings, mainly on ethics and conduct yet in beautiful verses.[115] In the praise-of-kings section, Nezami tacitly (or not) asks for compensation, a theme much explored and uncontested by others.[116] In doing so, he does not hesitate to remind the reader of his art of Sakhon.

All his five (or six counting, both volumes of his last one) are dedicated to or requested by kings, and he received remarkable compensation for his art including gold coins or fertile land. The dedications are *Makhzan al-Asrar* for Bahramshah, *Khosrow o Shirin* for Jahanpahlavan and his brother Qezel Arsalan, *Layli o Majnun* for Shervanshah, *Haft Paykar* for Karparsalan; *Shrafnameh* for Abubakr Saljuqi, and *Kheradnameh* for Ezedin Arsalan.

HOMELAND

Nezami's has numerous constructs around Iran, its kings, and its land. In numerous verses, he also refers to the country or its people as Ajam (Iran, Persians), and he juxtaposes it with Tazian (Arabs). Nevertheless, he remains respectful to all peoples. Some of his protagonists, including Layli, Majnun, Maryam, and Alexander, are not Iranian. In the following example in which he praises Shervanshah, he puts much effort into the alliteration topic, repeating the "sh" sound as in shah. Here he praises the king.

What a special king, to be the king of Shervan	خاصه ملکی چو شاه شروان
What is Shervan? He deserves to be the king of all Iran.	شروان چه! که شهریار ایران[117]

He does not speak of Iran frequently and certainly not as frequently as Ferdowsi. However, when he does, it is expressed as an exalted view of the country, insinuating that it is the best country, and the local king deserves the best through sovereignty under the king of the kings. Elsewhere, when he refers to Iran, he remains respectful and romantic in his portrayal depicting it in the image of the ancient Persia and as the heart of the world.[118]

The world is the body, Iran its heart	همه عالم تن است و ایران دل
I am not shy in making this comparison an art	نیست گوینده زین قیاس خجل
Yes, Iran is the earth's heart	چونکه ایران دل زمین باشد
The heart is better than the body, no doubt.	دل ز تن به بود، یقین باشد

Seeing Iran as the center of the world is a familiar construct in classical literature, but it is also similar to Nezami's notion of the Earth being the center of the universe. Of course, it is equally difficult to assign a nationalist ideology to Nezami simply because of such lines. He does not seem to be overly preoccupied with regional or broader politics. Even in these short samples, we see a trace of his pictorial allegories, the picture being of the King of Iran, and the purpose being praise. In praise of the ruler Atabak Azam Mohammad Ilgez, using comparison and *qiyas*, Nezami equates him with Mohammad, the Prophet of Islam, over several lines.[119] One is portrayed as an ever-shining moon, and the other as an eternal king. One has freed the world from its oppression, and the other has established worldwide justice. Nevertheless, the argument that Nezami had no understanding of nationhood, Iran, and Persian identity because Iran only existed as a cultural nation is entirely based on analytical and historical models that do not have universal applicability. The reality is that Iran did not disappear under occupation and survived with the difference that at times it was more than one family that administered the "protected realms." The concept of *Iranshahr*, which is more comprehensive than a "cultural notion," continued to inform the identity of people across a vast expanse of land.[120]

In conclusion, *sokhan* or *sakhon* for many Persian poets such as Rumi, Hafez, and Sa'di represents the actual human speech, which might also function as a facilitator of desire, emotion, or dictum. Sometimes they insist that there is something concealed behind (the *pardeh*, curtain) the expressed words, just the same way that representation of wine and women have ontological implications. As for Nezami, this conceptualization of Sakhon with its various subjects helps us understand how in his work all philosophical as well as religious issues are framed in grand language for the sake of the superior goal of creativity. Existence, religious beliefs, holy books, Greek philosophy, and all branches of science are means through which Nezami practices his artistic language, his understanding of the art and the world, and his cherished art of Sakhon. He is, in a sense, a philologist, in its broad meaning, rather than, as many traditional analyses have portrayed him, a philosopher, or even a theologian. That is why, in order to understand Nezamian Sakhon, one hardly needs any outside referent. His poetic discourse is, in that regard, self-sufficient as he is constructing a notion the subject of which is itself. No other poet of the classical period has ever engaged so extensively in the explication of the process of Sakhon creation, Sakhon structures, Sakhon forms, and the epitome of Sakhon thoughts, as has Nezami, the wordsmith.

NOTES

1. Nezami-Sarvatyan (1984), 80.
2. This chapter is based on my article "Nezami Ganjavi, the Wordsmith: The Concept of Sakhon in Classical Persian Poetry," in *A Key to the Treasure*.
3. *Kolliyat*, 17–18.
4. It was also pronounced as sakhan, or in Pahlavi, as sukhvan or sakhvan (سخون), See *Dehkhoda* 1372–73.
5. Talattof (2000).
6. Ibid.
7. This approach is different from those who cast a descriptive light on Nezami's works, such as Meisami acknowledging the importance of sukhan to him.

8. Dabashi (1992).
9. Meskub (2004).
10. Some believe that like other terminology, the word Sakhon also has additional connotations in Sufi thought. It is safe to assume that when a devout Sufi uses the word, he might be referring to God's words.
11. See Rypka (1968), 235.
12. I collected these figures decades ago. Since then, electronic versions of Persian poetry have made keyword search easier. Other poets in whose work the word Sakhon appears frequently are Ferdowsi: 843; Naser Khusrow: 413; Owhadi Maraghe'i: 322; 'Attar: 238; Khaqani: 189; Anvari: 184; Vahshi: 157; Jami: 145; Dehlavi: 115; Sana'i: 144; Kashani: 141; Khwaju Kirmani: 106. The combined works of Rumi, Nezami, Sa'di, and Hafez contain more than 1400 occurrences of the term.
13. For more examples, see Kamran Talattof, "Nezami Ganjavi the Wordsmith."
14. Rumi (1996), 378.
15. Ibid, 111.
16. Rumi (1987), 117.
17. Ibid, 671.
18. Rumi-Nicholson (1898), 75.
19. Rumi (1987), *Daftar* 1.
20. For more examples see "Nezami Ganjavi the Wordsmith."
21. Based on Sa'di-Clarke (1985), 42; Sa'di-Yusofi (1996), 46.
22. Based on Sa'di-Anderson (1985), 8.
23. Based on Sa'di-Clarke (1985), 42 and Sa'di-Wickens (1974), 178–179; Sa'di-Yusofi (1996), 154.
24. Sa'di-Wickens (1974), 43, 177; Sa'di-Yusofi (1996), 62.
25. Sa'di-Yusofi (1996), 34.
26. Sa'di-Wickens (1974), 150; Sa'di-Yusofi (1996), 134.
27. Sa'di-Clarke (1985), 49; Sa'di-Wickens (1974), 36; Sa'di-Clarke (1985), 254 and 257; Sa'di-Yusofi (1996), 49, 57, 132, 133.
28. Sa'di-Anderson (1985), 70; Sa'di-Yusofi (1996), 52 and 162.
29. Sa'di-Wickens (1974), 122; 134; 135; Sa'di-Yusofi (1996), 115; 123; 124.
30. Sa'di-Yusofi (1996), 124.
31. Sa'di-Anderson (1985), 330, 158, 464; Sa'di-Yusofi (1996), 76.
32. Ibid.
33. Sa'di-Anderson (1985), 331; Sa'di-Forughi (1986), 124.
34. Sa'di-Yusofi (1996) *Ghazaliyat*, 87.
35. For more examples see "Nezami Ganjavi the Wordsmith."

36. Hafez, *The Divan of Hafez* by Reza Saberi (Oxford: UP of America, 2002), 98; Hafez, Divan-e Hafez, by Rahim Zulnur (Tehran: Zavar, 1988), 185.
37. Hafiz-Saberi (2002), 100; Hafiz-Zulnur (1988), 188.
38. Hafiz-Saberi (2002), 107; Hafiz-Zulnur (1988), 198.
39. Hafiz-Saberi (2002), 147; Hafiz-Zulnur (1988), 269.
40. Hafiz-Saberi (2002), 32; Hafiz-Zulnur (1988), 59.
41. Hafiz-Saberi (2002), 191; Hafiz-Zulnur (1988), 358.
42. More than 400 times.
43. Rypka (1968), 189.
44. Nezami's *Iskandaranmeh* is essentially in the mode of Platonic and Aristotelian influence. "One of the chief topics is the role of philosopher-minister assigned to Aristotle; in treating this motif Nezami underlines, as throughout his writings, the need of the just ruler for sound advisers." Arberry (1958), 126.
45. 'Urfi Shirazi goes a step further by writing ghazals in praise of silence, stating that silence is better than any speech, period.
46. It is often "parole, or harf" that requires an audience, sometimes with religious connotation with having God as the audience.
47. Nizami-Darab (1945), 120–122; Nizami-Sarvatyan (1984), 78.
48. Nizami-Dastgirdi (1988), 16–17.
49. Julie Scott Meisami, "Fitnah or Azadah? Nezami's Ethical Poetic," *Edebiyat*, N. S. volume 1, no. 2, 1989, 41–77.
50. For example, in that introductory section of *Makhzan al-Asrar*, Nezami might use certain words in some of his lines to refer to certain Koranic verses.

Line	Word	Koran
پرورش آموز درون پروران روز برآرندهی روزی خوران	Ruz/Day	Surah An-Naba- 11: "And made the day for livelihood."
اول و آخر به وجود و صفات هست کی و نیست کی کاینات	Aval o Akhar / First and Last	Surah Al-Hadid- 3: "He is the First and the Last, and the Outer and the Inner, and He has knowledge of all things."

Such customary evocations exist in many of the introductory parts of his book, and they are often places where he intends to exhibit his creativity and knowledge. These are also perfunctory, a necessary part of poetry of the time, an expected aspect of the product, that if absent would in the eyes of readers of the day diminish the poem.

51. Nizami-Darab (1945), 122–123.
52. Nizami-Dastgirdi (1988), 18–19.
53. In *The World of Persian Literary Humanism* Dabashi recasts the classical Persian literature, known as whole as *adab*, or a combination of literature and etiquette as Persian literary humanism.
54. Nizami-Meisami, 23.
55. *Kolliyat*, 433.
56. Nizami-Meisami, 100.
57. *Kolliyat*, 482.
58. Nezami-Sarvatyan, 80.
59. Nezami-Darab (1945), 125–126; Nizami-Sarvatyan (1984), 84.
60. *Kolliyat*, 141.
61. *Kolliyat*, 332.
62. *Kolliyat*, 1259.
63. *Kolliyat*, 290.
64. Nezami-Atkinson (1915), vii.
65. *Kolliyat*, 343–44.
66. *Kolliyat*, 306.
67. *Kolliyat*, 306, starting with (خواهم که به یاد عشق مجنون).
68. *Kolliyat*, 314, starting with (در سحر سخن چنان تمام).
69. *Kolliyat*, 325.
70. *Kolliyat*, 12.
71. This 36-line passage is tucked between "In Praise of Malek Fakhr al-Din Bahram Shah ben Davud" and "On the Status and Rank of this Book." It is not clear if Bahram Shah was indeed the king who would be compensating him for that book.
72. Nizami-Clarke (1881), 111 and 123–4.
73. *Kolliyat*, 615.
74. There is an alternative reading in *Kolliayt* (1372).
75. See van Ruymbeke (2000) and Khazrai (2000).
76. *Kolliyat*, 857.
77. Nizami-Clarke (1881), 110.
78. *Kolliyat*, 612.
79. Ibid.
80. Ibid.
81. Ibid.
82. He writes:

لغت همه علوی چو از آن نمت بگردد / صلب دگر بپوشد به سیاق معانی

نتی که شعر دارد چو از آن زبان بگردد / چه نوشتن آید از وی چه رسد به ترجمانی

83. Occasionally, however, he denies he is concerned with any of them at all: "I know nothing of meaning nor am I aware of form / for meaning and form have left my heart and my eyes" (Ibid, 201).
84. Nezami Ganjavi (1988), 117.
85. Nezami-Meisami (1995), xxv.
86. Khaleghi Motlagh, (1991).
87. Ghanoonparvar (1991).
88. For the versions with dots see Nezami-Dastgerdi, 17 and Nezami-Sarvatiyan (1984), 81.
89. Naderpur (1991).
90. See Jafari (1991) and Sarvatiyan (1989), 37, 40.
91. Nezami Ganjavi (1983), 226.
92. Nezami Ganjavi (1988), KS11, 7, with alternative reading in Nizami-Dastgirdi (1372).
93. *Kolliyat*, 18.
94. *Kolliyat*, 820 and 944.
95. Ferdowsi, *Shahnameh*, ed. Khaleghi-Motlagh (1987–2005).

سخن هر چه گویم همه گفته اند / برو باغ دانش همه رفته اند

96. Raduyani (1960), 201–212.
97. Nezami Aruzi, *Chahar Maqaleh* (Four Discourses), translated by E. G. Browne in *Journal of the Royal Asiatic Society*, July and October 1899), at Persianpakhum.org, Chapter I.
98. Ibid.
99. Justine Landau, "Nasir al-Din Tusi and Poetic Imagination in the Arabic and Persian Philosophical Tradition," in A. A. Seyed-Gohrab, ed., *Metaphor and Imagery in Persian Poetry*, Brill (2011): 15–65. J. Landau's work also confirms these notions to "shed some light on Naṣīr al-Dīn Ṭūsī's contribution to 'that art whereby the poet arranges imaginary propositions.'" Ibid., 15.
100. Z. Ansari, Life, *Times and Works of Amir Khusrau Dehlavi*, (New Delhi: Amir Khusrau Society, 1975), 171.
101. *Kolliyat*, 409.
102. *Kolliyat*, 409, Davis 210. The first line of the passage reads:

Her life seemed tasteless, saltless, but then heaven   این بی‌نمکی فلک همی‌کرد
Rubbed salt into the wounds she had been given.   وان خوش نمک این جگر همی‌خورد

103. Davis, *Layli and Majnun*, trans. 210.
104. *Kolliyat*, 409.
105. Christine van Ruymbeke, "Nizami's Poetry versus Scientific Knowledge: The Case of the Pomegranate," in *The Poetry of Nizami Ganjavi*.

106. J. Christoph Bürgel, in his article "Occult Sciences in the *Iskandarnameh* of Nizami," in *The Poetry of Nizami Ganjavi.*
107. *Kolliyat*, 354 (lines 77, 79).
108. *Kolliyat*, 33 (lines 43–44).
109. *Kolliyat*, 354 (line 80).
110. *Kolliyat*, 94 (lines 13, 17, 21).
111. Sai'di expresses this concept as (فهم سخن چون نکند مدعی):
112. Nezami in particular, uses *baligh, moakad kenayeh*, and *makineh* types of *tashbih.*
113. *Kolliyat*, 602 (line 10).
114. *Kolliyat*, 417.
115. The passage starts with this line,

شاها ملکا جهان پناها / یک شاه نه بل هزار شاها

116. An example of this the passage that starts with (از یکر این عروس فکری).
117. *Kolliyat*, 307.
118. This nostalgic image is not solely based on Zoroastrian principles and imageries. Sometime shapes and items or the behavior of characters is also indicative. In some stories, kings are still wearing a horned crown.
119. It starts with this line:

یکی بزج عرب را تا ابد ماه / یکی ملک عجم را از ازل شاه

120. Nezami Ganjavi was born only 49 years after the Persian political theorist, Nezam al-Mulk Tusi. His concept of Iran could not be too old or distant.

CHAPTER 3

Women and Love in the Works of Nezami, Ferdowsi, and Jami

Women feature in the works of Nezami Ganjavi (1140–1202), Abolqasem Ferdowsi (932–1020), and Abd al-Rahman Jami (1414–1492), three major classical Persian poets, to differing degrees.[1] All three poets are skillful in their portrayal and distinguished from poets such as Hafez or Rumi, who are not closely concerned with characterization.[2] If they refer to Shirin, for example, or to her relationship with the Persian king, they do not feel the need to elaborate, because they assume the names they invoke will naturally conjure the needed sentiment.

Although these poets' portrayals of their female characters also vary considerably, it is possible to compare them since all three have written love stories. Specific stories are common to at least two of these authors. Their stories include shared characters, often based on historical figures. Moreover, Nezami was inspired by Ferdowsi in a significant way and referred to his work, while Jami was inspired by Nezami and referred to him. Perhaps for these reasons, prominent scholars of classical Persian literature, including Meisami, Bürgel, and Moayyad, have compared some of their female characters. However, the existing literature on the topic does not provide reasons for such diverse characterizations; rather, it merely offers engaging descriptive analyses. This comparative study of the portrayals of women will seek to clarify the ambiguity surrounding the ideological positions of these poets. Such clarification carries broad significance. In postrevolutionary Iran, for instance, the interpretation of these

© The Author(s), under exclusive license to Springer Nature Switzerland AG 2022
K. Talattof, *Nezami Ganjavi and Classical Persian Literature*,
Literatures and Cultures of the Islamic World,
https://doi.org/10.1007/978-3-030-97990-4_3

poets' works has become the subject of intense debate among cultural and literary critics, many of whom are widely divided over Islamic discourse and state ideology. Although Nezami's work has always been subject to various opposing readings in Iran, these differences have become political in recent years. Encouraged by the ruling elite, advocates of the state ideology use these poets' works to further their ideological objectives. An analysis of their portrayals of women shows that the three poets do not belong to the same ideological paradigm, and forced religious interpretations limit the understanding of their literary significance.

There is an inconsistency even within the religious or mystic readings of Nezami's work, and here I will point one of them regarding the characterization of women. While A. A. Sa'idi Sirjani has read Nezami's works from a non-ideological point of view, a host of other Muslim critics offer merely religious readings of the poet's work. Such varying approaches have produced highly diverse images of the poet's beliefs and attitudes. For example, Sa'idi Sirjani, pointing to Nezami's positive portrayals of characters such as Shirin and Layli [Layla], presents the poet as progressive and culturally liberated, especially regarding women's issues.[3] Yet, we should remember Nezami was influenced by the Persian ancient thinking and Zoroastrian dualism, and, therefore, he does not stop at only portraying the positive aspects of his female characters, but he also goes on to versify possible and contextualized shortcomings of some of them. In his stories, a woman might act hurriedly, another might treat people condescendingly, and in certain situations one might use trickery and deceit. However, Sarvatian, a prolific scholar bringing a peculiar Islamic point of view to the poet's work, claims that the writer promoted the Islamic hijab (veiling of women) and implies that Nezami's female characters do not necessarily represent women but are instead symbols, codes, and secrets that often carry religious meanings.[4] Sarvatian also states that Nezami has portrayed human nature and sensuality as deceitful procurers and wisdom as a wealthy world traveler.[5] Sarvatian's conviction is most probably based on a story in the *Iskandarnameh* (The Book of Alexander) in which Alexander tries to convince the women of the city of Qifchaq to wear the veil. However, in addition to all the historical inconsistencies and ambiguities that mark this last work of Nezami, as Matini states, Nezami's voice in this story is neutral and stops short of corroborating Iskandar's views.[6] Moreover, he disregards the fact that even in *Iskandarnameh*, women are portrayed as free members of society who participate in all sorts of activities. They play music, fight on the battlefield, and provide deep insight into social and philosophical issues. As with Sarvatian, Fatamah Alaqih offers a traditional interpretation of women's roles in Nezami's writings when, in a critique of *Khusraw and Shirin,* she concludes that Shirin appears in the story simply to exalt the spirit of Farhad, a male character deeply in love with her.[7] 'Alaqih disregards the central significance of Shirin in the story and the fact that in his narrative, Nezami often disassociates himself from characters who struggle with virtues. 'Alaqih's interpretation of women in Nezami's works stems from her belief that women in gnostic lyric poetry form the basis for the ascension of gnostic men's spirits.[8] Ahmad Mahdavi Dameghani's statement on Nezami's religiosity is expressed directly in the title of his article (text of a speech), which reads as "'Aqayed-e Nezami dar Tohid va Sefat-e Barita'ala" (Nezami's beliefs about God's Unity and Attributes of the Exalted Almighty). He locates Nezami's poetry in the middle of the then intense medieval debates between religious scholars (Arab and Persian) over the still forming Islamic theology and jurisprudence. He argues that Nezami was directly inspired by Koran, hadith, and the prophet's tradition because in his firm and sharp religious beliefs, his poetry is not based on dry philosophical reasoning. Here, Mahdavi Dameghani is a little more specific about Nezami's alleged religiosity. However, his thesis begs the question: Weren't the other Islamic theological scholars to whom Nezami is compared also inspired by Koran, Hadith, and prophet's tradition? If not, what did then inspire them? He further reiterates the dictum that whatever Nezami has [achieved], he owes it to Koran.[9] What is not mentioned is Nezami's numerous other sources of inspiration and working materials such as Persian myths and legends, Zoroastrian thoughts and philosophy, and the poetry of previous poets such as Sana'i and Ferdowsi. In general, these interpretations display the problematics of the discourse on sexuality in Iran, as interpreters try to disassociate Nezami from this aspect of human activity. As a Muslim poet, Nezami did render religious themes, but post-revolutionary religious critics attempt to portray those themes according to the exigencies of their own time.

I maintain that Nezami, reflecting on human love, offers a favorable and consistent concept of love and its diverse forms in his presentation of female characters. He portrays complex, multi-dimensional characters in their roles as lovers, heroines, rulers, and even educators and challengers of men, as he places them in a variety of contexts. Given the patriarchal nature of twelfth-century Iranian society, such a portrayal of women seems anachronistic, unlikely, and puzzling. Comparing Nezami's characterization of women with that of Ferdowsi, who wrote approximately two centuries before him, and Jami, who appeared approximately three centuries after him, further illustrates Nezami's unique position.

Although these and many other classical poets, as Meisami asserts, may in one way or another address themes in their love stories such as self-knowledge, ethics, and the protagonist's suitability as a lover and king, they differ in the way they characterize women.[10] Ferdowsi seems to follow the logic and necessities of epic writing in his characterization of women, and female characters are not, therefore, the focus of the stories in the *Shahnameh* (*The Book of Kings*). The women in Ferdowsi's work are described in terms of their relationship to the heroes. Jami, embracing the dominant traditional culture, portrays women in a highly negative, unflattering manner.[11] In his work, homosexual love, relatively common in certain Sufi expressions, overshadows his characterization of women. I do not quarrel with either those who view Ferdowsi's artistic and historical importance as equal or superior to Nezami's or those who feel that Jami's work is sufficiently significant to count him as one of the great Persian poets of the classical period. My contention relates to the relevance of the characterization of women to the genres and discursive contexts of the three poets. And such an approach is especially problematic when a distinction should be made between women in Jami's allegorical work and the notion of women presented by orthodox Islam.

Nezami's education in several branches of science and learning, and his personal experience, contributed to his unique portrayal of women, love, and relations between men and women, making them among his major themes. Through his treatment of such themes, he brings a progressive and humanist approach to the characterizations of Shirin from *Khosrow o Shirin*, (*Khosrow and Shirin*, 1180), the female characters in *Haft Paykar*, (the Seven Beauties, 1197), and Layli from *Layli o Majnun*, (*Layli and Majnun*, 1188).

Examples of such descriptions are provided throughout this book. Nezami's concise and powerful lines about Shirin show how completely the storyteller defines his characters.[12] The author depicts Shirin's ethics in terms of Zoroastrian value system.[13] Her virtues manifest in every encounter she has with other figures. The poet also depicts her physical attributes in the first patch, equating her with a young, beautiful, radiant, moonlike, fairy mermaid. Tall, long, beautiful, braided black hair, sweet lips, pearl-like teeth, and intoxicating scent are adjectives and metaphors that construct a pictorial allegory by depicting a garden with a pond and a mermaid on the surface and thus she narrates the beloved character on an additional level. The second passage, which includes more than these two samples, describes Shirin's wealth and status as a successful woman. The third part portrays her social life as independently single (*nadarad shuyo*), prosperous and happy (*kamrani* and *shadi*), and stronger than men.

In the early part of the story, the description is of Shirin bathing in a pond in a green prairie on her way alone to the capital of Persia to meet the Persian prince. In the scene, the naked Shirin looks like a shining star in a green galaxy and like a pearl in the blue water. That depiction has become iconic; one that has inspired classical and contemporary poets, artists, and miniaturist of the past and present, as well as fiction writers such as Mahmud Dowlatabadi in the depiction of Maral in a similar situation in his monumental novel, *Kalidar*. Khosrow and Golmohamad, the male protagonists of these two works, arrive at the scenes to witness their beloved bathing, intensifying their longing for her.[14]

Aware of the position of women in pre-Islamic Iran and the cultural context of his own time, Nezami demonstrates familiarity with the psychological aspects of women's experiences. *Khosrow and Shirin* and the Seven Beauties portray several women in pre-Islamic society, while *Layli and Majnun* presents a woman within the social context of the early Islamic period. As Mehdi Zarghani also points out, in his *Khosrow o Shirin* and *Haft Paykar*, Nezami offers an understanding of the human body that is rooted in the pre-Islamic Persian notion of the body, while in *Layli o Majnun*, he remains loyal to the context of the original tale in which Islamic jurisprudence oversees body and bodily contacts.[15] However, verses in the latter romance might ambiguously suggest contacts between the lovers. Moreover, as we will read in later chapters, the absence of lovemaking does not make their relationship mystical or their love for Sufi, which is otherwise conflicted, ambiguous Sufi love, within which the body is supposed to be annihilated.

Khusraw and Shirin recounts the love between the Sasanid King Khosrow Parviz (590–628) and the Armenian, or possibly Zoroastrian, Shirin.[16] It is a complicated story. Shirin, an affectionate, strong, and honest woman, plays polo, goes on picnics with her maids, and swims naked in ponds. She hears about Khosrow, sees his picture, falls in love with him, and rides without an escort to the capital, Mada'in, to meet him. She discovers that Khosrow is an irresolute and inadequate person and challenges him, attempting to make a responsible and caring man of him. Many years go by and Khosrow changes to some extent. After they marry, she continues to ascend morally and spiritually by good deeds and thoughts, both of which are basic principles of Zoroastrianism. When Shiruyeh kills Khosrow and tries to marry her, she commits suicide.[17] Throughout the story, Nezami affectionately portrays Shirin. He shows enormous sensitivity to the happy and tragic aspects of her life. Some scholars believe that Shirin, in fact, represents Nezami's wife, Afaq.[18] However, he portrays other women in the story as equal and, in some cases, superior to men— capable even of ruling a country. As we shall see, Nezami's sympathetic portrayal of Shirin as affectionate, strong, and straightforward can be better appreciated by contrasting it with Ferdowsi's version of the story in the *Book of Kings*, in which Shirin is assigned negative characteristics.[19]

Nezami's romance genre written in the couplet meter has the quality of lyricism to some extent, contributing to his unique characterization of all women (and some men). Almost all medieval historiographies refer to the historical Shirin as a maidservant who becomes Khosrow's (often abused) secret mistress. As mentioned, Ferdowsi, too, remains somewhat loyal to his historical sources. Nezami does not seem to have relied on just the *Shahnameh* alone. Some scholars believe that Shirin in Nezami's work is different (and elevated to the status of a princess) because Nezami based the characterization on his beloved wife Afaq.[20] However, even if we had the correct information about his other sources, it would not prove that Nezami has embedded a coded message in that characterization, requiring a key to decipher. Nezami recalls his wife Afaq when portraying Shirin's character is not solid proof that Shirin represents all the traits and characteristics of the poet's wife. Nezami's religiosity will be later discussed further, but here, if the construction of Shirin based on Afaq were a valid argument, then another question arises. Why would a supposedly mystic or pious Muslim poet want an Armenian princess to represent his wife? The two women could have been similar somehow, but they belonged to two different eras, cultures, and religions. Suppose we are to base our analysis on specific attributes. In that case, we may also surmise that Shirin's character in Nezami's work could have been based on the Anahita, the much-beloved Zoroastrian goddess. After all, according to Zoroastrian narratives, Anahita was not only strong and beautiful but possessed numerous virtues. One of those myths even portrays a scene where she swims in a pound and drinks from its water to become pregnant with Zoroaster's child. Could have that imagery contained a hidden Zoroastrian message, requiring a key to decode it? The relevance of Anahita's question is to support the notion that Nezami seems to have rebelled against all hitherto treatment of Shirin's character, historical and or fictitious, by portraying her significantly and anachronistically different from any of the known and existing sources.

The characterization of Shirin is not the only innovation rooted in Nezami's genre in general and his profound view of humanity and love in particular. Farhad (whose love for Shirin is a shorter tragic romance and a touching story within the book of *Khosrow o Shirin*) is a highly educated engineer, so he would somewhat qualify to have a chance to earn Shirin's reciprocating love. Nevertheless, at the same time, Farhad represents another unorthodox view of love and life.[21] The genre factor explains these differences between the character of Shirin and her encounter with two lovers in *Shahnameh* and *Khosrow o Shirin* more effectively than differences between historical sources, which might or might not show significant discrepancies.

The characterization of each woman in the Seven Beauties also highlights Nezami's unique, humanistic, and eloquent representation of women.[22] The "frame story" of the book revolves around the Sasanid king Bahram. It includes seven stories told to the king by seven princesses of seven climes on each of the seven days of the week and in seven different beautiful and colorful domes.[23] Each tale features fulfilled or thwarted love.[24]

On Tuesday, the "princess of the fourth clime" residing in the "red dome, a Slavic princess, tells Bahram the story of an admirable, discriminating, beautiful, wise, and learned king's daughter who concludes that no ordinary man deserves to be her husband.[25] The poem refers to her as the Slavic girl, ruddy face lady, and then named Lady of the Fortified Citadel (*banu-ye hesari*), the same character named Turandot in Giacomo Puccini's opera. Suitors wishing to gain this princess's hand in marriage encircle her castle. She eventually tires of rejecting them. Frustrated, she moves to a stronger fortress on a high mountain, a fortress that pushes its head into the clouds, where she can dwell and be spared the great plague of burdensome suitors. She arms the castle with numerous talismans to keep away men of inferior intelligence. Any man able to navigate the deadly traps and find the castle entrance will be made to answer four riddles to discover whether he is worthy of her love. Therefore, such a man must be of noble lineage, brave, strong, sufficiently cunning to disarm the talismans and to find the entrance, and clever enough to solve the riddles. Suitors try to reach the castle but fail and lose their lives. One young prince comprehends the vast amount of knowledge needed to win the princess. He goes away to study and learn the necessary skills and wisdom. After a long journey, he returns, successfully enters the fortress, and solves the riddles. The princess finds him worthy of marriage. They make love.

Now he kissed her cheek, at times her lips.   گاه رخ بوسه داد و گاه لبش
Sometimes tasted her pomegranates [breasts], at times her dates   گاه نارش گزید و که رطبش [26]
[lips].

In mystical and religious readings of Nezami's poetry, often such portrays are ignored. Those critics repeat their conviction that Nezami was pious because his language was "clean," for example, he did not grossly portray sexual scenes and did not mention human sexual organs; that he had *effat-e kalam*, modesty of words or chastity of speech. Nezami sees sexual drive in its natural sense and frequently portrays it to *Haft Paykar* and *Khosrow o Shirin* to the extent that some parts of these books might be referred to as *Havasameh* but in a classy style. Generally, the reason the lack of such natural portrayal is considered clean goes back to the pretentious ideological ethical system, which is in fact more contemporary. I argue that the reason for the absence of a successful modernization process, a pervasive discourse of modernity in Iran, and freedom of the interpretation of classical text (or even printing and reading a substantial number of forbidden texts) is that any public and theoretical discussion of modern ideas and philosophies has lacked the necessary academic, intellectual, national, and most importantly historical debate over the seminal subjects of sex and sexuality. Even if some statements were made within the realm of popular culture about sexuality, their meanings were limited to sex instead of covering all of which makes a person sexual, regardless of their sexual identity. Yet fundamentalism found such statements erotic enough to embark on a moral campaign to repackage and present their view of sexuality as more virtuous and even as revolutionary.[27] A mere ideological reading of classical texts, depriving their authors and their literary characters of their stories, contributes to the suppression of modern discourse of sexuality and to the lack of a history of sexuality.[28] Besides, a so-called cleansed language does not make a poet a Muslim or the other way around. Many Muslim authors wrote about human sexuality, including Obeyd Zakani. To be sure, the Zoroastrian religion also encourages good (yes, chaste) speech. The reason for this emphasis on Nezami's "clean language" is perhaps because Nezami does indeed talk about sex, sexuality, and women's bodies. No analyst talks so much about *effat-e kalam* in, say, Hafez's poetry.

Going back to the story of "The Lady of Fortified Citadel," even the way she speaks to her father reflects confidence in her abilities: "Dearest Father, forgive me, but I must leave you. Provide me with provisions for travel."[29] Rarely in stories of the same period did daughters have the tenacity, let alone the resources, to reject a system in which patriarchs arranged women's marriages. The princess's search for wisdom in both herself and her husband forces a comparison with men who act without thinking. Nezami further demonstrates their inferiority by presenting the princess's ultimate victory. Furthermore, the final love scene nullifies any notion that Nezami's metaphors represent religious symbols and refutes the claim that Nezami's story narrates a metaphorical union between God and humankind, as traditional interpretations suggest. This scene does not support Jafari's notion that love in Nezami's work is directed to God, nor does it bear out Sarvatian's statement that Nezami's female characters represent not real women but symbols, codes, and secrets, often carrying religious meaning.[30] Although Nezami uses a good number of metaphors to refer to the female body, "breasts," "cheek," "sex organ," "naked arms," "stature," and "lips" are too literal, and pomegranate, pistachio, and silver palm, cypress, and ruddy red are well established stand-ins in Persian literature for female features to just be dismissed as mere symbols.

STRETCHING MYSTIC INTERPRETATION

The man who manages to solve the riddles and surpass all other obstacles to reach the princess proves that he is brave and learned in all sciences and thus deserving. To learn all this, he goes to an older wise man for help; an act all other men who were killed in the process had failed to do. This consultation has strengthened the mystic reading of the story, according to which, the successful suitor is perceived to be a disciple (morid) and the older man to be an elderly Sufi mentor (pir or morshed).[31] I believe this whole concept of morshed or pir versus morid or salek (the spiritual adviser, the wise guide versus the disciple, the devotee), which became perfected in the story of Rumi and Shams is an ineffective, misleading as a probable universal explanatory model for understanding causality. It is hard to justify that in this story of the "Lady of Fortified Citadel," a little-known character who helps the suitor of the princess teaches him all knowledge and skills and prepared him for unknown challenges in such a brief time, no matter how imaginary the story might be. First, any student who needs to learn new knowledge might seek advice from a knowledgeable person;

the teacher does not have to be a mystic. Second, Sufi mentors are not characteristically known for knowing all the sciences of their time and tricks. Third, the man's goal was to earn the love of a woman, and he did. There is no indication that he united with God or earned an "immaterial love." Finally, why would a Sufi poet seek to convey such a rudimentary message through such a complex story with a Zoroastrian context, a story that easily lends itself to much more profound interpretations?

MORE CARNAL LOVE STORIES

Furthermore, a group of women feast and drink in a garden in the story told by "the Persian princess." Two persons responsible for guarding the area during the party capture a young curious man trying to enter the garden through a breach in the creek. Nezami portrays the scene as:

He entered the garden to watch	شد درون تا کند تماشائ
And dance with them like the Sufis	صوفیانه برآورد پائ
Using the garden inspection as an excuse	گوش بر نغمه ترانه نهد
To listen to the song and music.	دیدن باغ را بهانه نهد ³²

Here the word "Sufiyaneh" does not mean that the curious young man was a Sufi; it means he intended to take his cloth off or act like a thief. Both meanings agree with Nezami's general negative views of the Sufis. They discover that he owns the garden and that the party was taking place without his knowledge. The women allow the garden's owner to enter, and he sits in a hidden corner, watching the group as they revel and play music. One girl discovers the man's presence and becomes interested in him. They fall in love, make out away from the group, and try to make love several times. The party ends, and the girl's father and others later find out about the incident. However, the women are not punished or accused of wrongdoing. Some, in fact, seem to understand the passionate girl and her desire. The girl is not contrite and feels no reluctance or restriction in talking about herself, her feelings, or her ill-fated attempts to make love with the man. In the concluding scene, the community helps the young couple marry.³³ Although Nezami's tale here tacitly points to the necessity of marriage for legal intercourse, he again represents female desire, even outside wedlock, as neither sinful nor blasphemous. Since they describe their inner feelings, the female figures are more expressive, eclipsing the male characters. Such portrayals of women and the centrality of their roles lend the poet's work an anachronistically modern quality. His contemporaries do not share such an approach.

Yet another story from the Seven Beauties, "Dastan-i Bahram ba Kanizak-i Khish" ("The Story of Bahram with His Slave-Girl"), features a female character named Fetneh, who rejects traditional, patriarchal customs. Like Shirin, Fetneh, one of King Bahram's slaves, is also present in Ferdowsi's *Book of Kings,* where, as will be seen later in more detail, she appeared in a radically different light. The differing treatments of this character by Nezami and Ferdowsi reflect fundamental differences in their genres and portrayal of sexuality.

In Nezami's version of the story of King Bahram's slave-girl, the woman is renamed Fetneh (meaning revolt or sedition) from Azadeh (meaning free or noble), her name in Ferdowsi's version.[34] Fetneh rebels resolutely against the traditions and institutions of King Bahram's court. For example, hunting does not impress her, so she repudiates a cherished court custom. She then uses her wits to stay alive and challenge the king's beliefs.

Fetneh could accompany the king on one of his ritual hunting trips to witness the great skill with which he kills his prey. She avoids praising the king's hunting skills. Then she downplays the king's amazing performance in hunting an onager, stating that it only takes practice to shoot the animal so skillfully and that she does not consider it an art. The king is filled with rage and asks one of his army commanders to kill her. Fetneh reasons with the officer, persuading him to spare her life so that if the king later regrets his harshness, the officer will not be in trouble. The commander sends her to a faraway place where, as part of her work, every day she carries a calf on her shoulder up 60 stairs to the palace roof. As a result of this, she becomes so strong that she is able to carry the animal even after it is a fully-grown ox.

Meanwhile, Bahram remains under the sad impression that Fetneh was executed. One day, however, he visits the palace and sees her carrying the ox. He tells her that with practice, everything is possible. Fetneh reveals her identity. He is happy that she is still alive and apologizes to her. Fetneh in turn apologizes and attempts to justify her comments on the hunting trip. Nezami's Bahram is wise enough to see that Fetneh was right; by marrying her, he acknowledges her superior wisdom.

This is not the only time in *Khosrow o Shirin* that a man falls in love with a woman by hearing her descriptions. Such passages are pertinent to both discussions of women's characterization and Nezami's alleged religiosity and Sufism. Khosrow becomes interested in both Shirin and Shekar before meeting them. Here is the story of the latter. The king asks his audience (primarily rulers and noblemen) to tell him where a woman (kuban, the good ones) deserving his praise can be found. The following several verses start with *yeki goft*, or someone said. Each speaker offers the name of a realm and the descriptions of the girls/women of that region.

In what part of the world and domains	که خوبانی که در خورد فریشند
Do reside praiseworthy girls?	ز عالم در کدامین بقعه بیشند
One said, Rum offers beauty like jewels	یکی گفتا لطافت روم دارد
And Rum has beautiful gems.	لطف گنج است و گنج آن بوم دارد ³⁵

The last person suggests a beautiful girl in Sepahan (Isfahan) named Shekar (sugar) and offers more details and descriptions than the previous contributors to convince the king. It works. The passage ends with two lines—the penultimate is the last description of Shekar, and the last line is about the king establishing a new way of having sex with another woman possible. The two lines read:

Whoever sleeps with her for one night	کسی کاو را شبی گیرد در آغوش
Will never forget that night	نگردد آن شبش هرگز فراموش
The king fell for those heartening words of love	ملک را بر گرفت آن دلنوازی
He created a fresh basis for making love.	اساسی نو نهاد از عشق بازی

The passage is also an allegory formed around the *yeki goft* phrase, and those words mean a girl. In these lines and those in between, several different words come to mean a girl(s), each after *yeki goft* (one said). These words include *khuban*, (the good ones, fair girls, beloved), *letafat* (tenderness, a pleaser), *delaram* (one that calms the heart, a lovely girl, a sweetheart), and *laleh* (tulip, an enthusiastic lover). The last one, *laleh*, like words such as pomegranate, dates fruit, pistachio, and treasure, has a sexual connotation reinforced in the following line. The carnal sexual desire and passionate, lustful aspect of this story segment are not secret. Khosrow wants to sleep with another beautiful woman (in addition to all his mistresses) to elicit Shirin's jealousy and provoke her to sleep with him. However, in Nezami's characterization of Shirin, she belongs to a noble social class, a princess with pride and *kherad*. Mahin Banu, Shirin's aunt and practically a mother to her, is portrayed as a wise and rational ruler of Armenia. She advises her niece, "Not to submit her body to Khosrow before getting married to him because to him you would simply become another mistress." If fact, Mahin Banu's preemptive prudent advice, sense of rationality, the strength of character, and virtuous traits continue to inspire Shirin throughout her life. For her, the Armenian Mahin Banu is as profound as the Zoroastrian *Minuye Kherad* (spirit of reasoning). Shirin can use these virtues because she has dangerously fallen in love with a careless Persian prince. She feels compelled to leave her utopian women-ruled society and ride to the den of the "demons," all thanks to Shapur's shrewd and scheming and successful tactics to place Khosrow Parviz's portrait within her sight. Even in dealing with Maryam, a Roman emperor's daughter and Khosrow's official wife who goes out of her way to prevent sex between her husband and Shirin, the spirit of Mahin Banu's rationality comes to help. It is as if Mahin Banu fulfills the author's desire to protect his beloved heroine.

There is no need to argue that the book of *Khosrow o Shirin* prominently portrays love, lust, and sex; the author himself refers to it as *shahvatnameh*, the book of concupiscence, far from any type of religious categorization. What is needed is an explanation of the complex characterization and complexity of each section of the book and how these sections form a formidable poetic narrative. Furthermore, one of the intricacies of the story is that Nezami portrays several types of love and longings (none of which is even remotely mystical or platonic). Khosrow's love for Shirin, at least in the beginning, is purely carnal, lustful, derived from a sense of male sexual entitlement, rooted in where male sexuality and power meet. Shirin's love for Khosrow also begins superficially and only based on looks and desire. However, it turns rational, *kherdmand* particularly due to her admirable virtues, strengthened by the life-changing advice she receives from Mahin Banu. Throughout the story, Shirin tries to act based on kherad to be rational and reasonable in her daily life and her relationship with the man she loves, just as Mahin Banu had taught her. This characterization, an enormous aspect of Nezami's narrative, has no roots or sources in Islam or Sufism.

Farhad falls madly in love when he meets Shirin to receive her instruction for building a tunnel to carry her much-needed daily fresh milk from the pasture into her castle. His love is burning, a painful desire, with a crazy intensity. Shirin's feeling for Farhad is ambiguous and grows at most into sympathy. Later Shiruyeh, Khosrow's son, seems to have fallen in love with Shirin. However, his feeling is perhaps nothing by a desire to conquer all that was his father's, which explains the book's brilliant and tragic end when she commits suicide next to her husband's lifeless body.

Khosrow's love for Shirin is primarily rooted in his tense physical attraction toward her. When he is in Armenia looking for Shirin, he holds the most extravagant party in his camp. He hears that Shirin has gone to Ctesiphon (his capital city Madaen) after him, but all Khosrow does is dispatch Shapur to find her. The segment entitled "Majles Bazm-e Khosrow va Baz Amadan-e Shapur" (Khosrow's Leisure Banquet and Shapur's Return) is an extended pictorial allegory that reveals the nature of the prince's desire.[36] He is searching for his beloved Shirin in Armenia, and while waiting, he engages in one of his favorite activities; a party with musicians and cupbearers at his service. But the way Nezami constructs the surface story of the allegory to convey or foreshadow the mood of the party and the mentality of the prince (the second layer of the allegory) is yet another remarkable example of the author's storytelling prowess, his literary techniques, his intention to entertain his readers, and his profound understanding of *kherad*, reason, and rationality. Here, he demonstrates how the infamous concept of *bikheradi* (irrationality) can cause distress and disaster.

According to three passages there, looking for Shirin is not the sole reason for his travel to Armenia; he is also trying to escape his father's additional planned punishment for destroying a farmer's house and livestock. The narrative of the passage, however, remains focused on the banquet: describing colors, fruits, the aromas and scents, the tastes and types of fine foods and wines, dark red fire in a golden brazier with the diffusing musk and pussy willow logs burning on its top, sounds, and shapes of birds which are not even present but are named in Persian songs appropriately performed. With the usual sense of relativism, which stands against the emphatic "know this" (*bedan*) certitude of Sufism and "go through the course" (*taye tariq*) Sufi stages, two of Nezami's verses challenge the enduring proverbial dictum. The first refers to the saying that "there is no color beyond black." The verse rejects it by saying that the redness of fire comes after the blackness of the charcoals and that the black hair of a man turns white later when he is aged.[37] He also features fruits and foods that are served and helps readers feel them with their senses. All this point once again that for Nezami, love, often portrayed as sensual and worldly, is personal but ultimately a literary motif, an element in his literary allegories. Finally, at the end of the scene, as if he is supporting Khosrow's desire to enjoy his time, he argues that life is short. We must cherish every moment of it, a notion that later became more fully explored in the poetry of Khayyamian and Rumi, notions which can be taken as afront to the otherworldliness of the dominant religion.

This segment also confirms that Nezami portrays all sorts of sensual and emotional relationships (consensual or reciprocated) in other love stories, imaginatively, historically, and realistically. In *Layli o Majnun*, as we will see in more detail, the protagonists' love is intense and improbable. Both have no desire or even ability to seek other desirable alternatives for sexual satisfaction despite the constant longing. On all these occasions, let us have no doubt, the lovers express the desire for physical contact, and this, too, should encourage a literary reading of the poet's stories.

Nezami wrote during a period when women were strongly believed to be impaired in intelligence (*naqes ul-aql*). His humanistic approach to rhetoric and his understanding of women as equal set him apart from the dominant literary discourse of his time. In fact, Bürgel and Meisami have also pointed to Ferdowsi's and Nezami's differing portrayals of this character as a means of underscoring their contentions about Nezami's work and personality. Bürgel states that "seldom is the humanism of Nezami more palpable than in the alterations he made in this story."[38] Meisami states that "the story is paradigmatic, demonstrating Nezami's conception of his poetic task and his specific intent in The Seven Beauties, displaying the devices used to achieve his ends, and clarifying both his relationship to his surfaces and his departure from the epic tradition embodied in Ferdowsi's (ca. 1010) *Book of Kings*, on the heroic values of which both this episode and the poem as a whole provide a commentary."[39] In general, Meisami's study sheds light on the moral seriousness of romance and on the integration of literary elements in Nezami's poetry.[40]

In Nezami's tragic romance, *Layli and Majnun*, Layli's father removes her from school to prevent her from seeing her childhood love, Majnun, originally named Qays until he goes mad (*majnun*). He later forbids her to think of Majnun and gives her hand in marriage to an older man, Abd al-Salam. Majnun goes mad and wanders in the desert, living with wild animals. During the lover's separation, Majnun's parents and Abd al-Salam die, but the situation does not improve. Finally, after a miserable life, Layli dies while speaking about Majnun to her mother. Upon receiving news of her death, Majnun goes to Layli's tomb and dies there.

Nezami illustrates how social restrictions prevent Layli from speaking out. Throughout the tale, we hear little from Layli directly because she has no one to trust and is afraid to reveal her love for Majnun to others. She hides her pain, even from her parents, to avoid disgracing her tribe. So, she suffers, laments, and finally dies completely unfulfilled. Layli is correct in believing that she would damage her family by disobeying tradition, which holds that love outside marriage or marriage not arranged constitutes a sin. Yet Layli's last words to her mother reveal not only her love for Majnun but also her condemnation of those cultural restrictions. In her confession to her mother, she states, "I am dying because this is not a life." It is a critical indication of the emotional deprivation enforced by the cultural constraints of that time.

Even under such miserable conditions, Layli does not submit to her fate easily; in fact, she resists vehemently.[41] She shows more emotional fortitude than Majnun; for instance she complains less about her own misfortune. She writes a letter to Majnun suggesting plans to escape with him, condoling Majnun over his father's death, and detailing their love circumstance.[42] This letter demonstrates Layli's superior strength. She suffers as much pain or more, and yet continues to function within society and bravely refuses sexual intercourse with her husband.[43] Unlike Majnun, whose behavior demonstrates his surrender. The letter, written in the form of an elegy, also shows Nezami's empathy for Layli. Although she is not as outspoken as Nezami's other female characters, she is portrayed as a victim of the traditional culture and a prisoner of a male-dominated society, making Nezami's characterization of Layli as impressive as his characterizations of other women.

Nezami approaches the subject of sex in keeping with the settings of his stories, which he refers to occasionally as *Havasnameh*, The Book of Passion (or Lust). In the stories of Shirin and the characters of the Seven Beauties, set in more open societies, Nezami explores the complexities of this subject. He avoids sexuality in the story of Layli, because in her conservative society she was deprived of any realization of her sexual self, and, therefore, no lovemaking scene is described and no words of passion with sexual connotations are exchanged between the lovers.

We hear little direct testimony from Layli because, as Nezami mentions in introductory verses, the social context gives him less room to illustrate her public appearance. The way he describes Layli is different from the way he describes his ideal protagonist, Shirin. Nezami wrote *Layli and Majnun* reluctantly. The story was written on the court's command and not by his own choice.[44] He had to elaborate about how after the conquest of Iran by Islam, the season for earthly love was gradually lost to the desire for repentance and salvation. In *Layli and Majnun,* he criticizes a society steeped in tradition. Despite the lack of desirable context, he weaves another artistic love story, portraying a deprived Layli, deeply in love, who has no choice but to surrender, yet passively resists. She does not completely give in to her fate. She never submits to the husband she does not love, although Islam stipulates that a wife must yield to the husband's sexual demands. On one occasion, she even punches her husband, knocking him down. In that society, the perception of love was different from that which Nezami portrayed in *Khusraw and Shirin* and the Seven Beauties. In these works, in the context of what he presents as pre-Islamic open society, men and women seem to be more equal, and women have the right to enjoy life, love, and sex. He selectively promotes personal and cultural freedom in both works.[45]

In a segment entitled, "Majnun Learns of Layli's Marriage," Zeami quotes the storyteller on the status of Majnun, who abject with a broken heart is wandering from one pasture to another and awaiting news from his moon-like beloved. He was lying down by thorny bush when a camel rider, resembling a pitch-dark demon, weaving like a poisonous snake (a sharp-tongued) appears to him and informs him that Layli is married. The rider tries to convince him to forget about Layli, who, as he passionately believes is just like all other women, unfaithful, disobedient, guileful, seditious, fickle, and what not (Kokliyat **368**).

Each day she's with him, always, face to face,	باشد همه روزه گوش در گوش
Clasping her husband in her close embrace.	با شوهر خویشتن هم آغوش
Her days are spent in kisses, hugs, caresses,	کارش همه بوسه و کنار است
So why should you care how her love progresses?[46]	تو در غم کارش این چه کار است[47]

With each word, Majnun further breaks inside.[48] As if breaking terrible news in such terrible dispraise voiced demonically is not enough, the rider goes on yet another long, vilifying grumbling negative enunciations about women in general.

Women can be your friend, but in the end,	زن دوست بود ولی زمانی
You'll find out that they've found another friend,	تا جز تو نیافت مهربانی
And when she is cuddled by another love	چون در بر دیگری نشیند
It won't be you that she" be thinking of!"[49]	خواهد که دگر ترا نبیند[50]

In his major book, *Layli and Majnun: Love, Madness and Mystic Longing in Nizami's Epic Romance*, Ali Asghar Seyed-Gohrab provides a detailed analysis of this scene.[51] He writes, "This chapter demonstrates the interdependence between the content and tone of a monologue and the framework provided by the narrator."⁵² Without the camel rider's biting blister, "which literally breaks Majnun, the monologue cannot be fully understood."⁵³ Seyed-Gohrab also addressed a few scholars' misreading of the passage. Rarely do characters have negative views of women. Even here, Nezami does not wait too long to make the demon-looking rider retract and tell Majnun the truth about Layli's loyalty to him and her lack of sexual relations with her husband. Revealing the truth makes Majnun regain his senses and ability to stand up from his fallen, pathetic position. Given that demons do not play a role in this tale and that an unknown rider cannot have such intimate information about Layli's bedroom, this segment may be indeed one of those Majnun's internal debates triggered by hearing the news of her marriage. The next part is titled Majnun complains to the wind about Layli. Either way, the rider seeks forgiveness and offers to help him; so, he is not too devilish to be unable to redeem himself.

Nezami's liberal portrayal of sexuality is also demonstrated through metaphors for male-female relationships, carnal love, and men's and women's sexual organs. In the Seven Beauties, he refers to women's genitals as *ganj* (treasure), *ganj-e dor* (treasure of pearl[s]), *ganj-e gohar* (treasure of gem[s]), *khazineh* (treasury), *ganj-e qand* (treasury of sugar), and *dorj-e qand* (jewel box of sugar).⁵⁴ He also defines it somewhat with the use of the word *pesteh* (pistachio) to leave no doubt about his meaning. In addition, he also refers to the hymen and virginity as the *kan-e la'l* (mine of rubies), *dar-e ganjkhaneh* (treasure house door), *qufl-e zarrin* (golden lock), *mohr-e gohar* (jewel seal), and *mohr* (seal). Regardless of his occasional resorting to a male-constructed notion of virginity (mostly uttered by characters), these references to love and sex and the female body do not specifically denote any particular Sufi trend. Interestingly, they are entirely ignored in Sufi or religious interpretations. In the Sufi literature and, in fact, in much of the Persian poetry written after Nezami, the body, particularly the female body, disappears. In contemporary literature, being chaste is the cornerstone of an unmarried woman's overall virtue. While it had become increasingly acceptable for a young man to have sex (available via burgeoning prostitution houses and other forms), preservation of the hymen was still, in the 1970s, a cultural imperative. It served as the proof of a woman's morality and virtue and for the sake of a man's self-confirmation when he consummated the union and broke the hymen.

How may such openness and progressive characterization be explained? And if Sufism did not provide the driving force for Nezami, what inspired him throughout his career, and what links his diverse works in *Five Treasures*? Bürgel's contention—that Nezami was concerned with promoting humanistic values—contributes to an understanding of the diversity and depth of the poet's work.[55] However, I believe that Nezami shows sensitivity to a variety of social and cultural issues. Living in a multicultural society, he made use of a unique opportunity to embed in his text elements that elevate works: universality of human experience, tolerance, and lessons from history. **Equally** important, I argue that Nezami was extremely preoccupied with the art of speech perse and not so much with jurisprudence or any other Islamic themes/concerns that he used as raw materials. For him, this art was the sublime. These characteristics explain why a Marxist, a Zoroastrian, a feminist, and a Muslim theologian may all find ideological interest there. It is because his work is art before anything else. Nezami's language is not (perhaps deliberately as will be explained) faithful to matters of fact, as is most evident in *The Book of Alexander*, for example, where he brings together in one room Alexander, Plato, Balinas, Socrates, Thales, Hermes, and Aristotle. His interests influenced his language as they developed throughout different periods of his life. And this influence is precisely what makes him a distinct rhetorician, far from an ideologue, boasting that he could have written *Layli and Majnun* in 14 nights instead of 4 months, or from an artist satisfying different tastes.

Of all these issues, however, he devotes his Sakhon (eloquent rhetoric) particularly to love and women in his poetry. His education, his liberal position on social issues, his knowledge of diverse societies, and his personal experiences lead him to present progressive views of women. And in presenting this liberal interpretation of love and of women's social roles, he subverts the dichotomy of love and morality. He celebrates the union of good and happiness: to be good does not mean to suppress passion. In accomplishing these ideas, he has benefited from a strong imagination and wealth of metaphors. These aspects have influenced poets after him and distinguish his work from that of Sana'i, Ferdowsi, who to a limited degree influenced him in terms of genre, characterization of Shirin of *Khosrow o Shirin*, and characterization of Vis of *Vis o Ramin*, respectively.[56]

In addition to personal traits, two other factors explain Nezami's profound interest in human sensibility and portrayal of love, among so many different themes and motives. As described, the first factor is related to Nezami's preoccupation with Sakhon and his desire to perfect language and imagery. This fact led him to read, speculate, and acquire knowledge of other cultures and religions. And his concept of Sakhon not only runs throughout his work as a significant theme itself but also, as Dabashi stresses, the importance of language and the idea of sokhan in Nezami's provided Nezami with an identity.[57] Dabashi states that for Nizami, being is conceived by sokhan, which is used "not only to convey the meaning but also the creation."[58] I would like to think that *sokhan* has a somewhat broader meaning and implication for Nezami. That *sokhan* could be conceptualized as eloquent rhetoric (always expressed in the form of poetry) in his overall literary discourse.

Another evidence of Nezami's main preoccupation is the fact that his books include more than 100 verses that begin with the word sakhon, tens of derivatives of the word such as *sokhandan* or *sokhanvar*, meaning a person who demonstrates an oratorical, eloquent, and poetic manner when writing or speaking, and compound verbs and words such as *sokhan afarin*, *sokhan parvar*, *sokhan ravan*, *sokhan shinas*, *sokhan gostar*, all meaning an eloquent rhetorician who values words, an excellent writer or orator. This preoccupation goes beyond frequent use of the concept; Nezami emphasizes that he holds a high opinion of Sakhon, particularly in its poetic forms, and considers poets to be creative artists of nearly divine status. Because of such a prominent place in poetry for the concept of poetry and literature, his portrayal of women and love, like other subjects, finds its way in the hearts of the readers all over the region. Because Sakhon is so important to him, Nezami assigns the poet a high status in *Layli o Majnun*. He ranks his verses with the Quran, an ambitious aspiration for his time, particularly as such a claim stands against Islamic belief that the Quran could not and cannot be written or imitated by a human being. In The Book of Honor, he compares himself with kings. In The Book of Happiness, he considers himself a great poet, imitated by others.

Secondly, Nezami offers a liberal understanding of Islamic discourse that does not limit his learning from other cultures. His impressions and his love for the prophet as expressed, for example, in *Layli and Majnun*, are mingled with his other cultural impressions. Departing from a Manichaeist or Zoroastrian dichotomy of good versus evil, he subverts the prevalent dichotomy of love and morality by presenting both as good. In his view, to be a good rhetorician required flexibility, sensibility, and responsiveness to a given situation. Nezami's interest in ancient Iranian culture and in philosophy, and his peculiar interpretation of Zoroastrian teachings as illustrated above, may further explain his liberal approach to women and sexuality. Indeed, his understanding of these teachings was more philosophical and therefore different from their idealization by many authors of books of kings in preceding centuries, especially in books written about the history of kingdoms in Iran. Moscati describes ancient Iranian civilization as follows:

> [T]he function of ancient Iranian civilization is principally historical and religious in its nature. In the historical field, the tolerant liberalism, which combines different people into a harmonious empire, has repercussions incalculable in their extent upon the maintenance of civilization...In the religious field, Zarathustra's teaching achieves the highest point of ancient oriental intellectualism. In his conception of the universe, the forces of logic are already active.[59]

As explained and will be further demonstrated, Nezami upholds similar qualities and assigns them to some of his characters.

Dustkhah states that in Zoroastrianism, according to God Ahuramazda, the female angel Anahita is equal to the male Mehr, and the woman is an equal companion of man. In fact, in the Zoroastrian religious text, *Gathas*, Zoroaster lets his daughter, Puruchist, decide who should become her husband.[60] We hear an echo of this in a verse from Yasna 53: "I tell these words to these girls who are being married and to you."[61] Thus, both women and men are addressed in scripture equally. We hear an echo of these influences in Nezami's writing.

It is not necessary for a poet to have a progressive and fair view of women to be inspired by any religion but Nezami refers to this ancient culture frequently. Even in *Makhzan al Asrar*, he calls upon the prophet.

Do not stay in Arab land, come to Iran	سوی عجم ران منشین در عرب
Ride the dark horse of day and night.	زرده روز اینک و شبدیز شب[62]

Indeed, one of his friends criticized him for reviving Zoroastrianism by writing *Khusraw and Shirin*. Instead of answering the critique, Nezami read some of the verses to his friend and made him praise the poet for the beauty of the poem. This is probably a hint from Nezami himself as to how he expected his poetry to be read. Once again, the dichotomy of good versus evil is a major theme in his works and sometimes constitutes the only theme, as in the section of the Seven Beauties titled "Khayr va Shar" (The Virtuous and the Evil), which helps explain Nezami's underlying philosophical beliefs.[63] He contends with the concept of good versus evil as he portrays the evolution of characters such as King Khosrow or the warrior Alexander from their youth. Nezami then may have derived this binary pattern and epistemological element from Zoroastrian dualism. His positive characters always seek to ascend, cognizant of philosophy and sometimes of prophecy.

The poet's acceptance of the concept of duality leads, for example, to the portrayal of various characters from a variety of regions and religions. Or it leads to an imaginative self-portrayal as half *serkeh* and half *angabin*.[64] Another binary opposition surfaces in Nezami's description of his own destiny. In *Iskandarnameh* (The Book of Alexander) he writes about how he explores history, past poets, and new artistic areas.

With each turn in life,	به هر منق گردش روزگار
A learner must seek a new way.	ز طرزی دگر خواهد آموزگار
He warps the old tune,	سرآهنگ پیشینه کج رو کند
To renew and usher in another world.	نوائی دگر در جهان نو کند
When the players begin the game,	به بازی درآید چو بازیگری
Another figure will appear from behind the curtain.	ز پرده برون آورد پیکری
With that figure, in a magical way,	بدان پیکر از راه افسونگری
He will steal peoples' hearts for a time.	کند منق خلق را دلبری
When that old figure becomes decrepit,	چو پیری در آن پیکر آرد شکست
A young figure will appear.	جوان پیکری دیگر آرد بدست[65]

Through such binary depictions, Nezami presents his protagonists as constantly working to improve their attitude to an extent that they might look different from their historical image and from their depiction in the *Book of Kings*. As honest, combative individuals, the female characters are more successful in expeditions and as they attempt to amend themselves, provide a model for the dishonest men.[66]

Nezami's sensitivity may also derive from his experiences of being in love and married three times. He provides a chronology of his life and the deaths of his wives. Writing stories, he says, is pleasurable and can ease his pain in difficult times. This again attests to the importance of women in his life.

I have a strange destiny in poetry	مرا طالعی طرفه هست از سخن
whenever I write an old story anew.	که چون نو کنم داستان کهن
In that celebration when I pour the sugar,	در آن عید کان شکر افشان کنم
I lose a sweet, smiling bride.	عروسی شکر خنده قربان کنم
When I made the *halva* of Shirin	چو حلوای شیرین همی ساختم
I had to give away the *halva* in my house.	ز حلواگری خانه پرداختم
When I enclosed the treasure of Layli,	چو بر گنج لیلی کشیدم حصار
I gave away another jewel.	دگر گوهری کردم آنجا نثار
Now that the wedding is over,	کنون نیز چون شد عروسی بسر
I give another bride to Paradise.	به رضوان سپردم عروسی دگر
With my grief for each bride, I don't know	ندانم که با داغ چندین عروس
how I can write the story of Rum and Rus (Byzantium).	چگونه کنم قصه روم و روس
It is better that I not recall this past sorrow	به از آرم اندوه پیشینه پیش
so that I can enjoy myself with this story.	بدین داستان خوش کنم وقت خویش[67]

According to his chronology, he lost his wife Afaq as he wrote the story of Shirin; lost his second wife when he completed Layli's story; and then later he lost his last wife. The deaths of his wives signify important turning points coinciding with the completion of one work and the start of another. The above passage ties together four major aspects of Nezami's life: his cultural knowledge, the beloved women in his private life, the cherished female figures in his fiction, and Sakhon. His celebration of the creation of Shirin turns into lamentation over the death of his first wife, Afaq. The pattern repeats two more times, and yet he continues to seek a remedy for his grief in his art through Sakhon.

The love stories in *Haft Paykar* and his other books featuring women prominently are told through pictorial allegories. A few of the stories in *Haft Paykar* are not about love, but those too are often told by women. Even the title of the book is indicative of its content and emphasis on women. The title of *Haft Paykar* has been rendered creatively in a few diverse ways, such as Seven Domes, Seven Figures, or in French as Sept Portraits. An analysis of the story leads me to believe that Seven Beauties is closer to the original Persian. Numerous meanings of the word Paykar can explain the diversity of the translation of the word, from portrait to sculpture to the body (as its contemporary usage indicates more often). However, contemplating Nezami's countless use of the word, to him, the title *Haft Paykar* could have meant Seven Beautiful Girls. The narrative and the setting of the stories support this notion. Further, in some verses, the word "Paykar" can hardly be translated into anything other than the word "girl."

As the last example, let us look at a passage that is entirely devoted to the concept of love in *Khosrow o Shirin* entitled "Sakhoni Chand Dar 'Eshq" (Verses on Love), where the word *'eshq*, love, appears 26 times (once as 'eshqbazi, making love). The passage praises love offering numerous arguments about the importance and effects of love. It provides a few contentions about the diversity of love, its reflections, and its contexts. One can easily mark and separate these images, after which a shift in the passage's text occurs. Those verses show how he uses the images of nature and objects to speak of a person and internal feelings. Here a few lines from that section. (The section's first line, which is an introduction that makes a better sense of the rest of the lines, is omitted in Brat Zanjani's edition.[68])

There is no better poem for me to write than love poetry	مرا کز عشق به ناید شعاری [69]
May I have no other preoccupation than love so long as I live	مبادا تا زیم جز عشق کاری
	فلک جز عشق محرابی ندارد
The sky has no altar for praying but love	جهان بی‌خاک عشق آبی ندارد
The world is parched (notorious) without Earth (land of love)	غلام عشق شو کاندیشه این است
Be a slave to love, that is the idea	همه صاحب دلان را پیشه این است
All pure-hearted ones have made love their métier	جهان عشقست و دیگر زرق سازی
The world is love; otherwise, livelihood seeking	همه بازیست الا عشقبازی
It is all a game except for the lovemaking	
Don't be content eating and sleeping, donkey-like	مشو چون خر بخورد و خواب خرسند
Love a cat, even if there is no one else to like	اگر خود گربه باشد دل در و بند
If loving a cat, you feel like yourself and a victor	به عشق گربه گر خود چیرباشی
It is better than to be a lion and a drifter	از آن به کز با خود شیرباشی
If a magnet were not in love	که مغناطیس اگر عاشق نبودی
How could it steal its heart with such resolve?	بدان شوق آهنی را چون ربودی
If they were not on the path of love	و گر عشقی نبودی بر گذرگاه
The magnet would seek whereof.	نبودی کهربا جوینده کاه

The sky, iron, magnet, donkey, stone, passage, provision, and other elements (in the rest of the passage) come together to create images that can be enjoyed when imagined. However, they also tell the tale of human heart and love, which the poet applies to his characters' situations later in the story.

LOVE OR ILLUSION, RHYME OR RELIGION: IS THE HISTORY OF CLASSICAL PERSIAN LITERATURE LINEAR?

Let us discuss the verses quoted above further. Several scholars have written on the concept and the form of love in Nezami's work, and they all have referred to it as mystic or religious love based on the interpretation of those verses.[70] By focusing on love and mysticism, some scholars also understand Nezami as a link between materialist literature and mystic literature in the history of classical Persian literature. Furthermore, even if we consider the twelfth century a link between two periods distinct by two different worldviews, it still does not justify reading Nezami's poetry as the expression of mysticism. Such an understanding is based on their notion of an evolution in Persian literary history or some sort of qualitative shift in the Persian poetic styles. However, if a shift occurred, it must be decades if not centuries later, as evident in the authors' view on life and literature in such works as the 'Attar's influential Sufi poetry (Divan-e 'Attar), Juvayni's history book (Tarikh-i Jahangushay Juvayni), and later in Rumi's mysticism (The Masnavi). Such shifts (in worldviews, discourse, understanding of science, body, and sex, characterization, styles, and forms) occurred all the time, often disruptive to the notion of process or progress. In Nezami's work, more than ever before and perhaps even after, the body (particularly the female body) becomes the site of understanding, love, and self-awareness. In a later time, Rumi's sexuality is expressed in an extremely different style and genre. These nuances of the classical literature should inform our understanding of its history. Syed Mehdi Zarqai has written histories of Persian poetry based on several aspects of Persian poetry including genre.[71] Even in understanding the distanced classical literary history we depend on our reflection, hindsight, and the juxtaposition of events and documents, and in the process, we might downplay the autonomy of literature. There was no evolutionary process with or without a middle. However, what certainly had happened since the Samanids was the deepening of a new mentality, new religious thinking, the formation of a new identity, even more, a strange glorification of the conquerors (Muslim or Mongol or combined) due to a backlash to the frequent translation of materials from Greek and Persian into Arabic and intensified later after the Mongol invasion. All these unique traits were different from the aspiration of the earlier century when a revival of ancient glory would still seem a possibility. Nezami strived to stay connected to his roots as he worked with new material.

Of course, even this theory of a metamorphosis toward Sufi poetry is disturbed by eager religious readers. Some even present Ferdowsi's *Shahnameh* as the product of the dominant religion of his time. In fact, the *Shahnameh* has not been spared by the outdated Sufi mode and method of reading either. Sa'eb represents numerous other scholars who contribute to the Islamization of all things Persian when she writes, "We can find hidden and delicate streaks (traces) of mystic thoughts."[72]

Others perceive Persian literary history in terms of Islam and believe that Persian poetry was the production of religion (or was written for the sake of faith) since the tenth century starting with the Samanid and Ghaznavid dynasties.[73] de Bruijn writes, "The religious use of poetry, as I intend it in this discussion, may be defined as the use of the means at the disposal of the literary artist in the tradition of Persian poetry in general for specifically religious purposes. These means include the various forms of poetry, the stock of images, of topoi and figures of speech as well as the social conventions connected with the craft of the secular poet."[74] No evidence is provided to show that the opposite of this statement is not correct. **One can argue that poets used religion as materials, as subjects and motifs for their literary creativity made possible by their literary devices and figures of speech.** The approach that perceives religion as central to social and art histories is rooted in the fact that those scholars take religion and Sufism too seriously in terms of philosophy but divorced from their economic contexts. In doing so, the discussions do not distinguish between religion and Sufism as a way of life, as means of hegemony and poetry, be it ghazal or couplets as genres.

These scholars point to Nezami's selected poems on love in the introduction or the conclusion of *Khosrow o Shirin* and not the narrative itself. However, even those selected lines if read in the context portray a few variations of love, and not just a Sufi love for God.[75] **In fact, other types of love from the divine to profane, from fruitful to unfulfilled, from lyrical to lust, from consideration to obsession, from enflamed feeling to long-lasting infatuation are portrayed in *Haft Paykar*.** Nezami has also featured star-crossed love, mad love, as well as a triangle love (Khosrow, Shirin, and Farhad). Reading a passage of Nezami as solely a Sufi expression is tantamount to ignoring the enormity of Nezami's conceptualization of human sensibility and his creative imagination (which is now defined as a combination of conscious and nonconscious thoughts). Finally, in some of the examples in Sufi interpretations, God is not even addressed or mentioned.

In the passage above, Nezami talks about the love of the skies, love of a cat (to encounter arrogance and not necessarily as a Sufi guide), love of fire (not necessarily advocating Zoroastrianism), love for Ka'ba, love for taverns, and love of his wife. He talks about love between a magnet and iron, between Zoroastrians and fire. These are related to the themes he wants to render in the actual story that follows. Several verses indicate that love is also an earthly concept. He says that without love and making love, this earth, this life is all about making a living, and rest. The continuity of this world depends on love and lovemaking. Without them, the generations will disappear. A loveless person will look like a dead person even if they possess hundreds of spirits. He uses the natural pollination process in (the sex life of) flowers to refer to human lovemaking. Yet, love and inebriation can lead to idle worshiping. And yes, one can read any of these references as epitomized by ka'ba and tavern as the love for God. At one point, his visit to the court is analogized with a pilgrim visiting the ka'ba. However, Nezami does not juxtapose them to create a mystic system of thought in the manner of Shaykh Najm al-Din Razi (the author of *Mersad al-Ebad*, the description of the Sufi path) or in the style of Shaykh Abu al-Hasan ibn-e Ahmad ibn-e Mohamad ibn-e Jafar ibn-e Salebeh (who also features this cat anecdote). Neither did he live the way these great Sufis lived their lives. Nezami was a master of belles-lettres. His concept of love is universal, tangible, and social. It is not confined to the specific idea of love in Sufism. His portrayal of the bodies of Shirin, Layli, and numerous female figures in *Haft Paykar* is more detailed than Ferdowsi's portrayal of women warriors, closer to Gorgani's portrayal of women lovers and distant from all Sufi poets' portrayal of the bodyless beloved.

To be sure, the first line talks about the love of poetry. In the first line, the word *sho'ari* has several meanings, including slogan or motto, custom, device, habit, or even chanting.[76] However, I believe this is one of the cases of poetic license (*ekhtiyarat-e sha'eri*) in which the poet has the option to change the length of a syllable for the sake of rhyme or rhythm in *'aruz* prosody system. The word is *sho'ari*, or a poem, meaning writing poetry about love is a desired practice. To assure the readers that he is talking about his poetry and his story of ancient lovers Khosrow and Shirin, he ends the segment by saying that if anyone criticizes this book, the critique will display his wickedness instead of rewarding me.

The connection between the essay's succinct and thought-provoking discussion of Sohravardi's philosophy and Nezami's poetry is not elaborated. These two authors belong to two different disciplines and two different ideological discourses and establishing any supposed connection between them requires a more extended analysis.

Shirin's desire for Khosrow does not tell us anything about Sufi notions love and death because these concepts are parts of most romances and tragedies. If fact, love, betrayal, and death are central in many stories, and they are often the driving forces in romance and tragedies. Nezami does not say much about them in that concluding passage either. The segments in the introduction and conclusion to the stories are often longer than a ghazal or a qasideh. Sometimes they are thematically connected to the extent that they appear under the same title in some editions.

In the broader concluding segments of the book, Nezami speaks of a plethora of subjects and human experiences in addition to the brief references to love and death.[77] He ponders working hard to achieve goals, exercising frugality to succeed, finding the right tools in solving problems, using medical procedures, and medicine to regain health. He talks about chess, cities of Iran, justice, proper protection against cold and heat, remedies, Jesus, Galen, and Plato. He teaches using tricks to escape dire situations (the famous parrot story which appeared in the works of other poets). He writes about the causes for shame, digestive routines, gathering provisions (accomplishments) while still alive, and numerous other epigrammatic statements. These are all addressed to his friend to convince him that he is mistaken about his work, describing its verses as pearls within dark bay shells and himself as a lyre harp. More importantly, he writes these introductions to talk about his book and the possible manners its readers might receive it. He dismisses possible criticism of the book, saying that he will not listen to them. One of the criticisms, according to the poems, was that he revived the history of fire worshipers (Zoroastrianism) against Islam, and in response to that, he says that he has lit a light, placed it on a rood for people to take the light if they want and leave the rood in its place. In fact, to the friend who was mad at him for renewing the magi tradition by writing *Khosrow o Shirin*, Nezami only describes Shirin's character and beauty to change the friend's opinion of the book.[78]

He denounces the envious. He further says if my book is guidance toward the fire temples, know that I have ornamented its content with my blood. He says that he authored the book with toil, investing in it with his all being and connecting each drop of that being with verses of his poems. He talks about the happy effect of eating saffron in verse and soon after about his good voice singer, reciter who accompanies him in the courtly banquets, like all great poets. That is not the only compliment he gives himself. He says that other poets are mediocre compared to his sunny status, like a simple oil lamp that can light only a room and not the world. He continues to say that other poets are only famous in their hometown compared to his universal fame. He also predicts that after a hundred years passed, if anyone asks about his whereabouts, every verse will answer, oh him. Finally, he talks about compensation for authoring the book and assures that he has spoken of God and his unity at the end of the book to make up for whatever he has said in the romance part of the book. The verses make clear that the king wanted to give him the lordship of ten villages or ten fiefs, but when he saw the poet's lower expectation, he awarded him only one village. The end of the second segment is the real story; the previous pictorial journey through all those subjects served as a surface layer. That Nezami employs several issues of humanities directly and metaphorically in a passage to build a block of his romance or pens an extraneous segment should not be a surprise to his students. These sections of *Khosrow o Shirin* are long to quote and translate, but they are the typical complex amalgamation of subjects and themes used in his poetry. Nezami comes remarkably close to describing his sophisticated craft with one word. He has repeatedly referred to himself as a *motarrar* (a maker of patterned, ornate garments) poet.

In the discussions of portrayal of women and the story of Layli and Majnun, I discuss the topic of love, particularly star-crossed love. Although Nezami characterizes his female figures positively, he also alters his sources to present perhaps the most amiable and charming portrayals of women from a humanistic and progressive point of view. If a vice occasionally interrupts these mental imagery processes, it is to point to the presence of reality about these women's charming complex situations and a multidimensional portrayal of their characters. Such portrayal reflects his character, ideas, and high esteem for the women with whom he was involved, all of which by today's standards are elements of high morals and ethics. Love often materializes in the context of his understanding of gender.

Of course, the number of such pertinent verses about love is considerable.[79] Some of them hit a contemporary cord in a striking manner.[80] However, the overwhelming presence of other subject matters in the poet's work prevents us from seeing love as a sole constitutive concept. In this area, too, he seems to be deeply preoccupied with allegorizing the concept of love, as demonstrated repeatedly in *Khosrow o Shirin*.[81]

There is no better poem for me to write than love poetry	مرا کز عشق به ناید شعاری
May I have no other preoccupation than love while I live	مبادا تا زیم جز عشق کاری
Be a slave to love because the thinking is this	غلام عشق شو کاندیشه این است
Without the soil of love, the world holds no water	جهان بی خاک عشق آبی ندارد
I heard a lover was inebriating	شنیدم عاشقی را بود مستی
From there, he rose to idle venerating	و از آنجا خاست اول بت‌پرستی
The Zoroastrians who sit by their flaming shrine	همان گبران که بر آتش نشستند
Are in love with fire because they first loved sunshine.	ز عشق آفتاب آتش پرستند

In the first line, love is compared to one of the essential elements. In the next two lines, love is portrayed with two simultaneous stories hinting at a drunk, an idle worshiper, a Zoroastrian, a sun lover, and a fire worshiper. Nezami's son once associated him with Zoroastrianism because of his depiction of Khosrow and Shirin's story. Would it not limit the achievement of these lines if we argued that they are simply about love and ignore the sublimity invested in creating the allegories? Yes, love is simply another theme, albeit a predominant one, that informs the meanings, but it is not the driving and underpinning cause, even though the concept of love could be understood as an ethical system in such paradigms as mysticism. Love, like religion, constitutes a theme for Nezami to display his art of Sakhon, driving him to take a tender and progressive approach toward women.

There are occasions in Nezami's poetry where he metaphorizes love playfully or surprisingly. In a verse in an early allegory in *Makhzan al-Asrar*, nature is the surface story to facilitate the meaning of the season changes on earth, which is supposed to be done by God. Yet, the author states that Sakhon can illustrate them too.[82]

He washed the face of the gold from baseness.	روی زر از صورت خواری بشست
He washed the flower's redness/menses with rains.	حیض گل از ابر بهاری بشست

This one verse also represents the complex, contemplative, exaggerated, and yet odd references and connotations of the entire segment. He refers to Koranic verses, and he renders other subjects, including nature, as an homage to rulers. Here, however, in the above verse, the word *hayz* is used to mean red by association, raising questions. In its dominant meaning, the word means menstruation, which has been tenderly treated in association with roses and thus leaves no choice but to read it as red.

Such poetic insinuation stands against the mainstream religious and traditional dictum in which an understanding of women's bodies was profoundly different, incomplete, or even profoundly faulty. He refers to this natural bodily function and women's womb the same way in connection to the zodiac description in one of his stories of ascension (me'raj), which appears in *Khosrow o Shirin*.[83] As mentioned, in some Sufi poetry, the love for a young man becomes the symbolic significance for a mystic love, a notion that is absent in Nezami's work. As opposed to many Sufi poets, he never weaved a homoerotic tale. To interpret the concept of love in the above lines as Islamic concept of love for God limits the reading and isolate the segments from which they come from the romances to which they are annexed.

Ferdowsi is known for his magnificent and monumental epic poem, the *Shahnameh* (the *Book of Kings*), which consists of some 50,000 couplets.[84] This book is a literary representation of ancient Iran and its dynasties. Based on material from mythical, heroic, and historical periods of Iranian history, Ferdowsi's *Book of Kings* presents a mixture of epic and love stories versified in lucid language that uses nearly exclusively Persian words. Women constitute about one-fifth of the characters in Ferdowsi's *Book of Kings*.[85] Presented as lovers, wives, servants, and even brave warriors, these female characters are fully developed, with beauty, coquettishness, and kindness. They are compared to the sun, stars, gardens, flowers, trees, and idols.

As part of the Islamization of the classical Persian literature that had a limited representation in western scholars of Sufism but is now in full force in Iran, Ferdowsi's work is being criticized for all sorts of things. One criticism is that *Shahnameh* includes too many anti-women notions and verses. The example these Muslim critics provide is almost all utterances by the fictional character whose views Ferdowsi and the spirit of the tragedies are not in agreement. This chapter does not seek to review or find disparaging verses. Instead, it will show why the characterization of women in *Shahnameh* is different from the one in *Panj Ganj*. However, these women do not figure as importantly as male heroes and always occupy peripheral roles. Moreover, some characters such as Sudabeh, Zanbandavi, and Malikhah are portrayed as villain, impetuous, or at best hypocritical.[86] Even positive female characters such as Sindukht, Rudabeh, Tahmineh, Farangis, Jarireh, Manizheh, Gordafarid, Katayun, Gurdieh, Shirin, and Rushanak are either beguiling and fallible or good only because they act like men. This does not mean that Ferdowsi's book is antifemale. Nor does it mean that the poet practiced male dominance in his personal life. As is evident in the book, he benefited from his wife's cooperation in the versification of the stories. Moreover, as mentioned before, his female characters are certainly more memorable than those described in the sources Ferdowsi used. It simply means that because of the nature of epic writing, allegorization of these women serves the purpose of mere symbolic glorification of the men who possess them. Such glorification of the possession of women is characteristic of most epics. The epic, a long narrative poem recounting glorious heroic deeds of national heroes, deals with myths, heroic legends, history, religious tales, and edifying morals. As with Ferdowsi's book, such legendary narratives gained central importance during a time when nations had to struggle for a national identity. Indeed, during a critical period following the Muslim conquest of Iran, several authors such as Daqiqi, Moayyad Balkhi, Ahmad Balkhi, Mansur Razzaq, and Asadi Tusi wrote their own versions of *The Book of Kings* or similar books. It was a time when small dynasties tried to link their lineage to the pre-Islamic dynasties. A main function of this genre was to glorify the past and thereby present an ideal model of a heroic society. In such a genre, women are present to preserve the heroic lineage, to be abducted by the victorious force, or to be recovered by the heroic men of her family. This perhaps explains the difference between Nezami's understanding of Zoroastrian teachings, as least as regards women, from that of Ferdowsi. In any case, the women close to the heroes are portrayed as sublime and superior models in beauty and servitude to their men.[87]

Additional evidence suggests that this characterization of women is dictated by the genre of *The Book of Kings*. The love scenes and lyrics that embellish the book show Ferdowsi's loyalty to his sources. As Meisami has noted, Ferdowsi acknowledges the "truthfulness of his presentation."[88] The book is based, for the most part, on the prose *Shahnameh* that was based on a translation of the Middle Persian history of the kings of Persia, *Khvatay Namak* (*The Book of Kings*). Before Ferdowsi, another poet, Daqiqi, had versified this history; however, due to his early death, he finished merely 1000 verses. Ferdowsi's perception of his sources is not, however, as creative as Nizami's. Disparaging remarks about women are common, although non-heroic characters such as the King of Yaman, King of Hamavaran, or Afrasiyab express them. Such expressions are rare in Nezami's work. By allowing these men to speak, Ferdowsi remains faithful to his art. He creates a masterpiece from the historical documents in his possession.[89]

Moreover, in Ferdowsi's stories, in contrast to Nizami's, women more often fall in love with men first. The reason for this might well be that the male hero must remain as "righteous" as possible. Each of these love stories functions as an introduction to an epic in which the real themes are birth, life, battles, or the death of a hero. The "Rudabeh and Zal" love story, for example, is an introduction to Rostam's birth. And of course, in terms of its historical and fictional significance, the birth of Rostam is not comparable to Rudabeh's love experience. She is only a peripheral character, a good example of many such characters. Tahmineh's expression of love for Rostam functions as an introduction to the birth of Sohrab, another significant highlight of the epic. Love acts only as a catalyst for tragedies, and women do not play an essential role. Such a subordinate role for women is not only apparent in a structural and thematic sense but is also often expressed in some verses, albeit often expressed by characters.

Tahmineh, who serves the tragic story by giving birth to the hero, exemplifies such female characters. Rostam spends a night at the court of Samangan. There, Tahmineh, who had fallen in love with Rostam based on rumors about him, attempts to seduce him so that she can have his child.

Further, perhaps may the creator   دو دیگر که از تو مگر کردگار
place your child in my womb.   نشاند یکی پورم اندر کنار ⁹⁰

Rostam is amazed by her beauty and spends a night with her, and she gives birth to Sohrab. He grows into a strong and brave man and is killed mistakenly by his father in a long, tragic battle. Tahmineh's assertions, therefore, only serves the purpose of setting up the tragedy of Rostam and Sohrab. The fact that she initiated sex is inconsequential.⁹¹ Once the child is born, she all but vanishes. Her goodness is assured because, as Ferdowsi's Shirin says, "a good woman gives birth to a boy,"⁹² perhaps implying her goodness been diminished or non-existent had she given birth to a girl .

Quite unlike Nezami's portrayal of the same character, Ferdowsi's Shirin is delinquent and weak. In *The Book of Kings,* she appears on Khosrow's way to remind him of their former love to manipulate him. He is portrayed as morally weak, promiscuous, and responsible for the death of innocent people. Shirin, now Khosrow's lover, poisons Maryam—the King's princess—out of jealousy. Shiruyeh, Maryam's son, appears justified in berating Shirin now as a murderer.

| You only know witchcraft and bad behavior | همه جادوئی دانی و بدخوئی |
| You are the most sinful person in Iran. | به ایران گنگار ترکس توئی [93] |

Shirin defends herself and denies any wrongdoing, including the poisoning of Maryam. With some flattering moves, she persuades Shiruyeh (now king after the death of Khosrow) to think better of her.

Azadeh, one of King Bahram's female slaves, is a beautiful harpist who accompanies Bahram on a hunting trip. Bahram, the good hunter, shoots two gazelles skillfully in the way Azadeh had requested. However, instead of praising the king's skill, she criticizes him for hurting the poor animal. Bahram kills her brutally under his camel's hooves and seems to be justified because she challenged his authority. He concludes that he should never have taken a slave girl on a hunting trip. Meisami aptly indicates that Ferdowsi's includes this story to epitomize his epical and heroic values, such as brevity and hunting skill, and for this reason, the description story of Azadeh is short.[94] As can be seen, Nezami's departure from Ferdowsi's depiction of this woman is radical. For Nizami, the story of Fetneh is, in Meisami's words, "an emblem of the larger cosmic circle, symbol of the forces of wisdom, justice, and love that maintain the order and harmony of that circle."[95]

Among all these figures, Sudabeh may well represent the first evil female character. Not confined to this story alone, she embodies all "beguiling women," drawing on the trope of women's guile in classical Persian tales. She is the daughter of the king of Hamavaran, who decides to throw off the yoke of Persia. Kay Kavus, the Iranian king, attacks the unruly Hamavaran region and captures it. He takes Sudabeh, intending to bring her back to Iran to marry her as tribute and to guarantee peace between the two countries. Bitter over the defeat, Hamavaran's king conspires to imprison Kay Kavus. Sudabeh remains loyal to her husband and accompanies him into prison until Rostam, the book's foremost hero, saves them. Several years later, Sudabeh falls in love with her stepson, Siyavosh, a handsome, artful, and popular man, the product of the king's casual sex with another woman. She unsuccessfully tries to trick Siyavosh into sleeping with her by seduction and threats, and even attempts to marry off one of her daughters to him to provide further opportunities. However, the good Siyavosh abstains and does not deviate from the righteous path. Finally, she desperately besieges him.

She held his head and undressed	سرش تنگ بگرفت و یک پوشه چاک
She had no shame or fear.	بداد و نبود آگه از شرم و باک

Siyavosh resists and manages to set himself free. She causes a scene by tearing her dress, beating herself, and accusing Siyavosh of making advances toward her and of an assault that killed her unborn child; although, she was not pregnant. After a second accusation and in order to find the truth, King Kavus makes a huge fire and asks Siyavosh to pass through, believing that if Siyavosh is telling the truth in denying the accusation, he will emerge from the fire unharmed. Siyavosh passes the test successfully and volunteers to fight the Turks, only to be banished to a foreign land where he is killed. Sudabeh herself ultimately dies at the hand of Rostam for contributing to the death of Siyavosh. Sudabeh's trickery is contrasted with the honesty and grace of a hero for whose death Rostam never forgives her.

The tale hardly leaves any alternative reading of Sudabeh's character. She represents ultimate guile. She betrays her father, her husband, her country, and her love. In small and remote villages of Iran, Siyavosh remains to this very day the ultimate symbol of martyrdom for truth and righteousness. Rostam, the mighty symbol of national consciousness, who considers Siyavosh his own son, kills Sudabeh by cutting her in half with his sword. King Kavus watches the killing passively.

In short, Ferdowsi does not seem to have needed to express the sensitivity toward women and women's issues later exhibited by Nizami. Ferdowsi was much preoccupied with reviving the Persian language and with other issues related to writing a national epic. Moreover, he may have lacked the sort of personal experience that enabled Nezami to show such perceptiveness and sympathy toward issues of gender. Although Ferdowsi's wife was apparently quite literate and played music, and although he describes her beautifully in the beginning of the story of "Bijan and Manizheh," telling us that his poems depended on her contributions as she read the sources to him while he versified them,[96] it seems unlikely that she played as important a role in his life as Afaq played in Nizami's. Other than this, little is known about Ferdowsi's life and his relationship with his wife. Nezami Aruzi, a twelfth-century writer, states that Ferdowsi was a landowner with sufficient income to support his only daughter. What is clear is that he advocated the dominant movement among writers: to contribute to the revival of what they perceived as Persian society through this art. Moreover, by writing epic poems, he remained faithful to his sources and followed the conventions of the genre. Through his treatment of similar themes and characterizations, Nezami in contrast brought a progressive and humanist approach to the portrayal of women, embodied in Shirin from *Khosrow o Shirin* (*Khosrow and Shirin*, 1180), the female characters in *Haft Paykar* (the Seven Beauties, 1197), and Layli from *Layli o Majnun*, (*Layli and Majnun*, 1188), other women he mentions in his narrative or introductory parts of his books.

Jami, a poet of the last years of the Timurid epoch, is considered the last great classical poet. A leader of the Naqshbandi order of dervishes, he devoted his life to saintliness and the study of Arabic and Persian and became a critic, a prolific writer, and a biographer of Sufi personalities. His works include the *Baharistan*, "a memoir of famous Persian poets"; *Lava'ih* ("Splendors" or "Flashes"), a collection of articles concerning the principles of mysticism; *Ashii'at al-lama'at* ("Rays of the Flashes"); elements in the Fakhr al-Din Iraqi book *Lama'at: Sharh az Shuruh-i Qarn-i Hashtum Hijri*; work on the *Nai-nama of Jalal al-Din Rumi*, *Nafahat al-uns* ("Breaths of Fellowship"), a biography of 614 Sufi saints; and the translation of the *Tabaqat al-sufiyya* by Mohammad b. Husain Sulami of Nishapur.[97] His *Masnavi haft awrang* (Seven Thrones) includes several historical romantic poems. Referred to as "khatam al-shu'ara" ("the last of the poets"), the prolific Jami is known as an imitator even though he shows creativity in characterizing figures such as Yusuf and Salaman, portraying them differently than others who portrayed these characters. He primarily imitated Nezami both in form and in motifs, going so far as to borrow entire stories, such as *Layli and Majnun*. Women characters are also present in his work. Generally, the earlier classical works influenced literary activities during the fourteenth and fifteenth centuries, and poets such as Sa'di and Nezami were widely imitated. However, in contrast to Nezami, Jami's main thematic concerns revolve around Islamic jurisprudence, *hadith*, morality, and, most important, Sufism. Such differences between Jami and Nezami—and Ferdowsi—reflect the various times and places influencing these poets' work. Jami lived in a time and place in which he could easily enjoy the generosity and favor of the rulers of three dynasties, Al-i Kart, Timurids, and Gurkans, all of whom supported poets. Yet for most of this time, disorderliness marked the period.

Disturbances that can be dated back to the Mongol invasions, and which finally developed into the disruption and disorder of the period after Shah Rukh's death, occasioned a serious decline in civilization and deterioration in thought. At the beginning of this period a few of the scholars, poets, and writers of the interval between the Mongol Il-Khans and the Timurids were still alive and affording contributions to science and literature. But apart from these few, and with the possible exception of those who had gathered at the court of Sultan Husain Baiqara at Herat and who were didactic rather than original, we hardly hear of any important or justly celebrated men of learning or science until the latter part of the ninth/fifteenth century.[98]

However, "with the coming of Timur, Herat experienced the beginning of a new age. It was an age of splendor that witnessed the city's rise to an apogee in cultural achievement that has only on rare occasions been equaled in urban history."[99] It was during Husain's reign (1469–1506), Herat reached its cultural peak. During this time, "it was the most refined city in Asia, the center of Persian and Turkish culture, and the capital of a prosperous province."[100] All these factors helped in shaping poets' literary enunciations. Jami also lived in a period when Sufism was a major ideological discourse. The purpose of art had come to mean making sense of all earthly aspects of life in terms of Sufi theology. Poets especially were expected to recast earlier literary monuments in this new mode. Jami's creativity was manifested in the way he reinterpreted, redefined, and rewrote the love stories of Nezami and other stories he found interesting.[101]

In Jami's work, negative characteristics and generalizations define women. Their major attributes include betrayal, deceit, and disgrace. *Salaman and Absal* exemplifies Jami's attitude. A powerful and prosperous Greek king wished to have a son but wanted to refrain from having contact with women, whom he and his vizier believed were all lustful and inferior. Finally, the wise vizier finds a solution.

Without lust, he released the sperm from his backbone and laid it in a place that was not a womb.	نطفه را بی شهوت از صلبش گشاد در محل جز رحم آرام داد[102]

True, the utterance is assigned to a character and should not necessarily be taken as the opinion of the author; however, the idea is so bizarre that one wonders how it might have been formed. The king assigns an assertive nanny, Absal, to care for the child. The child grows up to become the handsome Salaman, whose beauty is equated to that of Joseph. These two fall in love, and the king's attempt to separate them and to convince his son to stay away from women fails. Salaman and Absal fight against all odds to save their love. However, the force of morality and the continuity of the kingdom are too powerful to defeat. At the end, Absal dies and Salaman takes up the "righteous path" of his father. From the beginning, Jami seems to uphold the king's perspective by portraying Absal as beguiling and deceptive. Even in describing Salaman's falling in love with her, Jami's eloquent language warms about the charm of women who could lead men astray.

When, for all Salaman's self-control and propriety,	چون سلامان با همه حلم و وقار
Absal's coquetry did its work on him,	کرد در وی عشوهٔ امسال کار،
the prick of her eyelashes pierced his heart,	در دل از مژگان او، خارش خلید
the snake of her tress' lasso bit him,	وز کند زلف او، مارش گزید
his strength was bowed by her eyebrows,	ز ابروانش طاقت او گشت طاق
her lips made honey bitter to his palate,	وز لبش شد تلخ، شهدش در مذاق
her magic narcissus-eyes robbed him of sleep,	نرگس جادوی او خوابش برد
the ring of her curls robbed him of power.	حلقهٔ گیسوی او تابش برد
Then his tears flowed bloodstained over his cheek,	اشک او از عارضش گلرنگ شد
the memory of her mouth strangled his joy.	عیشش از یاد دهانش تنگ شد
He saw her restless ringlets on her cheek,	دید بر رخسار او خال سیاه
he became restless with the desire to embrace her.	گشت از آن خال سیه حالش تباه
Yearning brought him out of the veil, but	دید جعد بیقرارش بر عذار
inwardly he still mediated well,	ز آرزوی وصل او، شد بیقرار
thinking, 'if God forbid!- I once taste the savour of union	شوقش از پرده برون آورد، لیک
that savour will prove fatal to my soul.[103]	در درون اندیشهای میکرد نیک
	که مبادا گر چشم طعم وصال
	طعم آن بر جان من گردد وبال[104]

Jami's language here is shrewd. He unnecessarily exaggerates the association of love and pain that is a characteristic of the classical period. It is not clear whether the poet is carried away by his rhetorical power or is communicating a literal pain that his male protagonist somehow endures upon falling in love. Absal's eyelashes pierce Salaman's heart, her tress's lasso bites him, her eyebrows subdue his strength, and her lips make honey bitter to his palate. Given the idea that the "savour of union" with her will "prove fatal" to Salaman's soul, it is not unlikely that in Jami's discourse on sexuality women may cause pain. This is a constitutive element of love and sexuality in such religious discourse in the medieval Islamic world.

Eventually, after going through a rough time, they decide to jump into a huge fire that Salaman has set for this purpose. However, the king, who has been secretly watching them, saves Salaman and allows Absal to burn.

Soon after, Salaman, with the help of the vizier's new trick, manages to forget about her. There is a section with a title that cannot justify as being the words of a character. It reads:

In Condemnation of Women, Who Are the Focus of That Passion Upon Which the Child's Existence Depends	در مذمت زنان که محل شهوت موقوف علیه فرزندان است

In that section, Jami provides his lists with women's deficiencies. The passage starts with these lines and goes on for some length.

What is woman? A thing deficient in reason and faith; there is nothing so deficient in the whole world. Know then that it's removed from the conduct of perfect men to be, month and year, the plaything of defective creatures; in the eyes of the perfect man, a leader by his knowledge, the defective's plaything is inferior even to the defective. At the table of munificence of the bountiful man there is no ingrate worse than a woman.[105] …	زن چه باشد ناقصی در عقل و دین هیچ ناقص نیست در عالم چنین دور دان از سیرت اهل کمال ناقصان را مخره بودن ماه و سال پیش کامل کو به دانش سرور است مخره ناقص ز ناقص کمتر است بر سر خوان عطای دولتمن نیست کافر نعمتی بدتر ز زن[106] …

The story of *Salaman and Absal* has a Greek origin. It would have been available to Jami through Ibn Ishaq's Arabic translation of the original Greek as well as through the references to the story in the works of Ibn Sina, Fakhr al-Din Razi, and Nasir al-Din Tusi.[107] It nonetheless includes a large amount of Jami's own amplification. Moreover, it is well situated in his general discourse on Sufism and what threatens it, namely womanly guile.

The story, as Jami indicates at the end, can be interpreted allegorically from a Sufi point of view. In Bürgel's word, "the fact that the mystical spirit, long present in the ghazal, has earned a permanent place in romance is verified by this epic and others such as those by 'Arefi (*Hal-nama*) and Helali (*Shah va gida*).'"[108] In *Salaman and Absal,* and similarly in *Yusof and Zulaykhah,* the demands of romance writing are eclipsed by the poet's ideological orientation and his perception of women. Even to the extent that these works can be considered works of romance, the misogynistic characterization of women discourages the reading of works within this genre, at least in the way it is possible to read similar stories by Nezami as works of romance. The poet's ideological points of view weigh centrally in the story, making a Sufi reading of it more possible. That Salaman is not born of a woman can be interpreted as a reflection of the need to create the most pious heir possible for the king. At the conclusion of the story, the fire does not burn Salaman, though he is in it just long enough to be purified. As Hadland Davis expresses it, "little by little Salaman came to regard his old earthly love as 'The bondage of Absal,' a thing merely of the senses, whereas by his new knowledge, this love, belonged to the 'Eternity.' And so this beautiful little poem, to put it as briefly as possible, tells of the love that binds and fetters and is corruptible, and of that other Love that is incorruptible."[109] More significantly, many critics have read the story as Sufi symbolism related to wisdom, moral truth, and self-control. However, such reading does not change the fact that it contains the poet's general notions that women are "deficient," "ingrates," "bare of...fidelity," and full of "craftiness," and "treachery." As Jami frequently asserts in the stories, it is his true belief that women are unfaithful, weak, and crafty by nature. This attitude is pervasive throughout his poetry. In *Salaman and Absal*, Absal represents ardent sexual desire and bestial, carnal love while the king represents reason, and Salaman the immortal soul.

Two points should be mentioned here. First, Jami is not the only poet in the classical period to hold a negative view of women. Such allegorical uses of women's images as symbols of unreliability were not only pervasive in Iranian medieval literature but also in many other parts of the world. Second, Jami's understanding of Islam and Sufism is not necessarily representative of the official view of these discourses. Muslim scholars such as Ibn Hisham, Ibn Hajar, Ibn Sad, and Tabari presented a radically different portrayal of women.[110]

The theme that love between men is more important than love occurring between men and women is fully developed in the stories of Farid al-Din 'Attar (d. 1230), such as *Mahmud and Ayaz*. In the case of Jami's anecdotes (*hikayat*), his distrust of women turns into disinterest. To convey a message regarding the *qiblah* (the direction to which Muslims turn in prayer), Jami versifies the same short love story three times, insinuating that love for a boy (or young man) may be mystical and might be interpreted as love for God. In a piece entitled "Story of that Young Beloved and the Amorous Old Man," Jami portrays a young man who is loved by an old man.[111] A young man sits on the eaves of a roof, and his beauty and coquetry kill those who fall in love (or long for union) with him. An old man with gray hair approaches the boy on the roof and declares his love for him. The young man tells the old man to look in the other direction to observe his brother, who is 100 times more beautiful than he is. As soon as the old man turns around and realizes that the brother is not there, the young man pushes him off the roof. The boy expresses his private thoughts: "If he loved me why did he want to see another face?" The poet then steps into the first-person narration, concluding the poem with a vow to close his eyes on those who are not his friends lest he should weep blood day and night. If he did not benefit from the union, he would be mournful of the separation.[112]

Jami has included a similar story in *Subhat al-Abrar* (Rosary of the Pious, a collection of poetry about moral and Islamic issues), under the title of "Qiblah of Love." However, this time with no direct reference to the gender of the beauty. He refers to this beloved as a *chardah-saleh mahi* (a 14-year-old moon), a metaphor used most often for the young female lover. However, he immediately uses masculine adjectives such as *nojavan* (youth), leaving little doubt that he is talking about a male moon. Here Jami does not use a female figure to convey his mystical message that the *qiblah* in Islam (the actual site) and the *qiblah* in love (center of universe) function to focus attention on and to solemnize the beloved.

Both stories and another similar to them then beg the question, why are beloveds amoral only if they are women? We know that the modern concept of homosexuality was not a determining factor in such portrayals and the debate on sexuality in classical period is extensive. "The Islamic view of the couple based on the pre-established, premeditated harmony of the sexes presupposed a profound complementarity of the masculine and the feminine. This harmonious complementarity is creative and procreative."[113] However, what J. W. Wright Jr. states about homoeroticism in Arabic literature may have some implications in classical Persian literature. He writes that reading homoerotic texts "reveal complex parody and satire through which artists and writers metaphorically strengthen their social and moral positions vis-à-vis that dominant Islamic polity."[114] He views homoeroticism "as a reflection of sublime and often subversive ideals" and "represent a metonymical complex of beliefs and reactions."[115] For Jami, as a Sufi, then the love of God is the greatest love achievable on earth. Carnal love, on the other hand, is of value only if it signifies the greater divine love. The beauty of the boy signifies the light of God. Just as there is only one Mecca, there is only one true love, and if one genuinely believes in one God, one looks in Mecca's direction. Therefore, the beloved could be anyone, but Jami prefers young men.

However, it is quite possible to argue that homosexuality may serve to represent a criticism of some deviation from the true Sufi path. Analyzing a few homoerotic poems, Sprachman writes, "Like Sana'i's version of the homoerotic take, Sa'di's plays on the hypocrisy of Sufis who are more interested in self-satisfaction than self-denial."[116] And that "His primary purposes are to entertain and to poke gentle fun at outwardly ascetic but inwardly hedonistic Sufis." The absence of women in this story, nevertheless, further signifies the poet's indifference to them. Sarvatian's aforementioned statement about the symbolic value of women in Nezami's work could have been a profound assertion had he applied it to Jami's work. Both women and young men in the writings of Jami serve as symbols and designate broader religious and cultural issues.

Jami's *Yusof va Zolaykha* (*Yusof and Zolaykha*, 1509) might seem to be an exception to his negative portrayal of women. This story is based on the biblical (Genesis, chapter 39) and quranic (sura 12) love story that has inspired several other poets, including Gurgani, to rewrite it. It also resonates the story of Sudabeh and Siyavosh. Jami's version is arguably the best in terms of fluency, clarity, and poetic expression. Yusof, sincere and righteous, but lonely, is his father's most beloved son. His jealous brothers torture him for a long time before selling him off to slavery in Egypt. There, the gluttonous, self-indulgent Zolaykha, the wife of Potiphar, buys Yusof at an auction. Deeply in love after having several dreams about him, she tries all her tricks to gain Yusof's love and to sleep with him. When she fails, she conspires to send him to prison. After he is freed, he continues to remain moral and virtuous. He leads Zolaykha to believe in God. Upon God's order, he enters into union with her. Following an inspiring dream, Yusof decides to leave this world. He receives an apple from Gabriel, smells it, and dies. Zolaykha, who suffers tremendously from his death, goes to his tomb, and lies there without saying a word. She then dies, in an ending like that of *Layli and Majnun*. In this story, as Merguerian and Najmabadi write on its Quranic version, "Yusof, through the concept of *Jamal* [beauty], stands in for the Divine; Zolaykha, through '*Ishq* [love], for a Sufi burning with desire for union with the Divine."[117] These authors also note that "even in the story's happy closure, it is Yusof and his sexual desire that are rewarded. In fact, one could argue that in an important sense and despite that clarity with which the Koran says, 'she desired him,' Zolaykha remains the 'object of desire' in narratives—namely, the desire and drive of the narrative to produce Yusof's victory over her temptation and his own sexual desire, thus establishing his merits as a righteous prophet."[118]

In Jami's version, Zolaykha is not so different from Sudabeh except that she has interfered with a prophet. And Yusof does not share Siyavosh's fate. That Yusof is a prophet accounts for the work's significance not only as a piece of symbolic reference, but also as a story that ends happily. Zolaykha stands for the untrustworthy female and the temptation that men must resist by virtue of their wisdom. More importantly, a prophet is after all supposed to proselytize, and this is what he achieves in the end. Zolaykha improves, but Sudabeh is cut in half.

It is worth emphasizing that Jami's antipathy toward women causes him to depict them negatively, even when the stories are not originally his. He often expresses his views directly rather than through characters, leaving no room for literary interpretation. In, *Subhat al-Abrar*, he discusses the dichotomy between men and women.

There is a manly woman in Mosul,	بود مردانه زنی در موصل
her head and soul reached to truth	سر جانش به حقیقت واصل
like the sun, feminine in name,	همچو خورشید مؤنث در نام
but in knowledge, a complete man.	لیک در نور یقین مرد تمام[119]

That is, only men can recognize truth and obtain knowledge. Such perceptions underpin Jami's overall troubling portrayal of women and gender.

In his *Layli and Majnun*, Jami still seeks to drive conclusions about the eternal and mystic love and uses the events in the lives of the lovers as stages of a Sufi's journey. However, and to be fair, he has a more positive view of the female character and portrays her in a much better light than the other women characters of his other books. That is, Jami's Layli is more active and more present. Such a description does not contradict the context and does not harm the logic of his storytelling.

Why does Layli not marry Majnun after her husband dies? Was he not a significant obstacle on the path of the lovers' unification? Nezami explains the reason in a short one-liner as opposed to other questions and issues, which he lays out at length.

The Arab's custom is that after her husband died, a woman	رسم عرب است کز پس شوی
Should not show her face anywhere, to anyone.	ننماید زن به هیچکس روی

Of course, Nezami does not let this go unanswered. He unites them in his own way. Majnun goes to Layli's tomb, mourns her loss, and dies later. His burial is also as vividly illustrated as Layli's. Some versions of the manuscript are more detailed at this point.

Men made a tomb for him, and at his side   شستند به آب دیده پاکش

They laid his Layli as his longed-for bride: دادند ز خاک هم به خاکش

She was the lovely cup-bearer who brought   پهلوی دخمه را گشادند

Her king the wine of love that he had sought.   در پهلوی لیلیش نهادند

They were no longer blamed or sorned, but lay   خفتند به ناز تا قیامت

In peace, and side by side, till Judgment Day: برخاست ز راهشان ملامت

They'd kept one vow on earth, now they were given   بودند در این جهان به یک عهد

One cradle to be shared by them in heaven.   خفتند در آن جهان به یک مهد

A lovely Garden was laid out around   کردند چنانکه داشت راهی

Their earthly resting place and burial ground,   بر تربت هردو روضه گاهی

Unrivalled in its beauty and its fame,   آن روضه که رشک بوستان بود

A garden where the world's sad pilgrims came;   حاجتگه جمله دوستان بود

And there these votaries of love would find   هرکه آمدی از غرب و زنجور

Joy was restored to them, and peace of mind,   در حال شدی ز رنج و غم دور

No one would leave this garden willingly,   زان روضه کسی جدا نگشتی

Only when forced by necessity.[120]   تا حاجت او روا نگشتی[121]

In sum, it should be mentioned that all three authors, as Muslims, were sensitive to Islam, the question of women, and literary issues. However, the exigencies of their genre and the impact of the general understanding of Islam in their time influenced their impressions.

Although Nezami characterizes women in positive ways, he also alters his sources to present perhaps the most amiable and pleasing portrayals of women from a humanistic and liberal point of view in the classical period. If these images are occasionally tainted by a vice, it points to the presence of reality about these women's complex situations and a multidimensional portrayal of their characters. Such vice and flaws are portrayed within the context of human ascension to higher virtue. His poetry reflects his character, his ideas, and his high esteem for the women with whom he was involved, which seems to spill over for all women characters in his narrative poetry. It points to his deep understanding of the human psyche and the role culture plays upon it. Nezami's poetry is also a reflection of his time in that this period was marked by a renewed attempt to redefine the concept of Iranian-ness more from a philosophical point of view. It is a reflection of his place, an area marked by tolerance of several cultures. Nezami's love stories are, therefore, unique in terms of female characterization, and he stands out as an anachronism among the great Persian poets of different periods of classical literature for his progressive and positive characterizations of women.

In contrast to Nezami, Ferdowsi remains perhaps more faithful to his historical sources and portrays women according to the logic of the epic stories he versifies. In his monumental work, he seems to be more concerned with the Persian language and the genre it undertakes than with the problematics of gender representation; the genre carries out the labor. It is also possible to say that Ferdowsi ushered a literary revolution by portraying a beautiful, perceptive, and versified history and an identity of Iranians all the while emphasizing the place of Persian language in his conceptualization of that history and identity. Nezami, in his *Khosrow Shirin* and *Haft Paykar*, elaborated on the human relations of those aspects.

Five centuries after Ferdowsi and three centuries after Nezami, Jami inherited the rich literary tradition they left behind and creatively altered it to produce new masterpieces. He nevertheless represents a regression regarding the portrayal of women and denigrates the moral and intellectual capacity of women in some of his work. Thematically he had a new fixation: the problematics of an ideological representation of Sufism. He was deeply enmeshed in the discursive exchange, which did not necessarily prompt him to be sensitive to the cause of women or to portray them realistically.

NOTES

1. This chapter is an expanded version of "Nezami's Unlikely Heroines: A Study of the Characterizations of Women in Classical Persian Literature," in *The Poetry of Nezami Ganjavi*, 51–81.
2. Of course, one might even compare Nezami's characterization of women with that of Anvari (1126–1189), who lived closer to the time of Nezami. Anvari, known to know a few different fields of knowledge, also wrote numerous bold anti women's poems. However, he did not write narrative poetry featuring female figures.
3. Sai'idi Sirjani, *Sima-ye do zan* (Tehran: NoAvaran, 1991).
4. Behruz Sarvatiyan, *A'inah-i Ghayb, Nezami* (Tehran: Kalameh, 1989), 37, 40.
5. Behruz Sarvatiyan, Ed. *Makhzan al-Asrar-e Nezami* (Tehran: Tus, 1984), 283.
6. Jalal Matini, "Azadigi va Tasahul-i Nezami Ganjavi," in *IranShinasi*, 4, 1 (Spring 1992), 1–20.
7. Fatamah Alaqih, "Sima-ye Zan az Didgah-e Nezami" in *Farhang* 10 (1992), 317–30.
8. Ibid.

9. Ahmad Mahdavi Dameghani, "'Aqayed-e Nezami dar Tohid va Sefat-e Barita'ala" *IranShenasi*, 3, 3, (1991), 458–468.
10. Julie S. Meisami, "Kings and Lovers: Ethical Dimensions of Medieval Persian Romance," in *Edebiyat* 1 n. 1 (1987), 7.
11. Christoph Bürgel compares romance writing in the work of Gorgani, Nizami, Amir Khosrow Dehlavi, Jami, and others. See Christoph Bürgel, "The Romance" in E. Yarshater, *Persian Literature* (New York: Bibliotheca Persica, 1988), 161–79 and "Die Frau als Persien in der Epik Nizamis," *Asiatische Studien* 42: 137–55.
12. *Kolliyat*, 104. The passages start with the following line.
13. Nezami is not writing history, but we should keep in mind that Armenians followed Zoroastrianism for about a millennium before the Christianization of the region in the fourth century.
14. Mahmud Dowlatabadi, *Kalidar*, (Tehran: Farhang Mu'aser, 1989).
15. Mehdi Zarghani, *Tarikh-e Badan dar Adabiyat* (Tehran: Sokhan, 2019).
16. This is the year when Zoroastrians inhabited the Armenian region. For an informative study about historical Shirin, see Ghodrat Ghasemipour, "Shirin" Zaban va Adabiyate Farsi" Tabriz, 74, 244, 2021.
17. For a treatment of this text as a work of drama, see Peter Chelkowski, "Nizami: Master Dramatist," in E. Yarshater, *Persian Literature* (NY: Bibliotheca Persica, 1987), 190–213.
18. Abd al-Majid Ayati, *Dastan-i khusraw va shirin* (Tehran: Jibi, 1974), 27–29.
19. Ibid.
20. Ibid.
21. Farhad's passionate and unfulfilled love for Shirin has been sufficiently significant for some poets to entitle their version of this romance as *Farhad O Shirin*. Nezami's characterization of Farhad further points out his deep involvement with the human aspects of the Pre-Islamic Persian philosophies and lifestyle.
22. See the *Haft Paykar* by G. E. Wilson and more recently Julie Meisami.
23. Elements such as colors, numbers, and the names of weekdays play important roles in this book and indicate Nezami's awareness of some of the sciences of his time. See Meisami, *The Haft Paykar* and Georg Krotkoff, "Colour and Number in the *Haft Paykar*" in *Logos Islamikos: Studia Islamica,* ed. Roger M. Savory and Dionisius A. Agius (Toronto: Pontifical Institute of Mediaeval Studies, 1984).
24. Cameron Cross studies Nezami's intricate and complex portray of love and how one might understand its forms and types of love and their connection to colors, buildings, and sequences. Cameron Cross, "The Many Colors of Love in Niẓāmī's *Haft Paykar*: Beyond the Spectrum" *Interfaces* 2 2016, pp. 52–96.
25. Peter Chelkowski, "Aya upra-yi turmdut-i Puchini Bar Asas-i Kushk-i Surkh-i Haft Paykar Ast?" *IranShinasi* vol. 3 no. 4 (Winter 1991), 714–22.

26. Nezami, *Haft Paykar,* ed. Dastgerdi (Tehran: IbnSina, 1955), 233.

27. In the absence of an open treatment of sexuality by the advocates of modernity, the religious fundamentalists have used their notion of sexuality to provoke resistance to modernization, affecting the interpretation of literary texts. See, Kamran Talattof, *Modernity, Sexuality, and Ideology in Iran: The Life and Legacy of a Popular Female Artist* (Syracuse: Syracuse UP, 2011), chapter 2.

28. According to David Halperin, *How to Do the History of Homosexuality* (Chicago: UPS, 2002), the history of sexuality is not the mere history of sexual classifications; it includes a history of human subjectivity.

29. Ibid.

30. See M.T. Jafari, *Hikmat, Irfan, va Akhlaq dar Shir-i Nezami Ganjavi* (Tehran: Kayhan, 1991) and Behruz Sarvatiyan, *A'inah-i ghayb.*

31. Some scholars apply the *pir and morid* model in many situations even today, and it has, in my opinion, become a cultural woe. Many have explained the 'improvement' in the works of Forough Farrokhzad using this model, seeing Golestan as a mentor who changed Farrokhzad. They impose a Rumi-Shams relationship on her relationship with Golestan forgetting that the latter does not even feature in any of her writings. As an example, see Naser Saffariyan, *Ayeh-ha-ye Ah* (Tehran: Dur Negar, 2002), 124.

32. *Kolliyat,* 556.

33. Nizami, *Haft Paykar* (1955).

34. He has renamed other female characters such as Ferdowsi's Qaydafeh to Nushabeh in *Sharafnameh.*

35. *Kolliyat,* 203. The passage starts and ends with (که خوبانی که در خورد فریشند) and the line after.

36. This segment appears in Nezami, *Khosrow va Shirin* edited by Barat Zanjani (Tehran: U-Tehran, 1997), 63–67 and in *Kolliyat,* Introduction (Tehran: Behzad, 1999), 126–127. The first line starts with (یکی شب از شب نوروز خوشتر).

37. The proverb goes, "Baalaa tar az siyahi rangi nist," meaning you have hit rock bottom. Furthermore, Nezami says, there is an amber color after the charcoal lights, and a white/grey color after one's hair turns white due to aging.

38. Christoph Bürgel, "The Romance" in E. Yarshater, *Persian Literature,* 161–79.

39. Julie S. Meisami, "Fitnah or Azadah? Nezami's Ethical Poetic," in *Edebiyat* N. S. vol. I, no. 2, 1989, 41–77.

40. Julie Scott Meisami, *Medieval Persian Court Poetry* (Princeton, N.J.: Princeton UP, 1987).

41. For a discussion of Layli's character, see A. A. Sa'idi Sirjani, *Sima-yi du zan,* 24.

42. Barat Zanjani, *Layli o majnun-i Nezami ganjai* (Tehran: Tehran UP, 1990), 113.

43. This passage (*Kolliyat*, 60) shows Layli's ability to face and deal with the harsh reality of her life. It begins with this (ایلی بودم ولیکن اکنون).

44. Jan Rypka, *History of Iranian Literature* (Dordrecht, Holland: D. Reidel Publishing Company, 1968), 211.

45. Many saw the defeat of the Sasanian Empire (224–642) which marked the beginning of a regression in the Persian world. For Nezami, *Khosrow o Shirin* represented the era before the defeat when an "urban" love is portrayed in the domes or gardens, and *Layli o Majnun* belonged to the post-invasion time when the unfulfilled love is portrayed to trigger tribal wars.

46. *Layli and Majnun* by Nezami Ganjavi, translated by Dick Davis, 104.

47. *Kolliyat*, 369.

48. See Seyed-Gohrab, *Layli and Majnun: Love, Madness and Mystic Longing in Nizami's Epic Romance* (Leiden: Brill, 2003), 198–200.

49. *Layli and Majnun* by Nezami Ganjavi, Dick Davis, trans, 106.

50. *Kolliyat*, 369–70.

51. Seyed-Gohrab's *Layli and Majnun: Love, Madness* is a comprehensive study and among several explanations, the book argues for the possibility of double meaning and thus the double reading of Nezami's story as a mundane love story featuring a madman's love and an allegory and expression of mystic love, 200.

52. Seyed-Gohrab provides a detailed analysis of this scene in his major book, *Layli and Majnun: Love, Madness and Mystic Longing*, 198.

53. Ibid., 198.

54. Arjang Maddi, "Barrasi-e Suvar-e Khiyal dar haft paykar," *Farhang*, 10 (Fall 1992), 331–408.

55. See Christoph Bürgel, "The Romance" in E. Yarshater, *Persian Literature* (NY: Bibliotheca Persica, 1988), 161–79.

56. Nezami compares his *Makhzan* to Sanai's *Hadiqatu' l-haqiqat*, (The enclosed garden of the truth) and his romances to Ferdowsi's *Shahnameh*.

57. Hamid Dabashi, "Harf-i Nakhostin: Mafhum-i Sokhan dar Nazd-i Hakim Nezami Ganjavi" in *IranShenasi* vol III, no, 4, (Winter 1992), 723–40.

58. Ibid, 733.

59. Sabatino Moscati, *The Face of the Ancient Orient* (Chicago: Quadrangle, 1951), 111.

60. Jalil Dustkhah, *Avesta* (Tehran: Murvarid, 1983), 9.

61. "Yasna," 53.

62. [29] *Kolliyat*, 23.

63. From *Haft Paykar*.

64. *Khusraw O Shirin*.

65. From *Haft Paykar*, 1168.
66. In *Layli and Majnun*, he passionately talks about his mother too.
67. *Kolliyat*, 1196.
68. Barat Zanjani, *Khosrow va Shirin-e Nezami* (Tehran: U-Tehran, 1997), 22.
69. Because the word She'ari has a few different meanings, this half line can also be rendered differently. For example, it can read, "For me there is no chanting/mott/custom/device/habit better than love." However, it must be rendered in a way that makes sense when combined with the second half. This line is included in the editions by Dastgerdi and Sarvatiyan but is omitted in Zanjani's edition.
70. For example, see M. Mashhadi, and Esfandiari. "Tahlil-e Bonmayeh-haye Erfani Khosrow o Shirn" in *Pazhuheshnameh Erfan* 19, 2018, 162–183 and articles in Peter J. Chelkowski, ed. *Reza Ali Khazeni Memorial Lectures in Iranian Studies, V. 2*, (Salt Lake City: University of Utah Press, 2013).
71. See for example, Mehdi, Zarghani, *Tarikh-e Adabiyat-e Iran va Qalamrov-e Zaban-e Farsi* (Tehran: Fatemi, 2019).
72. Maryam Sa'eb, Ta'vilat-e Erfani dar Shahnameh, Mo'aref, 34, Bahman 1384. Streak is for *rageh* (vein, seam), a rather vague word for this occasion.
73. See the chapter entitled "The Religious Use of Persian Poetry" in J. T. P. de Bruijn *Pearls of Meanings: Studies on Persian Art, Poetry, Sufism and History of Iranian Studies in Europe* (Leiden: Leiden UP, 2020), 161–172.
74. Ibid.
75. See *Kolliyat*, page 95 (line 1 and 4): Section 12, "Sokhani chand dar eshq."
76. *Kolliyat*, 96.
77. *Kolliyat*, 284–288; 'On the prologue of the book' and 'denouncing the jealous.'
78. *Kolliyat*, 96–97. The most pertinent passage starts with (ز شیرین کاری شیرین دلبند). Then he makes yet another connection to the pre-Islamic religions by evoking Mani's book of drawing, *Arjang*, a reference that changes the friend's criticism: he advises Nezami not to cover copper with gold and instead to take a path of abstinence and chastity to receive more gold. This verse has two levels of meaning related to the content of the book and the resulting compensation. Of course, Nezami disagrees with him.
79. The section in *Khosrow o Shirin* on love starts with (مراکز عشق به ناید شعاری).
80. Another passage from *Khosrow o Shirin* exemplifies the centrality of love in the life of his hero. It starts with (می و معشوق و گلزار و جوانی).
81. *Kolliyat*, section 12, page 95 (line 3–4 and 12–13).
82. *Kolliyat*, 2 (line 39).

83. *Kolliyat,* 282 (line 16), and in the following line from his Me'raj story.

ز حیض دختان نغش رسته / ز رفعت تاج داده مشتری را

84. Prior to Nezami, Ferdowsi pioneered the portrayal of women characters in epic stories. Therefore, this segment could have come before the discussion of Nezami's work for chronological purposes; however, this book is focused on Nezami's work. The discussion of other poets serves substantiating the arguments.

85. The article, M. Dabir-Siyaqi, "Chihrah-i Zan dar Shahnamah" in *Kitab-e Paz,* 20–78, counts to 32 named women and 35 other women without name in the *Shahnameh.*

86. Obviously, this is not to suggest that Ferdowsi does not sometimes portray men negatively.

87. See C. Bowra, *Heroic Poetry* (London: St. Martin's, 1961).

88. Julie S. Meisami, "Fitnah or Azadah? Nezami's Ethical Poetic" in *Edebiyat,* 1, n. 2 (1989), 44.

89. For information about this work, see E. G. Browne, *A Literary History of Persia,* 2 vols.; J. Rypka et al., *History of Iranian Literature* (Dordrecht, D. Reidel, 1968); Dick Davis, Epic *and Sedition: The Case of Ferdowsi's Shahnameh* (Fayetteville: University of Arkansas Press, 1992 and Olga M. Davidson. *Poet and Hero in the Persian Book of Kings,* (Ithaca: Cornell UP, 1994).

90. Ferdowsi, Abolqasem, "Rostam va Sohrab," *Shahnameh,* edited by M. A. Furughi. (Tehran: Javidan, 19--.), 83–98.

91. On this important scene of lovemaking, Seyed-Gohrab writes, "It is difficult for Muslim audiences to identify with a story in which intercourse outside marriage is not condemned. In the oldest manuscript of the *Shahnameh,* Ferdowsi tells how Rostam and Tahmineh spend the night together, and how Tahmineh becomes pregnant, without making any value judgment. But in later manuscripts, and especially in naqqali retellings, this passage is modified." See, Seyed-Gohrab, "Corrections and Elaborations: A One-Night Stand in Narrations of Ferdowsi's Rostam and Sohrab," in *Iranian Studies,* Vol. 48, No. 3, 2015, 443–461. Such textual modification is part of the renewed post-1979 Islamization of the Persian culture including the poetry of Nezami Ganjavi and Forough Farrokhzad, all as part of the mystification of Persian poetry. The poems that do not lend themselves to a mystical or religious reading are often ignored or excluded from official sites. In a study of such poetry produced from tenth to fifteenth centuries, R. Zipoli writes, "These genres include invective, cursing, lampoon, satire, diatribe, mockery, facetiae, social criticism, burlesque, parody and the like." See, Riccardo Zipoli,

Irreverent Persia: Invective, Satirical and Burlesque Poetry from the Origins to the Timurid Periode (10th to 15th Centuries) (Leiden UP, 2015), 11. Also see Paul Sprachman *Suppressed Persian: An Anthology of Forbidden Literature* (Costa Mesa: Mazda, 1995).

92. See M. Islami-Nodushan, "Mardan va Zanan-i Shahnamah" in Hariri, ed. *Ferdowsi, Zan, va Terazhedi* (Babol: Kitabsara, 1986).
93. Ferdowsi, Abolqasem, "Rostam va Sohrab."
94. Julie S. Meisami, "Fitnah or Azadah? Nezami's Ethical Poetic" in *Edebiyat* N. S. volume I, n. 2, 1989, 46.
95. Ibid, 63.
96. Abu al-Qasim Ferdowsi, *Shahnameh*, 195.
97. See also Thibaut d'Hubert and Alexandre Papas (ed.), *Jāmī in Regional Contexts: The Reception of ʿAbd al-Raḥmān Jāmī's Works in the Islamicate World*, ca. *9th/15th–14th/20th Century* (Leiden, Boston: Brill, 2018).
98. Peter Jackson (ed.). *The Cambridge History of Iran*, volume 6, *The Timurid and Safavid Periods* (Cambridge: Cambridge UP, 1986), 913.
99. Shannon Stack, *Heart: A Political and Social Study, Dissertation*, ULC, 1975, 241.
100. Terry Allen, *Timurid Heart* (Wiesbaden: LRV, 1983), 15.
101. In some of his other works such as those on Sufism, he imitated Attar.
102. Abd al-Rahman Jami, *Masnavi-i Haft Awrang*, edited by M. Mudarris Gilani (Tehran: Sa'di, 1958), 331, *Salaman va Absal*, ed. Muhammad Rawshan, (Tehran: Asatir, 1994), 118.
103. Jami, *Salaman and Absal*, trans. Edward FitzGerald, edited, prose translation by A. J. Arberry (Cambridge: CUP, 1956), 174–175.
104. Ibid, 341.
105. Jami, *Salaman and Absal*, trans. Fitzgerald, 160.
106. Jami, *Masnavi-i Haft Awrang*, 330.
107. Jami, *Masnavi Haft Urang*, 28.
108. Christoph Bürgel, "The Romance," in *Persian Literature*, no. 3, ed. Ehsan Yarshater (New York: Bibliotheca Persica, 1988), 175–77.
109. Hadland F. Davis, *Wisdom of the East: The Persian Mystics, Jami*. (London: John Murry, 1908), 23.
110. Fatima Mernissi. *Women and Islam*, trans. Mary Lakeland (Oxford: Basil Blackwell, 1991), viii, 126, and 128.
111. Jami, Abd al-Rahman, *Silsalat-al-zahab* (Golden Chain) in *Masnavi-i Haft Awrang* (Tehran: Sa'di, 1972).
112. G.H. Yusofi, *Chishmeh-ye Rowshan* (Tehran: Ilmi, 1970), 269–78.
113. Abdelwahab Bouhdiba, *Sexuality in Islam* (London: Saqi, 1998), 30.
114. J. W. Wright Jr. and Everett K. Rowson, eds. *Homoeroticism in Classical Arabic Literature* (NY: Columbia UP, 1997), xv.
115. Ibid, xv and 3.

116. Paul Sprachman "Le beau garcon sans merci: The Homoerotic Tale in Arabic and Persian" in J. Wright and Everett Rowson, *Homoeroticism in Classical Arabic Literature*. 192–209, 196.

117. Gayane Merguerian and Afsaneh Najmabadi, "Zolaykha and Yusof: Whose Best Story?" *IJMES*, 29, no. 4 (November 1997), 485–508.

118. Ibid.

119. Jami, *Subhat al-Abrar*, 495.

120. Davis, 254.

121. *Kolliyat*, 415.

CHAPTER 4

Faith, Facts, and Fantasy: Stories of Ascension and Nezamian Allegory

Thus far, I have shown that Nezami uses a variety of concepts, subjects, and themes related to love, women, speech, science, and religion to construct intricate poetic allegories. To continue the challenge to the notion that religion or mysticism was an overwhelmingly important source of inspiration and creativity for Nezami's literary output and to demonstrate that his approach to all these concepts was literary (Sakhon), I point out the way non-ideological readings of his poetry are possible by analyzing the highly religious story of the ascension of Mohammad to heaven or *me'raj*. The story of ascension, which appears in all of his five books, is yet another literary portrayal based on exceptionally religious and yet fantastic material. It is another excellent example of Nezami's poetic process of imagination and pictorial allegory in general and the expression of his cosmic knowledge. In Chap. 7, I will provide a comparative study of another fantasy and mythical story by Nezami to further illustrate that he has used similar allegorical techniques regarding another highly imaginative story that has no intent to preach Islam.

To be sure, there are clear religious connections in all five poems on the story of ascension, but as my analysis shows, they can be understood in terms of their literariness.[1] That is, in those five depictions, the poet demonstrates his understanding of not only the religious symbolic signification of the story but just as much displays his knowledge of astronomy in his

© The Author(s), under exclusive license to Springer Nature
Switzerland AG 2022
K. Talattof, *Nezami Ganjavi and Classical Persian Literature*,
Literatures and Cultures of the Islamic World,
https://doi.org/10.1007/978-3-030-97990-4_4

day, which are all rendered playfully, masterfully, and eloquently.[2] To be certain, images constructed of names, colors, and shapes of the zodiac and its constellations permeate numerous other parts of his *Five Treasures*. In those lines, Nezami does magic with his words.

There are two common types of scholarly analysis of Nezami's stories of ascension. The first group explains why/how the components of this story of ascension appear in Nezami's works. They might elucidate what they call the mystic concepts embedded in the poems. They might further believe that the stories of ascension as poems were close to Nezami's soul, explaining that "from traditional material which he knew well, Nizami exercised his talent, affirmed his preferences, and produced an original work" of mysticism.[3]

Other prominent scholars who read Nezami's ascension stories to signify the poet's absolute religiosity and advocacy of his religion embrace a second type of analysis. Countless books and articles have been written in Iran to promote the idea that the portrayal of the story of ascension in *Five Treasures* is yet another sign of the poet's complete devotion to Islam and his piety. Some take it further and claim Nezami was actually a clergyman who also wrote poetry. Some analyses have compared his stories to the numerous early Arabic sources on me'raj to discern which Islamic school of thought he promoted in the poems. This emphasis and exaggeration regarding Nezami's religiosity and piety are not limited to academia. The false notion is now quite popularized. In an article in *Kayhan-e Farhangi*, Qomshe'i equates the Me'raj poems in the works of Sana'i, Khaqani, and 'Attar in terms of their religious quality and in the way all three have written their work in accordance with Koran.[4] The problem with both types of readings is that they ignore the fact that Nezami included five poetic pieces on a popular subject using popular science of his time in his books in the same way that he artistically renders the topic in other segments. He did not write ardent articles, treaties, or religious books of interpretation.

Thus, I propose reading these variations of the story of me'raj in terms of what I call Nezamian pictorial allegory, which I will explain further in the next chapter. It is his way of taking an object or a concept and connecting it with meanings that exist outside the text to form his narrative. His type of *ebham* (ambiguity) and *iham* (double meaning, polysemy, pun) are present in these me'raj constructs where the thematic aspects of the verses, their connections to science, truth, and myth all contribute to the modes of figuration that can be found in all stories of ascension in all of Nezami's books. The description of constellations and figures of ambiguity, substitution, and simile are derived from the inner logic of the structure of Nezamian allegories. Nezami's pictorial allegory is a self-generating system of literary techniques and figuration, which by the way, explains the difficulty or sometimes untranslatability of some of his verses. His use of the names of stars, the heavy onus he puts on the shoulder of the colors, and his unlikely pairing of images all speak to his playfulness with language and his Zoroastrian understating of the cosmos as a living body. Nezamian figuration is thus more serious than his outward messaging. It shows his focus on form.

This chapter, therefore, offers an alternative to the religious or mystical reading to help further address Nezami's understanding of poetry in which he indeed possesses a systematic and, if you will, a theoretical approach far from any ideological motivation, that very notion of Sakhon. This chapter also supports the argument for the need to read the works of Nezami without attributing, ascribing, or assigning any ideological advocacy to the poet. In this analysis, I am inspired by the work of Jacque Le Goff, who does not recommend the study of the culture of the Middle Ages from a Marxian viewpoint because classical imaginative works are not mere ideological representations of the infrastructure; the imagination sometimes shapes other realities.[5]

Classical Persian literature is rich with imaginative stories depicting fauna and flora with emphasis on specific animals and birds, fairies, jennies, and the descriptions of the celestial spheres and religious myths. One such religious theme revolves around the notion of Mohammad's trip to heaven to meet God; a journey called the Me'raj. Some consider the journey as one of this prophet's miracles, even though he did not initiate it in many accounts of the story. The journey consists of his night travel to Jerusalem (mentioned briefly in the Koran in the short Asra' and Najm) and his ascension (me'raj) to the heavens. The Koran is the originator of the story, but other anecdotal versions over time have added details. Fleshed-out versions of the tale tell of the archangels Gabriel and Michael meeting Prophet Muhammad and preparing him for his meeting with God. Gabriel provides a mythical winged creature Buraq (that looks like a human-headed flying steed), to transport him overnight from Mecca to Jerusalem and then from Jerusalem to heaven (me'raj). Mohammad and Gabriel proceed through seven levels of heaven (in a sense, the seven rings around the Earth) to reach the throne of God. Numerous Persian poets have recast this miraculous myth.[6] Nezami has versified the story of the ascension in almost all of his books, collectively known as the Five Treasures

(*Panj Ganj*). Fouchecour, Burgel, Gohrab, Asfrayeni, Hematian, Porshekuh, Vafai have written on this topic and for the most part explained its religious significance. This chapter raises several new questions about Nezami's approach to this specific tale. Why has Nezami portrayed the story of ascension in all of his works? How do these presentations differ? What do they tell us about the author's approach to literature and poetry? Generally, critics of Persian poetry take his telling of the tale as a sign of his own fervent religious and/or mystical belief. This chapter provides a comparative analysis of the portrayal of the story of ascension in Nezami's works to find the central driving motifs in his various portrayals and renditions of the story. The chapter further compares Nezami's presentation of the story of ascension (from all his five books) with those presented in Shiite and Sunni sources of me'raj and with works of other poets and authors who recounted the story in their literary works as well. I intend to explain Nezami's evolving literary thoughts through his rendering of the story and how each version in each of his masterpieces corresponds to his notion of the concepts of rhetoric and poesy more than his faith.

Nezami writes poetry that revolves around religious motifs, particularly in his first book and in the introductory parts of his romances, which are not intrinsic to the books' entire content and stories. In them, he praises God, Mohammad, the kings, and his own poetry and fuses these with other themes. Scholars of Nezami have, for the most part, relied on those segments in their interpretations that advocate for the poet's religiosity or mysticism. In particular, his renditions of the story of ascension in those introductory parts have led literary scholars to dig deep into them in search of Nezami's ideological beliefs.

I propose reading these variations of the story of Me'raj in terms of what I call *Nezamian pictorial allegory*, his way of taking an object or a concept and connect it with meanings that exist outside to form his narrative. This leads to his type of *ebham* (ambiguity) and *iham* (double meaning, polysemy). Nevertheless, from a literary point of view, these me'raj constructs, the thematic aspects of the verses, their connections to science, truth, and myth all contribute to the modes of figuration found in all the stories of all of Nezami's books. The description of constellations and figures of substitution and simile are derived from the inner logic of the structure of Nezamian allegories. Nezami's pictorial allegory is a self-generating system of literary techniques and figuration, which by the way, explains the difficulty or untranslatability of some of his verses. His use of the names of stars, the heavy burden he puts on the shoulder of the colors, and his unlikely images all speak to his playfulness with language. Nezamian figuration is thus more significant to him than messaging. The fact that these allegorical patterns match with and are ornamented by the sound of music of the poem (markedly in the initial syllables and the couplets' rhyming syllables) is a testament to the superiority of his poetic process over the intended or resulting unintended meaning. The qualities are most manifested in the segment parts of each of those versions. Generally, classical Persian literature has undoubtedly been enriched by the possibilities that form, chronograms, numerology, and other techniques can offer. The story of ascension is merely Nezami's chosen lunch pad to construct a poetic, pictorial allegory because likely all his readers were already familiar with it.

I have shown before that such essential concepts and themes related to love, women, speech, and even the holy site of the Muslim faith, the Ka'beh, serve as materials for Nezami's work, which construct intricate poetic allegories. The story of ascension is yet another literary allegory and clearly a proper one for his type of pictorial allegory, that provides a premium theme for his poetic process of imagination and the expression of his cosmic knowledge. As in his other allegorical constructs, all five representations of the ascension story might have an ambiguous and abnormal religious connection too, but as the following analysis shows, they are understood better in terms of their literariness. In fact, in those presentations, the poet once demonstrates that he understands the messages of different religions and his contemporary astronomy, which is all rendered playfully, masterfully, and eloquently.

The Sources of Me'raj

This story is briefly referenced twice in two chapters, Asra' and Najm, of the Koran, According to these verses, God takes Prophet Muhammad from Mecca to Jerusalem and from there to the heavens or to the highest layers of the skies.[7] The verses state that he shows Mohammad the mysteries of creating the universe, and Muhammad gets a chance to learn new meanings as well as the chance to meet the previous prophets. The verse also repeats the common phrases about the prophet praying to and praising God. That is it. Many hadiths or collections of traditions containing sayings of Mohammad also produced a significant body of exegetical works of those few verses that tell a more complete and more vivid tale. Those verses and the explanatory renditions have since provided poets a poetic motif.

It is a common knowledge that the hadith or sayings of Prophet Mohammad are of secondary importance to the Koran but are used in Islamic jurisprudence to understand more fully the Koran. Hadith were collected by early followers and then studied and extrapolated upon in collections of hadith. These collections came to differ somewhat in the hands of different factions of Islam. Sahih Muslim's hadith documents include the most famous hadith regarding the ascension in chapter 74 of the book *Kitabi al-Iman* (The Book of Belief), which describes the night journey and the ascension/me'raj. Below is a summary of the story according to that book of hadith.[8]

> I was brought al-Buraq, which is an animal white and long, larger than a donkey but smaller than a mule, who would place his hoof a distance equal to the range of vision. I mounted it and came to the Temple (Bait Maqdis in Jerusalem), then tethered it to the ring used by the prophets.

> Then he took us up to heaven. Jibril then asked the (gate of heaven) to be opened and he was asked who he was. He replied: Jibril. He was again asked: Who is with you? He (Jibril) said: Muhammad. It was said: Has he been sent for? Jibril replied: He has indeed been sent for. And (the door of the heaven) was opened for us and lo! we saw Adam. He welcomed me and prayed for my good.

> Then we ascended to the second heaven. …. When I entered 'Isa b. Maryam and Yahya b. Zakariya (peace be upon both of them), cousins from the maternal side, welcomed me and prayed for my good.

> Then I was taken to the third heaven …I saw Yusuf.

> Then he ascended with us to the fourth heaven. Idris was there.

> Then he ascended with us to the fifth heaven, and I was with Harun.

> Then I was taken up to the seventh heaven. …. and there I found Abraham.

> Then I was taken to the Distant Lote tree, whose leaves were like elephant ears and its fruit like big earthenware vessels.

> Then Allah revealed to me a revelation and He made obligatory for me fifty prayers every day and night.[9]

The story continues with meetings with Moses who advises Muhammad to negotiate the number of prayers to be required by Muslims and basically to ask for a lighter obligation. Mohammad takes the advice and succeeds in arguing for just five prayers a day.

Other versions of the stories might differ in terms of the time of departure, the place of departure, the orders of the meetings, and so on. In one case, the means of transportation is not Buraq, that unique mount. It is rather a ladder, a tall, tall ladder. The explanation for that is the fact that the Arabic word "m'eraj" can also mean ladder in addition to ascension. The accompanying commentaries to these books of hadith are also numerous and varied. Some points of contention in the commentaries include the exact timing of the departure and return, the exact point of the departure, the number of stops, and even the purpose of the trip. There is no universal agreement on the number of trips he takes to heaven either. They also differ in the interpretation of the nature of the trip as to whether this trip was spiritual, or occurred in a dream, or if Muhammad was actually physically transported to heaven. Though most believe that he did travel to heaven physically.

VIEWS ON THE NEZAMI'S STORY OF ASCENSION

Nezami has versified the story of the ascension in the introductory sections of all of his books. The story consists of 68 verses in *Makhzan al-Asrar* (*The Treasure House of Mysteries*), 43 verses in *Khosrow o Shirin*, 66 verses in *Layli o Majnun*, 78 verses in *Haft Paykar* (the Seven Beauties), and 77 verses in *Iskandarnamah* (The Book of Alexander). Contrary to Islamic writings on me'raj, Nezami does not seem to emphasize overtly any specific interpretation in any decisive way, particularly in terms of the nature of the trip (spiritual, physical, or dreamlike) and the details such as the point of departure. For example, regarding the nature of the trip, in *Khosrow o Shirin*, he remains vague and in his *Layli o Majnun*, he tends to represent Prophet Muhamad's journey as physical but merely for the purpose of storytelling. He also seems to have been talking about a single trip in all his five different poetic portrayals as opposed to others who believed that there could have been more than one visit. These minor points can prove that his motivation had not been ideological. And the reason for this diversity seems to be more related to his word choices in the quest for beautiful versification and allegorization of the story. An analysis of these stories can also show the poet's ability to compose allegory, construct imagery, and exhibit knowledge in a poem or even in one single verse of a poem as well as his improvement in doing this over time.

Countless books and articles have been written in Iran to prove that the portrayal of the story of ascension in Five Treasures is yet another sign of the poet's complete devotion to Islam. Some take it further to claim he is indeed a clergyman who also wrote poetry. Some analyses have compared his stories to the numerous early Arabic sources on me'raj to discern which Islamic school of thought he promoted in the poems. For example, in his well-researched article, Said Porshekuh and Abasali Vafai try to show that three Arabic books on the story of ascension had influenced Nezami.[10] There are some similarities in all these stories, no doubt. However, a survey of these books shows that the core of their account is similar to what Sahih Muslim has portrayed in his detailed and widely accepted hadith. They all focus on the prophet, the people he meets, and the greatness of God. However, Porshekuh and Vafai are right that Nezami's portrayals are comparable with these books regarding the time and place of departure, meetings, and purpose. However, Nezami's portrayals differ slightly in some details, even though the core of the story is the same in all of the five versions. This may be because he could have been inspired or informed by Sana'i (another Iranian poet) or the hadith attributed to Umm Hani (one of Muhammad's relatives). Nezami in fact mentions her.

Even though most, if not all, scholars see the Islamic or mystic beliefs as constitutive in the life and literature of Iran and the Middle East, many of them also pay attention to the rhetorical aspects of such expressions of religiosity and their literary values. Such a reading can in fact explain some of the complex meanings. For example, de Fouchécour explains the prophet's journey taken place in seven stages.[11] He writes, "A similar form of religious agnosticism is present in the hymns on God. The same Ash'arite (whether Hanafi or Shafaei) attitude is also palpable in Nizāmī's emphasis that Muhammad did see God at the summit of his ascension, clarifying his opinion in the unending debate on the *visio beatifica*."[12] He further states, "The higher orders of demons, saints, prophets and angels appear in Nizāmī's work, though he does not give a description of the cosmos, as does Qazvvini in his 'Aja'ib al-Makhluqat."[13] However, to me, Nezami is not genuinely concerned with this debate. While in *Makhzan al-Asrar*, he insinuates that the God can be seen, in Kheradname, he takes a slightly different position. It is not easy to prove that Nezami changed his religion, but it is possible to know that he writes based on his poetic exigencies. He writes more on Kherad in his last two books, once of which is entitled Kheradnameh (the book of reason), and in doing so, he becomes closer again to Ferdowsi's understanding of this ancient concept.

Asghar Seyed-Gohrab elucidates the mystic concepts embedded in the poems and explains that the story of ascension is also similar to the story of Bahram in Nezami's other book, *Haft Paykar*. He states that in both cases, a journey begins from within the actual material existence and passes through seven stages (consisting of the real and imagined worlds) symbolized by the seven planets.[14] Seyed-Gohrab reads these journeys as Sufi expeditions. He writes, "at each stage during his passage through the spheres of the planets, the Prophet leaves behind one aspect of his material being even as he offers something to the planets, until he has totally divested himself of all worldly entity."[15]

THE STORIES OF ME'RAJ IN NEZAMI'S *PANJ GANJ*

Even if we assume that Nezami's source is inspiration is the Islamic myth of ascension and that he had no knowledge of *Ardaviraf-namag* as a forerunner of me'raj stories, we still cannot conclude that his goal in his renditions was to promote religiosity. Let us look at these five poems comparatively and structurally to understand their signification and process of allegorization for Nezami. It is true that in one place or another, all five poems mention angels and the prophets. Moreover, all five versions point to the time of the start and end of the journey (at nighttime); the means of transportation (Buraq, a human-headed flying stallion); the place of meeting with God (skies, heaven); and the gift the traveler brings back (God's intercession). It is also true that in all these, and despite all the differences, Mohammad is portrayed and praised as a central character. Other references to religion include the mention of other angels, prophets, and holy sites. However, these repeated religious references are only one small part of each poem. In all of them, the plot is that Muhamad, accompanied by Gabriel and Michael, departs on a Buraq at midnight from the Ka'beh; goes to Jerusalem[16] and from there to heaven; meets a few other figures, including some past prophets; and then returns to the Ka'beh still at night bringing with himself the news of God's intercession.

This core plot, then, is not Nezami's creation. However, when the five renditions of the story are studied comparatively, it becomes clear that the poems accomplish more than reiterating that simple plot. In reading these versions together, we should be aware of the distinction between two conceptual sets: religion and religious symbolism versus knowledge and literary metaphors.

Sharafnameh	*Haft Paykar*	*Layli o Majnun*	*Khosrow o Shirin*	*Makhzan al-Asrar*
Intro: the journey, Boraq	Intro: time, place	Intro: desire, journey	Intro: time, place	Intro: time, praise
شبی کاسمان مجلس افروز کرد	چون دگدمید در جهان تنهن	ای نقش تو معراج معلی	شبی رخ ثاقله زین ذبر قالی	نیم شبی کان ملک فیروز
شب از روشنی دعوی روز کرد	تخت و عرش بست معراجش	معراج تو نقل آسمانی	به خلوت در سرای ام هانی	کرد روشن ملک گیش فروز
سرایرده هفت سلطان سریر	سر بلندیش راز پایه بست	از هفت خزینه در گشاده	رسیده جمرئیل از بیت معمور	نه خاک از دیده عماریش کرد
برآورده گوهر به چوبی حریر	جبرئیل آمده براق به دست	بر مهد کبر قدم نهاده	براقی بری سیر آورده از نور	کرد راه در هرم کاتنات
سرسپری پوشان باغ بهشت	گفت بر باد نه ببی خاتی	از حوصله زمانه تنگ	نگارین پیکری چون صورت باغ	کرد و هم در هرم کاتنات
به سرمزی آراسته کار و گشت	تا زمهوت گرد اغلاکی	بر فرق فلک زده شهاماف	سرش پکر از لکام و رانش از داغ	هفت حط و چهار حد و شش جهت
محمد که سلطان این سپه بود	پاش شب را ز خیل خانه خاص	چون شب علم سیه برداشت	نه باد از ابر نهسان درخشان تر	روز شده با قدمش در وداع
ز چندین خلیفه ولیعهد بود	مرح برق این بناق داراست	شون کی تو رخس راه برداشت	چو دریای ز گوهر گرده زینش	زامشی آمده شب در سماع
سرنافه در بیت اقصی گشاد	برشین کاشف این بناق ترامت	خلوتگاه عرش گشت جایت	دگاشته وام کس زوری نشایش	نیده اخبز گران خواب گشت
ز دانش زمین سر به اقصی نهاد	چوکاه کبر بناقت آورده	پروار بری فارک پایت	فوی پشت و گران نعل و سیه خیز	کم سیاه از خواب خلان تاب گشت
ز بند جهان داد خود را خلاص	به جنبت براق آورد	بر پرزده از سرای هانی	بدین غیز سین و ذر در شن نیز	با نفس کله ازین دامگاه
به معشوقی مرشبیان گشت خاص	مهد بری گرد ران که ماه توانی	جمرئیل رسید طوق در دست	وشق تنگ چشم هفت دره	مرغ نلش رفته به آزمگاه
بله بست از این کوی هفتاد راه	بر کواکب دوان که شاه توانی	کز مهر تو آسمان کمر بست	از آن خانی شده پیش شهنشاه	مرغ زیر در اندیشه یعنی قلک
ز رفتن زه در بارگاه	شش جهت را ز جوار میع براز	نظاره است در چه هستند	چو مرغی از اندیشه پیش شهنشاه	مرغ الهیش قفس پر شده
دل از کفر نه حجره نیما خانه	ز فلک را به جوار میع براز	Zodiac, Angels	به اقصی الغایت القصی رسیده	قلیش ازین قفس سکتز شده
به حجز از آسمان تاخته	برون جسته زین جعفد چرخ جست	برخیز هلا نه وقت خواب	نموده لبیا را آینه خویش	گام نه گام او چو تحرک نمود
فرس رانده در سماک چرخ جعاد	از لائی شباذده زیرش چرخ جعاد	جمان را درآر سر به نعمد	تو زتفطیل امانت رفته پیش	میل به جهت سوای به کبرگ بود
و ارگی شذاده زیرش چرخ	عطر سایان شب به کابی کند	عطر سایان شب به کابی کند	چو گرده پیشوانی لبیا را	چون دو جهان نیده بر از داشت
سلبانی چو خورشید در نور غرق	سبز پوشان در انتظار که کار	سبز پوشان در انتظار که کار	گراقه پیش راه کبریا را	سر ز بی سپده فرو باشد
سهیلی بر اوج چرخ ثلاثه	نارنجان مصر این بر کار	نارنجان مصر این بر کار	برون رفاه چو وهم تیز هوشان	پای ازان پایه که درپیش داشت
ادیم یمین ز رنگ از او نا	تو عاشق خفته یوسفوار	زمره کبود سنر پوشان	ز خرگاه کبود سنر پوشان	پایان ازان پایه که درپیش داشت
بریایم دیی ملکه لؤلؤ سمی	خیز تا در تو بهت نظر کند	از زیر نقش بر فرق	تازور کو در یاید از شرق	رخش بلند لخورش افکند دست
روینده جو لؤلؤ بر آبریشمی	هم کشد و هم مرتع پاره کند	طاور شب را که خوبش درباب	خود را وجود پوشان	هاشیه را بر گکت هر گه همت
نه آهو بلکه نافاین در مشگ بی	اسمان را به زیر پایه خویش	چون نرولان آسمان گیر	زمین کرد از صورت مالی	بحر ز خین نان شد و او گوهرش
نیز دیدن آهو برآموده در	مرغ مالاره بلنذ	اسمان را به زیر سایه خویش	به سامل گاه قطب آورده کشتی	برد سپهر از بی کنوار مرش
از آن خوش حذان که آبد کمان	موکب روی و کمین زد وفات	از ابن اخز بر امبر سایه خویش	خوربنید ره سیاد از به چشتی	Cosmic, Angels
آز آن نیز روشن که غیر از گمان	درکش آهوان قعس را به کمند	موکب روی و کمین زد وفات	جهره مامع و کرد	گوهر آب که کرد شب معنبرین
شکاندش و هم طوای بدراند	شبروان از آ شکوفه نه چو جراغ	موکب روی و کمین زد وفات	چو هرده کرده لبیا را	گاو فلک برد ز گاو زمین
نوز بازدم سه ماده ماه داشت	تاره زبوبائی چون شکوفه باغ	دزکش آهوان قعس را به کمند	کمان را اسخوان بر گلیه کرده	او سنه پیشگانی این سفر
به علم کشانی فرشته وار	شب شب تست و وقت وفت دعامت	دزکش آهوان قعس را به کمند	تو را روی ساخنه درای	از سراذان یافح و ز هوز کمر
نه علم کشانی که خبر کند	پاک خوامی هرآنچه خواهی خواست	شبروان از آ شکوفه نه چو جراغ	رحم بر مادران دم بسته	خوشه کبرو سنبلز سلحفه
به شرنانی در شب جرا گشت	تازشگر که فرشکان را آرش	شبروان از آ شکوفه نه چو جراغ	رحم بر مادران دم بسته	سیله را بر اسد اند اخته
که شریانی جو آهو جذا گفت	خیمه زن ز ز بهت تازه دامان بشتاب	شب شب تست و وقت وفت دعامت	ز جمین دختران نامز رسته	کا شب او را که قدر قدر همت
چو ما آمد شب جراتی مست	قائل خامی تست هفته	دی ما بخابی دام آزفته	رغعت ناه تازه دختری را	زهره دنب سه ماه تزار او به دست
چذان شد که تا نیزوگام او	شب نما و صبح هزار باغ	شده هزارت کارگه	ربوده ز آفتاب اتگذری را	منگ و زن از که قدر همت
نسی بر ز حنش ازاد او	سر براوز به مهر بر کشیده	شب نما و صبح هزار باغ	ز جمره ماه جوز را پکی نیز	زلاکه به مقدار تزاز او بود
مگر خود آدم بر نظر سیام	جدول به سر برآور او را کشدی	تاج شب که شاهنه افروز	چو نوسف شریای درد او باز	ریچکه نوش از دم سنبری
تو برآور از آن اب ذخشائی دست	روی بر کنده ناش راز را به کند	سر براوز به مهر بر کشیده	چو نوسن وقفای در جود داشت	نور ز هم در بی کنوار سری
بیسر ز آن خائی را و دور	تا به حق القدم را قدامت	جدول به سر برآور او را کشدی	ثریا در کلیش مانده مدهوش	چون ز کمان قمر شکر ز شام ریخت
بر آور از آن تیزی گام او	چون محمد ز جمرئل به راز	رفق روی تو گرد ز راش	به سرخی حمایل بست بر دوش	زهر از کمان خواننه أین لنیا
مین جربئل که آن ربنا گفت	گوش کرد آن این گوش نواز	سفت دوری ستون تیراو شدی	وز ر زینی که مطر بر افشانده	ستر که آن کاف خشم مندری
خیمه زن در شب جذا گفت	از سحن حمی چون تماس داد	طلبز کان شده وقت بخش	وز زور دینه ریحان آن گان	یوسف بلوی شده جونی کتاب
تازشگر که فرشکان را آرش	جو محمد از حهان گوشه	رفق روی تو نیز گرد از راش	تهده چشم خود را مهر مانع	بونی جوان تاخته جون لؤ اب
زانجا که چان بک اسه راند	این گام و قدری که چان شده مود	بنخش که در جان لؤ اب	تهده چشم خود را مهر مانع	ناک خرخز تخت جُ لؤ اب
قاندام را ار زان جای شده	این گام و قدری که چان شده مود	جو جریان رفت زا این جهان خصارا	تهده چشم خود را مهر مانع	لشگر گل خیمه به صحرا زده
دوران نواسی را بمادی	جو بیرون رفت زا این جهان خصارا	بن جربئل که را بغاب زد	ربای خزتا در صحرا با صحرا	ربیع زمین یافته رنگ دبیع
داده در دهند هزار خوشه	داده در دهند هزار خوشه	رکاب اقلاند ز صحرا سا صحرا	بادن پرداخلی طاووس اخضر	ربیع زمین یافته رنگ دبیع
بناش نظر تو مهر بز مازا	بناش نظر تو مهر بز مازا	رکاب اقلاند ز صحرا سا صحرا	بادن پرداخلی طاووس اخضر	عذر گوم خواننه ز سما
Cosmic, constellations,	به طف جربئل با صحرا	از مطلع عرش تا به همر	از مطلع عرش تا به همر	سبز کوکب قدمش میدرید
پس آدگه قلم بر حذاد ز دست	به طفاش گذاشی به پر چم	عنان بر ز ت رکابش باز پس گشت	سراقبل آمد و بر بر نشاندش	سفت دکراف طهش میکانید
طلاش طبیعت به نامید داد	هم طاش آمد و بر بر نشاندش	سراقبل آمد و بر بر نشاندش	سراقبل آمد و بر بر نشاندش	تاف شب آکده ز مشک لبان
به شکرانه قرصی به خوررشید داد	هم طالسک ره را ز با شکستی	وز آنجا بر سر سذره رساندش	نعل به راه نکانده سم مرکش	از شب تاریک بدان اتفاق
به برع داد آنش خشم خویش	هم خان آخده بر بر که کلام	وز آنجا بر سر سذره رساندش	وز آنجا بر سر سذره رساندش	برق شده پویه پایه بری
به حشم انذران ره را نسبرفت پیش	در شب خود آن سراج منیر	هم بال افکند و به شد به خزر	جریده بر جریده نقش میخانه	کبک وش آن تاریک بدان اتفاق
رطونت ره از د بر مشتری	گرن از آن طوق دان که نگات	(الله محکم) ز نور خوانده	ز آنجا بر سر سذره رساندش	برق شده پویه پایه بری
دگلیش خار ز دو انگاشتوری	از آن طوق ان که نگات	مکالیات نشده بر از	ز آنجا بر سر سذره رساندش	فاخنوی گشت نیر هنی
سواد خشم به کیوان میود	بری کرد بر بری نشانده	واورده به خواجه تاش ذبگر	بنابان رخش سبر ماک ایت	سذره دیده همد ز پی خمانی
به جذ گوهری پاک با خود درد	تاریش زور و آزاره به دست	اسرافیل فنده به چای	تو به استقیش آمد ذ شت در فرش	عرفی گریه باش زه زده ذاشش
جذان گرد بر ماند و شیا تاب	جون آر در آورد و طایی پای	همه بوای سماء به روی قوین	طرز زد بر سرری گلب کیوان نوین	شب شذه ز هر دود داناه بکری
شذه با گرفر مائه و شیا تاب	کبک طوی خرام جسن ز جای	رفرف کند شده بر روی خویش	قدم برگ ز روی خویش بر داشت	زان گل و زان دریشان گشنه ذاشت
رافی با وکذه چیار مطلب	حون از در آورد و طایی پای	برده به سری سذره گاهت	حجاب کلیات از پیش برداشت	نرگس او سرمه مازاغ داشت
ز ده دست در بی به فکر گاه او	جون از در آورد و طایی پای	جون از بر سذره گاهت	حجاب کلیات از پیش برداشت	جون گل آزین پایه فیروزه فرش
کمر بر خیز کوه بر گیر	ر از فتادن مه چون گذار داد	اوراق حذوت در نوشتی	مکان را ر آمد غم شکستنک	دست به دست آمد تا سقف عرش
گرینه گویاره حبیبت جوانذ	شب تاله و دبر زبر گلف عرشی	تا طارم بلنذ عرشی	محمد در مکان بی شکانی	همفرانش سیر نزاذاده خواست
به هاروندپس خاضر و موسی دوان	سح و زان تمام بلنذ	سوح زنان نذاش بیختانی	بل شکنته و بر انذخاه	بل شکنته و بر انذخاه
مسبحا گویه گوییم ز موبگ روان	وهم عبدی که جون گذار د ناام؟	خداوند جهان را ببیجهت دید	او بخیر چو عربان داد	حلقه زانی جو غربان راه
نه انذازه آنکه یک رعن کنند	سرحش عقل از در جوانروزي؟	هفتا حجاب ر بریدی	به هر مصووی کنش رقمس بر آور	پرده نشویان که در خیال ذاشت
تباه ذاودی جون در جوانروزي؟	بود زار اهروین همه تشگ	وز آنجا رفته سری ذرخت	به هر موي بلش جشمی بر آور	رفت بدان راه که هیمه نمود
به اردای کوی چشم زخمی که دی بر هم از ناک گذشت	بود ز ار او و ریش همه تشگ	هج ناخ گذاشای و هم شذه	و زان نذاش لاه داشای قدک	این قذنان زازها آگه زود
زمین و زمان را ز پس درنوشت	با جون بی آخویش همه تشگ	دلش در چشم و چشمش بر دلش بود	و زان نذیش لاه داشای قدک	هر که در راه آخرش گفته بود
ننده ز تعجیل داوذ او	با جون بی آخویش همه تشگ	ز زحمت تحت وفوق رستی	خطاب آمد که ای مقصود درگاه	زو سر راه آموزش خود بذماند
کس از گرد بر کنده ذ او	با چون گشیر قطب شمالی شذ	در ختبه خاص قاب قوین	تو را حاجت که مقصود است	بر هر خشتی باد مضاج بود
پر بیابان نیرشی در از باد نگذار	در سیرنی مسک آن در جذول	ز زحمت تحت وفوق رستی	درخوار؟	عرش بنان مالده منجاج بود
	کاه رامع نمود و گفنا اهزار	خیمه خاص قاب قوین	سرای فضل بود ز بنخل خالی	جون بی همه خرق قلم ذر کشید
	Seeing God	Seeing God		

فلک تیو پزدلها ماند باز	چون محمد به رقص پای براق	هم حضرت ذوالجلال دیدی	برات گنج رحمت خواست حالی	ز آمدی عرش علم برکشید
تابید تنش در رسدهای دور	نر نشت این صحفه را اوراق	هم سر کلام حق شنیدی	گه کاران است و ا دعا کرد	تا تن هستی دم جهان میپرد
به روحانیان بر جسدهای نور	راه دروازه جهان برداشت	از غفلت وهم و غور ادراک	خدایش جمله حاجتها را کرد	خواهید جان را به تن میپرد
در آن راه بهراه از اوارگی	نوری از دور آسمان برداشت	هم نودین وهم شلونت پاک	چو پوشید از کرامت خلعت خاص	چون به عرش به پایان رسید
همش بار ماندہ همش بارگی	Cosmic, Angels Prophets	درخواسته خاص شد به نامت	بیامد باز پس با گنج اخلاص	کار دل و جان به دل و جان رسید
پر جبرئیل از رهش ریخته	میپرید از مشازل فلکی	از قربت حضرت الهی	گلی شد سرو قدری بود کامد	تن به گهر خانه اصلی شتافت
سرائیل از آن صدسه بگریخته	شاعر احی به شهیر ملکی	باز آمدی آنوادکه خواهی	حالش رفت و بدری بود کامد	دیده چان شد که خیالش نیافت
ز رفتن گذشته به فرسدگها	ماه را از خط جمایل خویش	گلزار شکافته از جبینت	خلایق را برات شادی آورد	دیده که نور ازلی بیابش
در آن پرده بنموده آهنگها	بر عطارد ز نظر کاری دست	توقف کرم در آستینت	ز دوزخ نامه ازادی آورد	سر به خیالات فرو نابش
ز دروازه سدره تا ساق عرش	زهره را از فروغ مهانی	آورده برات رستگاران	ز ما سر جان چون او نازلیی	راه آدم پیش قدم در گرفت
قدم بر قدم حصمت افکنده فرش	برقمی برکشید دیمانی	از بهر جو ما گناهکاران	یقینی باد هر دم آفرینی	پرده خلقت ز جهان برگرفت
ز دیوانگاه عرشیان برگذشت	گرد راهش به ترکیب مهر	ما را به محل که چون نو شامی		کرد چو ره رفت ز هدایت فزون
به درج آمد و درج را نوشت	تاج زرین نهاد بر سر مهر	زانها که تو روشن آفتابی		سر ز گریبان طبیعت برون
جهت را ولایت به پایان رسید	سبز پوشید چون خلیفه شام	بر مائه شفاعت اگر نذلی		هستی از غفلت روشن نلی
قطیمت کو برگل از نوران رسید	سرخ پوشی گذاشت بر بهرام	دریای مروتت رایت		آمد در منزل خویش نلی
زمین زاد تا آسمان شاخته	مشتری را از فرق سر شامی	خضرای نوشت جبت		خیرت ازین پرده مباشل گرفت
زمین و آسمان را به جایی رساند	در دسر دید و گشت صندل سای	شدبی تو به خلق بر مروت		حیرت ازان گوشه عدلش گرفت
که از بود او هیچ با آن رسید	تاج کیوان چو بوسه زد لادمش	بر بشاختر از این نبوت		پرده در اندلخته نیمت وصال
چو شد در ره نیمتی چرخ زن	از خوامان چو شیر زنجیری	هر که از قدم تو سرکشیدد		از در تعظیم سرای جلال
برون آمد ز هستی خویشتن	برخوابی به شیر زنجیری	دولت قلیش در کشید		پای شد آمد بسر انداخته
نمود آن سر او قدساله او	هم رفیقش از ترکلاز افتاد	در منظره ابد نشسته		جان به تماشا نظر انداخته
رهی رفت بر زیر و بالا نابر	هم بر اقلن ز پویه باز افتاد	باغ ارم از امید و بیمت		رفت ولی ز رحمت یافی نداشت
حجاب سیاست بر انداخت	منزل آنجا رساند کز دوری	جزت نه و ناقه نیست		جست ولی رخصت یافی نداشت
ز بیگانگان حجره دربداشت	دید در جبرئیل دستوری	ای مصند آسمان نوشته		چون سخن از خود به در آمد تمام
Hearing/Seeing God	سر برون زد ز مها میکابل	جون گنج به خاک باز گشته		تا سخنش یافت قبول سلام
در آن جای کلنیانه نامیده جای	به رمضکاه صور اسرافیل	از سرعت آسمان خرامی		Seeing God
درود او از محمد قبول از خدای	گفت از آن تخت نیز رفت گرای	سری بگتانی بر نظامی		آیت نوری که ز وراثنی نود
کلامی که بی الت آمد شنید	افغان و سفر و هردو ماده به جای	موفوت نقاب چند باشی		دید به چشمی که خیالش نود
لفظی که او نهانی بود دید	همرهان را به نیمه ره برانداخت	بر برگ خواب چند باشی		غیش را بی حرض و جوهرست
چنان نبود که حضرت ذوالجلال	قطر دریا بی قطر بی محیط گذشت	برخرد را نقاب رخ بر اندازی		گر حرض و جوهر از آسم ترست
نه ز آن سود صحبت به نه از این به خیال	قطر دیر قطر در چه بود نوشت	این مغره ز پشت بار برگیر		مطلق از آنجا که نه پنداشتی
همه دیده گشته چو نرگس تش	لردبان سلامت از کمند نیاز	وین پرده ز روی کار برگیر		دیدنش از دیده دلش نگاشت
دانگته یکی خار پیرامش	سر برون زد ز عرش نورانی	رنگ نیاز او مه سفید بزای		کوری آن کاسی که دیده نگاشت
در آن نرگس حرف مکی ده ماشت	در خطرگاه سر سجماتی	هندی ز مهد علمی مغازی		تو بیمر دیده به چشمی دگر
ماگو زاغ کم مهر ما ز ماغ دنداشت	حیرتش نور خطر بیری خرد	یک عهد کن این دو سویدا را		دیدن آن پرده مکانی نود
گذر بر سر خوان اخلاص کرد	رحمت آمد لگام گیری کرد	یک دست کن این عقد ثریا را		رانی آن راه ز مکانی نود
هم آو خورد و هم بخش سه خاص کرد	از این ناقه بسوی او ادنی	جون تربیت حیات کری		هر که ره آید به جز نظرگاه ماه
دلش نور اخلاص الهی گرد	از دنی رفت سوی او ادنی	زان همه مشکلات کردی		از جهت بی جهتی راه یافت
یقیمی نگر تا چه شاهی گرد	چون حجاب هزار نور رسید	زان نافه به داد بخش طبی		هست ولیکن نه بجز بجای
سوی عالم آمد رخ افروخته	دیده در نور نفس نبود آنجا	باشد که به ما در ده نصیبی		هر نه جایی نیست بیاشد خدای
چنان رفته و آمده بود پس	گامی خود دید نرسید آنجا	زان لوح که خواندنی تر به بدایت		کافر بود دین ثباتش سکن
که ناید در اندیشه هیچکس	Seeing God	در خاطر ما فکن این معنی		جهل بود دین جهانتش سکن
ز گرسی که چون برقی پیمود راه	گامی چو خود بود فراتر شد	وین صرف نه که پاکیش بیصرف		خورد و شرابی که حق آمیخته
نشد گرسی هیچ خبر از خوابگاه	دید معود خویش را به درست	در دفتر ما نویس من بادی حرف		جرعه آن در گل سار آمیخته
نداکه که شب را چه احوال بود	دید زایده خویش را به درست	بنمای به ما که یه چه نامیم		لطف ازل با نفشتی هستین
چو شلید کا خود یکی سال بود	دید بر یک جهت نکرد مقام	وز بک گر ز جهت نهان تو		کسمت حق نازگتی و نازمین
برآید با پیران علمی	زیر و بالا ز پیش و پس چپ و راست	آی کار مرا شامی از تو		لب به نماز خلده بیراشته
اگر شد به یک لحظه او جان مست	شش جهت گشت و شش جهت بخامت	نوری نه از نظامی از تو		است خود را ز جهت یافت
به آر گوهر جان نازرش کلم	بی جهت شد جهت گریز کدد؟	زین نل به دما قناعی کن		همتی از گل که توازگر شده
ثنا خوانی چار بارش کم	زین جهت هم جهت گریز کلد	وز بهر خدا شفاعی کن		جمله مقصود میسر شده
گیر غار چهارزده و گوهر چهار	بی جهت را جهت ندارد کار	تا پرده ما فرو گذارد		پشت قوی کرده از آن برگاه
فروشنده را با فضولی چکار	تا نظر بر جهت نیست هرگز	وین پرده که بهست نه ندارد		روی بر آورد بدین گرگاه
به مهر چلی گره چها محکم بیم	جهت از تشویش و اضطراب نر نیست			زان سفر عشق میز آمد
ز عشق عمر نیز خالی نیم	چهت از دید چون جهان نهان باشد؟			بر نفسی زده و باز آمد
سبیدون در این چشم روشن دماغ	دین بیجهت چون جهان نهان باشد			ای سخت مهر ز ربانای ما
اویکر شمعت و عثمان چراغ	از نبی جز نفس نبود آنجا			بوی تو جداداروی جهانای ما
شده چار تکبیر دولت تمام	همگی را جهت بود آنجا			دور سخا را به تمام رسان
زهی پیشوای فرستادگان	در احاطت جهت کجا بود سجد			ختم سخن را به نظامی رسان
پذیرنده مظر افتادگان	شربت خاص خورد و خلعت خاص			
به آغاز ملک اولین رایتی	جاسش اقبال و معرفت باقی			
به پایان نور آخرین آیتی	هیچ باقی نماند در باقی			
گزین کرده او سر عالم توئی	باماداری دمه هزار ز درود			
تو تو گر کسی باشد آن هم توئی	ای ز اوج آن ز مدار فرود			
توئی قفل گنجهاها را کلید	هرچه آورد گاه باران کرد			
در نیک و بد کرده بر نامید	ای نظامی جهان پرستی چند			
به شب روز ما را به پی نذلی	بر بلندی برای پیش بلند			
سبیل کو زده کاشی امتی	کوشی تا بلندی سری یابی			
من از آستان کمترین خاک او	وین ز دین محمدی یابی			
بمین لا غری صید فتر اک تو	طل را گر طفره دارد پس			
نظامی که در گنبه ده شهربند	رستگاری به نور شرع شلاس			
میاد از سلام تو دلهر مند				

Because the rendition of that simple plot requires imagination, one might conclude that the second conceptual set, that is, knowledge and literary metaphors, predominates over religion and religious symbolism. However, even if we assume that both groups are present, literary criticism must determine their relation to avoid assigning the renditions to the realm of ideology.

All five poems consist of three broad sections that sometimes overlap. In the first section, Nezami talks about the time and the place of the beginning of the prophet's journey to the skies, elaborates on his desire for the journey, and offers powerful praises to him and other mentioned characters. The second part of each poem consists of eloquent descriptions of the cosmic knowledge ending with a vivid portrayal of the constellations and the zodiac regarding their shapes and colors. The reader has to be familiar with that science to understand the metaphors, similes, and references in this section. This second section of the five poems might also return to the angels and/or the past prophets who appear on Mohammad's path or whose names might be evoked by a reference to a star. Finally, the third section of all five poems contains a brief description of the moment the prophet sees, meets, or hears God. As it is customary with Nezami and other poets, the last section of all five poems includes a reference to Nezami himself in which he asks for prayers on his behalf along with other prayers, praises, and acknowledgments.

THE STORY IN *MAKHZAN AL-ASRAR*

The first section of the story of ascension in *Makhzan al-Asrar* renders in verse the idea of the prophet's initiation of the journey. It begins with comparing Mohammad with the midday sun and placing him within a sense of time and space where the journey begins. In many different ways, it describes the night, the seven skies, four elements, and six directions in which he says goodbye to Earth. Nezami understands the seven skies as seven rings that loop around the Earth, and the Earth is sitting right in the middle. This portrayal insinuates a physical journey; however, there is a decisive line in the third section indicating that the journey was taken in one breath. Many celestial concepts are also mentioned in various creative ways. What is most consistent are the references to the signs of the zodiac. The poet here demonstrates his ability to play with certain words and concepts in diverse ways without being too concerned about the consistency of the plot, putting all his effort into creating unprecedented imagery. Angels are flying with the prophet, but they fall behind. Even the horse that is so fast, that is synonymized by Rakhsh (a legendary horse that belongs to the hero of the *Book of Kings* and whose presence is felt even in this story of Nezami), cannot catch up. The constellations begin to dance in his support. All these moments are vividly portrayed and are rendered by playing with words through devices such as alliteration, allusion, amplification, and analogy, to name a few.

The *noh falak* (nine firmaments, nine skies) consisted of seven stars plus two on the top of those. The last one is often referred to as *falak al-aflak* (the firmament of the firmaments). They look jubilant. Here is an example.

The gem of the night, in the perfumed night	کوهر شب را به شب عنین
Took Taurus of the constellation from the Taurus of Earth	زمیگاو فلک برد ز گاو
Was gifted a crown from Cancer and a victory from Gemini	او ستده پیشکش آن سفر
The grape hyacinth shaped Virgo	کرجوبا تاج و سرطانار
He placed Virgo on Leo.	ساختبسلبلبر کرو خوشه
	انداختبلسدسنبله را بر 17

The context is that Nezami portrays the material world (Haram-e Ka'enat) in which the Sun (Mohammad) shines and provides light for all. At the same time, Mohammad is so fast that the angels (and Rakhsh) cannot keep up with him in the ascension process, and then the sky behaves like a Sufi who turns into dancing. Thus, the moon, the Taurus, took away the earth, Mohammad, that night. Again, this is not the first or the last time Nezami portrays the cosmic formations. About Teucros in *Haft Paykar*, Ziva Vesel writes that images of the cosmic cupola in the Palace of Khavarnaq "could be the pictorial description of either the thirty-six decans, or the three hundred and sixty degrees of the ecliptic" or "they could also be a reminiscence of archaic pictorial traditions collected in a book attributed to Teucros."[18] In the above line, the description becomes a report of some game.

As Christoph Bürgel explains, de Fouchécour has noticed that Nezami's verses on cosmology indicate the importance of the sphere's planets and the stars, which for him constitute the world order. For Nezami, de Fouchécour writes, "the world is embedded or enshrouded in the nine spheres of the Ptolemaic universe (i.e., the seven planetary spheres [which includes the sun and the moon], the sphere of the fixed stars; and the encircling sphere). These represent time and fate and are usually expressed by metaphors such as the 'seven' or 'nine snakes'."[19] Of course, the numbers seven (for its pre-Islamic significance, his book Seven Beauties, and its use in popular stories), nine (for its astronomical relevance), and four (for its use in astronomy and popular medicine, four elements and four directions) feature frequently in the five poems. Nezami purposefully references the constellations and the months of the year and the shapes and the "associated" colors described in vivid detail. In these verses, all colors have meanings, and the implications are sometimes indicative of a human's feelings.

Despite its forbidden or unclear status in Islam,[20] astrological science in Persia has a long history starting around the eleventh century with the works of such scientists as Abu Mash'ar Balkhi and Abd al-Rahman Sufi. These expanded in the following centuries into the works of Biruni, Khayam, Kharazmi, and Kuhi. This knowledge seems to have been based on *The Almagest*, written by Claudius Ptolemy (c. AD 100–170), in which he documents a mathematical and astronomical model for the apparent motions of the stars and planetary paths.[21] However, there are other indications that it could have been informed by the ancient Persian sources. We know that the Persian astronomer Rahman Sufi Razi (903–986), also known as Azophi, wrote and translated works on astronomy (and added pictures to his textual descriptions in his book) during the rule of the Delimites (Daylamian) and that the astronomy book of Ptolemy was translated into Arabic in the ninth century. These were only part of the activities and fascination with stars and planets before and during the time of Nezami. Based on the available knowledge from the Greeks, Arabic, and Persian sources, poets and prose writers were familiar with this science.[22] Several studies show that the Zoroastrian astrologists had also held similar views and understating of the sky and its constellations with a level of precision.[23]

Nezami's *Makhzan al-Asrar* has been the most ardently touted source for those who understand Nezami as an Islamic ideologue. However, its story of ascension is not the only so-called religious poem that lends itself to literary analysis or that might cast doubt on the poet's signification. In the big picture, such an analysis shows that religion, too, is simply a theme for him here. To be sure, the portrayal of Mohammad in this book is dissimilar to any other ideological descriptions. In this book, the prophet is not engaged in any bloody battle, he takes actions such as this journey for the sake of love, and most pertinently, the journey often occurs in short time (a description that came along much later), which indicates a radically different interpretation of the me'raj from standard Islamic sources. His portrayal of his religion is a literary portrayal, which is the most substantiated indication we have about his faith.

THE STORY IN *HAFT PAYKAR*

An analysis of the story in the Seven Beauties prompts an even stronger urge to pay attention to Nezami's stress on the poetic trade. In the first two lines, the Earth feels too confining for the prophet. Gabriel shows up with a Buraq and invites the prophet to accompany him on a cosmic journey. In the following 20 verses, Gabriel first briefly describes the Buraq's speed as faster than lightning. Then he explains the deserving higher status, beyond this Earth, which the prophet will achieve due to the journey.

Over both worlds, your banner will follow.[24]	بر دو عالم روان شود علت

From their seven roots, uproot the six directions, the nine spheres unfix From their four nails: pass by the Fish and bend the heavens to your wish.[25]	شش جهت را ز هفت بیخ برآر نه فلک را به چار میخ برآر بگذران از سماک چرخ بلند قدسیان را درآر سر به کمند

This version starts by saying that the world was too small for Mohammad's crown, a ladder (Me'raj), and/or Gabriel, and the horse he brought helped/instructed him to go through the skies to God. In this context, Nezami makes another pictorial allegory. Mohammad is told of all the wondrous things he can do. For example, in the two lines above, he is told to uproot or conquer all six directions (east, west, north, south, up, and down) of the world and the seven skies and tame the nine spheres but using four nails, pivots, or elements. Still, you will pass the Arcturus and the constellation Virgo. Even here, Nezami frames Gabriel's speech in terms of space and time. Everyone here and there will love the prophet more. The following six lines after the two above show how effectively the two communicated. In the next 16 verses, the central portrayal is the speed with which the Buraq launches toward space, both northward and then southward.

All these segments are versified with care, paying attention to the sounds, alliteration, and interconnections of the metaphors. Perfume makers of the night (*atr sayan shab*) or nightwalkers (*shab ravan*) refer to the stars; wearers of the Green (*sabz pushan*) refer to angels, and blossoms of the orchards (*shekufeh-e bagh*) refer to light/stars. These references are clear to Nezami's readers who understand the poet's passion for words and his penchant for creative pictorial use of words. Nezami also employs the shape or the characteristics of several birds, including the eagle, the partridge, and the peacock, as similes to convey other meanings and pictures such as soaring, apogee, the moon, and the four elements (four eagles). His attempt to portray this journey as a cosmic adventure in this section reaches grandiose proportions.

Its speed outstripped the Poles' swift course: one moment south, the other north.[26]	با تکش سیر قطب خالی شد گر جنوب و گر شمال شد

That is, with one leap, he outperformed the journey between the poles, both the south and the north. One interpretation of the line is that the Earth (or its poles which were believed to be most active) became fixed at its north and south poles. This image would be consistent with the other astronomical knowledge presented in the poem. Whether riding south or north pole, with his canter and one jump, he left behind the earth.

The lines above and the following one portray the trip to elevate Mohammad's status, making him look like he is the guardian of the earth and a special guest in the skies above those angels. In this portrayal, the lines use descriptive or foretelling astrological and astronomical images, such as bending stars to respect him, immovable poles to acknowledge his greatness, shining mount to carry him upward, the universe's four corners and four columns to locate him, the night's imbuing and perfumed stars that lit his path, angels in green garments walking on the carpet made of the blossoming, chiaroscuro morning lights to greet him, an eagle flying to the other world to indicate his speed, moon offering silky light to guide him, seven colors of seven planets to tell a secret to him, the Saturn's headache to be tacked by him, and the directionlessness of God to warn him. Nevertheless, "eyes might observe God," because the valuable flying particles were also observed early on the path. It is how these theological concepts are expressed in prosody that is impressive.

However, we should pay attention that a scene, event, character, or a natural element might be versified, integrated, and narrated more than once in Nezami's work but each time differently further indicating his preoccupation with Sakhon and allegory rather than the subject alone. As an example, we look at an allegory that is constructed around a frequently used word. The word night, *shab*, in its symbolic and natural sense appears several times in each of these ascension stories. However, it has appeared numerous times before all over his poetry though never in a dull picture, always using new imageries (even geometrical shapes), similes, and metaphors. In *Makhzan al-Asrar*, there is even an entire segment dedicated to "Describing the Night and Knowing the Heart," as the subtitles go. Nezami expresses his own inner thought apparently in one of those emotionally low moments and reminds himself of the sage words. The night is primarily a dominant metaphor in the first 15 lines so that it reflects his inter-feelings as well. Then, toward the end of this prelude, he is inspired by a voice about writing and what to think. In other words, he is as preoccupied with the literary images (pictorial language) as with subjects (allegorical renditions). Most of the difficulties of understanding some of Nezami's poems are related to this combination.

I have provided the Persian lines in the endnote.[27] Here, I would like to render those lines in prose to illustrate my point better, even though such a paraphrasing cannot convey all the techniques, including the sound created by alliteration and expert juxtaposition of the words. This rendition also shows that without knowing Nezami's references (or looking them up), they might not make sense in the first reading or when rendered into other languages. The passage goes:

As the Sun dropped its shield onto the earth and the earth its shield into the water, the universe dwindled from its breathing and gained more yellow color than the painters' colorful yellow flowers. However, as he, the Sun, dropped his shield, his army pulled their sword to cut his head. It is just when the cows (Taurus) who are adorned with the rough, tough neckless fall, all those around pull their sword. Children in the care of the night pearls are nevertheless chained by feet by the day's rattle bell. Anticipating the deal of the night worriedly, a refreshing potion was made from the dust. To tend to the passion of this young night, the nursing sky made a delightful philter on earth. The earth added water onto a mix of love fire from Jesus' breath. That sweetened beverage cured maladies that coexisted, the mad house now arranged. After drinking that delightful earthen sherbet, the love sickened night poured a goblet of blood [red color] onto the horizon, ushering in the dusk and twilight. That anxious, maddening love now exposed, and the young night dressed as black as the ink of a pen, head to toe. That interior color reflected outwardly to the extent that fate considered it an infidel. Each breath out of playfulness, the night has created a night game with delight. In the game, the night covered the fine linen-like moon with flowers and at times threw round golden coins on the face of round Venus. In that night when there was no light, in that heavenly garden where no nightingale sang, I mixed my heart blood with Sakhon, and I created fire from my compassionate splendor. In my poetry, as the words took forms alone, I began to think of an admonition. I was inspired by a call to invest all my power, and it will repay.

He ends the segment with complimentary lines about himself and his Sakhon. Expert readers will make more sense of the passage, but even a literal rendition shows how far Nezami's imagination flies when creating his pictorial allegories. It is with this ability that he found the Me'raj stories an appropriate subject for all his books. One thing in common in such descriptions is Nezami's use of cosmic structures to portray the inner and outer shapes and conditions of the subjects of his muses: subjects including religion and wine, prayers and sex, and conflict and peace (all of which are entertained by contemporary astrology). Such a vivid animation and animating quality of the surface story of pictorial allegories give agency to natural elements to tell or foretell the story in the second layer of the construct. To consider the night, *shab*, as a mere metaphorical stage (Sufi or not) that changes with the arrival of the day (a spiritual transformation) does not hold in the case of Nezami because it plays a significant role in his allegory sometimes independent of the daylight and sometimes as a force that overcomes the light of the day too.

It is striking how he attempts to portray this journey as a cosmic adventure. He uses the middle segments of the tale to delve into the descriptions of stars. He does this in all five versions and so demonstrates his mastery of the language but also his intimacy with the astronomical science of his time.

When he with Buraq's dancing feet /
inscribed that volume, sheet by sheet,
He left behind the worldly road /
and far above the heavens soared;
Cut through the station of the sky /
with angel's wings, a broad highway.
From his own verdant nature, he /
gave to the moon new verdancy.
His silver-work to Mercury gave /
the bluish shade of leaden glaze.
O'er Venus, from the moon's bright light /
he drew a veil of silvery white.
His dust, as he attacked the heavens, /
set on the sun a golden crown.
Green-robed like Caliph of the West, /
red garments bright to Mars he left;
And, finding Jupiter consumed /
by pain, rubbed sandalwood thereon.
when Saturn's crown his feet had kissed, /
he placed its flag in ambergris.[28]

چون محمد به رقص پای براق
در نبشت این صحیفه را اوراق
راه دروازه جهان برداشت
دوری از دور آسمان برداشت
می‌برید از منازل فلکی
شاهراهی به شهر ملکی
ماه را در خط حمایل خویش
اداد سر سبزی از شمایل خویش
ماه را در خط حمایل خویش
داد سر سبزی از شمایل خویش
بر عطارد ز نقره کاری دست
رنگی از کوره رصاصی بست
زهره را از فروغ مهتابی
برقعی برکشید سیمابی
گرد راهش به ترکتاز سپهر
تاج زرین نهاد بر سر مهر
سبز پوشید چون خلیفه شام
سرخ پوشی گذاشت بر بهرام
مشتری را ز فرق تا پای
دردسر دید و گشت صندل سای
تاج کیوان چو بوسه زد قدمش
در سواد عبیر شد علمش

Mohammad starts his journey with a fast moving, dancing Buraq and leaves the gates of this world. What this section conveys is also in accordance with the knowledge of his time. The poetic exaggeration in this segment from *Safarnameh* is that the prophet determines seven colors for the seven stars he is passing by while the moon's axis is his baldric (sword belt). The ascribing of the colors stands out and exaggeration becomes the aim. The moon is green because it is the ruler of the night. Mercury became the color of a black and white pearl as it tapped into the silver. Venus gained its silver color due to a moonlike ray. The mighty Sun gained a golden crown. Mars took the bold red color. Mars is *Bahram* in Persian, which is also the name of the king protagonist in the stories of the same book. What Mars, Ares, and Bahram have in common is a connection to war. The naughty Jupiter naturally becomes rosewood and sandalwood. And Saturn became black as it kisses.

According to this system, there are 12 signs that stand for 12 periods of a year and for 12 months. Stars are also divided into a variety of regions of varied sizes, each referred to as a constellation. Different images and shapes of animals and objects are formed when these stars in a constellation are mentally connected with lines. Each constellation is named according to its shape. Today, the International Astronomical Union has divided the sky into 88 constellations, and each has a precise boundary and specific group of stars.[29]

He also extensively explores the constructed connections between the days of the week with their corresponding start, shape, and their assigned color. However, the portrayal of the days of the week is not limited to these relationships. Nor is the list of the starts he pictures limited to these seven corresponding ones.[30] As it will be discussed, in a section in *Layli and Majnun*, both charts are combined.

THE THIRD SECTION

After the sections on astronomy, Nezami returns to Mohammad describing his transformation due to the journey. Yet, he does not take the opportunity to offer any particular doctrine and interpretation of what he is imparting. His portrayal of the journey can be read as a journey into the skies or a journey within the self. He mentions that it became possible for the traveler to see God, but the verses imply no literal meaning. Angel Michael also does not show up in any consistent way. And to be sure, the poems soon turn into the description of a state of weightlessness, directionless-ness, and ecstasy, all conveying an ephemeral sort of meeting with God. One verse refers to the letter/bill of riddance he brings back with himself. All of these are done rather quickly and in noticeable brevity. Yet, Nezami continues to use the same literary devices, making his poems beautiful and intriguing in terms of form. These sections, like the first ones, are also shorter than the second section on astronomy.

Nezami focuses on the trip itself and, more precisely, on Mohammad's views during the trip. He compares the prophet's moods with the constellations. He plays with the names and the names of the shapes in the zodiac. Like in his other poems, he is so preoccupied with imagery that he is sometimes carried away with his alliteration, similes, anagrams, and enjambment thereby halting the story from meaningful progress. If people are referenced, it is done through allusion or juxtaposition. Therefore, another way of reading and understanding Nezami's stories of ascension is to focus on or perceive his use of literary techniques and his knowledge of astronomy. To be sure, at his time and in that historical era, fascination with astronomy and astrology was even higher than preoccupations with the hadiths and their sources. The Abbasid Caliphs also followed activities and discoveries related to astronomy. The Persian scientist Abu Rayhan al-Biruni (973– after 1050) devoted much of his work to mathematics and astronomy. I am not sure to what extent, but this fascination could have been rooted even in the pre-Islamic Persian culture. After all, one of the discourses/chapters in Aruzi's *Chahar Maqaleh* is about astrology/astronomy, and it starts with a reference to Biruni.[31] After all, it is in *Khosrow o Shirin* where he foreshadows his fascination with astronomy. In an early short segment entitled "Spherical, Stars," he writes:

One said I have heard every star is a cosmos,	شنیدستم که هر کوکب جهانیست
having earth and a sky of its own.	جداگانه زمین و آسمانیست
Another said I had heard that too,	جوابش داد کاین ما هم شنیدیم
but I have not seen strong proof.	درستی را بدان قایم ندیدیم[32]

It should be mentioned that Nezami also refers to many pre-Islamic and Zoroastrian concepts, angelic characters, and virtuous and philosophical ideas in other parts of his books. In *Layli o Majnun*, he invokes the images of Nahid, Zohreh, Venus as "the lover's glittering jovial rein of his saddle."[33] Several lines later, there is a segment in which Majnun prays to Venus and another segment in which he prays to Taurus. Both segments describe the stars with new adjectives. In *Khosrow o Shirin*, Nezami often equates the night's silence and stillness to the sleeping time of the constellation's northern forms and the stillness of the southern shapes to a nesting bird. Birds get pregnant, and they do not move away from their eggs.[34] (On some occasions, the depiction of the lining or the interaction of these stars and planets represents love relations between the male and female protagonists of Nezami's stories. Such depictions are part of the introductory segments of the poet's pictorial allegories.[35] The description also supports the earlier point I made that Nezami's portrayal is in accordance with the Zoroastrian understanding of the universe, cosmos, stars, and planets in terms of a living body.)

Overall, in rendering the story of ascension, Nezami uses the same skills and techniques he uses to deal with other subjects and topics with what are religious events but does not evoke a religious belief or fervor in his readers. Even the archangels (Gabriel, Michael, and Israfil) and God are not placed as prominently as the planets, the zodiac signs, the colors, and the shapes in his five versions. Providing five renditions of the mythical anecdote might therefore be seen as proof of his ultra-numinous claim that poets are on par with prophets and that his work is on par with, if not superior to, the texts that portray the same fantasy vaguely and fragmentarily. I believe that the essence and nobility of Nezami's literary endeavors are aesthetical and not ideological, and, therefore, his literary skill should be examined over and above his alleged devotion.

A LOOK AT THE STORY OF ASCENSION IN THE WORKS
OF SANAI AND KHAQANI

Countless articles and books take poets' versification of the story of ascension as a sign of piety and advocacy of Islam and its prophet.[36] This formula has been applied to Nezami as well. Mansoor Yarvaysi, who once wrote that Persian literature would have been monotonous and dull without Islamic teachings and Koranic verses and revelations, comments on the ascension story. He believes that "Of the concepts and subject matters that caused the Persian literary men to gallop their speedy steeds in that field was the concept the confirmation of the instance of Prophet Mohammad's ascension."[37]

Numerous poets before and after Nezami, including Sanai, Khaqani, Attar, Amir Khosrow Dehlavi, Salman Savoji, Jami, and others, have verified the story. Many of them are too upfront with their intention to promote religiosity. However, it is not easy to categorize Nezami beside any of these other poets.

Sana'i (1080–1131) in his *Hadiqat al-Haqiqa* (Walled Garden of Truth) and Khaqani (1120–1190) in his *Tohfat-ul Iraqein* (A Gift from the Two Iraqs), on the other hand, represent the story of ascension entirely within their Sufi or religious discourses and in the context of their ambition in employing Persian poetry in the service of his spiritual views.

Sana'i's 41-line poem of the story in his *Hadiqat al-Haqiqa* focuses on one theme, and that is the description of the prophet with acute flattery and flowery language.[38] True, there are a couple of references to stars and the sun, but the emphasis is on Mohammad. The first few lines set the poem's sentiment. In addition to using many Arabic and Quranic expressions, which creates some absurdity, the poem also mentions the ladder. His mashing this all together leads to some obscurity about the meaning of the ascension to the poet.

Taking steps to gain the crown	بر نهاده ز بهر تاج قدم
Feet on the head of the world and man	پای بر فرق عالم و آدم
His feet became the head of human's crown	پای او تاج فرق آدم شد
His hands became (a base for) the world's banner.	دست او رکن علم عالم شد[39]

In other words, his poem consists of one section but seems to want to touch on many of the topics or images in Nezami, which consists of three sections. Sana'i's poem is in a section of a book about the traits of the

prophet, and the book itself is about the poet's view of Islam and his philosophy of religion. As such, Sana''i's situation and work are different
from Nezami's poems that include the ascension story as a part of the
introductory sections to his books of romance.

Khaqani, like Nezami, conveys the sense that the prophet was physically transported to heaven and God. However, as discussed above, this
notion for Nezami is simply an excuse for the literary description of a
fantastical journey, whereas, for Khaqani, a belief in the journey's physical-
ity is part of his religious and philosophical belief system. Nevertheless, in
his 23-line poem on this story, Khaqani offers an exciting description of
Buraq as part genie, part horse, and part human who has grazed in heaven
since before the creation of humans. The rare references to the stars in the
poem are to illustrate this creature.

The eternal field has not seen ever	میدان ازل ندیده باری
Such a rider on the back of the heavens	بر پشت فلک چو سواری[40]

While Nezami and Khaqani share the Ash'ari (Sunni) interpretation
and notion according to which Mohammad could see and indeed saw God
with his own eyes, the two differ in the use of this theological reference.
The content and purpose of his ascension poem are not surprising.[41]
Khaqani states:

He saw the holy threshold with his eyes.	درگاه قدم به دیده دیده
He heard the answer to his call with his ears.	لبیک به گوش سر شنیده[42]

Even in this reference, Nezami takes the opportunity in the *Makhzan
al-Asrar* to play with the word "seeing" (*didan*). Based on a religious
reading, the repletion might appear as an emphasis on the Ash'ari belief
that God can be seen with human eyes. However, Khaqani, who believes
in the same idea, does not feel a need for repetition. Therefore, it is possible to listen to the sound of the word didan and hear the music that
Nezami creates with his verses.[43]

This literary approach applies to all other aspects of the story. It is safe
to say that Nezami uses the story to prove that he can versify it better than
his predecessors. This assertion is not too hypothetical if we remember
Nezami's praise of his own work, his awareness of literary techniques, and
his notion of Sakhon, all of which I discussed in previous chapters. He
conveys the notion of his ability to versify other legends every time he

does so. He deserves this recognition because in versifying this story of ascension, he marvels, epitomizes, and encapsulates the beauty of the constellation in his words. He also presents the prophets, the horse, the lights, and colors in fascinating verses. Moreover, and to be sure, no other poet was as creative and imaginative in the versification of the story.

In sum, Nezami's expressions on astronomy might go beyond the realm of popular culture and shared beliefs of his time, but they only show his familiarity with the field yet not expertise. As he frequently equates and associates the days of the week with a star and a color, he demonstrates his wordcraft as he creates extraordinarily vivid and sometimes multi-referential images. I posit that the essence and nobility of Nezami's literary endeavors are aesthetical and not ideological, and, therefore, his literary skill should be examined over and above his devotion to his source materials—the Koran and the hadith. The source of his creativity should be sought in his work and not his possible religiosity. These poems highlight Nezami's illustration of his sublime literary skills, his ability to construct allegories, and his knowledge of astronomy. His artistic, poetic portrayal of the added elements to the story of ascension eclipses the story itself and the religiosity of the story, which initially consisted of a few brief verses. When Nezami undertook the task at the request of the Sharvan Shah Akhsatan to verify the oral, short, and fragmented story of the characters of Layli and Majnun, he expressed reluctance because the story not only belonged to an unfamiliar land, but he also did not see in it enough material to compose his own version.

Nevertheless, Nezami assembled that fragmentary material into a beautiful poetic narrative that inspired tens of other poets to follow suit. As mentioned, in applying the concept of the divine logos to Persian poets, one must be careful since such a concept is more in line with the ideology of scholasticism in which a sweeping distinction between medieval Christian philosophers and theologians and their philosophical exposé and theological writings did not exist. Unlike the scholastic authors, the Persian poets did not all use their entire rhetoric to justify and elaborate on faith. Nezami is no exception. For him, every other subject, including faith, was subservient to the word.[44] For him, the most essential aspect of his work was the Sakhon and its form.[45]

There is another piece of support for my arguments regarding Nezami's literariness (as opposed to discursiveness) of his poems on the story of ascension. Astrology, horoscope, and their related practices (including writing or reading books on the topic) are or were forbidden in Islamic tradition, perhaps because those practices and fortunetelling would be considered an attempt to intervene in God's plan. Whether there was a distinction between astrology and astronomy in twelfth-century Persia, Nezami constantly uses the position, colors, and images of the zodiac and the constellations to foreshadow an event. More pertinently, he uses the word "tale," which refers to horoscope and to the name of a portentous eastern constellation tens of times. Clearly, in his poetry, Nezami does not pay any attention to this Islamic ban, and instead, he provides the "key" to "all that is hidden" and "all that is unknown" by trying to show what he knows about the earth, the sky, the sea, and the time of the death of the leaves, all of which are knowledge and details that the Koran attributes only to God. I will not go as far as to say that Nezami was a heretic, but perhaps a somewhat secular (to the extent that the twelfth century could allow) poet. However, I can say with confidence that Koranic verses were simply other sources of reference to him and sometimes he could be subversive toward them. It suffices to look at the Koranic verse that justifies the punishment for those who practice or try to benefit from the field of astrology and fortune telling. It reads, "And with Him are the keys to the ghayb (all that is hidden), none knows them, but He and He knows whatever there is in [or on] the earth and the sea; not a leaf falls, but he knows it. There is not a grain in darkness of the earth nor anything fresh or day but is written in a clear record."[46] Yet, the Muslim literary scholar Behruz Sarvatian, whose edition of *Panj Gang* displays his challenging work and interest in Nezami's poetry, sees the poet's poetic intervention with the "secrets" in a different light. In his book titled, *Aineh-ye Ghayb-e Nezami Ganjavi dar Masnavi-ye Makhzan al-Asrar* (The Hidden Mirror of Nezami Ganjavi in *Makhzan al-Asrar* Masnavi), in which he carefully extracts useful information about Nezami from his poetry, he argues that Nezami considers himself the hidden mirror or more precisely the mirror that reflects and sees the hidden.[47] Nezami says that, but Sarvatian offers several reasons for his finding hoping to justify his own interpretation. First, the poet lived in seclusion to pray for many, many years, which transferred "his heart into a mirror of divine secrets." Second, his poems have come from the hidden world. Of course, this is an unreal and absurd claim, and he does not (cannot) prove such a superstitious claim. However, in the book, Sarvatian offers several reasons (not proofs) for these unbelievable qualities in Nezami. First, his magic ability is related to his belief in women's abstinence or piety, which is not true because Shirin and few others from *Haft Paykar* made love in a few scenes, and even Layli was craving contact with her beloved all the time. The second is the poet's opposition to epic writing, which for Sarvatian is more than a mere genre; it is a genre best used for the portrayal of ancient Persia. I discussed the question of genre in Chap. 3 on Portrayal of Women and Love and showed its role on three poets' work. He also mentions Nezami's knowledge and information about geography for several reasons, making little sense because the poet talks about geography mainly through his poetry and for the sake of poetry. Besides, Nezami's alleged "knowledge of east, west, north, and south" does not support the alleged poet's preoccupation with the so-called hidden, secret world. While the extent of Nezami's knowledge of geography is not clear, we know that he depicts his fictional regions with as many details as necessary. In the story of "Khayr va Shar" from his *Haft Paykar*, the road the two characters travel cannot be forgotten. Many other parts of the book are based on the common assumption regarding Nezami's mysticism, but it also substantively and skillfully engages with and refutes many claims about Nezami's ethnicity and language.[48]

Nezami speaks of astronomy, astrology, and horoscope (tale') like in the rest of his poetry but with an intense focus. This alone, I could argue, would disqualify Nezami as a Muslim poet because Islam sees astrology and horoscope as harmful, perhaps an interference of God's work, and thus at least officially forbidden, *haram*. However, the approach and argument are literary and as such, the chapter engages with his five versions of the story. That, of course, does not mean that Nezami was not a Muslim; it means that he was not promoting it.

To be sure, Zoroastrianism, particularly its Zurvanism branch or movement, has a tradition of studying space as the "heavenly sphere" regarding the time of creation, its origin, purpose, and its (limited) future. The good Zodiac constellations consisting of stars and planets were positioned vis-à-vis the evil planets. Even the book of *Minuye Kherad* speaks of stars and planets when speaking and explaining life and reason. It reads, "Ahur Mazda brought happiness to man, but if man did not receive it, it was owing to the coercion of these planets."[49] That does not mean that Nezami was a Zoroastrian either. It is even improbable that he used the Islamic story of ascension to promote a Zoroastrian preoccupation with astrology, even though he was perceived that he promoted Zoroastrianism by writing *Khosrow o Shirin*.

Again, Nezami boasts about the high place of poetry, how his book is on par with the holy book, and how poets rank as high as the prophets, a blasphemy according to official Islam. It should not be surprising if he also calls himself or his book a mirror. Although some passages of his works function as more than a mirror, they are the 'Cup of Jamshid,' and a palimpsest. The basis of this self-awareness is also *kherad* (universal reason), particularly the way it was defined by Razi, the philosopher of Ray, and its implication in defining the Koran.

In addition to Sanai and Khaqani, other Persian poets use the outer space and the zodiac in their poetry. Rumi's space images resemble Nezami. However, most of these poets do not concern themselves with a complete presentation of the zodiac and constellations as Nezami does. Not because their portrayals serve a message about a religious or philosophical message, but because they are not as extended and as complex as Nezami's references, they are not as miraculous; they are often random and short.

In his pictorial allegories, Nezami uses the stars (like other natural features) to facilitate a sensual connection with his passage's main point, which varies from one book to another and from one segment of a book to another segment. In a 36-line introductory section to *Khosrow o Shirin* entitled "The Reason for Authoring This Book," he begins with a description of the sky at night. He weaves a passage that features birds, animals, nature, philosophy, gems, stars, and the planets Mercury and Venus. Then, he compares himself with Ferdowsi, Jesus, and Moses to say that he deserves rewards for authoring this book even during this "uncertain" time. The passage starts with these expressions:

> When the Sun, as the king of the skies, sat on its throne, prosperity overtook the world. Prior to that, the universe was under the royal black numerals, and it would need a king. Then the birds played their drum and the Sun sat on the sky's moving throne. I am nevertheless sleepless and thus drunk, and my pen is in my hand like a sword. What kind of Sakhon should I offer to help increase the value and status of the language?

Then he ends this fantastic journey through words and images by talking about himself even more directly. 'When I am in need, help me, and when I am saddened, console me. I might be satisfied with a piece of bread, but I can still perforate and craft a dose of diamond well. Even though munificence is rare these days, I can still bring a bird from the sky into the room through a small hole, and I can break the earth open to bring a fish out of the chasm.'[50] The passage insinuates that he can perform miracles as Jesus and Moses did. Nevertheless, he is not happy that he might not be compensated [due to the region's historical chaotic condition].[51] His references to the planet *Atarod* (*tir*) or Mercury, the innermost planet in the solar system, in this passage raises the question about Nezami's awareness of the symbolic significance of this planet in other cultures. In Greek mythology, Mercury represented the God of commerce. Merchants prayed to this God for prosperity and wealth. Mercury is also associated with eloquence, and it is called *dabir-e falak* in Persian (The sky's writer). Here Nezami implicates both attributes. His reference to *Zohreh* (Nahid) also reminds of the splendor of the Roman Venus. Referring to his writing ability and demonstrating it in that same passage, he says that he made the pen in Mercury's hand come to a halt, ending his dominance over eloquence. Furthermore, if that is not enough, the softness of his own Sakhon made Venus jealous, feeling she is wearing a thorn instead of silk. Considering his poetry as a miracle and magic and evoking the names of prophets such as Moses and Jesus, Nezami congratulates himself as he does in other parts and creates a representative pictorial allegory.

In the next two parts of this chapter, I will discuss astronomy/astrology and religion in some of Nezami's poetry. This discussion will help understanding Nezami's use of various themes and subjects and how they are not symbolism of each other.

Astronomy: The Solar Calendar, Change of Season, Nature

I have already discussed Nezami's knowledge and fascination with the zodiac and its constellations and how he uses them in his poetry in this chapter in his stories of ascension. It is essential to be reminded that he uses his knowledge and ability to create unprecedented imageries in many other parts of his *Panj Ganj*. Nezami starts writing about Layli's death, a climatic part of the story, in a section of the book titled "The Arrival of Autumn and Layli's Death." The description of autumn is long, and it shows two things. First, Nezami was familiar with meteorology or at least how the weather affects nature, including gardens, trees, leaves, flowers, and the wind and the land. That does not mean he was a natural scientist. Second, the description of nature upon the arrival of the autumn foreshadows the state of Layli's being and her looming death. As the fall arrives and the leaves fall to earth, so will Layli die in her autumn of life. This shows that he knew how to employ words in a genius way to construct his narrative, allegories, and stories combining them with the calendar and the change of seasons. The resulting pictorial allegory also shows the poet's ability to weave words from his various fields of knowledge as beautifully as one can imagine and as playfully as the somber occasion allows. The passage starts with this verse.

When autumn leaves are falling, it's as though	شرطست که وقت برگیزان
Blood drips in droplets on the earth below.[52]	خونابه شود ز برگ ریزان [53]

He creates an allegorical description of the arrival of autumn. The poet features first the autumn, stating that it is inevitable for the leaves to fall in autumn. The blood, the life that flows in each branch, drips out of the tiny holes of the tree's body and vanishes. The golden ewer of water cools down, and the face of the garden turns golden yellow. The branches' bark grows blisters, and their leaves ambitiously search for gold but fall into the ground below instead. Narcissi flowers pack their clothes, mounted to depart, then the boxwood tree gets dethroned. The jasmine sullies, the rose mourns, and then a lock of dust sat on the top of the grass, twisting like Zahak's snake. When the hostile wind blows from far, leaves have no choice but to fall down. The descriptions continue until a turning point where he starts writing about Layli with (لیلی ز سریر سر بلندی / افتاد به چاه دردمندی), meaning. Just like the leaves and flowers, Layli, too, fell from her higher status into the well of agony and grief. Of course, in describing Layli's condition, the poet refers to all those autumn sceneries again, displaying the care with which he has chosen his words. As opposed to some other poets, Nezami is not repetitive in the enunciations of his meaning. He hammers down all aspects of seasonal changes, all of them fresh and some complex and complicated. Amazingly, when he describes Layli's state of mind and body, he returns to nature to its components and seasonal change as metaphors but more directly related to her life, as if she was one of those flowers or trees from the previous section that faces autumn's transformations similar to one's life.

NOTES

1. Surely, the concept of ascension existed before Islam as documented in the books such as *Arda Viraz(f) Nameh* in Middle Persian and the inscription of the Kartir (Mobad of Hormozd).
2. Ziva Vesel in "Teucros in Nizami's *Haft Paykar*" offers valuable information about Nezami's knowledge of astronomy. In "Nizāmī's Cosmographic Vision and Alexander in Search of the Fountain of Life," Mario Casari

analyzes the poet's knowledge of classical authors and the science of his time. See, Bürgel and van Ruymbeke, *eds. A Key to the Treasure.*
3. De Fouchécour, C. "The Story of the Ascension in Nizami's Work," translated from French by Kamran and Arjang Talattof in *The Poetry of Nizami Ganjavi*, 179–188.
4. See, Sayed M. Qomshe'i, "Tasvir-e Me'raj dar Ash'ar-e Sana'i, Khaqani, va Nezami" in *Kayhan-e Farhangi*, Isfand 2006, 245.
5. Jacque Le Goff, *The Medieval Imagination*, trans. Arthur Goldhammer (Chicago: University of Chicago Press, 1988), 6.
6. His view is not dissimilar to the views of the Greek poet Parmenides who wrote, "not only does the cosmological part of the poem tell us how the cosmos is arranged, it also tells us how the cosmos, humans and animals all came into being." See, Andrew Gregory "Parmenides, Cosmology and Sufficient Reason" in *Apeiron* 2014; 47(1): 16–47 (https://core.ac.uk/download/pdf/16229153.pdf).
7. There is one verse in the *Sura Asra* and a few more in *Sura Najm.*
8. Complete text, https://sunnah.com/muslim:162a.
9. These and 'Bait Maqdis' are quoted from the site above.
10. The books are *Ketab al-Me'raj, al-Me'raj al-Nabi,* and *al-Asra va al-Me'raj*. See, Said Porshekuh and Abasali Vafai, "Barrasi Tatbiqi Me'rajih-haye Khamseh Nezami," in *Pazhuhesh-haye Adabiyat Tatbiqi* 1 and 2, 1392, pp. 23–51.
11. de Fouchécour (1989), 99–108; English translation in de Fouchécour (2000), 179–88.
12. Ibid, 32.
13. Ibid, 32.
14. Asghar Seyed-Gohrab "A Mystical Reading," 181–193.
15. Ibid.
16. Based on sources such as Tabari's work, scholars argue that Jerusalem was a later addition to the hadith/story.
17. *Kolliyat*, 6.
18. See Ziva Vesel "Teucros in Nizāmī's Haft Paykar" in *A Key to the Treasure*, 245.
19. J.C. Bürgel "Nizami's World Order" in *A Key to the Treasure*, 17–52, 41.
20. Islamic sects and scholars reject the notion of the influence and impact of celestial phenomena including stars, moons, and galaxies in predicting life, weather, rain, and the future.

كتب المنجمون ولو صدقوا / وعلامات وبالنجم هم يهتدون (Nahl, 16)

21. See "Almagest: work by Ptolemy" at https://en.wikipedia.org/wiki/Almagest.

22. In today's astrology, there are 88 constellations, and their shapes include 42 animals, 29 objects, and 17 human or mythological characters. Some ancient people recognized most of the northern constellations.

23. In 1952, Behruz wrote a concise article on this topic. Zabihollah Behruz, "Taqvim va Tarish: Az Rasad Khaneh Zartosht ta Rasad-e Khayyam" in *Iran Kode*, 15.

24. Ibid, page 422, line 22.

25. Nezami Ganjavi, *The Haft Paykar*, trans. Meisami 6.

26. Ibid., 8, 423.

27. *Kolliyat*, 19–20. It begins with (چون سیر انداختن آفتاب).

28. Nizami-Meisami (1995, 8, ll. 38–47.)

29. Referring to the sun's movement in the celestial sphere and constellations over a year forming Ecliptic Constellations, divided into 12 equal parts (every 30 degrees). The 12 signs include Aries, Taurus, Gemini, Cancer, Leo, Virgo, Libra, Scorpio, Sagittarius, Capricorn, Aquarius, and Pisces.

30. See the chart above.

31. Nizami Samarqandi, Ahmad. *Chahar Maqaleh*, ed. M. Qazvini (Leiden: Brill, 1948), 85.

32. *Kolliyat*, 261.

33. *Kolliyat*, 384.

34. *Kolliyat*, Introduction by Sa'id Qanei, 422–424.

35. See *Khosrow of Shirin*'s passage that starts with (زبان بکشاد گوهر ملک دلبند).

36. See well-written and relevant chapters in *A Key to the Treasure*.

37. See ensani.ir/fa/article/download/240284. He writes that Persian literature without Islamic teachings and revelational verses and concepts is numb and boring topics.

38. A. Sana'i', Hadiqat al-Haqiqa (Tehran UP), 196. His hands became the base of the world's science. However, hand and banner match head and crown better.

39. Ibid. Sanai, Abu al-Majd. *Hadiqatu' l-haqiqat*, (The enclosed garden of the truth) (Tehran: Hirmand, 1996).

40. See, *Tohfat al-Eraqayn*, 73.

41. On the religiosity of this poet, Anna Beelaert writes, "These na'tiyas in particular, but many of his other panegyrics as well, more specifically those dedicated to mystical and religious figures, have an ethical and pious content (*zohdiyas*)." See, Anna Beelaert "Khaqani Shervani" in *Encyclopedia Iranica*, XV, 5, pp. 523–529.

42. Khaqani, *Tohfat al-Araqayn*, 42–76.

43. It begins with:

آیت نوری که زوالش نبود / دید به چشمی که خیالش نبود (43)

44. This topic was covered in Chap. 2.
45. The form will be discussed further in the last chapter.
46. *Koran* 6:59.
47. Behruz Sarvatiyan, *Aineh-ye Ghayb-e Nezami Ganjavi dar Masnavi-ye Makhzad al-Asrar* (Tehran: Sabzan, 2006).
48. He said he was sad to receive a book by R. Azadeh, *Zendegi va Hunar-e Nezami* Ganja-i (Baku, Baku Science Academy, 1979), and he engaged with that book as well. Ibid, 8.
49. *Minuye Kherad*, 48, 4. On page 26, numbers 7, 8, and 9, the book offers a broader picture.
50. Nezami Ganjavi, *Khosrow va Shirin-e Nezami* edited by Barat Zanjani, 8. The first and last verses and two in middle that are most pertinent:

چو طالع موکب دولت روان کرد / سعادت روی در روی جهان کرد

عطارد را قلم مسمار کردی / پرند زهره بر تن خار کردی

چو عیسی روح را درسی درآموز / چو موسی عشق را شمعی برافروز

گر از دنیا وجوهی نیست در دست / قناعت را سعادت باد کان هست

51. This historical situation is related to the delay of Nezami's ownership of the land he had been awarded/promised because of the change of power and rulers—from Toghril Shah, who requested it, to Qezel Shah, who fulfilled the promise of compensation.
52. Nezami Ganjavi, *Layli and Majnun*, translated by Davis, 233.
53. *Kolliyat*, 410.

CHAPTER 5

Wine and Identity in the Works of Nezami and Rudaki

Like other literary traditions, Persian poetry features and celebrates wine and wine-drinking parties, giving rise to the *khamriyat* subgenres, which in the words of Paul Losensky "provided a well-established repertoire of topoi and tropes on wine, its vessels, and the servants, entertainers, settings, and manners appropriate to the courtly banquet. Such parties by their very nature depart from the normal routines of daily life and violate the precepts of Islamic law."[1]

Through his lyrical (*ghazal*) poetry, Manuchehri (d. 431/1040–1041) contributed to the popularization of a few themes including wine-songs (*khamriyat*).[2] In fact, whenever discussing the theme of wine and wine-making in classical Persian literature, the poetry of Manuchehri always comes to the fore. He was a poet at the court of Sultan Shihab ud-Dawlah Mas'ud I (1030–1040) of the Ghaznavid dynasty. He is best known as the poet of lavender for his poems on natural beauties, but he also excels in the description of vineyards, wine, and winemaking, using many original images and metaphors. Even in Iran today, many quote him nostalgically.[3]

| Three things adorn the noble's feast | در مجلس احرار سه چیزست و فزون به |
| no more do they require; Kebab, wine, and lyre.[4] | وان هر سه شرابست و ربابست و کبابست |

© The Author(s), under exclusive license to Springer Nature Switzerland AG 2022
K. Talattof, *Nezami Ganjavi and Classical Persian Literature*, Literatures and Cultures of the Islamic World, https://doi.org/10.1007/978-3-030-97990-4_5

However, many scholars, including Iraj Bashiri, believe that Manuchehri "was continuing the tradition of Rudaki whose 'Madar-e May' (Mother of Wine) qasideh sets the scene for a series of works on the theme."[5] Manuchehri had apparently read Rudaki's poems, perhaps including poems that have not survived and as such, it is not surprising if their work had points in common. In fact, Julie Scott Meisami, William Hanaway, and Jerome Clinton have pointed out the similarity between the themes and mode of expressions in the work of these two men and the longevity of their poetry.[6] Speaking more broadly on the significance of the wine trope in Persian poetry, Asghar Seyed-Gohrab comments that, "Persian poetry is rich in the genre of wine literature. In the first centuries of the appearance of New Persian literature, wine was a standard subject for the majority of authors. It appears in various poetic forms, from ghazals and quatrains to panegyrics and masnavis. In prose texts, it is a theme that is widely treated in 'mirror for princes' books such as Qābus-nāmeh (completed 1082–83)."[7] Similarly, Dominic Parviz Brookshaw provides a literary analysis of a number of these poems, conceptualizing them as the "Persian wine production myth."[8] This type of poetry first led to the establishment of specific forms in Arabic and Persian literature, first as *khamriyat* and then later, and more Persian in nature, as *saqinameh*.[9]

Writing about Abu Nuwas (756–814) and early Islamic wine poetry, Yaseen Noorani addresses the problematics of qasideh arguing that poets supported (and depicted) in their works a specific view of power and society whereby those with "moral self-integration" were considered upstanding individuals who were justified in being the leaders and in engaging the court's entertainments (or in supervising activities at court). Moral self-integration throughout in this case means self-control, the repressing of desires and impulses that might, if unleashed, appear unseemly, disrupt the court, or mar its image as serious and stately.[10]

Meisami offers an analysis of the wine poetry of Abu Nuwas, who also personifies wine and uses it as a replacement of the *mamduh* (the praised one). She writes: "Wine thus becomes an object of adoration as well as praise, and the poet's journey to the tavern a pilgrimage to her holy shrine … The fact that wine is also described in concrete terms (colour like rubies, scent like musk, bubbles like pearls, and so on) does not detract focus of desire, praise, and worship."[11] But most pertinently, Meisami, in her study of the issue of structure in Persian and Arabic poetry, comments on this particular poem of Rudaki, stating that the trope of "daughter of the vine" turns into "the object, not of desire, but of sacrifice," which is also an early example of the treatment of this topos in a narrative.[12] Elsewhere, in a short and informative study of "Mother of Wine," she concludes that the "early Persian qasida thus emerges as an analogue of the Persian court, as if absorbing into itself both the macrocosm of the world-garden and the microcosm of the private world of the self, to become a poetic microcosm whose formal divisions and the varied genres it is able to incorporate, making it the ideal vehicle for conveying the many facets of the world of the court."[13] There is no doubt that the fall of the Persian Empire and the Islamicization of many aspects of Persian culture (starting in AD 633) did not affect the long-lasting pre-Islamic tradition of wine drinking at the royal court. Wine drinking and writing about it continued well into the following centuries.[14]

NEZAMI'S PORTRAYAL OF WINE

The portrayal of wine in Nezami's poetry often occurs for the exigency of the narrative. However, drawing on the Bakhtinian concept of chronotope, which I will enlarge upon below, I argue that wine in Rudaki's poem, "Madar-e May" (Mother of Wine) and the poem itself convey the sense of a much larger worldview beyond the court. In addition to its use as an analytical tool and its connection to the concept of the chronotope will help me examine the imagery presented in the subject of my inquiry. The poem also conveys a worldview that is based on specific identity, one modeled on the Sasanians.[15] These components are presented, elaborated, and structured seemingly to reverse the rupture—the interruption in Persian history caused by the Arab invasion (AD 633). The underlying message of the poem can be interpreted, as "it is good that we are writing poetry in our own language."

The fact that fine wine poetry began with the pioneering and panegyric works of Rudaki, a poet in Bokhara and at the court of Nasr ibn Ahmad, the Samanid ruler of northeastern Persia during the first half of the tenth century, leads us to the important and instrumental role played by the poet in what is regarded as the Persian cultural renaissance that took place almost three centuries after the Arab conquest of Persia.[16] All this should explain why Rudaki is considered the father of Persian poetry, but also should tell us something about his era and the court that supported him.

Wine poetry exists across cultures from ancient to contemporary periods. Literary scholars are sometimes challenged to decide the real/physical or transcendental meanings of the concept of wine in some of those poems. Similarly, Persian wine poetry lends itself to contradictory inter-pretations. Do these poems express a literal or metaphorical meaning? Beyond this frequently posed question, we also strive to understand how a wine poem is relevant to its time and social context. What do the wine-drinking scenes reveal about people at the time of their creation? Finally, how can we compare poetic wine tropes in the works of different poets?

Literarily, countless numbers of Persian verses, lyric ghazals, and short poems revolve around or contain references to wine. The word "wine," *sharab*, appears in its numerous synonyms (such as may, *badeh, mol, shar-bat, nabiz, mol...* and even with associated words such as *piyaleh, jam, qadah, rayhan*) or in its myriad epithets and allusions (*dokhtar rez* or daughter of roses, *jam* or cup, *khun-e rangin* or the colorful blood, *sabu* or jug, *khomreh* or wine press, *kuzeh* or earthen jar, *jor'eh* or draft, or *sas-ghar* or wineglass). In addition, some poets have a book, or a long seg-ment of poetry dedicated exclusively to the wine motif. Such works are referred to as *khamriyat khamrieh* (also known as *badeh seta'i* and *badeh-gani*) and *Saqiameh* (the book of the cupbearer, bacchanalian verse), all of which can be categorized as the poetic book of wine and tavern. Most of such works were composed in the form of masnavi starting with an order-ing verb such as *biya* (come) and *biyar* (bring), features that made the poems feel like an epic and suitable for classical music even more so in the contemporary era. In the word of a contemporary poet, Hooshang Ebtehaj known by his pen name H. A. Sayeh,[17]

Oh cupbearer, come and bring that wine resembling light	بیا ساق آن می که چون روشنی
That will no doubt end this demoniac night	به روز آرد این شام اهریمنی
Give to me, so from this dreadful damnation	به من ده کزین دامگاه هلاک
I am rescued, liberated, thanks to the sparkler wine.	بر آیم به تدبیر آن تابناک

This highly political contemporary verse, which was written in support of and inspired by leftist Marxist political ideas, only partially confirms the characteristics of wine poetry. This is most clear in the portrayal of his society (of the 1970s), which is done in a gloomy, depressing, and desper-ate light. And interestingly, in this secular poem by a secular poet with modernist aspirations, the wine does not seem to be literal; like several other references, it is simply an allusion to few different things including blood (of the fallen anti-king fighters).[18] In classical times as well, wine was both discussed literally and as a metaphor for other things.

Khamriyat poems focus on the description of the wine and all the thoughts the poet might have while drinking and ponder why they are drinking. In *Saqinameh* (the book of the cupbearer, bacchanalian verse) type, the poet or the narrator calls upon the *saqi* (wine server) for more wine while lamenting about all his personal and social predicaments in life. As such, the subject of his speeches can and does often go beyond the description of the wine or wine-drinking settings. An associated sub-genre is the *moghaninameh* (book of musicians) in which the poet speaks about similar issues with the singer (present in the tavern) requesting more songs. These two were often combined. During and after the Safavids, and due to the rise of interests in such poetic expressions, the genre became more uniform and more popular than ever before. At this time, a religious element was added to the poems and that was the praise of a religious character, but poets continued to praise the king, his court, and the past pre-Islamic kings and characters.[19] Moreover, when they mentioned wine, they meant literal drink. Nevertheless, in some cases, the expressions of love (often for another male) were added to the genre. In other words, even we recognize wine poetry as a subgenre; although, its contents and themes changed over time.

Scholars generally think that early poets such as Rudaki, Farokhi, Manuchehri, and Moezi wrote about wine in a literal sense, and then with the rise of Sufism, poets wrote about wine in a metaphorical sense. I am not sure if we can draw such a clear-cut line, because not only did poets continue to write about the literal wine after Moezi, but the earlier poets, such as Rudaki, also used wine and the winemaking process (in their literal sense) to approach broader social issues. Moreover, the genre benefits from the popular conception that a drunk tells the truth (*masti* or *rasti*), and, therefore, the poet or the speaker in the poem feels free to draw upon numerous social predicaments as assertively as possible, which otherwise would not be easy to express in public. The candor and acuity of the criticism would have not been probable without the real or at least the imaginary effect of the real wine. This style of candid poetry intensified during the more severe social conditions. In particular, as the case of Rudaki indicates, the poetic wine often represented natural wine, and drinking rituals had extended implications. I explain the real wine theme in his poem in terms of the Bakhtinian chronotope, which can illustrate how the poet tackles the issues of the Samanids' cultural and national identity. Scholars also mention Sanai, Attar, Rumi, Araqi, Hafez, and even Nezami as examples of the poets who treated the wine motif merely as a metaphor. It is difficult to prove that is the case, because the wine in their poems often seems to refer to the legitimate wine of paradise or the wine of knowledge, particularly in the cases of Hafez and Nezami.[20]

Another common characterization of wine in the works of Rudaki and Nezami is the association of wine with the kings and nobles (more so in Rudaki's case). This notion is shared by other poets and is itself a pre-Islamic and ancient characterization.[21] However, in a rare verse, Nezami calls for providing a cup of wine to all the city's residents. The passage entitled "Borhan-e Qate' dar Hodus-e Afarinesh" (Decisive Proof of the Occurrence of Creation) includes another subsection entitled "The Beginning of the Proof," and together is a relatively long part.[22]

In the passage, Nezami compares his art of Sakhon with other grand notions.[23] The first comparison is between his artistic practice and the royal court public receptions. On the latter, he states that on such occasions, the kings (should) serve wine to all the people of the city like a cloud that rains generously and without hesitation. They also (should) listen to people and provide them with guidance. They (should) give loans to people and legitimize the loans too. And then Nezami says that just like those kings, I am the king of Sakhon, giving away beautiful Sakhon, a sweet gift that they can use in their life. This passage is not proof that Nezami was an early socialist; it proves that he provides a colorful first story to get to his point about the high status of the art of Sakhon.

However, in the entire passage, which consists of 100 verses, Nezami accomplishes more poetic objectives. As the title of the segment suggests, it is about creation. He states that there is no way of knowing the secret (origin) of creation as there is no effortless way of knowing its rationale and form. Then he mentions the sky and its layers and stars, the earth with its mountains, wind, clouds, vegetation, rivers, waters, and vast landscapes, and finally how wisdom, knowledge, and reasoning (*kherad*) might help make sense of all this, all that is the story of the creation. Such a reasoning approach to the concept of creation is far from Islamic mystical philosophy. Thus, focusing on the passage's poetic objectives is the most fruitful reading of the segment. However, the poet, not so subtly, lists some of his frequent poetic subjects. And one line also seems to convey a further connection between those common subjects, the story of creation, and his Sakhon creativity.

Presume a cluster grows from a seed	گیرم که ز دانه خوشه خیزد
Who gives it the form with which it keeps?	در قالب صورتش که ریزد

In the second half of the verse, the question (the answer to which should) is rhetorical. We can assume that a twelfth-century poet is likely thinking within a religious paradigm when he thinks of the myth of creation and the world's origin. The evolution of species via natural selection as a theory came much later. As such, one can argue that even an infidel at that time had to be thinking within the same paradigmatic belief system. Even if a poet does not write about Islam or writes against it, we cannot assume that he was not a Muslim. However, here, Nezami suggests a second layer of meaning beyond the question of faith. He wants his readers to see that his Manasvi poems, metaphorical constructs, love stories, and pictorial allegories are the forms he has used to present those thoughts, ideas, and religious information. Like the myth of creation, the origins and sources of his knowledge should not be given much thought because it cannot be found. For example, there is little information about the myth of creation beyond its earlier Mesopotamian versions. Nezami's verse is, therefore, a tacit reference to the core of his matière, which is referred to more directly in the second layer of this detailed allegory. The next segment in his work is titled "The Cause for the Composition of the Book," which draws upon similar concepts regarding his creativity.[24] On other occasions, he compares his art of speech with the Koran and his literary creation with the miracles of prophets. Based on such comparisons, he is constructing another type of pictorial allegory to say that he is *khoda-ye Sakhon* (The Lord of Literature).

Many scholars consider Nezami as the inventor of the *saqinameh* subgenre following the assertation by the seventeenth-century Fakhralzamani Qazvini (d. 1631) who stated this in his *tazkereh* (biography or book of "who is who") about wine poetry writers.[25] In later periods, other biographers pointed to other potential inventors.[26] No matter, Nezami certainly wrote extensively about wine in his works, and many imitated him thereafter. Nezami's vaulted position among poets notwithstanding, wine is not treated from an ideological perspective or as a matter of social, mystic, and hedonist theme or concept in any of his poetry, as he did not write an independent *saqinameh*. He includes wine poems in the supplemental parts of his romances and naturally in the romance narratives as the stories might call for it. The poems in the introductory and ending parts of the stories in his two-volume final book *Eskandarnameh* (The Book of Alexander) are the reason he is understood to be the creator of *saqinamen* type of verse; yet, there are extended number of verses in other books including his *Layli o Majnun*. Those books include chapters or segments

with the title of *saqinameh* with some of the most key features of this subgenre including the call for the wine server, requesting a song from the
musician, frequent use of the various meanings of wine, description of
wine using various and sometimes obscure terms (even for their time), and
the usual words of wisdom as well as personal and social statements.

Scholars often begin their discussion of Persian wine poetry with the
influence of Arabic poetry and in particular the works of Abu Nawas. As it
will be shown in the later part of this chapter, that comparison might be
justified in terms of forms and genre. Persian poets could have been influenced because they historically contributed to Arabic grammar, poetry,
and prose. However, the culture of wine, winemaking, and wine drinking
had a well-known history in Persia prior. Most descriptions of the festivi-
ties in which wine was served are based on the collective memories of the
pre-Islamic period, preserved in tales and texts. Nezami bases numerous
stories, rational, philosophical expressions, and cultural statements on
Persia's ancient history and Zoroastrian concepts. He alludes to his sources
of inspiration in all his books including in his *Kheradnameh*, one of the
two volumes of *Eskandarnameh*. He writes:

Oh music man, follow the ancient way	مغنی بیار آن ره باستان
Help me weave my story.	مرا یاری ده در این داستان 27

The ancient source of inspiration manifests itself clearly in Nezami's
word choice when writing about wine because he uses ancient forms of
words for wine such as *may* (a synonym of *sharab* which is more common
now for referring to wine) along with numerous musical terms often associated with the pre-Islamic musicians such as Barbod. Even in *Makhzan
al-Asrar*, he addresses Bahram Shah with the pre-Islamic analogies and
references to wine.

Drink wine, you have the music and a cupbearer	میخور می مطرب و ساقیت هست
No reason to be sad, your fortune is forever.	غم چه خوری دولت باقیت هست 28

In the previous line, Nezami mentions Fraydun, the legendary character of the *Book of Kings* and later in this and other books, the poet shows
that by music, he refers to the pre-Islamic musical work of Barbod
or Nekisa.

Analyzing Nezami's wine poetry can further contribute to the general
discussion of his professional and literary approach to poetry. In his wine

poetry, he speaks to both the singer and the cupbearer and explains why he has summoned them. His characters are described as persons who might or might not drink wine. Like in his treatment of other subjects and themes, here, too, he spends much of his efforts on the construction of images with his incredible lexical ability. Here, as well, it is all about pictorial allegories.

In addition to the introductory parts of *Khosrow o Shirin*, Nezami wrote on wine as a crucial element of his storytelling and characterization. For example, early in the story, Nezami provides a vivid description of his protagonists by describing the Sassanian Prince Khosrow's nonstop drinking escapades in the presence of Princess Shirin.[29] In the section, which is titled "Khosrow Seeking Pleasure in the Meadow and Hormoz Punishing Him," Nezami creates pictorial allegory revolving around the concept of drinking and wine (using such variation of the words as *sharab, may,* and *nuss*).

He spent the night drinking with friends,	نشست آن شب بنوشانوش یاران
Drinker of morning draughts, with full cups	صبوحی کرد با شب زنده داران
In the house, with songs or dance	سماع ارغنون گوش می‌کرد
He kept drinking the crimson wine.	شراب ارغوانی نوش می‌کرد[30]

Khosrow, with his guards, goes out on a fun expedition. He approaches a village surrounded by a beautiful pasture, fresh grass, a hunting site, and a proper place for an outdoor feast and delectation. He begins to drink his "ruby-red" wine and continues the feast and beguiling his day until the sunset (conveyed by metaphors such as yellow flower and yellow wall). Consequently, he begins to behave recklessly. While highly intoxicated, he makes his men confiscate a house in the village where he continues partying, drinking, and listening to music throughout the night. As a result of this outing, he and his men damage the meadow and inflict pain on the residences nearby. As if invading and smashing someone's house is not enough, his horse kicks another person to death. In addition, one of his servants steals the grapes from one of the local gardens. When his father, Hormoz, a "true Zoroastrian," hears about these brutalities, he punishes the son by taking his favorite horse, giving his bed to the owner of the house, and breaking his musical instrument, among other measures.

Nezami then concludes that the fire of Zoroastrianism has warmed up the world and that Muslims should be ashamed of their religion (which does not encourage them to seek justice the same way Zoroastrians do).

According to the tale, Hormoz punishes his son for his actions and not necessarily for drinking even though it was excessive drinking that contributed to the tragic events.

The plot is simple. A son behaves badly, and his father punishes him. The goal, as in other cases, is to provide an allegory with a twist and a surprising conclusion, which happens to be about drinking wine, the notion of justice, and the practice of justice. I have emphasized a few times that Nezami does not intend to advocate for religion. Here, he is saying that non-Muslim religious kings also have a strong or a stronger sense of justice and saying so provides a surprise ending to his story. Besides, the comparison between Zoroastrians and Muslims is one of the common literary conventions used by Nezami and many other so-called mystic poets to encourage Muslims to act more properly. I am not of course using such lines to engage in polemics. Referring to or elevating Zoroastrian culture, moral codes, and past glory is also another theme he uses rather often to advance his narratives.

Neither should the wine-drinking scenes in which the color and taste of wine are portrayed and described in tens of tangible and earthly ways be taken as an indication of Nezami's liking or disliking (particularly from a religious point of view) of drinking. The man drank too much over a prolonged period, and he acted criminally. That is the entire function of the wine; it is neither Hafez's wine nor a wine from paradise (*sharab al-antahur*). Here wine is simply part of the story, and it is not a metaphorical construct. It is real because drinking too much of it led to calamity. Of course, this prince does not learn from his mistakes, and we find him drinking and acting improperly throughout the story in which Shirin also strives to correct him, "make a man out of him." In another scene of the outdoor party and drinking, we read the following line in which the wine and love are juxtaposed. However, only the latter proves to be intoxicating to the king.

Wine and love conspired with an oath	شراب و عاشقی هٔدست گشته
Making the king drunk by them both.	شهنشه زین دو می سرمست گشته[31]

If we avoid the common typo which connects do and may, we can easily see that Nezami considers both love and wine as ecstatic, capable of providing ecstasy (the Persian word *sarmast* literally also means head-drunk).

Throughout the poem/story, wine seems to have played an intensifying role, along with the expression of the characters' feelings and love. However, each segment can also be read as an allegory of its own. The following part narrates the story of a lion that attacks Khosrow's campsite while he and his entourage are having fun. It details the demise of the lion at the hands of Khosrow, and how the incident led to establishing the tradition of carrying a sword at all times. Again, there is not much hidden meaning there. Nezami's second intention is the usual, he demonstrates his skills with words. The second part includes and plays with the name Shirin and the word *shirin* (sweet), manifesting an extensive auditory use of the "sh" sounds as in words such as *tamasha* (gazing), *behesht* (paradise), *sharab* (wine), *shir* (lion), *bisheh* (woodland), *lashkar* (army), *shetab* (swiftness), and *aysh* (pleasure), just to count a few. He constructs one of his pictorial allegories with a short but relatively complete subplot. It goes something like this. Khosrow and Shirin, are relaxing, laughing in the outing spot in a meadow where their cupbearer serves them wine. Suddenly a lion appears and charges toward them. The king who is not carrying his sword or any other weapon on him, attacks the lion and knocks him out with his bare fists. Shirin begins to kiss him all over starting with his hands. After that incident, it became a necessary custom for the kings to have their sword ready at hand.[32]

Nezami has numerous one-line poems where he seems to recommend moderate wine drinking, which is in line with his attitude toward many other aspects of the lives of his characters. At the end of *Layli and Majnun* where he praises Shervanshah, he offers advice, too. One is:

Be strong, be patient	قادر شو و بردبار میباش
Drink wine but be conscious.	می میخور و هوشیار میباش[33]

The above verse shows that according to him, drinking wine is fine but he does not assign the functions to the wine the way Rudaki does, and that he does not promote excessive drinking the way a huge cohort of Persian poets such as Hafez does.

On this theme, he has constructed more pictorial allegories. In an introductory part of *Layli and Majnun* he writes:

Saki, thou know'st I worship wine;   ساق به کجا که می‌پرستم
Let that delicious cup be mine.   تا ساغر می دهد به دستم
Wine! Pure and limpid as my tears,   آن می که چو اشک من زلالست
Dispeller of a lover's fears;   در مذهب عاشقان حلالست
With thee inspired, with thee made bold,   در می به امید آن زنم چنگ
'Midst combat fierce my post I hold;   تا باز گشاید این دل تنگ
With thee inspired, I touch the string,   شیرپست نشسته بر گذرگاه
And, rapt, of love and pleasures sing.   خوام که ز شیر کم کم راه
Thou art a lion, seeking prey,   زین پیش نشاطی آزمودم
Along the glades where wild deer stray;   امروز نه آنکسم که بودم
And like a lion I would roam,   این نیز چو بگذرد ز دستم
To bring the joys I seek for home;   عاجزتر از این شوم که هستم
With wine, life's dearest, sweetest treasure,   ساق به من آور آن می لعل
I feel the thrill of every pleasure: کافکند سخن در آتشم نعل
—Bring, Saki, bring the ruby now;   آن می که گره‌گشای کارست
Its lustre sparkles on thy brow,   با روح چو روح سازگارست ³⁵
And, flashing with a tremulous light,
Has made thy laughing eyes more bright:
Bring, bring the liquid gem, and see
Its power, its wond'rous power, in me.[34]

This follows the conventions of the *saqinameh*, in which the narrator calls upon the cupbearer to bring him wine as he shares his griefs and reasons for his need to drink. In this section, titled "Remembering some of my Dead Relatives," he assigns new importance to wine, and he connects it with the concept of Sakhon. He worships wine as a drink that can help him overcome grief, encounter dangers (lions), and assist him in embracing his beloved Sakhon.[36] This call by which the author seeks help in writing poetry (Sakhon art) appears in other books such the *Book of Alexander* where he constructs pictorial allegories using the names of his characters.[37]

Of course, those scholars who read Nezami's work as a manifestation of his devotion to Islam or Sufism interpret the wine in his poetry as a symbolic wine, which according to the reading above is nearly impossible. As explained in the chapter on Portrayal of Women, many of the poems and segments of *Khosrow o Shirin* describe wine's attributes and scenes of wine drinking in which music and other types of entertainments are also performed. Such descriptions do not lead themselves to religious or mystic or metaphorical reading. Nevertheless, as mentioned, some scholars, such as Sarvatiayn, interpret every element as a sign. Some might create doubt about a literal reading in other ways. For example, a wine-drinking party in a section of *Khosrow o Shirin* entitled "Khosrow's Leisure Banquet and Shapur's Return," which I discuss in the chapter on Portrayal of Women has been doubted.

Barat Zanjani, whose efforts in creating a credible edition of this book are historical, considers the mention of a rooster's singing as a reference to a call for prayer, that is, the rooster is flapping its wings in the morning to remind the required five Muslim daily prayers. Given the context and historical facts, a drum and bronze horn were played at the court to indicate a special occasion. The verses say that a long-necked, large body wine container (*sarahi*, which was used to serve in parties) announced the time for drinking (in times like a rooster). More specifically, it says that the wine is served at the right time, as the rooster also often sings on a timely basis, playing off another adage.[38] It might not be relevant here, but is believed that rooster had a symbolic significance in ancient Persian as well and was a companion to a divine entity called Soroush. The passage is just about wine, which matches the description of birds grilled on a golden brazier containing a red fire made of pussy willow and other aromatic woods. Birds, red wine, goblets, the sound of music are all elements of a pictorial allegory that strives to convey the mood and manner of the prince and his close companions. Reading the poem, even as unlikely call for five prayers would not apply to Nezami regardless because only the Shiites pray five times, and he did not belong to that denomination. Finally, a Zoroastrian prince and his companions camping in Armenia during the pre-Islamic era would not need a reminder of religious duty that was not even invented yet.

Here is another way of looking at these problematics of reading of Nezami's work. Behruz Sarvatian, the highly accomplished editor of Nezami's work, well read, and studious scholar, has quoted this poem, which he believes the scriber of Hafez's divan has included it in the beginning of the book to argue, among other statements, that Hafez had been inspired and influenced by Nezami. What is perplexing is the following comment by Sarvatian: "Mysticism is the main factor in the unity of thinking and coordination of thoughts among our poets."[39] Obviously, there has hardly been a unity of thinking and coordination of thoughts over a long period of time in any literary tradition except in what became known as party literature formulated by A. A. Zhdanov.[40] In fact, many scholars who read Nezami's poetry in Sufi or religious terms often emphasize on particular words, such as mysterious (*raz guneh*), secrets (*asrar*), and mysterious codes (*ramz* which is none but a symbol), and they come to believe that Nezami had some secret knowledge and a secretive mission or at least what to speak about the secrets of creation and the creator. That is the word key (*kelid*, a word used by Nezami himself), which can help reveal and decode that which those mysteries hold significant. Sarvatian uses the words secret, code, and key to explain Nezami's meaning, perhaps insinuating that the poet is talking about God in a symbolic and allusive language. Numerous scholars share this notion that there are secrets and codes in the works of Nezami and that Nezami holds the key for accessing those secrets and codes or knows something about the key. Other scholars who offer a more secular reading of the poet's work have not challenged this notion. Sarvatian writes:

> The majority of *Makhzan al-Asrar* is similar to Hafez's *Divan* from the point of view of the codes that are hidden in words and scholastic theology (kalam). But, the myth of *Khosrow and Shirin* is constructed with codes in order to criticize the pre-Islamic Iranian history through the love affairs of the Iranian king with a chaste and prayerful woman and express what he had held in his heart through codes, riddle, and insinuation.[41]

However, such secrets and codes (which are merely symbols) do not remain covered and hidden, as the poet points to their existence in his allegorical constructs.

As evidence of this encoding, Sarvatian quotes a somewhat convoluted line which does not exist in some of the editions, reveals nothing about the "key."[42] The reader remains baffled by the characterization of *Khosrow o Shirin* as a criticism of the pre-Islamic history of Iran, a notion that is more used as a contemporary justification of the invasion of the Persian Empire.

He continues, "The story of the masnavi of *Layli o Majnun* is founded on the mystical codes and riddles. And *Haft Paykar* is itself seven secretive mystical, political, social, and moral myths." Sarvatian believes that by authoring the *Iskandarnameh*, Nezami also waged a war against Ferdowsi's *Shahnameh* (*Book of Kings*). One might ask what happened to the notion of "the unity of thinking and coordination of thoughts among our poets?" All these views support the last 40 years of the state's cultural attempt and policy of dichotomizing Iran and Islam for the benefit of the latter. Basically, by quoting a few lines from the *Iskandarnameh*, these scholars maintain that Nezami acknowledges that the book contains secrets and codes, as troubling as the state cultural policy itself. Interestingly, the line that Sarvatian and others quote is in a section (in an edition that includes the line) that starts with another verse.

| Oh cupbearer, bring the wine quickly! | بیا ساق آن باده بردار زود |
| For without wine, I cannot be happy. | که بی باده شادی نشاید نمود[43] |

However, neither Sarvatian nor Noruzi mentions that verse, which is representative of many other descriptions of wine and its use in the construction of what has become to be known as the *saqihameh* in the book of *Iskandarnameh*.

How can they explain the "secrets" in Nezami's writing by reiterating that there are secrets in them? Even if Nezami were to convey some secrets and codes, we should now be able to figure them out given the fact that we have a better and faster access to libraries, science data, religious philosophies, and other sources of knowledge. A similar methodology can be applied in explaining the concept of wine in the works of other Persian poets including Khayyam and Hafez, ignoring their highly realistic portrayals. It is interesting to notice that these poets sometimes even speak of the harm that alcohol can inflict upon bodies.

For Nezami, wine is yet another concept and theme that helps him construct his pictorial allegories and move his narrative forward. He also offers a moderate approach to wine and wine drinking when he speaks to readers directly or when he depicts it through the words of his characters. He does not prohibit it as Islam would recommend and instead takes the same approach to wine as the approach to the practical wisdom of *Minuye Kherad*, which also recommends the benefits of drinking wine in moderation. If wine were a code or a metaphor, he would have not needed to write so much about it in so many vivid and realistic depictions.

Rudaki's Portrayal of Wine[44]

It is almost a tradition among the scholars of classical Persian literature to start their study by reminding readers that Persian poetry was inspired by Arabic poetry. This notion is employed in the analysis of Rudaki's poetry more than other poets' work because of his early appearance in Persian poetry.[45] However, lyric/vocal type of poetry by Persian poets woven in early decades of the classical period were more influenced by the ancient, pre-Muslim invasion, tradition of poetry and lyricism, ways of thinking, logic, and legends. In some of his poems, Rudaki looks at wine through the same literary conventions.

Live happily with the beautiful women	شاد زی با سیاه چشمان، شاد
for the world is none but myth and wind.	که جهان نیست جز فسانه و باد
Be happy that you lived on this earth	زآمده شادمان باید بود
just do not think of the past and your birth.	وز گذشته نکرد باید یاد
This world is none but clouds and wind, alas	باد و ابر است این جهان، افسوس
bring forth the wine, let us be free facing menace.	باده پیش آر، هر چه باداباد

We can see a similar notion in the poetry of Khayyam and Hafez. However, in his longest poem, "Mother of Wine," Rudaki delves into the topics of wine and wine drinking.[46] Like many other classical Persian poets, he uses the word "wine" in several forms and associated terms not only in that poem but also in many of his other verses. However, he surpasses all other poets in such descriptions when he presents the process of winemaking in a highly allegorical poem entitled "Mother of Wine." Through contextual and historical analyses and by drawing on the Bakhtinian concept of chronotope (to be defined in more detail below), this chapter argues that this poem—written in the form of *qasideh*—is unusually and well structured, organized, cohesive, and thematically unified. In addition, it reflects the national culture of the tenth- century Samanids as they saw themselves to be the continuation of the pre-Islamic Sasanians. As I shall show, it does so through synchronic and diachronic portrayals and references.

First, who and what had influenced Abu Abdollah Jafar ibn Mohammad Rudaki (859–940/1 CE) in his portrayal of wine? From where did he draw his inspiration? Was he inspired by Arabic qasideh and strove to write similar poetry? Even though Rudaki, like many other classical Persian poets, refers to wine in much of his poetry, he surpasses his peers in his descriptions of intoxication, the production of the wine, and celebration in his "Madar-e May" (Mother of Wine), written between 943 and 945. The poem is unique in its narrative quality, prosody, layered meanings, and complex metaphors. Indeed, it not only meets the conditions of a good qasideh (i.e., it rhymes properly, uses archaic terms, names, locations, and people, ends with a praise of the patron, etc.), but it also transcends the well-defined boundaries of the poetic form. Moreover, the poem seems to have been written to be performed before a live audience and, as such, it includes elements of the discourse of the Samanids (819–999): the first native dynasty after the Muslim Arab conquest of Persia, who saw themselves as the successors of the pre-Islamic Sasanians (224–651). It does so through synchronic and diachronic portrayals and references. On the one hand, the poem refers to the contemporary characters and geographical places in all directions, and, on the other hand, through symbolism, makes references to the Persian past. Here is where one might think of the Bakhtinian concept of chronotope to explain the poetic maneuvers over time and space in order to make it possible to use the synchronic and diachronic aspects of Rudaki's poem as a way of revealing its meaning.

In literary theory today, the chronotope, in its basic sense, is used to show how time and space are configured in language and discourse. Borrowing the term from the natural sciences, the Russian philosopher and scholar Mikhail Bakhtin (1895–1975) defined it as "the intrinsic connectedness of temporal and spatial relationships that are artistically expressed in literature."[47] Use of the chronotope and Bakhtin's complementary concept of heteroglossia (the presence of two or more viewpoints in a text) can thus inform our understating of the narrative poem in an analysis of the way in which it plays with time and space. In the case of Rudaki's poem, an ontological connection to the Sasanian era can be shown. Looking at the poem in this way, wine (and its effect) can be seen to influence the temporal and special relations in the poem. In other words, it influences the narrative's chronotope.

| We will host a banquet fit for kings, | مجلس باید بساخته، ملکانه |
| halls with roses, jasmine, and mallows. | از گل و از یاسمین و خیری الوان |

Since the wine is ready, a kingly banquet is in order. And the banquet itself becomes a space filled with flowers. The concept of the chronotope is used principally to refer to the intrinsic connection between temporal and spatial dimensions within a literary work. However, and in the case of Rudaki, what if references to time and place, in a sublime manner, catapult the readers outside the text? In addition, as Bakhtin and other writers on literary theory have shown, literary conventions and the dominance of particular genres are influenced by the society and culture of the time. In Rudaki's work, we can see how descriptions of wine are used to articulate Persia's past and present history and Persian language as the desired utterance, for example, within the poem, is praised for being the ideal language for a poem on wine and identity as a central focus.

Moreover, "Mother of Wine" reflects emphatically the fact that its author lived during the rule of the Samanids who in many ways differed from the Ghaznavids and other early native rulers. After all, as an affiliate of the court of Nasr ibn Ahmad (913–43) of the Samanid dynasty, Rudaki was effectively a minstrel or poet-musician, a role that gradually disappeared in the following periods. Likely, Rudaki's concept of wine is also rooted in pre-Islamic cultural nuances that resurfaced during the time of the Samanids. To be sure, the concept of wine changed a generation or so after Rudaki in the works of such great authors as Sana'i (1080–1131/41) who seems to have been inspired by different issues related to a different period.

Examination of the poem from this viewpoint might provide insights into what has been characterized as a Persian renaissance. Scholars such as G. Lazard and L. P. Elwell-Sutton have discussed the rise of early classical Persian poetry in the cultural and historical context of the Samanid period.[48] More recently, in his PhD dissertation, Sassan Tabatabi has tried to explain the emergence of the Samanids' literary renaissance in terms of the weakening of the caliph's power and the distance of Khorasan from Baghdad.[49] It is true that the cultural, linguistic, and historical connections between the Samanids and the Sasanians are not accidental. However, the Samanid context requires further examination. That is, a renaissance does not come about merely through support of Persian literature by the state, and a state cannot thrive merely by being separate from another center of power. It takes many other factors, such as social and cultural, to reestablish a nation and thereby launch a renaissance.

THE ANATOMY OF AN ALLEGORY

In the Persian language, there are numerous metaphors and similes to describe wine, vineyards, and grapes themselves, often based on the attributes of the beloved. The palm of her hand, her hair, and other attributes might be used to describe vine leaves, the stems of the vine, or the whole plant. Conversely, grapes and wine have been used as images to evoke the physical appearance of the beloved—her eyes, scent, and other alluring features. Furthermore, many words and phrases, for example words to describe the beloved or human relationship, have come to describe elements of the process of wine production. As alternatives for the word "vine" alone, poets have used the synonyms *tak, rez,* and *mow.* For "wine," they have used similar terms or synonyms such as *sharab, may,* and *badeh, aab-e aatash zaay* (literally, "fire-breeding water"), *khamr,* and even the Arabic word *nabiz.* Rudaki, like many other classical Persian poets, uses some of these works and all associated vocabulary in his poetry, but he also places wine as the subject of his phrases more than ten times in "Mother of Wine" as he elaborates on the description and the process of winemaking. He also uses numerous adjectives such as aged, happy, angel haired, fragmented, spring, and many others to describe the drink before he shifts to the other subjects of the poem.

But what are the other subjects of the poem and why has the poet used wine and winemaking as his setting to entertain and perhaps even to express a broader picture of the polity of his time? A literal analysis of "Mother of Wine" indicates that the poem is based on one of the Nasr ibn Ahmad courtly gatherings even though there is no direct mention of the emir himself. The story behind its composition also might shed light on the context. Said Nafisi quotes *The History of Sistan* stating that Emir Bu Jafar had insulted an impudent emir, Makan, who had been disobedient toward the court. Nasr ibn Ahmad is grateful to Bu Jafar for his actions, and so Rudaki, in his role as court poet, writes a piece praising Bu Jafar for his laudable behavior. According to some sources, Makan also pays Rudaki not to lampoon him in the poem. Nafisi also refers to another incident in which emir sends a few expensive gifts to Abu Jafar, along with Rudaki's poem, as a token of friendship.[50]

The structure of Rudaki's poem, its messages, themes, and its musical cadences (and whichever way it might have been recited) all likely served the purpose of entertaining an audience. Yet, in focusing on wine, Rudaki's work reveals certain qualities that have not been fully replicated in the work of his imitators or those who were otherwise inspired by him even if the latter group was not concerned with the Samanids' preoccupation with identity.

To illustrate these qualities, I have translated the poem into English as an addendum to this chapter, and I have divided it into three segments based on the three subjects which I believe are covered by the poet.[51]

In the first segment, Rudaki talks about the fermentation process of wine, where the juice is separated from the grapes and mixed with other ingredients, creating a chemical reaction that results in the production of wine. As mentioned, the description (particularly as a poetic subject in tenth century) is unique and, for the most part, realistic; the process needs the same essential ingredients for fermentation to take place, even if this is poetically described. In today's local winemaking (and drinking) practices, which still continues in some Iranian households even after the 1979 Revolution that officially shut down winery and vineyard, the sugar and yeast added to the grapes convert the glucose and fructose into ethanol, a technique also used to some extent to produce beer. For the first stage of fermentation, Rudaki seems to suggest separating the grapes/juice (*bachche*) from the vine (*madar*) to start the process.[52]

To sacrifice the mother of wine,	مادر می را بکرد باید قربان
you must first take away her child and lock it up.	بچه او را گرفت و کرد به زندان[53]

However, the suggested seven months, a much longer period than would be needed elsewhere, might have to do with the specific climate of the place. The average temperature in that region in contemporary times is 14 °C.

Until it has nursed for seven months	تا نخورد شیر هفت مه به تمامی
From early Spring until Autumn's crest.	از سر اردیبهشت تا بن آبان

As for the second phase of fermentation, in which the wine is usually siphoned into a sealed container, Rudaki seems to be in line with recorded techniques. He vividly illustrates the stage in which the "must" begins to bubble within hours after the process has begun, with clear reference to the process of extracting the sediment, lees, and dregs.

Yet the child's caretaker will wipe the froth	مرد حرس، کفکهاش پاک بگیرد
From its dark face and so make it shine.	تا بشود تیرگیش و گردد رخشان
When the child is calm at last	آخر کارام گیرد و ن چند نیز
The guard then caps the brine.	درش کند استوار مرد نگهبان
When finally settled, smooth and clear,	چون بنشیند تمام و صافی گردد
It becomes a lustrous deep-toned crimson.	گوهی یاقوت سرخ گیرد و مرجان

The detailed poetic process explains the quality and specification of the wine to some extent. In line with proper wine-evaluation techniques, Rudaki points out that a good-quality wine should have a fine color and aroma.

Red as a carnelian of Yemen	چند ازو سرخ چون عقیق یمانی
Or precious gem from Badakhshan.	چند ازو لعل چون نگین بدخشان
When you smell it you think of roses,	ورش بوی، گبان بری که گل سرخ
Scent of Ambergris, musk, or myrobalan.	بوی بدو داد و مشک و عنبر با بان

He then suggests keeping it for an additional period after this stage to ensure an especially good wine, wondrous as the "shining sun."

Throughout this first section, the poet demonstrates both knowledge and humor. This knowledge was likely derived from still extant but changing discourse about wine; since the pre-Islamic knowledge and practice of winemaking was to be replaced with a more mystic approach to the subject in the following centuries. Only a few poets after him have written about wine so extensively or in such a literal celebratory manner. Rudaki's praise of wine was of course anomalous not only in the post-Islamic context of his time when wine would have been officially unwelcomed but also in terms of what wine symbolized in later literary works. In fact, in later poetry wine was even employed as a metaphor for something unearthly or spiritual. Dick Davis writes: "A subdivision of this mysticism is the set of ideas metaphorically expressed in Persian poetry by wine, drunkenness, the opposition of the rend (approximately "libertine") and the zahed ('ascetic'), and so forth."[54] In the Introduction to his *Borrowed Ware: Medieval Persian Epigrams*, Davis explains how the non-religious poetry of the tenth century turned into panegyric and then mysticism,[55] a secular approach, particularly in eastern Iran, that might have its roots in pre-Islamic culture.

There is no doubt that wine has a long history in Persia, stretching back to pre-Islamic times.[56] Indeed, evidence of winemaking in Persia points to it being among the earliest anywhere. An article by Patrick McGovern on the topic begins with: "In a very real sense, my research into ancient wine begins with Iran."[57] It is part of a publication that offers all sorts of evidence, including images of articles from ancient sites and extracts from poetry of the Islamic and pre-Islamic eras. In a highly idiosyncratic piece, Joobin Bekhrad traces the history of the Persian wine tradition in his article "Ramblings of an Iranian Wino" pointing out to a fathomable continuity to this date.[58]

The presentation of wine production and consumption (and the subsequent intoxication) in the poetry of Rudaki and other Persian poets is somewhat different from that of the ancient Greeks in that they believed that the gifts of Dionysus could harmfully send the thoughts of men to "topmost heights." Plato stated that wine "makes the person who drinks it more jovial than he was before, and the more he imbibes it, the more he becomes filled with high hopes and a sense of power, till finally, puffed up with conceit, he abounds in every kind of license of speech and action and every kind of audacity, without a scruple as to what he says or what he does."[59] So even if wine was consumed, influential Plato's view seems to have been sober and serious whereas the subject is presented in a light-hearted, playful fashion in Persian poetry, as exemplified in Rudaki's poem.

Rather than dwelling on the effects of drinking wine and the dangers of intoxication, Rudaki focuses instead on the joy and splendor of the feast in general. His verse is infused with a spirit of light-heartedness that is perfectly matched by the epigrammatic form in which the poem is written. Even in the following, for example the second segment where he talks about the rituals connected with serving wine, and about how wine can contribute to a social setting, he retains a lightness of touch, and he uses playful exaggeration.

With a wine so perfectly aged	با می ِ چونین که ساخورده بود چند
Its robes o'er fifty years well worn.	جامه بکرده فراز پنجه خلقان
We will host a banquet fit for kings,	مجلس باید بساخته، ملکانه
Halls with roses, jasmine, mallows adorned.	از گل و از یاسمین و خیری الوان
Heavenly riches spread all over	نعمت فردوس گستریده ز هر سو
The likes of which no one else can best.	ساخته کاری که کس نسازد چونان
Golden garments, colorful new carpets	جامهای زرین و فرشهای نو آین
Perfumed flowers and a seat for every guest.	شهره ریاحین و تختهای فراوان
Isa's harp leads the moving music	بربط عیسی و لوبهای فؤادی
Along with the lyre, the lute and happy fife.	چنگ مدک نیر و نای چنگ جانان [60]

All the qualities that Rudaki describes—the color and aroma and terms such as shiny, aged, ravishing, sparkling, and tasty—suggest something more resembling a cabernet sauvignon than another type of wine (such as the native, heavy, sherry-type Shirazi, and Khulaar wines); playful speculation apart, he fancied a wine that would help him reclaim identity and history.[61] This segment lays the foundation for the third section of the poem: a panegyric in praise of the patron, in addition to which he also praises his own métier, asking indirectly for financial remuneration for his poem. Here the style of the writing moves from stylized and epigrammatic to more fluid and idiomatic.

Another interesting stylistic characteristic of the poem is Rudaki's choice of metaphors, which William Hanaway indicates are similar in their narrative style to the imagery in Manuchehri's verse. In both cases, the vines and grapes are personified. The vines are presented as a woman who is impregnated and gives birth to a child (the grapes), who is then taken away and slaughtered for its invigorating blood (the wine). Why some of these metaphorical expressions are seemingly so violent is a subject for another inquiry. In addition, another study is needed to provide the social and cultural context in which later poetry, especially the mystic poetry of Sana'i and Attar, began to do the opposite, namely, to use wine as a metaphor for individuals and society.[62]

Metaphor is not the only device at work in Rudaki's poem. As the above extracts indicate, all figures of speech are at play in his verse, including simile, analogy, antithesis, panegyric, and hyperbole.[63] The use of such literary devices in "Mother of Wine" indicates the complexity/sophistication of Persian verse at this period.

THE POEM'S PERFORMATIVE AND RHETORICAL ASPECTS

Reading the final segment of the poem, it becomes clear that beyond the theme of wine, winemaking, and the effect of wine, the poem has broader cultural and political significance which, contrary to Hanaway's comments on the poem, also indicate a profound complexity and rhetorical sophistication.[64] It uses various literary devices not only to praise the patron but also reflects a depth in historical consciousness. True, the wine made for the reception Rudaki describes is sparkling and ravishing. It has been produced with care and skill. However, it is the ambience of the gathering at which the wine is served that constitutes the main focus of the poem. The party is filled with jubilance, songs of prosperity and success, and soaring grandiosity. It is in this section of the poem that the poet/artist/musician frees his imagination in conquering the world, perhaps in reestablishing the former grandeur of the Persian Empire. In fact, there is a literary trace of the pre-Islamic music of Barbod (d. 628) in Rudaki's work.[65] Indeed, Nezami Aruzi, writing in the twelfth century, points out the connection between Rudaki and Barbod.[66] This poetic grandiosity in "Mother of Wine" is pointed out by Julie Scott Meisami.[67]

Rudaki was not as candid as Daqiqi in advocating Zoroastrianism or the return of the pre-Islamic era, but he does so allegorically in the poem. He believes that the glory has already returned. He verbally conquers many of the areas that were once part of the Persian Empire to impress his readers with not so much the power of influence but rather the power of imagination. He mentions Badakhshan, Tanjeh (Morocco), Ray, Oman, and Sistan:

The wine scares away old worries to Tanjeh
While new hopes arrive from Oman and Ray.

انده ده ساله را به طنجه رماند
شادی نو را ز ری بیارد و عمان

In evoking these, he banishes care to distant parts and looks optimistically to the central areas of Iran. He also drinks to the health of Ahmadibn Mohammad, who is, by the way, the "greatest free man and the pride of Iran."

They drink to Bu Jafar Ahmad ibn Mohammad
The noblest in the land, glory of Iran.

شادی بو جعفر احد بن محمد
آن مه آزادگان و مفخر ایران

He refers to natural landmarks, such as the mountains of Sieam, Joudy, and Ararat, again while imagining a revived august nation, a sublime geographical journey—a chronotope of location indeed.

May his face be more brilliant than the Sun
May his good fortune endure longer than Mounts Ararat 'n Sahlan.

طلعت تابندهتر ز طلعت خورشید
نعمت پایندهتر ز جودی و ثهلان

In all this, Rudaki is not thinking simply in terms of the area ruled by the Samanids. After all, not long before that, the Samanids had interrupted the dynamics of Saffarid's rule over the eastern Islamic world that had lasted for 40 years. It was not long ago that they added to their Khwarazm land, Transoxiana and Khorasan, extending domination into the depth of Sistan. They kept an eye open for Fars and Kerman as well. However, in his poem, he is reconstructing a nation on an even much larger scale. He allegedly versified Kelileh o Demneh, (the Indian fables which go as far back as 500 BC), and that, too, supports this notion about Rudaki's historical consciousness. Unlike Ibn Muqqafa (Firoozabadi, AD 724–759), who was murdered for translating and completing his manuscript of *Kelileh o Demneh* by the Muslim caliph, Rudaki neither felt nor faced any retribution for rendering the book in a new form. He was perhaps rewarded by the Samanid court, an indication of time's lenient and historical consciousness about the Middle Persian literary heritage.

Rudaki's discourse also exhibits some diachronic aspects when he names individuals. The people he mentions—Sasan, Rostam, Dastan, Socrates, Plato, Jesus, Moses, Shaf'i, Hanifah, Sofyan, Loghman, Amram, and Amr ibn al-Layth[68]—are a mixture of historical, philosophical, and religious figures who have played a role at one time or another in the Persian Empire and afterward. The list of august names, designed to flatter his patron, also includes himself as he writes, "My poems rival Jarir's, Ta'i's and Hasan's, and I have the gift like Sarie's and Sahban." This is another chronotope, for example a reference to the way in which Rudaki brings together names of individuals from various times and places. He also graciously invokes the name of Bu-Omar and Minister Adnan as the persons who had encouraged him to write.

If Bu Omar had not given me courage	ورنه مرا بو عمر دالور کردی
If Minister Adnan had not let me,	وان که دستوری گردهی عنان
How could I have dared to praise the Emir	زهرهٔ کجا بودمی به مدح امیری؟
For whom God created earth and sea?	کز پی او آفرید کیتی، یزدان

These historical and geographical references, as well as a number of cosmic images, complete the final segments of the poem. In a sense, the poem re-represents the Samanid universe in its myriad cultural, political, and literary aspects, since this is how they pictured time and place as well. "Mother of Wine" reflects the Samanid self-image; they saw themselves as the continuation of the pre-Islamic Sasanians. After all, Saman Khoda, the founder of the Samanid dynasty, believed himself to be a relative of the Sasanian Bahram Chubineh.[69] The poem triumphs through synchronic and diachronic portrayals and references.

Moreover, in the third section, when the poem praises the king, all the above names come together to add to the king's magnanimity and glory in the pre-Islamic references, as the poet had done before in his other poems.[70] The following lines in the section are historically related to Persian history and alien to the powers in Baghdad.

A fair king, sun of our times آن ملک عدل و آفتاب زمانه
Who lights the world and through whom justice lives on. زنده، بدو داد و روشنایی گیهان
There is no one like him among the sons of Adam آنکه نبود از نژاد آدم چون او
Nor will there be, I speak not on a whim. نیز نباشد، اگر نگویی بتان
Man is made of earth, water, fire, and wind خلق ز خاک و ز آب و آتش و بادند
But this king of Sasan was forged from the Sun. وین ملک از آفتاب گوهر ساسان
Through him this dark land found glory. فره بدو یافت ملک تیره و تاری
Through him this desolate world Eden has become. عدن بدو گشت نیز گیتی ویران
If you are a philosopher seeking a wise path, ور تو حکمی و راه حکمت جویی
Learn his moral precepts, study hard his codes سیرت او گیر و خوب، مذهب او دان
Observe, he is pure and noble پاک اخلاق او و پاک نژادی
He is gentle, generous and revered. با نیت نیک و با مکارم احسان
When you hear his voice you smile ور سخن او رسد به گوش تو یک راه
And Saturn's ill fortune is reversed. سعد شود مر ترا نحوست کیوان
If you see him upon his throne ورش به صدر اندرون نشسته ببینی
You'd swear that Solomon's returned to life. جزم بگویی که: زنده گشت سلیمان
...   ...

Even if Mars himself joined the fray, ور به نبرد آیدش ستاره‌ی بهرام
He'd soon fall victim to his sword. توشه‌ی شمشیر او شود به گروگان
From the clouds only drops of dark rain fall, ابر باری جز آب تیره نبارد
While he scatters bags of gold and rich brocade. او همه دیبا به تخت و زر به انبان
Compared to the great mercy of this glorious king, از (با رس) عفو آن مبارک خسرو
Vast desert and steppe seem bound within a narrow field حلقه‌ی تنگست هرچه دشت و بیابان
He is the lord of Nimruz, a victorious king, آن ملک نبروز و خسرو پیروز
He is a tiger while his rival is the quivering fawn دولت او یوز و دشمن آهوی نالان
The name of Rostam, son of Dastan, demands respect رستم را نام گر چه سخت بزرگ است
Yet lives on only in our king, our savior. زنده بدوی است نام رستم دستان ٧١

The reference to such names as Khosrow, Rostam, Bahram, Esfandyar, in the extract above and elsewhere in the poem as well as the use of purer Persian words (as opposed to the extant Arabic or Arabized forms such as *gah* vs. *vaqt* or *pil* vs. *fil*), are telling in themselves regarding the mindset of the poet and the court. Cyrus the Great is mentioned elsewhere in the poem to promote "chastity, affability, humanity, and liberality" with the king in the same way Scipio observed them according to Xenophon in his *Cyropaedia*. It is also a known tradition of within Cyrus' Persia to ponder the nation's exigencies over wine. In the Tajik movie about Rudaki titled *Rudaki: Sargozasht-e Yek Shaers*, the emir commands the poet to drink wine before asking him to improvise his famous qasideh. Referring back to the concept of chronotope, it seems that the time (chrono) in the poem is inseparable from the defined space (topos) of the poem, with the former functioning as a dimension for the latter. Rudaki's chronotope of "perspective" in the context of this poem functions as the geographical dimension of time and the temporal dimension of geography, just as a chronotope is supposed to work. These dimensions make the event described in the poem representable and flowing, just like the wine that is being poured into the goblets of the guests at the party. We are indeed witnessing a chronotope of wine.

WINE, POETRY, AND THE SAMANID REBIRTH

Those who apply the European concept of renaissance to the Samanids, in all likelihood also wish to imply that there was a rebirth of interest in ancient Persia. Rudaki's poem reflects some of the elements of this renaissance, even though it is written in an allegorical qasideh format with only tacit references to the pre-Islamic past. It reveals that the Samanids' vision of the past and their vision of the past show how they viewed themselves as equally important forces in launching a cultural rebirth, which they hoped would lead to a revival of the great nation. A movement did indeed begin and it expanded during the ninth and tenth centuries. Moreover, I would like to believe that the Samanid renaissance was at least a creative movement in the history of Persia (and creativity then came to be a core concept in the changes that occurred in Europe): an Eastern renaissance effectively preceding the more enduring, comprehensive, and consequential Western Renaissance albeit with no obvious connection between the two. Creativity can be seen not only in the realm of literature, but also in the visual arts, in coinage, in the use of the Persian language, in governance, and even in the implementation of foreign policy. Abu Abd Allah Jayhani, the premier under Nasr II, has been credited with implementing a Sasanian administrative system and for reaching out to neighboring countries and states.[72] The mausoleum of Emir Esmail (built between 892 and 943), one of the few remaining architectural examples of the Samanid era, seems to have been perfectly adapted to its surroundings and yet reflects the influence of architecture of the Sasanians (and Zoroastrian temples in particular). It is in this context that one can imagine, as the Samanids did, Rudaki delighted by the publication of his poems, standing in front of the ruler at the court with a goblet in one hand and the other hand gesticulating as he recites the "Mother of Wine," just as the Zoroastrian minstrels recited their own work a few centuries earlier. Upholding ancient festivals during the time of the Samanids—including the New Year (*Noruz*), *Mehrgan*, *Sadeh*, the celebration and commemoration of the defeat of Zahhak (the mythical prehistoric villain in Persian epics), and other cultural and historical moments—is another indication of a historical continuity or historical reconstruction. This emphasis on native culture, a sort of nationalism, to counter foreign domination was not new in the history of Persia. Already, centuries before, the Arsacids and the Sasanians sowed the seeds of discontent among the Iranians against alien domination. They used coins in particular as a medium for expressing their discontent.

The Samanid renaissance lasted for nearly two centuries (819–999). The fruits of the new era were first reaped when Nasr I received the license to govern all of Transoxiana in 875.[73] One of its other major accomplishments was the establishment of Persian language as the literary medium. This was for the first time that Persian was granted permission to be used in this way since 697 when Umayyad governor ibn Yusuf decreed that Arabic notation only should be used and prohibited Pahlavi script, including Persian.[74] When Persian developed further as a written language two centuries later, Iranian legends were versified under Samanid patronage in the *Books of Kings*. In fact, Rudaki's poetry can be seen as a prelude to the creation of Iran's national epic, Ferdowsi's *Shahnameh* (*Book of Kings*), completed after the eclipse of the Samanids around the turn of the tenth century.[75] To be sure, the fact that under the Samanids Bukhara had become a thriving cultural center provided the context in which Rudaki was able to crystallize the language and imagery of Persian lyrical poetry, thereby paving the way for Ferdowsi's gigantic accomplishment.

Persian literature developed amid the use of other languages and in the context of some sort of multiculturalism and tolerance for the other. Herodotus once described the Achaemenids as a tolerant people, and that characterization is in full display in Rudaki's poem. Contrary to many *Shahnamehs* (*Books of Kings*) that were already in circulation during Rudaki's time, he does not put too much emphasis on Persian roots as a major component of identity. This starts with an open attitude toward philosophy and religiosity. He writes, in reference to his patron (to explain himself):

If you look at him philosophically	آن که بدو بنگری به حکمت گوی
You exclaim: Here are Socrates and Plato of Yunan.	اینک سقراط و هم فلاطن یونان
If you look at him theologically	ور تو فقیهی و سوی شرع گرای
You exclaim: Here are Shafa'i, Hanafi, and Sufyan.	شافعی اینک و بوحنیفه و سفیان

In many verses of the poem, reference is made to all races and ethnic groups, and religions unite at the time of coming together in celebration of the wide spectrum, reminiscent of the Achaemenids' cultural policy. The king enjoys good relations with distant rulers. He is particularly fond of the Fatamids in Egypt, who along with other rulers in other non-Iranian territories are also mentioned and celebrated while drinking wine.

When Rudaki speaks about his patrons and compensation, he shows that the intellectuals were not alienated from the ruling elite during the Samanid dynasty. The following lines, taken from the beginning of the section on being rewarded financially, also indicate that the Samanids were generous and supportive of their poets.

Hand over hand he gives so much.	با دو کف او، ز بس عطا که ببخشد
Noah's flood is rendered obsolete	خوار ناید حدیث و قصه توفان
Verily, due to his generosity.	لاجرم از جود و از مظاوت اوی است
The price of a eulogy rises and that of silence depletes.	نرخ گرفته مدح و صامتی ارزان
Poor poets go to him with empty hands;	شاعر زی او رود فقیر و تهیدست
Return, and recompense in gold and coin report.	با زر بسیار بازگردد و حملان
He rewards poets with such benefits and perks	مرد سخن را ازو نواختن و بر
And most learned men may be hired at the court.	مرد ادب را ازو وظیفه دیوان

To support this point, one might also consider the works of Rudaki's contemporaries. They were impressive in numbers, but their works are not voluminous.[76] These include Shahid Balkhi, Daqiqi, Kasai Marvazi, Manjanik Tarmazi, Tayeb Khosrovani, and most importantly the first well-known female poet, Rabeh Qazdari. As in Rudaki's poetry, themes of love, music, happiness, nature, death, and bravery are also common in their works.[77] Most were familiar with the tradition of ancient music symbolized in the legacy of Nakisa and Barbod and their profession of *khoniagari*, which continued into the Islamic period with the same features at least until twelfth century.

Some literary activists in Iran either ignore Rudaki's multiculturalism or read his poetry from a purely nationalistic or religious viewpoint. As mentioned above, certain scholars, such as Nafisi, regard Rudaki's dedication to the Persian language as the most significant of his achievements, as if he wrote in Persian merely for the sake of saving or reviving the Persian language. Throughout his seminal book on Rudaki, Nafisi is concerned with the purity of Persian culture and sees Rudaki as a protector of that purity.[78] That might have been one of Rudaki's aims, but in "Mother of Wine" he seems incredibly open to other traditions as well. However, and to be fair, sometimes in the works of intellectuals of the late nineteenth and early twentieth centuries, "Persian" equates with "Iranian." What this means is that such writers do not wish to exclude minorities, as some of them in fact belonged to ethnic minorities in Iran. More recently, Edarechi, who opens his informative book on Rudaki's contemporaries with the words "Poetry is mixed in Iranian race," argues that the Samanids' use of Persian was for the purpose of unifying the land.[79] This assumes that Rudaki could have written poetry in other languages, yet did not.

Rudaki's poem has also been the subject of religious interpretation, just as the works of other classical poets, such as Nezami (twelfth century) or Hafez (fourteenth century), have been in the last few decades. In her book *Asman va Khak: Elahiyat-e She'r-e Farsi az Rudaki ta Attar* (Heaven and Earth: Theology of Persian Poetry from Rudaki to Attar), Tajmah Asefi tries to show the influence of Islamic theology on the Persian poetry of the Samanid, Ghaznavid, and Seljuk periods. The author not only wants to show that there are manifestations of religiosity and mystical belief in the poetry of these periods, but also somewhat contradictorily contends that Rudaki takes the side of the rulers in his works. Clearly this contention is a projection of the so-called morality of the current official discourse, which is never practiced any way. She refers to only a few religious manifestations in the works of Rudaki to come to a major conclusion about the poet's religiosity.[80] However, Rudaki's poems defy excessive or overwrought religious or mystical interpretation. In fact, despite the sophisticated allegorical implication of the poem, it gave rise to a type of wine poetry that is now known as *badeh seta'i*, the admiration of wine, a synonym for *khamriyat*. It is drinking for a cause: to drink wine, to praise the wine, and to recognize one's identity.

A contextual reading of "Mother of Wine" is, therefore, revealing of the poet's worldview against the social and political backdrop of the Samanid dynasty, dwelling on themes of time, geography, wine, and the concept of Persian identity—all a reflection of what has been termed the Samanid renaissance. It could be argued that other post-Islamic native dynasties—the Khwarazm-Shahs of Khwarazm, the Buyids of Ray and Shiraz, the Kakuyids of Isfahan, the Ziyarids of Gorgan and Tabaristan, and, a little later, the Persianate Ghaznavids of Khurasan and India—should be considered as players in that Persian "renaissance" since they too provided a cultural medium in which such luminaries as Mutanabbi, Avicenna, Biruni, and Firdausi appeared and thrived. However, this qasideh of the Samanid era documents a number of chronotopes through which time and space seem united and are expanded historically and geographically revolving around the concept of identity. The unification of time and space through which the Iranian identity is expressed has, since the Samanids, become a pattern indicating how, after being defeated by a foreign invader or as the result of internal turmoil, Iranians gradually rose to reassert their cultural identity. We have witnessed this pattern every time Iranian cultural identity has been tested by foreigners or by fellow Iranians: in the post-Hellenistic period; in the post-Arab-Islamic era; in the post-Mongol era; in the post-Turkic era; in the post-Anglo-Russian rivalry era; in the post-Ale Ahmad era; and finally in the post-1979 Revolutionary era. It seems that the pattern is the distinction, the glory, the grandeur, and itself the identity. History tells us that this nation, since the Samanids, and despite the vicissitudes of time, has remained aware of that generic cultural identity. All wineries, including the renowned, and lucrative brands of Shiraz Kholar and the Kurdish province Sardasht, were closed down after the 1979 Revolution, but what do they have now? Thousands of mini wineries erected in basements or attics. When they drink their homemade wine or the smuggled foreign brands, they also recite wine poetry. The wine poetry has even found its ways in calligraphy and art galleries.[81] Rudaki's celebration of wine and Persian identity is still quite relevant.

Beyond the fascination with wine and winemaking, what happens in "Mother of May" is the idea of shaping the greater Khorasan and eventually Iran in its approximate entirety. This also explains Rudaki's high regard for both Abu Jafar and Bal'ami. Rudaki compliments them and places them in a prominent spot in the banquet hall.

A row reserved for chiefs and ministers,	یک صف میران و بلعمی بنشسته
A row for elders and those of noble life.	یک صف حران و پیر صالح دهقان
They drink to Bu Jafar Ahmad ibn Mohammad,	شادی و جعفر احمد بن محمد
The noblest in the land, the glory of Iran.	آن مه آزادگان و مفخر ایران

Bu Jafar is the ruler of Sistan and Bal'ami is the vizier of Abu al-Fazl. If these two men worked well with his favorite Samanid ruler, Amir Nasr, and remain loyal to him, all "four lands of the Sun" could join to facilitate the reality of the greater homeland more effectively. Nezami's poetry imagines and concerns itself with the world of humanity, a world with Iran at its heart.

For Nezami, the cause is to drink the wine, to produce Sakhon, and to praise Sakhon. Here, too, one can mention the Islamic verses, hadith, verdicts, and laws that forbid drinking to prove that Nezami was not even a true believer let alone piety minded as he is referred to in almost all Persian scholarship of recent decades. Some may argue that wine was technically forbidden but widely available at the court, but the same scholars also credit Nezami (correctly or not) for not being associated with any court or, as Zarinkub states, for being a hermit (*ozlat neshin*). Once again, the contention of this project is not to disprove Nezami's faith. What is most pertinent here is that Nezami does not write too subjectively about and does not advocate Islam, Sufism, specific ethical codes and morality, the history of the Arab Muslim invasion of the Persian Empire, the Muslim story of the prophet's ascension to paradise, and wine. He simply fictionalizes them in his pictorial allegories that together constitute his romances while benefiting from his rational and informed views of all these other themes and motifs.

NOTES

1. Paul Losensky, "SAQI-NAMA," *Encyclopædia Iranica*, 2016, at http://www.iranicaonline.org/articles/saqi-nama-book (accessed 19 May 2016). Shahab Ahmed explains the Islamic notion of divine revelation, ambiguity, aestheticization, polyvalence, figural art, music, law, philosophical ethics, and political theory. He speaks of Muslims drinking wine. The book also confirms again that many versions of Islam (some idealized or imagined by the author) have appeared throughout centuries. See Shahab Ahmed, *What is Islam?: The Importance of Being Islamic* (Princeton: Princeton UP, 2016).
2. Alireza Korangy, *Development of the Ghazal and Khāqānī's Contribution* (Wiesbaden: Harrassowitz Verlag, 2013), 7.
3. The original poem is in Manuchehri Damghani, *Divan-e Manuchehri*, 3rd ed. (Tehran: Zavvar, 1968), 7. This qasideh starts with:

آمد شب و از خواب مرا رخ و عذابست / ای دوست بیار آنچه مرا داروی خوابست

   The variations of the verb *fozun beh* (the more the better) at the end of the first half of the verse include *fozun nah* (nothing more) and *fozun deh* (increase them), more and less convey the same meaning.
4. A fluent rendition of the verse by Dick Davis reads, "When those who know what's what / Get together to dine, / We want three things, no more: / Kababs, and music, and wine."

5. For a complete translation of Rudaki's "Mader-e May" see, Kamran Talattof, "What Kind of Wine did Rudaki Desire?: Samanids' Search for Cultural and National Identity," in *Layered Heart: Essays on Persian Poetry*, ed. A.A. Seyed-Gohrab (Washington: Mage, 2018), 127–171.

6. See Julie Scott Meisami, *Structure and Meaning in Medieval Arabic and Persian Poetry* (London: Routledge, 2003); Hanaway, "Blood and Wine"; and Jerome W. Clinton, *The Divan of Manuchiri* (Minneapolis: Bibliotheca Islamica, 1972).

7. Seyed-Gohrab, "The Rose and the Wine: Dispute as a Literary Device in Classical Persian Literature," *Iranian Studies*, 47: 1 (2013), 69–85.

8. Dominic Brookshaw, "Lascivious Vines, Corrupted Virgins, and Crimes of Honor: Variations on the Wine Production Myth as Narrated in Early Persian Poetry," *Iranian Studies*, 47:1 (2013), pp. 87–129.

9. Paul Losensky describes a Book of the Cupbearer as a poetic genre in which the speaker, seeking relief from his hardships, losses, and disappointments, repeatedly summons the *saqi* (Arazi; Hanaway; Soucek) or cupbearer to bring him wine and the *moghanni* or singer to provide a song. Paul Losensky, "Saqi-Nameh," *Encyclopædia Iranica*, online, (accessed on 19 May 2016).

10. Yaseen Noorani, "Heterotopia and the Wine Poem in Early Islamic Culture," *IJMES*, 36:3 (August 2004), 345–66.

11. Meisami, *Structure and Meaning*, p. 332.

12. Ibid.

13. Julie Meisami, "Poetic Microcosms: The Persian Qasida to the End of the Twelfth Century," eds. Stefan Sperl, Christopher Shackle, *Qasida Poetry in Islamic Asia and Africa* (Leiden: Brill, 1996), 137–82, 139.

14. A few articles in Bert Fragner, Ralph Kauz, and Florian Schwarz (eds), *Wine Culture in Iran and Beyond* (Vienna: AAS, 2014), discuss this topic.

15. The Tajiks during the Soviets in the 1950s seem to have held this view when they made a movie *Rudaki: Sargozasht-e Yek Shaer*.

16. On this cultural transformation see, Richard Frye, "Development of Persian literature under the Samanids and Qarakhanids," and "The New Persian Renaissance in Western Iran," in *Islamic Iran and Central Asia (7th–12th Centuries)* (London: Variorum Reprints, 1979).

17. Hooshang Ebtehaj, "Saqinameh" in *Masnavi*, available at https://xaka-meh.com/.

18. Also Manuchehr Jokar, "Molahezati dar Sakhtar-e Saqinameh," *Pazhuheshhay-e Adabi* (no. 12–13 summer-fall 2006), 99–121.

19. Ibid.

20. Why does the poet use *wine* so many times if he intends to convey a religious concept? Could the equally frequent use of the word *sin* be an indication or even a retelling of a "dichotomy?" Does he promote the same

approach to life as Khayyam? How can one take the wine to mean something other than wine in these lesser-recited verses which starts with "An invisible singer called me from the corner of the tavern" or "Oh musician play a song, and wine-bearer bring me wine," without ruining their imaginative and structural beauty?

21. This concept is best portrayed in "Zartoshtnameh" by the poet Zaratosht Bahram Pazhdu where the prophet gives wine to Goshtasb. On religious significance of wine in ancient Persia, see Marijan Molé, *Culte, mythe et cosmologie dans l'Iran ancien* (Paris: Presses universitaires de France, 1963).

22. *Kolliayt*, 302–305.

23. *Kolliayt*, 305. It starts with:

در نوبت بار عام دادن / باید همه شهر جام دادن

24. *Kolliayt*, 305.

25. *Tazkereh Paymaneh* (The biography of the goblet) by Golchin Ma'ani also mentions As'ad Gorgani and Hafez as pioneers.

26. Other biographers later mention other poets as the inventor of the genre.

27. Nezami, *Kheradnameh*, in the section on "Alexander's Private Meeting with the Seven Scientists."

28. *Kolliyat*, 13.

29. *Kolliyat*. Ibid.

30. *Kolliyat*, 100.

31. *Kolliyat*, 140.

32. See, *Kolliyat*,140. It begins with,

نشسته خسرو و شیرین به یک جای / ز دور آویخته دوری به یک پای

33. *Kolliyat*,417.

34. Nizami Ganjavi, *Laili and Majnun*: A Poem translated by James Atkinson (Allahabad: Panini, 1915): https://persian.packhum.org/main.

35. *Kolliyat*, 317.

36. See,

مغنی بیار آن ره باستان / مرا یاری ده در این داستان

37. This is in the section about the meeting of Alexander and the seven scientists, where Nezami creates an allegory with the names of his characters. He calls upon Moghani frequently in *Iskandarnameh* as well.

38. Khorus-e bi-mahal or an untimely rooster.

39. Behruz Sarvatian, "Falak joz Eshq Mehrabi Nadarad," in *Adabestan* (Khordad 1991, 18, 34–39. It reads,

---

"عرفان عامل اصلی وحدت فکری و یکرنگی معنوی سخنان شاعران ماست"

---

40. Kamran Talattof, "Comrade Akbar: Islam, Marxism, and Modernity," *CSSAFME* 25:3 (November 4, 2005), 634–49.
41. Behruz Sarvatian, "Falak joz Eshq…"
42. And Sarvatiyan is not the only scholar who has used this line to justify the existence of secrets and codes.

نظامی چند ازین رمز بهای / مگو تا از حکایت وافائی

---

43. Ibid.
44. For an extended version of this section and the complete translation of "Madar-e May," see, "What Kind of Wine did Rudaki Desire?"
45. Some of these assertions are influenced by the writings of Mohammad Ghanimi Halal.
46. It is believed that of Rudaki's work, only 1000 verses have survived. Among the poems that have been lost is his versified *Kelileh O Demneh*. He died at the time Ferdowsi was born. It is still not clear whether he was blind or not and if he was since birth. Some agree that his poetic style is Khorasani, and his poems do not contain many Arabic words. He composed in the forms of *masnavi*, *qet'eh*, *qasideh*, and *ruba'i*, the last of which he is considered to have invented.
47. Mikkail Bakhtin, *The Dialogic Imagination*, ed. Michael Holquist, trans. Caryl Emerson and Michael Holquist (Austin: UPT, 1981), 84.
48. Jerome Clinton, "Court Poetry at the Beginning of the Classical Period," in Ehsan Yarshater, *Persian Literature* (Albany: Bibliotheca Persica, 1988), 77; G. Lazard, "The Rise of the New Persian Language," in *Cambridge History of Iran*, vol. 4 (Cambridge: CUP, 1975), 595–632; and L.P. Elwell-Sutton, *The Persian Meters* (Cambridge: CUP, 1976).
49. Sassan Tabatabai, "Rudaki, the Father of Persian Poetry" (Dissertation, Boston University, 2000).
50. Said Nafisi, *Mohit-e zendegi va ahval va ash'ar-e Rudaki* (Tehran: Ibn-Sina, 1962); 309–10. Makan ibn Makan was one of the leaders of the Daylamians and ruled Taberestan, Ruyan, and Ray.
51. See, Kamran Talattof, "What Kind of Wine did Rudaki Desire?"
52. I first studied the poem in an old edition of Rudaki's collection that was later reprinted as A. Jafar Rudaki, *Divan-e Rudaki* (Tehran: Javan, 2001), 41–49, consulting other editions.
53. All lines are from the same edition mentioned above.
54. Dick Davis, "On Not Translating Hafez," *New England Review*, 25 (2004), 1–2.

55. See Davis, *Borrowed Ware: Medieval Persian Epigrams* (Washington, DC: Mage Publishers, 1997).
56. See Ehsan Yarshater, "The Theme of Wine-Drinking and the Concept of the Beloved in Early Persian Poetry," *Studia Islamica*, 13 (1960), 43–53.
57. Patrick E. McGovern, "Iranian Wine at the 'Dawn of Viniculture,'" in *Wine Culture in Iran and Beyond*, eds. Bert Fragner et al., 11–12.
58. See Joobin Bekhrad, "Ramblings of an Iranian Wino," *Reorient: Middle Eastern Arts and Culture Magazine* (September 13, 2016), at: file:///C:/Users/talattof/Desktop/Ramblings%20of%20an%20Iranian%20Wino.html.
59. Plato, *The Laws* (London: Penguin, 2004), 649a.
60. Rudaki, Divan, 41–49.
61. Other poets also describe their favorite type of wine and their desired quality in a wine. Centuries later, Hafez describes his wine as red, lavender, crisp, delightful, garnet like, two years old, bitter, homemade.
62. There has been debate about the use of wine in the works of Sa'di and Hafez. It is believed that Sa'di uses it as a metaphor, as exemplified by the following poems where *sharab* (wine) and *masti* (intoxication) are used in multiple metaphorical meanings.

غافلند از زندگی مستان خواب / زندگانی چیست مستی از شراب
از شراب شوق جانان مست شو / کانچه عقلت میبرد شربت و آب

63. These are common figures of speech in Persian:

استعاره، مدح، اغنات، تشبیه، مراعات نظیر، تطابق، تضاد، اغراق

64. See William Hanaway, "Blood and Wine: Sacrifice and Celebration in Manuchihri's Wine Poetry," *Iran*, 26 (1988), 69–80.
65. Askar Rajabzadeh in a speech at a conference on the commemoration of native languages in Dushanbeh argued that there are even similarities in the life stories of Rudaki and Barbod (Cultural Center of Iran, 1385/12/4). See also Firoozeh Khazrai, "Music in Khusraw va Shirin," in *The Poetry of Nizami Ganjavi*, 163–78.
66. See, Ahmad Nizami Samarqandi, *Chahar Maqaleh*, ed. M. Qazvini (Leiden: Brill, 1948), where he writes:

از آن چندین نعیم این جهانی ---که ماند از آل سامان و آل ساسان ثنای رودکی ماندست و مدحت---نوای باربد ماندست و دستان

67. Meisami, "Poetic Microcosms," 139.
68. Amr ibn al-Layth was the younger brother of the dynasty's founder, Ya'qub ibn al-Layth al-Saffar, and the second ruler of the Saffarid dynasty of Iran from 879 to 901.

69. See Zabihollah Safa, *Tarikh-e Adabiyat dar Iran* (Tehran: Amir Kabir, 1977), 204.

70. Praising Nasr ben Aham, Rudaki portrays the king superior to Hatam in conducting charitable deeds and to Rostam in war craft and strength; this brings the ultimate compliment and a connection back to the pre-Islamic culture which has understandably never ceased to exit.

حاتم طایی توئی اند محا   رستم دستان توئی اندر نبرد ئی، که حاتم نیست با جود تو راد   ئی، که رستم نیست در جنگ تو مرد

71. Rudaki, Ibid.

72. Elton Daniel, *The Political and Social History of Khurasan Under Abbasid Rule* (Minneapolis: Bibliotheca Islamica, 1979).

73. Safa, *Tarikh-e adabiyat dar Iran*, 356.

74. See ibid., Ehsan Yarshater, *Persian Literature*.

75. Ibid.

76. Analytical works by Said Nafisi, Ahmad Edarechi Gilani, Abbas Eqbal, Iraj Afshar, Foruzanfar, Qazvini, Paul Hern, and E. G. Brown all shed light on this topic.

77. These two lines of poetry one from Marvazi and one from Tarmazi are relevant here:

بکشای راز عشق و بهفته مدار عشق / از می چه فایده ست به زیر بنین

بدان منگر که می نهی است / می خور بوقت الورد شرب الراح جایز

78. Nafisi, Mohite Zendegi.

79. Ahmad Idarechi, *Sha'iran-i Ham'asr-e Rudaki* (Tehran: Bunyad, 1992), 15, 17.

80. Tajmah Asefi, *Asman va Khak: Elahiyat-e She'r-e Farsi az Rudaki ta Attar* (Tehran: Daneshgahi, 1997).

81. "Khayyam Gallery," one of the tens of galleries available online, focuses on wine. The cultural dispute regarding Hafez's wine poetry has also found its way into the art of calligraphy and social media.

CHAPTER 6

Nezamian Pictorial Allegory
in *Layli o Majnun*

In this chapter, I focus on the story of *Layli o Majnun* to elucidate the sophisticated aspects of Nezami's allegorical poetry, which I conceptualize as Nezamian pictorial allegory. A Nezamian pictorial allegory is a short, structured, and interconnected passage with a surface story constructed using descriptions of science, religion, religious references, nature, space, man-made gardens, and animals, and a second level story focused on his characters or events. The Nezamian pictorial allegory differs from a parable or fable. The surface story might not convey a philosophical message or lesson. Its purpose is to show (or boast about) the dazzling possibilities of words, when juxtaposed and coordinated in terms of sound, shape, and meaning. The descriptions are sometimes hyperbolic, but the juxtaposition of words for shapes, colors, and moods is often staggering. For example, the surface story in a Nezamian pictorial allegory might be about a splendid garden with a night sky filled with stars above and animals within all juxtaposed with a second story about a character's dealing with a jubilant or distressful situation. As opposed to conventional stories, the ones by Nezami do not promote any particular religion, but rather serve to move his story along in an eloquent way to showcase his mastery of the language. In this chapter, the reader will gain a better understanding of the Nezamian pictorial allegory and the extreme flexibility with which an allegory can be used in classical Persian literature.

K. Talattof, *Nezami Ganjavi and Classical Persian Literature*, Literatures and Cultures of the Islamic World, https://doi.org/10.1007/978-3-030-97990-4_6

175

Countless sections in his *Layli o Majnun* include at least one Nezamian pictorial allegory. In reading these allegories, attention should be paid to meanings, metaphors, repetitions of multi-meaning words, the enjambment cases, the amphibolies, extra-textual and intertextual aspects, and anachronisms. In Nezami's *Layli o Majnun*, he employs all these techniques in a uniquely Nezamian style.

The original story of *Layli and Majnun* was recorded in Arabic in the late seventh century in Arabia. A poet named Qays Ameri falls in love with Layli Sa'd (fictional or not), and because of the intensity and insanity of his desperate unattainable love, he begins to speak or act irrationally, gaining him the nickname Majnun, meaning madman or crazy. To alleviate his pain, he publicly recites platonic poetry in praise of his unreachable beloved. This story became the subject of more elaborate inconsistent stories and consequently books over the next few centuries.[1] Outside of those Arabic sources, it was Nezami Ganjavi who, thanks to Manuchehr Shervan Shah's interest in romantic stories and encouragement from Nezami's own son, expanded that original anecdotal tale, versified it, and popularized it globally.

Nezami's version is divided into 46 interconnected segments and episodes (which themselves include sub-segments) in a highly logical order with a vivid description of each event in each of those segments. According to the extended Nezami version, Qays (later Majnun) is born into a wealthy family; meets Layli at school at a young age; and later they fall in love. Layli's father stops sending her to school in order to avoid controversy. Majnun goes crazy and becomes a wanderer in the wilderness. Majnun's father seeks Layli's hand in marriage for his son, but Layli's father rejects the match. One more meeting, a couple of heated exchanges, and two senseless and ironic wars waged on Layli's tribe by Majnun's supporters do not prevent Layli's eventual forced marriage to another man with whom Layli never sleeps. Later, the lovers' parents and Layli's husband die one after another. These tragic events and deaths are described vividly thereby revealing the inner feelings of the characters.

Furthermore, Majnun's unlikely connection and relationships with animals and nature during his wandering times in the deserts and mountains are illustrated and expanded several times. Later in the book, the lovers exchange beautiful letters. Eventually, Layli dies because of her deep trauma due to her broken heart and her losses and longing, and Majnun dies on her tomb soon after. Her family buries his remains beside Layli's.

Nezami's *Layli o Majnun* offers a wealth of examples of his pictorial allegories, features through which he enhances a simple, anecdotal tale, and develops the originally flat characters into sophisticated, evolving protagonists. He is so focused on his Sakhon that the story's progress is often given secondary attention. As Seyed-Gohrab puts it, "The anecdotes are mostly very short, only loosely connected, and show little or no plot development. They commonly refer to only a few aspects of Majnun's physical or mental condition, his love-frenzy, his poetic talent and his reclusive lifestyle."[2] Nezami details Qays' intensifying mad love for Layli in a way that justifies the man's acquired nickname of crazy.[3] The resulting book inspired tens of poets (in Persian and other languages of the Persianate world) and beyond to write their version of the story. Other prominent poets, including Rumi and Sa'di, have made frequent references to beloved Layli or the star-crossed lovers, albeit without as much character development or storytelling. As we will see, hardly any of the copycat stories hold a candle to Nezami's version. The production of this book attests to Nezami's professionalism showing that when he decided to write, even as an assignment given to him by the ruler, he sought perfection.[4] Some lines and aspects of this narrative poem have continued to be part of the daily parlance of people. However, most importantly, this poem provides numerous examples of how the poet constructs his mini allegories.

Most versions or editions of *Layli o Majnun* have about 46 sections. The first ten sections are introductory parts consisting of the customary praise of the prophet of Islam, the king, and the poet's skill (a practice that Nezami follows in all of his books). The last segment is also dedicated to the piece's commissioner, King Shervanshah. The segments in the middle are divided based on a logical connection of the story parts, such as "the beginning of the story," "Layli and Majnun Falling in Love," "On the Quality of Majnun's Love," and "About Layli".

Like Shakespeare's *Romeo and Juliet*, with which Nezami's *Layli O Majnun* has been compared,[5] the eastern romantic story includes a star-crossed love journey, a rivalry between families and other male suitors, battles, deaths, and detrimental personal and social consequences. However, the former presents more dramatic subplots, including meetings and marriage between Romeo and Juliet, the prolonged street fights between the Capulet and Montague families, and suspense in depicting the lovers' deaths. Instead of an emphasis on dramatic effects (more suited for plays), Nezami's romance focuses more on the descriptions of inner feelings, the descriptions of the mental states of the characters, and pronouncedly the descriptions of the world around them from earth to skies. The few dramatic events depicted are brief, loosely connected, and even to an extent incomplete. They show little or no contribution to the plot development, and the battle between the two tribes, in particular, demonstrates the rather astounding depth of Majnun's love for Layli because he participates in the war, but does not know what he is doing. The war explains the depth of his love better than Nofal's discussion over dinner with Majnun on the very topic of Majnun's physical or mental conditions, his love-frenzy, his poetic talent, and his reclusive lifestyle. Layli's mental and physical descriptions and the praise, sometimes with the usual poetic exaggeration of her beauty and emotional strength, all also occupy the bulk of the work. We see a Layli who loves and longs for Majnun but is not as broken up by the pain of separation and deprivation as Majnun is.

Both Shakespeare and Nezami create postulating prototypical love stories in their language with these similarities and differences even though their authors use different techniques to achieve a literary sublime. Both have inspired literary creativity globally and throughout the ages. Both have also been read and re-read from a variety of perspectives.

However, a good majority of scholars of Persian literature who read Persian poetry and even romance and narrative poetry in terms of religion, mysticism, and Sufism see Nezami's masterpiece as an aspiring Sufi work and its author as a Muslim mystic. This means that they see the work as a text that promotes simplicity and abstinence and thus a reflection of Sufi faith. The truth is that carnal love, erotism, and sexual longing in the story's society, and by extension, its religiously conservative region had no choice but to be channeled through other means, including a veil of religion itself, or mysticism, or other forms of self-denial. However, this seems to have been related most poignantly to the public expression of sex and sexuality. The reflection of the unfulfilled, unreciprocated love became a hot poetic topic because, for the most part, it reflected the reality of the minds of the lovers while sexual relations of all sorts existed, though poets could not explicitly depict them. Nezami, as every chapter of this book has tried to illustrate, was not guided in his creativity by any religious vehemence. If he were, it would not make sense to that he alludes to sex in a story about forbidden love in a restrictive society. However, when his narrative required, he did speak of lust and desire in *Layli o Majnun* and indeed of sex and sexual encounter in *Khosrow o Shirin* and *Haft Paykar*. His ingenious creativity and mastery of literary figuration were why his characterization of this book's protagonists is beyond comparison to what they were in the original anecdotes.

The various Arabic original stories were short, simple, and predictable.[6] Majnun falls in love with Layli; her father rejects his marriage proposal to

Layli, and this makes him a wanderlust, gloomy, and frail. Nezami compli-
cates, explains, expands, beautifies, and meticulously details that core story
and recreates it with extended descriptions of Majnun's pilgrimage to
Mecca, the interventions and attempts by his father, friends, and even a
local authority, Nofal, to unite the lovers or at least to ease his pain, and
yet all the sage advice he receives are all to no avail. Nezami presents these
through his allegorical approach. Readers are in awe when reading Layli's
letter to her beloved. Readers are amazed when picturing Majnun living
among wild animals in the desert. They feel distressed when witnessing
the forced marriage of Layli to an older man. The description of Majnun's
fall due to fainting upon a secret meeting with Layli appears pathetic.
Furthermore, Layli's punching (or slapping the face) her unwanted husband when he advances on her feels justified. All these are described in
detail and in clear context as construed and imaginative they may be. The
description of the transformation of Qays to an abstinent, fasting, uncon-
fident, infatuated, mortified, dejected, the selfless romantic poet leaves no
detail out.

Speaking of context, Nezami's love stories are not always unrequited.
In his *Haft Paykar* and *Khosrow o Shirin*, the lovers fall in love, and their
love is fulfilled. On those occasions, neither their parents nor their societies provide an obstacle in the lover's union. Despite any desire he may
have had, Nezami was not be able to change the ending of Layli and
Majnun's story. That does not prevent him from manipulating the settings
and the context (about which he was concerned when commissioned to
versify the story). He creates a more familiar place for the story's context
(reflecting his surrounding and cultural milieu) where the two lovers fall
in love at school and later meet clandestinely in a city-like setting with
houses and rooms rather than encampments and tents as in the Arabic version. In fact, in one of the early original versions of the story, Layli and
Majnun become friends because they were both shepherds. Nezami injects
into the story gardens (be it an orchard or a lush palm grove), flowers,
prairies, a variety of birds, wedding dresses, love letters, side-by-side
graves, allusions to paradise, and more, all for the sake of his Persian readers. The gardens are described very much the same way he described them
in his other narrative poem *Khosrow o Shirin*. He brings in his proven
knowledge of the constellations to add even more ornaments to the settings when needed.

Nevertheless, the dramatic changes in the context do not lead to a dramatic alteration of the characters' convictions. He leaves them to function

as the product of their circumstances and believes in their personal qualities. As in his other works, this book contains a little literary analysis and
literary historiography of its own.

The above descriptions allow us to go back to an earlier point about the
story's interpretation. The book's description of earthly qualities features
human love, lust, behavior, bewilderment, and tragedy plus the addition
of affirmative wine poetry in the introductory section outside the story
make the book's designation as Sufi advocacy absurd and untenable. That
assertion is not easy to make even about the *Layli o Majnun* written later
by Jami, who was a confessed religious/Sufi believer. One or another version of the so-called mystical processes such as annihilation, love-madness,
self-sacrifice, and unification can be found anywhere in any form, whether
the author intended them to evoke religious fervor or not. Only in the Sufi
treaties or in self-proclaimed Sufi poets can we be sure that the presentation of Sufi elements and stages is not a mere brag about the knowledge
of that worldview. Most of Jami's work falls in this category.

Let us look at some of the poetic constructions within the story of *Layli
and Majnun*. At the beginning of the chapter titled "Layli and Majnun
Fall in Love with One Another," we read:

As beautiful as Joseph to men's eyes	هر روز که صبح بردمیدی
Each dawn the sun lit up the eastern skies.	یوسف رخ مشرق رسیدی
Like a ripe orange, lovely to behold,	کردی فلک ترنج پیکر
Turning the heavens from basil's green to gold;	ریحانی او ترنجی از زر
Layli sat with her chin dropped on her fist	لیلی ز سر ترنج بازی
So beautiful that no one could resist	کردی ز زنخ ترنج سازی
Her loveliness, and like Zuleikha's maids	زان تازه ترنج نو رسیده
Who cut their careless hands with sharpened blades,	نظاره ترنج کف بریده
Those seeing Layli's beauty felt such thirst	چون بر کف او ترنج دیدند
They were like pomegranates fit to burst.	از عشق چو نار می‌کشیدند
When Qais caught sight of her, his face turned sallow	شد قیس به جلوه‌گاه غنجش
As if it shared the dawn skies' golden yellow;	نارنج رخ از غم ترنجش
Their mingled scents were sweet, as though no care	برده ز دماغ دوستان رنج
Or sorrow could survive when they were there.[7]	خوشبوی آن ترنج و نارنج[8]

This passage revolves around the color of sun at dawn, using the two
words *naranj* (sour orange and the orange color) and *toranj* (an old term
referring to a variety of items including the fragrant bergamot fruits, fragrant apples, the combined colors in paisley). In addition, he uses the
word *nar*, an abbreviated form of *anar* (pomegranate, which was also
used before as a metaphor for women's breasts). Nar, as in Arabic, can also

mean fire. In addition to understanding the metaphorical use of these words, one should also be familiar with the reference to Joseph. It refers to his face when he reemerges out of the well in the biblical and the Koranic story here equated with the sunrise. The fifth line makes yet another reference to the story of Joseph, where several women see Joseph and become so distracted and awed by his beauty that they accidentally cut their hands while peeling their oranges. The similes regarding the situation in which hands are injured and the metaphors of Joseph standing like a sun before Layli, the frequent use of the fruits and their colors, however complex, are simply tools for the broader construct of a scene which is not precisely a parable or fable. It is an allegory without cause, short, picturesque, and uniquely Nezamian.

Such constructs might not further a so-called storyline or may deliver a simplistic line. For example, Layli appears in front of the lovers as she is analogized with the rays of the sunrise and the beauty of Joseph. But the combination makes the scene come alive in the reader's mind.

Here is another short example where Nezami constructs his narration around some of Majnun's body parts, which may be understood in terms of his allegory.

If I can't be with you, I won't complain	بر وصل تو گرچه نیست دسّم
Since it will mean that I can hope again.	غم نیست چو بر امید هسّم
A thirsty child dreams of a golden cup	گر بیند طفل تشنه در خواب
That's filled with water, and he drinks it up,	کورا به سوی زر دهد آب
But when he wakes, the dream no longer lingers	لیکن چو ز خواب خوش برآید
And thirsty he sucks and licks his fingers.	انگشت ز تشنگی بخاید
Pain racks my limbs, they and my body's frame	پایم چو دولام خویشر است
Seem bent into the letters of your name;	دسّم چو دو یا شکنج گیر است
Love for you overflows my heart, so be it,	نام تو مرا چو نام دارد
But others must not know of it or see it;	که نیز دوبا دولام دارد
It entered with my mother's milk, believe me,	عشق تو ز دل بهادنی نیست
He fainted and fell headlong to the ground,	وین راز به کس گشادنی نیست
And sadly those who'd watched him gathered around.[9]	با شیر به تن فرو شد این راز
	با جان به در آید از تنم باز
	این گفت و فتاد بر سر خاک
	نظارگیان شدند غمناک

The first three lines about hands and fingers (in their secondary meanings) serve as an introduction for the following two lines that are jaw-dropping in terms of the creative use of body, as well the letters of Layli's name as similes for Majnun's body parts. There are four letters in Layli, now Majnun's talisman, and the poet puts these words in his mouth. His legs are bent like the shape of the Persian letter L (curved, bent), and his hands like the shape of Persian letter I or Y (folded, coiled). The use of words for the body and head in the remaining lines of the passage is both literal and metaphorical. This, too is a sort of pictorial allegory in that it provides images of the body in the first layer to explain the man's physical and mental condition in the second layer, and this time both end with Majnun fainting and people gathering around.

A segment of the poem titled "Majnun's Father Takes Him on a Pilgrimage to Mecca" represents another example of the Nezamian pictorial allegory. It revolves around a pilgrimage to Mecca.[10] The purpose of the pilgrimage is to cure Majnun's love madness. There is an introduction and conclusion to this passage. Majnun's friends and family assemble to consult and seek a solution to his misery. After a lengthy discussion and debate, they unanimously believe that he needs to take a pilgrimage to Mecca (Ka'ba). His father arranges for the trip and takes the son along on the journey. Majnun goes along with the plan. As indicated in the first lines of the segment, when they arrive at the destination, the father reminds his son that this is not a game and asks him to pray for release from the chain of this debilitating love. Again, Majnun does not resist. Here the father holds Majnun's hand and begins talking to him.

And said, "my boy, this is no joke; it's where	گفت ای پسر این نه جای بازیست
Men can be cured of every curse and care;	بشتاب که جای چاره سازیست
Circle the ka'bah once, and you will find	در حلقه کعبه که دست
You can escape grief's circling your mind;	کز حلقه غم بدو توان رست
Just say 'O God, release me from this pain,	گو یارب از این گزاف کاری
Grant me Your grace, and make me well again;	توفیق دهم به رستگاری
Save me from this obsession, conform me,	رحمت کن و در پناه آور
Show me the way to health and sanity;	زین شیفتگی به راهم آور
Know love is my addiction and my master,	دریاب که مبتلای عشقم
Free me from love's injurious disaster.'"[11]	و آزاد کن از بلای عشقم[12]

However, when Majnun starts praying by the Ka'ba, he asks for the exact opposite of what his father had advised him to request. He first laughs, then cries, and after that jumps up toward the Muslim holy building like a snake uncurling. He prays that his love for Layli intensifies and deepens. It is a sublime moment.

He said, I'm like a knocker on a door,
A ring that waits but can do nothing more,
My soul is sold for love, and from my ear
May love's bright earring never disappear!
'Detach yourself from love,' these people say,
But knowledgeable folk don't talk this way!
My strength is all from love, so wouldn't I
Fall prey to death as well, if love should die?
It's love that's made me, formed me, fashioned me;
If there's no love, what could my future be?
And may the heart that has no love to hide
Be borne away upon grief's flowing tide!
....

O God, increase my need to glimpse the face
Of Layli always and in every place,
Take back the years that I have left, and give
Them all to her as added years to live.
I've withered to a hair in my despair
But I'd not have her lose a single hair,
And may the earring that I wear as proof
I'm hers be my continual reproof;
May my glass never lack her wine, my fame
Never be separated from her name.[13]

کامروز منم چو حلقه بر در
در حلقه عشق جان فروشم
بی‌حلقه او مباد گوشم
گویند ز عشق کز جدائی
کاپیست طریق آشنائی
من قوت ز عشق می‌پسندم
گر میرد عشق من بمیرم
پرورده عشق شد سرشتم
جز عشق مباد سرنوشتم
آن دل که بود ز عشق خالی
سیلاب غمش براد حالی
....
یارب تو مرا به روی لیلی
هر لحظه بده زیاده میلی
از عمر من آنچه هست بر جای
بستان و به عمر لیلی افزای
گرچه شده‌ام چو مویش از غم
یک موی نخواهم از سرش کم
از حلقه او به گوشمال
گوش ادم مباد خال
بی‌باده او مباد جام
بی‌سکه او مباد نام
جام فدی جمال بادش[14]

It is an astounding moment, and very much is unexpected. This happens again later as to how Majnun behaves on the battlefield when he and Nofal go to war against Layli's tribe.

In addition to the usual creativeness, this Nezamian pictorial allegory draws attention to another aspect of his work, particularly in this book, and that is his use of religion and religious references to bring readers' hearts close to the text. Ka'ba and Mecca, the epicenter of the rise of the Islamic faith, mean different things to different people or are catalysts for deep emotions. In the story, while neither the father nor the son gets their wishes fulfilled at that holy site, they both remain convinced in their beliefs after they returned from their unsuccessful journey. The father and son also ask their God for intervention and help. However, they ask for the opposite of the wishes of each other. The father's conclusion and report to the rest of the family is that the pilgrimage did not work and that there is no remedy to Majnun's pain. In other words, both the pilgrimage and Ka'ba become inconsequential religiously; however, poetically they serve as a sublime pictorial allegory.

The allegory builds suspense in the drama and tragedy of those lovers; they are willing to try anything, including the greatest of all Muslim acts, the pilgrimage to Ka'ba. In this case, the surface storyline is to seek a remedy by going on the pilgrimage. The "hidden" agenda is, once again, the construction of a sublime moment, the presentation of the surprising behavior of Majnun, and his subversion of convention. Pausing on a few metaphorical constructs within this passage sheds further light on the points I have been making. The lock of Layli's hair, albeit beyond the reach of Majnun, becomes a device to show how tightly this man's heart is entrapped, how his whole being is enslaved, and yet, the metaphor also stands for the access point to the sacred space. In the end, for him, her beloved hair becomes his Ka'ba. This sequence contrasts with all Muslim and Sufi beliefs. Nezami's reassignment of Majnun's Ka'ba also stands in contrast to the religious convictions and can be seen as almost sacrilegious. It would be too arbitrary to present this type of portrayal of Ka'ba as an advocacy of Islam, as many ideological readings do. Moreover, it would be too arbitrary to take Majnun's prayer for the intensity of his carnal love as the Sufi steps toward God, like many mystical readings do. To Majunun, Layli is a more tangible and desired destination for pilgrimage; Layli, as he says, is his Ka'ba, and Nezami supports his character by making the readers understand the depth of his love.

The following passage represents another larger layered allegory constructed around the concept of food, animals, and Majnun's malnutrition. It allegorizes, in a sense, the relationship between those elements.[15]

Better to be a fox whose belly's full	گرگی که به زور شیر باشد
Than be a mighty wolf that's vulnerable;	روبه به ازو چو سیر باشد
A hawk that's eaten well will have no need	بازی که نشد به خورد محتاج
To envy other creatures when they feed,	رغبت نکند به هیچ دراج
And mounting hunger makes sour food taste sweet –	چون طبع به اشتها شود گرم
What was disgusting now seems good to eat,	گاورس درشت را کند نرم
But when we're sick, sweet halva's like a curse,	حلوا که طعام نوش هر است
A poisoned food that only makes things worse.	در هیضه‌خوری به جای زهر است
Majnun was hungry, and he searched the ground	مجنون که ز نوش بود بی‌بر
For anything to eat that could be found.[16]	می‌خورد نواله‌های چون زهر [17]

The point of this short narration is to say that Majnun fed on anything he could find. However, to arrive there, Nezami weaves together several introductory lines about how and why foods are consumed and how such consumption might indicate one's character. Again, certain words and grammatical playfulness are repeated to create a somewhat independent short allegory.[18]

The two-line passage below repeats the words ear (*goosh*) and ring (*halqeh*) four times each, totaling more than one-third of the total words. Nevertheless, with them, the poet effectively describes Layli's painful anticipation for hearing any news of her beloved while masterfully assigning a different meaning to the words and juxtaposing them poetically.

Golden rings in her ear	در گوش نهاده حلقه زر
She listened at a ringing door to hear.	چون حلقه نهاده گوش بر در
Enduring the ring that enchained her	با حلقه گوش خویش میساخت
She never wished it on another.	وان حلقه به گوش کس نینداخت[19]

In two lines, the author describes Layli's appearance, constant anticipation, attempt not to submit to her fate, and her benevolence. The construct conveys the author's meaning because he assigns two meanings to those frequent words. *Halqeh-e gush* means earrings but also a "slave's earring" or collar and a doorknocker ring. The word *gush* is also used both literarily and to mean to listen. This short passage with which Nezami describes Layli's appearance and state of mind succinctly using extra-textual images also exemplifies the pictorial allegorical constructs that permeate his books.[20]

In the following section, the lovers write poetry and exchange poetic letters for a while. Despite hurtful rumors, they continue this line of communication and are somewhat satisfied with their images of each other with the help of the letters. It reads:[21]

And this is how love-messages between	زین گونه میان آن دو دلبند
This lovelorn pair passed safely and unseen.	میرفت پیام گونهای چند
The songs of nightingales could not compete	آوازه آن دو بلبل مست
With their melodious songs, they were so sweet,	هر نلمهای که بود بشکست
And many lovely songs were based upon	بر رود رباب و ناله چنگ
The lovers' story, and the songs they'd sung,	یک رنگ نوای آن دو آهنگ
And harps, and lutes, and flutes, whatever tune	زامشان معنی به نکته راندن
They played, it spoke of Layli and Majnun –	وز چنگ زدن ز نای خواندن
Their families' children heard these compositions	از نغمه آن دو هم ترانه
So often that they all became musicians	مطرب شده کودکان خانه
They suffered from these slights, and wept to hear	خصمان در طعنه باز کردند
The way such gossip made them both appear;	در هر دو زبان دراز کردند
A year passed by, in which they had to be	بودند بر این طریق سال
Content with dreams, and hope, and memory.[22]	قانع به خیال و چون خیال[23]

Thus, the storyline is that two lovers communicate through letters and their love poems that also reveal the state of their minds. Their adversaries hear about the lovers' indirect contact and begin to gossip and badmouth them. What is the cover story? None except that as usual, Nezami's goal is to tell the storyline through a cover story that illustrates an allegory and a metaphorical construct, which in this case is built around the musical concepts, compositions, musicians, and songs. Their poems are also elegant and appropriately melodious and even their enemies find out about them through hearing the music.[24]

In the beginning of a segment titled "Layli's Visit to the Orchard," Nezami eagerly describes the garden, its flowers, and the birds roaming around, yet another aspect he added to the original Arabic story to Persianize it. The passage is long, consisting of dozens of verses. It starts and ends with the following two couplets with nearly 70 verses in between, some of which will be reviewed later.[25]

The sun's rose drew its veil back, and its light	چون پرده کشید گل به صحرا
Made all the roses of the lowlands bright,	شد خاک به روی گل مطرّا
....	....
Once they were home, the pearl sought out her shell,	چون باز شدند سوی خانه
But she who'd learned her secret sped to tell.[26]	شد در صدف آن در یگانه

After describing the flowers, the tender layout, and pleasant weather, and the playful colors of nature, Layli is depicted in the orchard and later with friends in an adjacent palm grove, which is also described in similar terms as a garden. The description of the flowers and trees reminds readers of Layli's beauty, and the conversation/interaction between those natural elements indicate or mixes with Layli's "stream of consciousness." The dialogue includes the recitation of a love letter/poem composed by Majnun. The exchanges between birds and flowers and trees, the multiple meanings of the words used, the insinuations, and the similes all combined indicate a spectacular and overwhelming aesthetical force at play. After a short respite in the text's description of the scenes, images of the garden continue to flaunt its beauty in a few additional lines followed by a pivotal section when an old suiter seeks Layli's hand in marriage. Nevertheless, the visit to the breathing, lively orchard, and all the natural wonders it offers is personified as we read Majnun's somewhat oblivious and self-pity expression sung by a passerby and heard by Layli:[27]

As if a passer-by sang both the tune	قصهٔ غزل چو در مکون
And words of verses first sung by Majnun:	می‌خواند ز گفتهای مجنون
"O my veiled idol, whom I hope will be	کی پرده در صلاح کارم
Unveiled at last by no one else but me:	امید تو باد پرده دارم
"Flailing in blood, Majnun sinks to perdition	مجنون به میان موج خونست
And how does Layli fare? What's her condition?	لیلی به حساب کار چونست
Majnun is wracked with pain in every limb –	مجنون جگری همی‌خراشد
Layli draws all his strength and will from him;	لیلی ز نک از که می‌تراشد
Majnun's pierced by love's dart, the wound is deep –	مجنون به خندک خار سفته است
Layli lies sweetly, softly, sound asleep;	لیلی به کدام ناز خفته است
Majnun laments, his cries are never done –	مجنون به هزار نوحه نالد
Layli counts all her pleasures, one by one;	لیلی چه نشاط می‌سگالد
Majnun is branded and he writhes in pain –	مجنون همه درد و داغ دارد
Layli's all flowers and springtime's sweet refrain;	لیلی چه بهار و باغ دارد
Majnun is stricken by necessity –	مجنون کر نیاز بندد
Layli is free, and laughs spontaneously;	لیلی به رخ که باز خندد
Majnun's heart grieves that they must be apart –	مجنون ز فراق دل رمیداست
Layli is calm, all's well within her heart."	لیلی به چه راحت آرمید است
When Layli heard this, she began to moan	لیلی چو سماع این غزل کرد
And weep, as if her tears would wear through stone.[28]	بگریست وز گریه سنگ حل کرد[29]

Such alternating lines about Layli and Majnun permeate a good portion of the narrative. Here, the poet compares the lovers. The lines consist of Majnun's verses, which upon hearing Layli weeps. The mood in the orchard changes as does the tone of the text. Layli returns home. This allegory of the garden contains a storyline about interactions between flora and fauna overlaid with a storyline about the two lovers' interaction. In a reverse allegorical arrangement, the purpose of the passage, being the play with the names of flowers and colors, is more apparent than what is supposed to be describing the girl's state of mind and beauty. All these happen in a garden of beautiful employing rhyming words or using Henry Peachman's book title the *Garden of Eloquence*.

The poet relentlessly continues to build upon the same set of features to create new additional allegorical constructions. For example, a few lines after the above section, he dances around the word *bagh*, garden.[30]

The garden's gardener, poet-author of	فهرست کش نشاط این باغ
These words, brands with his speech this tale of love	بر ران مغن چنین کشد داغ
Layli, that moon who was so beautiful	کانروز که مه به باغ می‌رفت
It seemed she was a moon that's always full,	چون ماه دو هفته کرده هر هفت
Went one day to her garden, where her face	گل بر سر سرو دسته بسته
Was like a rose that topped a sapling's grace,	بازار گلاب و گل شکسته
And where her scent and beauty were so prized	زلفین مسلسلش گره‌گیر
Both roses and their attar were despised,	پیچیده چو حلقه‌های زنجیر
And as she walked her tumbling curls descended	...
As though they were chained links that never ended	از دین آن چراغ تابان
As he was passing by caught sight of her	در چاره چو باد شد شتابان
And thought no blossom could be lovelier. ...	...
The garden will be cleared of thorns; our rose	تا غنچه گل شکفته گردد
Will flower, her budding petals will unclose;[31]	خار از ین باغ رفته گردد[32]

The word "garden," like many other words, is repeated with different meanings and each time with double if not multiple meanings, as fitting subjects, adjectives, and similes.[33] The garden in the first line means the book on love between Layli and Majnun, and the gardener is no one but Nezami. After all, it is not the first time that he writes himself into his poetry. However, some have found this line vague enough to read it as a credit to the original tale and whoever authored it. The passage also returns to some of the previously metaphorized words such as flower, rose water, chain, ring, and so on to describe Layli's appearance when she, on her way to the garden, encounters a man who later comes to ask for her hand. The broader section about the marriage proposal also describes the man, but in more literal language. In the passage below, again, the repetition of words stands out as a literary technique.

Veiled Layli's secret was now out, her name	لیلی پس پرده عماری
A bandied byword for disgrace and shame,	در [آن] پرده دری ز پرده داری
And harps and lutes joined in, so that among	از پرده نام و ننگ رفته
Men everywhere the lovers' tale was sung	در پرده نای و چنگ رفته
By sweet-voiced singers, whose beguiling art	نقل دهن غزل سرایان
Enchanted each delighted listener's heart.[34]	ریحانی مغز عطر سایان
	در پرده [دفتر] عاشقان خنیده
	زخم دف مطربان چشیده[35]

The word *pardeh* (curtain, cover, etc.) appears six times in this passage. Each time, it conveys a slightly different meaning or a different connotation. These uses, which might not be easy to reflect in a translation, range from a curtain to secrecy to exposure (in its compound form), and musical concepts. Furthermore, Nezami entertains the same word within different constructs a couple of pages earlier and a few pages later.[36]

Nezami's unique allegories are sometimes built around one foundational word, which by repetition tease, spellbind, and intellectually delight the readers.

And were it not for shame he would have waged	گر شرم نیامدیش چون میغ
War on his own side as he stormed and raged –	بر لشکر خویشتن زدی تیغ
If scorn had let him, he'd have fiercely fought	گر طعنه زنش معاف کردی
Against his allies and the men they brought	با موکب خود مصاف کردی
And slashed his friends' heads off, did he not see	گر خنده دشمنان ندیدی
The sneering laughter of his enemy	اول سر دوستان بریدی
If Fate had willed it, he'd have drawn his bow	گر دست رسش بدی به تقدیر
Against his friend as often as his foe	برهم سران خود زدی تیر
And had his heart not stopped him, he'd have slain	گر دل نزدیش پای پشتی
His faithful allies on that dreadful plain.[37]	پشتی گر خویش را به کشتی

This passage portrays Majnun in a war, arranged by Nofal, against Layli's tribe. Even though the war is on his behalf and for his sake, Majnun cannot bring himself to harm anyone related to his beloved. It is an excellent case of psychological torment and internal conflict. The lines all start with the word "if." Despite some criticism of the unusual portrayal of that battle, this graphic description of Majnun's participation in the clash with confused thoughts and conflicted actions tells of a crazed love that drives Majnun to act upon his innermost instinct without much reflection.

Such paradoxes are inherent in tragedy and romance writing. Nezami uses paradoxical feelings and their descriptions everywhere in his work. As Seyed-Gohrab writes, "The importance of the romance for world literature lies in both the fascinating intensity of the love it portrays, and how love is seen to generate paradoxical emotions and responses."[38] Another similar occasion is Nezami's construct around the word farewell (*bedrud*). He writes:

You know you're as dear as my eyes anyway	با اینکه چو دیده نازنینی
Farewell, you will not see me until doomsday.	بدرود که دیگرم نبینی
Farewell, I am dressed to go, and, on my way,	بدرود که رخت راه بستم
To die on board my broken ship	در کشتی رفتگان نشستم
Farewell, yes, I have packed, and no delay.	بدرود که بار بر نهادم
On the way to the jaws of resurrection day	در قبض قیامت اوفتادم
Farewell, we are now strangers, to each faraway.	بدرود که خویشی از میان رفت
We hesitated, and the caravan is on its way	ما دیر شدیم و کاروان رفت
Farewell, I decided to flyaway	بدرود که عزم کوچ کردم
And when gone, there is no return on your way.	رفتم نه چنان که باز گردم
Once done with the sendoff,	چون از سر این درود بگذشت
He said his final farewell and returned home straightaway.[39]	بدرودش کرد و باز پس گشت

This summarizes the result and the conclusion of Majnun's father's attempt and struggles to convince his son to forget about that doomed love and return home. When he hears that Majnun prefers suffering the separation from his beloved over the comfort of home and hospitality of his parents, his insane world over sanity, Majnun's father is left with no choice but to say farewell. Majnun's father dies not much later.

The death of Majnun's father provides a few new creative poetic constructs. An example is a long construct that includes the frequent use of the personal pronouns (تو) and (من) (you and I), which is different from the usual standard conversational pattern of "you said" and "I said" in the way that only one character speaks on behalf of both, for example Majnun addresses his dead father.

Where can I seek you, find the love you taught me?	ای غم خور من کجات جویم
Who can I speak to of the grief you've brought me?	تیار غم تو با که گویم
You found it best to have no son, descended	تو بی پسری صلاح دیدی
Into the ground, and so your life was ended –	زان روی به خاک درکشیدی
For me though there is only bitterness	من بی‌پدری ندیده بودم
Now I've become this new thing – fatherless	تلخست کنون که آزمودم
I cry for help, but who can I cry to	فریاد که دورم از تو فریاد
Since help has always come to me from you?	فریاد رسی نه جز تو بر باد
You were my friend, my ally, and the source	یارم تو بدی و یاورم تو
Of all my heart's vitality and force,	نیروی دل دلاورم تو
You taught me what is right, you sympathized	استاد طریقم تو بودی
With all I sought and suffered and devised:	غمخوار حقیقم تو بودی
I'll be a phantom without you, no one,	بی بود تو بر مجاز ماندم
Alas that I am here and you have gone	افسوس که از تو باز ماندم
Don't use your absence as my punishment,	سر کوه دوری مکن پیش
I am ashamed enough and I repent,	من خود خجلم ز کرده خویش
Ah, how I blame myself, and weep and rave	فریاد برآید از نهادم
When I recall the good advice you gave	کاید ز نصیحت تو یادم
You were the happy trainer, I the colt	تو رایض من بکش خرامی
Who'd bridle at the bridle and then bolt,	من توسن تو به بد لگامی
You were an earring fastened to my ear	تو گوش مرا چو حلقه زر
With gentle guidance I refuse to hear:[40]	من دور ز تو چو حلقه بر در [41]
…	…

The brutal honesty as well as occasional self-pity of Majnun is well described as he thinks about and mourns his father's death. Nezami's romances are narrative poems that use rhetorical modes of expression and consist of the description of a series of interconnecting events, several scenes, plenty of images, and a few conversations. The poetic conversations, usually between the poet or a narrator and a person, an animal, or a natural element, are here between a living person and someone recently deceased. The poet also draws a universal picture of a father-son relationship.

Another construct revolves around the word *jan* (جان), which means soul, life, or dear. The word itself determines the nature, quality, and direction of the passage in a way that it can fit perfectly into the segment. In a segment titled, "Majnun Sings His Lyrics to Layli," Nezami writes:

And are our souls in separate worlds that you	با جان منت قدم نسازد
Can't step in my direction? Is this true?	یعنی دو جان بهم نسازد
Give me another soul to bear it, then,	تا جان نرود ز خانه بیرون
Or treat me better when you come again.	نایی تو از این بهانه بیرون
If you won't treat me generously, I fear	جانی به هزار بار نامه
My soul is leaving me and death is near	معزول کنش ز کار نامه
While any soul your lips speak kindly to	جانی به از این به بار در ده
Enjoys eternal life because of you.[42]	بایی به از این بکار درنه
	هر جان که نه از لب تو آید
	آید به لب و مرا نشاید
	وان جان که لب تواش خزانه است
	کنجینه عمر جاودانه است[43]

Although in terms of visual effect, this passage is not on par with some of the previous examples. It depicts well the mental status of Majnun, his despondency, and the dreamlike expectations he still keeps in his heart at that time of his life. He continues to place Layli in the usual higher regards. He goes on to make a plea. He asks her to take his life, liberate his soul from his confining body, and give him another life with a kiss. He sings that a life born out of a kiss is eternal, better than his current fleeting life void of her kiss. Thus, on the surface, the repetition of the word *jan*, in both of its meanings of soul and life, is combined with related terms (7 here, 15 times total) to depict an image that not only tells of Majnun's state of mind and expectation, but also foreshadows the end of the tale and the death of the two souls.

Of course, the inclusion of allegorical passages (with fables and anecdotes) in a more extended poetic narrative is not unique to Nezami. What is different about his work is his delightful manipulation of the grammatical elements, his creative use of words with double or even triple meaning, multi-layer imageries, and a meaning matched with an image: a picture on the first layer, and an explanation or description on the second layer. In all these cases, Nezami's pictorial allegories, their size notwithstanding and beautiful in their own right, also help drive the narrative forward. They also share similar features and literary devices.[44]

NEZAMI'S *LAYLI O MAJNUN* AND HIS IMITATORS' WORK

As we will see below, other poets have written their own versions of *Layli o Majnun*, or have included part of it, or referenced to it in their various works. Vahshi Bafeqi has a beautiful part of the story in his *Farhad o Shirin* (a variation of *Khosrow o Shirin*, which emphasizes the burning love of Farhad for the princess). A critical person tells Majnun to find a girl more beautiful than Layli because Layli truly lacks any beautiful features. Majnun gets upset and answers in beautiful verses, asking him to see Layli with Majnun's eyes. Here he is emphasizing that beauty is in the eyes of the beholder. Some of the verses of this passage have become part of common parlance among Iranians.[45] What is relevant is that we see a construct with the repetition of the body part as its core. The meaning is also complicated when we notice that the simple message of beauty is in the beholder's eyes becomes a song about love and perspective. Nevertheless, despite the beauty of Vahshi's portrayal and its similarities with Nezami's style, it lacks the exact features of pictorial allegory as it features a conversation without a surface image made of words.

Let us focus on comparing the work of Nezami with two other fabulous poets to learn more about Nezami's literary approach. As mentioned, the story of Qays (Majnun) was a short tale, mainly consisting of his lyrics, which he recited about his beloved. The basic story was circulating in the region and before being written down in two books Nezami was asked to versify it, which, as he has said, was done in four months. It is unclear how detailed the characters and the stories were developed in the oral versions. Its roots, according to Yan Rypka, go back to the Babylonians.[46] Yet, many other stories, including the Biblical and Quranic stories, have their roots in ancient Mesopotamia. Nezami's version is undoubtedly extended, developed, and contextualized in a way that reflects his Persian physical, cultural, and emotional settings. It has preserved the tribal and desert context of the original story, mainly when the poem speaks of limitations regarding women's situation and constrictions regarding sexuality. For example, even though the protagonists are still children, Majnun and Layli fall in love at school (in a *maktabkhaneh* at a young age), and then they do not get to meet until much later, and only briefly. We should recognize that the nature or quality of this school has to be of Nezami's own making because it is similar to the medieval Iranian schools in which students of different ages would learn a limited number of subjects, including reading, writing, and religion together. Alternatively, even though Nezami keeps the original names of people, places, and tribal customs, the way he describes them is mostly based on his own culture and surroundings, allowing him to draw on familiar emotions, characteristics of Persian gardens, changes of the seasons as in the northern climes, and Iranian philosophical and mental traditions—some of which (as explained before) were rooted in the pre-Islamic thinking of the Persians. Such creative nurturing of the bare bone original story should be considered a strength and can be explained by the poet's fascination with the art of Sakhon. He even adds episodes in which the lovers exchange letters and hear of each other in gardens, giving the poet a chance to exhibit his unbridled art of Sakhon, which is his virtuosity with the art of language.

Such additional context and prolonged descriptions are not as common in the works of Nezami's imitators. Their *Layli o Majnun* compositions are beautiful in their own ways and often share with Nezami the same typical tropes or the repetitive description of Layli's beauty, grace, and gentleness equating her to the moon or a pearl in a shell. However, they are different in significant ways. Ranking them in terms of beauty, elegance, and effectiveness of the poems and narrative is, to some extent, a subjective matter, but some are of Nezami's quality.

Under the Islamization of Classical Persian literature, a few scholars have argued that Jami's version is better and more realistic than Nezami's because the latter suffers from a few flaws.[47] One of the major flaws they claim to see in Nezami's version is that the two lovers meet and fall in love at a "very early" and "unrealistic" youthful age at school. They are "still children," the criticism goes. The truth is, however, that children can get attached at any age and never forget each other. Moreover, Nezami sees their love as a process that intensifies over time. Years elapsed between their meeting at school and their expression of burning carnal love.[48] It is ironic that these scholars also believe that the love between Layli and Majnun is mystical, which begs how young children could understand mystical and Sufi love or why children could not experience platonic love. Interestingly, in the version by Amir Khosrow, the lovers end up having sex in the desert, and in the version by Jami, a renowned Sufi, the lovers meet in the dark of the night many more times. In the Persian folk culture and music, even in most remote ethnic areas of the Persianate world as well as in the works of Eric Clapton or Giacomo Puccini, Layli, Shirin, and Nezami's other women characters are earthy women who epitomize love, beauty, and independence. Reading ideology into classical texts has the

potential to create gaps and contradictions in the interpretation and analysis. Classical literature is vast and has a long history, different from contemporary Persian literature (and other major Middle Eastern literary
traditions), which I have argued show close affinity with various contemporary ideological discourses. The Episodic Literary Movement model
may not apply to the history of classical Persian literature. Still, it explains
the different interpretations of this body of work since the early twentieth
century, perhaps best exemplified in the works of Kasravi and Hedayat,
Marxist critics, and the current Islamic readers.[49]

The second major problem scholars see in Nezami's version is the so-
called illogical behavior of Majnun, which in many other readings is in fact
a strong aspect of the story: the evidence of his craziness. To this I only
write what James Atkinson quoted from Shakespeare on the cover of his
translation of *Layli o Majnun*.

> The course of true love never did run smooth.
> Lovers and madmen have such seething brains,
> Such shaping fantasies that apprehend,
> More than cool reason comprehends.
> He will not be commanded.[50]

Majnun's behavior on the battlefield is the ultimate display of irrationality, yet that behavior introduced the lovers' depth of feeling and thinking, and the greatest extent of his craziness. In case we have forgotten, his
name is the madman.

Amir Khosrow Dehlavi and Abd al-Rahman Jami (whom I discussed in
Chap. 3 on portrayal of women) are believed to be among the most successful writers who, inspired by Nezami's work, wrote their own versions of
Layli o Majnun story.[51] Living two centuries after Nezami, Jami had access
to many more written Arabic versions and relied on them rather significantly, which explains why his version's environmental and cultural contexts
are mostly the tribal space and culture of that time and place. *Layli and
Majnun*'s story, written by Amir Khosrow Dehlavi and Jami is like Nezami's
in terms of the style, rhyme, rhythm, and most of the details of the events.[52]
There are, nevertheless, a few differences. For example, the ages of the couple and the places of their first meeting are different. In Jami's version,
Majnun is much older when he meets Layli, and when they meet in the
desert. This version lacks the numerous allegories and references that
Nezami makes to school and education. In Amir Khosrow's version (which
is the shortest of the three), the lovers are also older when they meet at

school and get the chance to see and talk to each other. Another difference is Majnun's relationship with his father and how his father understands his love for Layli and his situation. In Nezami's version, the description of this relationship and the changes that occur between them make sense to the contemporary reader. The episodes of Layli's marriage to Ibn Salam and Majnun's pilgrimage to Mecca (suggested and arranged by his father) fit well in the narrative beside other events that unfold. It is that marriage that breaks Layli, and it is that ensuing pilgrimage that explains the most inner feelings of Majnun. The marriage to Ibn Salam and the father's suggested pilgrimage does not exist in the version by Amir Khosrow Dehlavi. Despite being long, Jami's version includes only a few events that do not exist in other versions, yet another contrast with Nezami's work.

In Nezami's version, the father encourages his son to study science, particularly jurisprudence and medicine. In Amir Khosrow's version, the father encourages his son to learn science. In the version by Jami, known for his profound Sufi beliefs, the father wants his son to learn increasingly about religion. Jami tries to imply mystical stages on to Majnun's love within the story where there is none. Nevertheless, the best analysis and evaluation of Jami's version could also include a character analysis and how those implication of mysticism help make characters less realistic. But even then, that fictional characterization should not easily be taken to judge the authors' religiosity. In case of Jami, there are many other sources about his faith. This, too, is the opposite approach to the interpretation of contemporary literary movements and literary activities, which are most often formed and inspired by ideological paradigms and political positions.

Nevertheless, whether jurisprudence meant the law to Nezami or not, it is clear that his recommendation is in line with what he does in his work, covering all the sciences he knew and religion as well. Amir Khosrow, known for his more social and political approach and views does not surprise the reader by being a little secular in this portrayal. Jami, for being an actual religious and Sufi thinker, makes religion the suggested field of study. However, I retain my literary approach that what the characters say should not be taken as the author's thinking in the classical context as most of the materials already existed and the authors were primarily concerned with reworking preexisting themes, tropes, and tales even to the point of creating literary techniques. Sometimes even the narrator in the poetic narratives does not necessarily speak for the authors. Critics also tend to compare the structure of these poets' books and the way each is divided and includes chapters before and/or after the main story and from these divisions draw conclusions. These introductory parts are almost all irrelevant to the plots of the stories.[53] As I discussed in Chap. 4 on Faith, Facts, and Fantasy, even such direct poems that are not written on behalf of any fictional character or figure consist of fictional and imaginative allegories in Nezami's work. Moreover, writing such additional chapters of classical books of poetry was a common practice that most of the time aimed to please a ruler possibly for better compensation. Considering all this, it becomes clear that Nezami lets the logic of the narrative, the environment, and the forces of the protagonists' life events determine how Majnun's father behaves rather than a predetermined quality in the man.

The characterization of the lovers' agency in the works of Nezami and Jami is also strikingly different. Nezami is realistic about what a man or a woman could do or not do in that time and place. Yet, as I explained in Chap. 3 on portrayal of women and love, Nezami's Layli is a strong woman as opposed to Majnun who, maddened by love, exhibits extreme weakness in the face of the tragedies that strike both him and Layli. His elasticity simply helps him to move from one distressful situation to another. As opposed to numerous critics who praise Nezami's work for its presumed protagonists' platonic love relationships, Majnun and Layli have and do express physical longing for each other.

Moreover, the following lines in Behruz Sarvatian's version, the second of which does not appear in Dastgerdi's version, speaks of kisses and carnal love more directly.

In a love's religion, where there is no making love	عشقی که دل اینچنین نورزد
Less than a barley grain is the value of that love.	در مذهب عشق جو نیرزد
I do not expect much from your lips	چون از لب تو طمع ندارم
A kiss will be my sole souvenir.	بوسی که دهی به یادگارم[54]

A few lines earlier, he expresses concern that his beloved might lose virginity but finds respite in the fact that she has an iron will.[55] Even in Jami's version, the lovers' desire for carnal love is inevitable.

Layli untied her hair.	آن حلقه زلف باز می کرد
Majnun reached lustfully to grab her.	وین دست هوس دراز می کرد[56]

As mentioned, Nezami has been praised for his so-called effat-e kalam and his chastity of speech, but critics forget that he has his way of speaking about sexuality and sex, and his pictorial allegories leave some things up to imagination.[57]

Finally, Nezami's work has been consequential in popularizing even further the genre of *manzumeh nevisi* (writing a long fictional and romantic narrative poem in masnavi meter). Nezami's *Layli o Majnun* has, in particular, been imitated, translated into other languages, adapted into other art forms, and compared with other world literary masterpieces such as *Romeo and Juliet* mostly because of the logical progression of the events, the accessible characterization (including inner and outer qualities), explainable changes in the peoples' mood and behavior, creative contemplation on human traits, and a picturesque description of places and nature. To these, we can add countless poets and artists who did not write their own story of Layli and Majnun but did use the concept of their love and related imageries in countless ways in their poetry and paintings. In the concise and compelling words of Seyed-Gohrab, "It is remarkable how the love between Layla and Majnun has become a source of inspiration for generations of poets and artists, crossing the boundaries of languages, cultures, and religions. The romance lives on in pop songs, novels, poetry, and the visual and material arts, showing people's fascination with unrequited love, immense faithfulness, the madness that creates art, the relationship between male and female, and the mystery of love."[58] Perhaps we can agree that it was after Nezami and in the works of other poets and artists that Layli and Majnun's characters and their love became models and a prototype because of reading Nezami's work as literature. It is a story of star crossed, unfulfilled, and tragic love, the type of which can still occur to this modern-day in certain situation and places.

To give a last and general example of the poet's preoccupation with literary constructions, one can think about the other versions of the story. It is not easy to imagine the tragic outcome of the tale if Majnun got married instead of Layli. Nezami's version makes the most sense in the way that Layli is forced to marry an older man and yet remains loyal to her true love. It is not an exaggeration to say that there is no contradiction in the characters' behavior in Nezami's version except those contradictions that are the result of the characters' reality of life and actions. Where there is a contradiction, there is a good explanation for it. All this means that this brief comparison offers yet another example in which one can challenge the notion that Nezami was a religious advocate and confirms his skills in constructing his pictorial allegories using all the available literary devices and techniques of his time and perfecting his own.

NOTES

1. For information on the story's root, see Heshmat Moayyad, "Dar Medar-e Nezami: Naqdi bar *Layli o Majnun*" in *IranShenani*, Fall 1992, no. 15, 548–522.

2. Asghar A. Seyed-Gohrab, "*Leyli o Majnun*," *Encyclopædia Iranica* (accessed on 16 October 2017). In "Majnun's Image as a Serpent," in *The Poetry of Nizami Ganjavi*, he argues that in contrast to the early Arabic sources that refer cryptically to Majnun's emaciated body and his nakedness, Nezami uses images of the serpent, among others, to depict Majnun's physical appearance and his complex character.

3. On this narrative poem, see Seyed-Gohrab, Ibid.

4. Based on his own words, Nezami was initially reluctant to versify it thinking that it did not offer enough poetic material.

5. See Jerome Clinton, "A Comparison of Nizami's *Layli and Majnun* and Shakespeare's *Romeo and Juliet*," *The Poetry of Nizami Ganjavi*, 15–27.

6. For an analysis of this romance, see Seyed-Gohrab, *Layli and Majnun: Love, Madness and Mystic Longing*.

7. Dick Davis, trans. *Layli and Majnun* by Nezami Ganjavi, 7. A literal translation of line 5 of this passage reads: Upon seeing that young golden beauty, Joseph / The observant maids of Zulaikhah would cut hands, instead of their orange. Similarly, line 7 can read, Qays saw her emblazing amorous gestures / became pallid as he desired that golden beauty.

8. *Kolliyat*, 325.

9. Nezami Ganjavi, *Layli and Majnun*, trans., Dick Davis, 25. This rendition, which is based on Sarvatiyan's edition, appears to be shorter than the original Persian passage quoted here based on H. Vahid Dastgerdi's edition. Those verses are analyzed below.

10. *Kolliyat*, 335–36.

11. Davis, trans. *Layli and Majnun*, 26.

12. *Kolliyat*, 335

13. Davis, trans. *Layli and Majnun*, 28.

14. *Kolliyat*, 335–36.

15. *Kolliyat*, 337.

16. Dick Davis, trans., *Layli and Majnun*, 32.

17. *Kolliyat*, 337.

18. In the Sarvatiyan edition and the translation, the verse below, the third line in the quoted passage, is omitted.

خشکار کرسنه را کبیج است / باسیری نان میده هیچ است

It means to a hungry person, bread made with unrefined, low-quality flour will be as delicious as a cookie, and to an already full, satisfied person, bread made with refined flour is nothing. The verse includes some obscure terms, but it adds to the imagery as the passage is about food and nutrition.
19. *Kolliyat*, 343.
20. This passage is among segments omitted in Sarvatiyan's edition (and consequently Davis' translation). A comparative analysis of Sarvatiyan's editorial decisions might explain the reason for this omission.
21. *Kolliyat*, 344.
22. Dick Davis, trans. *Layli and Majnun*, 47.
23. *Kolliyat*, 44.
24. These verses are omitted in Sarvatiyan's edition that was the basis for the translation.

ژان هردو برهشم خوش آواز / بر ساز بسی برهشم ساز

واهشان ز بد گزاف گویان / خود را به سرشک دیده شویان

25. *Kolliyat*, 85–346.
26. Dick Davis, trans. *Layli and Majnun*, 48 and 52.
27. *Kolliyat*, 346.
28. Dick Davis, trans. *Layli and Majnun*, 52.
29. *Kolliyat*, 346. The length of this segment might be attributed to its subjects being gardens and nature, some of Nezami's favorite themes to versify throughout his *Panj Ganj*.
30. *Kolliyat*, 348.
31. Davis, trans. *Layli and Majnun*, 54.
32. *Kolliyat*, 347.
33. The translation has even elaborated on the description.
34. Davis, trans. *Layli and Majnun*, 57; based on Sarvatiyan's edition, thus somewhat different.
35. *Kolliyat*, 348.
36. Nezami Ganjavi, *Kolliyat Khamseh*, ed. Dastgerdi, 4th ed. (Tehran: Amir Kabir, 1987), 344.
37. Davis, trans. *Layli and Majnun*, 67.
38. Asghar Seyed-Gohrab "Longing for Love: The Romance of Layla and Majnun" in *A Companion to World Literature*, ed. Ken Seigneurie (NY: John Wiley & Sons. 2020), 861–872.
39. *Kolliyat*, 377.
40. Davis, Nezami's *Layli and Majnun*, 127–28.
41. Nezami, *Layli o Majnun*, ed. Behruz Sarvatiyan (Tehran: Tus, 1984), 210–11. This passage from page 379 in Dastgerdi's edition does not include a few relevant lines. The word *sarkubeh* in Sarvatiyan's edition is

sarkuft in Dastgerdi's version. However, the word *har dam* in Sarvatiyan's version makes more sense than Dastgerdi's choice of *mardom*.
42. Davis, 185.
43. *Kolliyat,* 403.
44. *Kolliyat,* 347.
45. A description in Vahshi Bafeqi's *Farhd o Shirin* also insinuates that beauty is subjective. It begins with:

اگر در دیدۀ مجنون نشینی / به غیر از خوبی لیلی نبینی

46. Rypka, Jan, and Karl Jahn. *History of Iranian Literature* (Dordrecht: D. Reidel, 1968).
47. Nezami's *Layli o Majnun* has been compared to Shakespeare's *Romeo and Juliet* (see Jerome Clinton "A Comparison...."). Before this, in 1941, Ali Asghar Hekmat provided a comparison between the two stories. In recent years, several scholars have compared *Layli and Majnun* of Nezami to other poets such as Amir Khosrow, Jami, Maktabi, and others in more detail in terms of the components of the story and segmentation of the books. See, Hasan Zolfaqari, Moqayeseh Chahar Ravayat-e *Layli o Majnun* in *Pazhuhesh-ha-ye Zaban va Adabiayt*, 1, Spring 2009, 59–81. Also, see Khadivar and Sharifi, "Eshterakate *Layli o Majnun*-e".
48. See the article by Zolfaqari, who has provided a useful, comprehensive comparison of the summary of the four versions. Hasan Zolfaqari, "Moqateseh Chahar Ravayat-e *Layli o Majnun*," *Zaban va Adabiayt*, 1, Spring 2009, 59–81.
49. See chapter Conclusion: Applicability of Episodic Literary Movement in Arabic and Turkish Literature p. 173 in Kamran Talattof, *The Politics of Writing in Iran: A History of Modern Persian Literature.* (Syracuse: Syracuse UP, 2000).
50. Nizami Ganjavi, *Laili and Majnun: A Poem Translated by James Atkinson* (Reprinted and published by Panini office, Bahadurganj, Allahabad, 1915).
51. See note 47: Nezami's *Layli o Majnun* has ...
52. Abd al-Rahman Jami, *Layli o Majnun* in *Masnavi-e Haft Awrang* (Tehran: Sa'di, 1972) and Amir Khosrow Dehlavi, *Layli o Majnun* (Tehran: Ketabchin, 1969).
53. The common introductory parts are Hamd or praise and laudatory chapters, Ne'at or describing God or the prophet, me'raj or the story of ascension, Sabab-e Nazm-e Ketab or the reason for the completion of the book.
54. Nezami Ganjavi, *Layli o Majnun*, 1st edition, edited by Sarvatiyan (Tehran: Tus, 1984), 244.

55. Ibid, 243.
56. Abd al-Rahman Jami, *Layli o Majnun*, section 10.
57. The examples presented are only a few of many.
58. Asghar Seyed-Gohrab "Longing for Love." 861–872.

CHAPTER 7

In Search of Religion and Dantean Moments in "The Story of Mahan"

Thus far, I have supported my arguments about the subjects, themes, and motifs in Nezami's poetry by comparing them with other Persian poets and passingly with Shakespeare. Like the chapter on the Story of Ascension, this chapter is about fantasy, myth, and pictorial allegories. It also responds to a growing trend in comparing Nezami to other religious authors of different literary traditions and unending comparisons of Nezami to great Sufi and religious thinkers and his poetry to Koranic verses. For example, in 2021, many scholars presented papers comparing Nezami and Dante and the similarities of their poetic concepts and beliefs, which, despite their excellent quality and educative values, confirm the need to expand the scope of my comparison. The two poets may share an interest of mystical love and a devotion to their faith but the reason for my anomalous comparison is to show that both poets use allegory as a central method and quite well, too. I argue that there are more differences between Nezami and Dante than there are similarities. They have separate agendas in their poetic goals. Yet a discussion of the two beside one another does elicit some interesting notions.

Nezami Ganjavi (1141–1209) and Dante (1265–1321) share unique, creative imaginations and eloquence. Even though they lived in different eras and diverse cultural settings, their literary works have a few thematic similarities, including their interest in religious symbolism and love poetry. They also share the ability to produce captivating images and tales. For

© The Author(s), under exclusive license to Springer Nature Switzerland AG 2022
K. Talattof, *Nezami Ganjavi and Classical Persian Literature*, Literatures and Cultures of the Islamic World, https://doi.org/10.1007/978-3-030-97990-4_7

example, Dante's enduring literary portrayals of the angelic and demonic characters in his *Divine Comedy* share some of the fictional and fantastical qualities of Nezami's of five iterations of the story of ascension and his story of Mahan from *Seven Treasures*. Moreover, in terms of form, they both make use of heavy allegory in the construction of their literary works.

Beyond these surface similarities, their works are profoundly different in their literary message and allegorical meanings. This chapter analyzes the concepts of love and religion as they appear in both poets' works. It also discusses the distinct functions of allegory in these poets' poetry.

As stated at the outset, a shared aspect of these writers' works is the place of love in their poems. Dante provides a doting description of Beatrice and his love for her. Nezami pens sweet poems in praise of his female characters, including Shirin (from *Khosrow o Shirin*) and Layli (from *Layli o Majnun*). However, because Nezami writes scant few lines about his love for his deceased wife, Afaq, a comparison between the two poets regarding love will have to focus mainly on the concept of love itself.

In Chap. 3 on love and women, I analyzed some of Nezami's love poetry and showed that he portrays carnal love as well as other types of love including a love that is divine or profane, fruitful or unfulfilled, lyrical or lustful, based on attraction or obsession, enflamed feelings or long-lasting infatuation in *Haft Paykar* and his other romances. The analysis showed that reading a verse, a few lines, or even a passage of Nezami as solely a Sufi expression of love one has for God is tantamount to ignoring the enormity of Nezami's conceptualization of human sensibility and his creative imagination. As for Dante, love, which is personified as an entity in Purgatory and Hell, is, ultimately, a divine concept, a notion related to God, embodied in Beatrice. The character of Virgil at one point in Dante's work explains that there are two principles concerning love; whom to love and how much and love for God, which cannot be mistaken.

> The natural is always without error,
> but mental love may choose an evil object
> or err through too much or too little vigor.[1]

For Nezami, carnal love is an option, and so is an elective love. He portrays them in the narratives of *Khosrow o Shirin* and *Layli o Majnun* and their introductory parts. Thus, the concepts of love are not exactly similar in the works of these poets.

There is no doubt that medieval religious books such as the Bible and the Koran influenced classical works of the time. However, some poets took it upon themselves to write and explicitly promote their religions, while some used a religious themes and motifs for literary purposes. Dante wrote the *Divine Comedy* to serve and help the Bible. As Kleinhenz notes, "The pattern of typology, allegory, and Providential history found in the tradition of biblical hermeneutics form the intellectual, literary, and theological bases of the *Divine Comedy*."[2] This chapter argues, in its comparison to Dante, that Nezami belonged to the second category. Nezami referred to Koranic verses as one of the many fields of common knowledge that enriches the thematic aspects of his poetry. I will return to a more general discussion of this issue shortly.

THE RELEVANCE OF ALLEGORY

The most vital area of comparison between their literary endeavors is their ability to construct colorful allegories. Dante's *Divine Comedy* is an enormous allegory, which conveys commentaries on, primarily and paradoxically, religion, politics, and love. Such subjects and themes also exist in the construction of what I term Nezamian allegories. This presentation reviews the allegorical and metaphorical aspects of some of these two authors' works. It analyzes the poetic hermeneutics, verbosity, and brevity with which they have composed their prosody.

Both Dante and Nezami use natural (and supernatural) motifs in their portrayal of their allegorical constructs. For example, Dante fantasizes a forest where he is lost, the place where he encounters Beatrice, and where Beatrice summons Virgil. In his use of natural (or supernatural) elements, Nezami often illustrates Persian gardens, prairies, and mountains, as well as the imagined connections of the stars with human life. Dante travels through the nine layers of Hell; Nezami takes the readers through nine levels of the skies. Dante comes out of the valley of disappointment to convey the hopeful message of salvation through Catholicism; Nezami takes his characters through tragedies to convey the redeeming quality of reason.

Nezami has verses about paradise and hell, and more so, he has used these words as adjectives.[3] In that regard, these concepts might be suitable for comparison with the extensive amount of verses Dante has written about hell and paradise. In terms of allegory, one might compare the story of Mahan from *Haft Paykar* with Dante's work to find more differences between them even in the portrayal of such common fantasies. To lay down a context for such comparison, let us first reaffirm our understanding of the nature of myth.

ALLEGORY OF ASCENSION

Nezami's five renditions of the mythical story of ascension as a myth constitute yet another Nezamian pictorial allegory, and in that regard, it resembles the *Divine Comedy* as an allegory. Nezami offers a highly religious story of the ascension of Mohammad to heaven or *me'raj*. The story of ascension, which has appeared in all of his five books, is a literary portrayal based on exceptionally religious and yet fantastic material. It is another excellent example of Nezami's poetic process of imagination and pictorial allegory, in general, and the expression of his cosmic knowledge in particular. To be sure, there are clear religious connections in all five poems, but as my analysis shows, they can be understood in terms of their sheer literariness.

Just as Dante's eventual ascension crosses through nine spheres of Heaven, including the Moon and many planets, Nezami colorfully portrays celestial bodies, including Mercury, Venus, the Sun, Mars, Jupiter, Saturn, and a few stars in those stories of ascension. Each of these celestial bodies is associated with one or another angel and some other religious characters. Both Nezami and Dante use the association of stars and planets with one or other aspects of human life, such as love. Dante's work also presents an eschatological purification process in seven stages, giving importance to the number seven. This digit also represents crucial concepts in Nezami's work for different reasons. Indeed, the number embodies a physical and spritual wholeness in many cultures. Moreover, like in *Divine Comedy*, in Nezami's various stories of ascension, angels and several past prophets are met in multiple levels, and all in a positive light, unlike Dante, who differentiates between them. Through their work, both have enriched their language in significant ways. However, *Divine Comedy* is a self-portrayal work; whereas, Nezami chooses the prophet of Islam as the protagonist of the journey. *Divine Comedy* is a commentary on Christianity (and other religions), a rendition of mystic eschatological purification in seven stages, and a political allegory that aims to criticize the dominant system whereas Nezami's stories are literary constructs hinging on widespread knowledge, and not preaching an ideology in a literary form. This comparison shows how we can somewhat effectively distinguish a mystical, religious literary work from a literary work that simply manipulates mystical and religious notions.

A LITERARY READING OF A LITERARY WORK: THE STORY OF MAHAN

Let us take a closer look at "The Story of Mahan" from *Haft Paykar*. On Wednesday of Mercury, Bahram Gur goes to the Turquoise Castle and, as in other cases, asks Princess Azargun of Maghreb to tell him a (sensual) story. Dressed in turquoise, she tells him the story of Mahan, which might or might not be sensual enough for the king's taste. An abridged version of the story is this. Mahan, an impressive, attractive young Egyptian man, slightly drunk, meets a business partner during a drinking party in a garden. The friend offers him a share of his newly gained treasure. Mahan hurries after him and ends up in a desolate desert. After a few more horrific episodes and encounters with demons and witches, he finds himself in a garden where he agrees to spend the night in a comfortable place in a sandalwood tree. However, he descended to feast with a beautiful princess who turned into a beast. Mahan weeps in remorse at having given in to those temptations. The immortal green prophet Khizr appears to save him. When Mahan awakes back at home, he finds his friends in blue mourning clothes, who had assumed he was dead. He, too, dresses in blue and joins them.

Scholars who believe Nezami was a Sufi writer should invest time in Mahan's story because it lends itself to such reading better than the stories of Shirin or Layli.[4] However, even if Nezami meant for the story of Mahan to represent a Sufi philosophy, I would still argue that the message is not strong and that such a quality is only part of a creative process.

To read the story of Mahan as a Sufi representation, one must read each episode as one of the stages of the Sufi path that leads a disciple toward unity with God. And these scholars often emphasize reading the story as a treaty of a Sufi (a religious man of a Sufi sect) and not even a versified story by an *aref* (an educated man).[5] Therefore, according to mystical analysis, the old man character or apparition of Khizr (or Khezr, the folkloric immortal prophet) can be perceived as the wise guide (*pir, morshed*). Accordingly, Mahan is ignorant, replete with human faulty traits, takes the Sufi journey through a path that challenges him over seven difficult stages aimed toward perfection and unity with God as represented by Khizr.

Nezami has added a few Arabic or Koranic terms that can help Sufi readers to substantiate their argument about the mystic meaning of the story. There is even the mention of a bird for some scholars to connect this story to Attar's version of Simorgh. Again, I believe this whole concept of *morshed* or *pir* versus *morid* or *salek* (the spiritual adviser, the wise guide versus the disciple, the devotee) needs to be reconsidered as an explanatory model for understanding causality.[6] The story of Mahan also portrays the challenges an imperfect *kherad* faces when encountering a dire situation. This portrayal seems to be influenced by the somewhat rational movements which produced the thoughts of Razi, the philosopher of Ray.

IT IS MORE THAN THAT: THE FABRIC OF A FANTASY

First, let us start with the word seven. The story of Mahan is presented in seven episodes, literally as in seven plays depicting four terrifying nights. Moreover, there is not much clarity about the origin of the story, except that number seven corresponds to numerous other (ancient) ways the number plays a structural role; it has nothing to do with Sufi stages. Most of Nezami's stories in *Haft Paykar* and his other books existed prior in far less developed or in even oral forms. In *Haft Paykar*, the stories told by the princess of each country or climate seem to have relevance with their land. In the case of Mahan's Egypt, such stories could have begun to shape in Alexandria since the time of Plato. Let us free the poetic construct from limiting Sufi interpretations; let us elaborate on the literary construct of each episode of the story, analyze them textually, and consider the alternative meanings and messages. We should keep in mind that in analyzing a myth or those stories of ascension, we are not looking for a rational explanation. We cannot ask why a character does this or that. Demons, ghouls (forest or desert demons), *divs* (devil, demon, jinn), and winged dragons (a wyvern acting more like a hydra) and the way they appear and disappear are not there to make sense. However, when Nezami, from the tongue of a character, refers to them as *bikherad* (irrational), we understand their metaphysical use.

Moreover, their understanding of Zoroastrianism still shaped the concept of demonic forces at Nezami's time. It was as dynamic as Ahriman, who would deploy these creatures as his weaponized army. The demons and the evil influences in Mahan's story can challenge the goodness, the powers of Ahura. This equation is quite different from its counterpart in Islam, and to some extent, in other Abrahamic religions, where the force of good, the deity, has absolute power.

Episode 1 On a summer night, Mahan Hushyar, a young handsome Egyptian man, is invited to a party in a nobleman's garden.[7] A few hours into the night, after long hours of drinking wine and eating delightful foods of all sorts and everyone enjoying other pleasures, he decides to take a walk. Half drunk and happy, he encounters one of his friends, Hayel, a business partner, who offers him a share of his newly gained treasure if Mahan follows him. Mahan follows him, but he feels he has gone too far, is 'off track,' and lost. Yet, he continues to trust the friend and follows him further, though his perception of time and place grows fuzzier.

This episode in a Sufi reading is interpreted as the author's rejection of greed, avarice, or material world. However, as discussed, Nezami has glamorized wealth and prosperity on numerous occasions. He has asked for compensation in numerous verses. And the character in the poem is, after all, posed to accept the offered money. Another meaning of this passage that reoccurs in the story and many other stories of Nezami is the question of misjudgment. Due to excessive drinking and intoxication, Mahan gets dizzy, and his judgment becomes impaired.

When Mahan's brain turned hot with wine	مغز ماهان چو گرم شد ز شراب
He saw the reflection of the moon and water roiling.	تابش ماه دید و گردش آب[8]

Mahan's first failure occurs when he is in a state of drunkenness, in a not-so-dark night in a palm grove far from the greens of the garden. It becomes apparent that a *div* makes him believe that they are friends and business partners, and thus Mahan follows him.

Episode 2 As he follows the friend for too long, Mahan begins to doubt his own perception. The next day, Mahan finds himself tired, dehydrated, and the so-called friend nowhere in sight. With no other option, he continues to walk and takes rest at the entrance to a cave. In his languor, he hears the conversation of a woman and a man named Hayla and horrible Ghalya.[9] The man approaches him and asks what he is doing in this forsaken land. Mahan tells them his story of his encounter with the friend in the garden and how the so-called friend dragged him out of that paradise. They say to him that the man who seemed to be his friend was, in fact, Hayel, one of the deceptive ghouls and *divs* of the desert. The couple takes Mahan with them bemoaning his bad luck at having been duped. *Ghouls* and *divs* used interchangeably are devious demonic creatures that can appear in human form to destroy them. We should remember that the ideas of divs (ghoul or devious spirit) have a long history in the Zoroastrian struggle against evil. The Zoroastrian book of *Vandida* written in the Avestan language, is a legal and jurisprudence book containing the anti-divs laws. As in the latter part of the mythical stories of the *Shahnameh*, divs and demons personified human beings' wicked traits, a frequent practice in numerous traditions. Nezami is clear in this episode; he even names the man who deceived Mahan in the garden as Hayel, the demon div of deception. However, Mahan's deficiency of good judgment is profound. He misjudges the couple as well. They leave him alone and disappear.

Episode 3 Mahan finds himself alone in a ditch at the next dawn. He keeps going until the dark, when he sees a horseman who also hears from Mahan his strange experiences and growing despair. The horseman says, "That couple was Hayla and Ghayla, the divs of evildoing. Still, you are lucky because they run away at dawn with the song of roosters." Again, the occasional mention of a rooster is perhaps a reference to Soroush, the Zoroastrian angle, who appears in this story as Khizr at the end as Mahan's subconscious. He offers his other horse to Mahan, who fails to ask himself why a rider in the middle of nowhere is giving him a horse. Once more, he misjudges a man and the situation.

Episode 4 After going for a while and passing a mountain, he arrives in a flat field and is delirious again. He feels he is in a desert of terror where he hears uncanny, delusive noises, and he sees thousands of dark shadowy devilish creatures who look like a combination of cows and elephants, having horns and trunks. They also carry a burning torch in their hands, a cowbell on their neck, while flames come out of their mouth, all trying to cajole him into doing this or that. From their now louder sound, Mahan's horse began moving around, prancing up and down. He realizes that the horse was a disguised seven-headed, four-legged, winged dragon from hell. He must battle this creature all day and night in utter fear in order to get rid of it and to move on. For the first time he acts, but still with no good judgment of the situation. It is clear how he does away with the winged dragon but not the thousand ghouls that were also moving toward him. Did he imagine all those in a state of delirium and dehydration? Was this episode a part of a longer drunken dream that started with his departure from the party in the garden?

Episode 5 The following day, Mahan looks around and finds himself past the hellish desert. Mahan rubs his eyes and sees a stretch of endless desert, hot as hell, covered with red and blood-colored, feeling like a leather carpet painted by a bleeding severed head, wild beats' trap, with poisonous air. His response is to run like smoke (dud) all day, so at night he gets out of that "hell." Nezami, instead of describing hell, uses hell as an adjective or simile. Mahan rubs his eyes and sees a stretch of endless desert, hot as hell, covered with red and blood-colored, feeling like leather carpet painted by a bleeding severed head, wild beasts' trap, with poisonous air. His response is to run like smoke (*dud*) all day, so at night he gets out of that "hell."

Episode 6 After that, he arrives in a lush green field with running streams. He washes up, enjoys the solace, and continues on his way until he arrives at a vast, deep shaft, a well system.[10] Deep in the bottom of the well, he takes a nap. Nezami does not mention purgatory (*barzakh*), however, this place in the well functions as a place between the hellish, demon-infested desert and the Eram paradise on the other side. However, as we will read, that Eram or paradise is also a production of perception.

When Mahan awakes, he carves his way out of the well into a fruit garden, and without hesitation he begins to indulge. The verses here explain the garden in terms of paradise. Nezami also refers to as Eram (the famous Persian earthly garden/paradise) with orchards and countless cypress trees and Buxaceae or marjoram plants. He sees tall, productive, and voluminous fruit trees of pistachio, apples, pomegranate, peach, banana, dates, pear, jujube fruit, fig, almond, orange, grapes, and honeydew. He begins helping himself.

Suddenly an older man shows up and scolds him for taking the fruits. However, he forgives Mahan after hearing his story and explanations. Here the reader is presented with the images of the divs, which are imagined according to ancient thinking, and Nezami inserts his usual dichotomized constructs, like hell versus paradise, through the words of his character.

In darkness is the key to light;	تیرگی را ز روشنی است کلید
Only in black can one see white.[11]	در سیاهی سپید شاید دید

This line refers to the previous shift in his unwanted journey when a hole and ray of light gives him hope at the bottom of the well, encouraging him to dig through the rocks to get to the garden, another magical moment.

As the wealthy older man tries to make sense of Mahan's story, he explains that those deceitful people are foolish and crooked, just like those *divs*. He then offers to adopt him as his son, give him his wealth, and find him a beautiful bride. He tells him about the future predicaments awaiting Mahan and warns him about all the forthcoming dangers. Finally, the older man takes Mahan to a heavenly palace-like place by a sandal tree in a paradise-like garden. He asks him to take a leather ladder to go up and stay there the entire night (and just that one night) and not descend under any circumstance. Here is Mahan's chance to think, evaluate, pose the question, and produce an evaluation of the events thus far. Does he, though, when he is enticed to descend and join a party with seventeen beautiful princesses? In a myth, we are not as concerned with logic; instead, we turn inward for answers. So, it will also be a chance for Bahram to think.

Enjoying the lofty comfort of the seat and the delight of the food, he begins to relax in the amber ambiance of the moon. Not surprisingly, at this point, the night arrives, and Mahan hears and sees 17 beautiful princesses with 17 other beautiful girls picnicking, partying, drinking wine, playing music, and singing seductive songs down below the tree. As if this is not enough to seduce Mahan, a gentle wind blows and reveals the citron-like breasts of those elegant, enthralling, enticing girls from under their white linen garments. The princess eventually invites Mahan to join. Of course, Mahan does not hesitate, he joins them, and makes love to one of them who seems to be leading the group.

All the natural metaphors rendered to portray the garden, sandal tree, the various fruits, and the wine reappear in this section in different forms and combinations to picture a sensual and suggestive scene of lovemaking, albeit of a Faustian nature.[12] A joss stick, the source of pure wine, ruby seal, and an agate, a carnelian refer to their sex organs and intercourse. This section might have satisfied King Bahram's craving for an erotic story, but the story has yet another twist. And yes, Nezami had "adhered" to "chastity of words" by using descriptive terms for body parts and actions.

The segment abruptly ends, and Mahan realizes that once again, a trick has been played on him; the beautiful girl turns out to be a haggish witch (which reminds one of the siren in Dante's tale) with an occultist nature. She also has a few sobering words for Mahan, asking him why he desired her only when she looked good. There is no rebuke for sexual desire; the enigma lies with the subject of desire.[13] Nezami portrays scenes with a beautiful princess and her beautiful entourage on several other occasions in *Khosrow o Shirin* and *Haft Paykar*, always vividly describing the women's lips, neck, body, and breast, occasionally even referencing their sexual organ. Such portrayals, which became a significant part of romance writing, are often associated with monarchs and royal courts, inspired by ancient history.[14] The late medieval European romance writers used similar techniques, albeit more liberally. Mahan's inability to learn from his previous mistakes and misjudgments is, however, of vital importance. He once again fails in his judgment. He ignores the foster father's condition, so easily forgetting why he is on the top of a tree, and not second guessing why so many pretty girls could show up at the bottom of the tree at that time of the night. Couldn't Nezami, the learned man, have used this archetype mythical tale to say something about the dire consequence of the failure to recognize patterns by which demons, ghouls, and ignorant people behave irrationally? In the morning, he opens his eyes, and he finds himself in an ugly place, in an inflamed hell replete with corpses, rotten bones, strange creatures, and feces. There is no sign of the previous night's paradise.

Episode 7 Mahan has no more excuses. This time, he has had many warnings. Mustn't he change now? He produces a primal scream, a scream you hear when "women give birth to a child," and he moves away as far as he can until he arrives at the site of a clear water source. He questions his perception; he washes up, repents, and asks God for forgiveness. The mythical immortal green-clothed prophet Khizr appears to him to take his hand. Khizr tells him that "because of your good intentions, I will help you go home."

I am Khizr, o pious man;	گفت من خضرم ای خدای پرست
And I have come to take your hand.	آمدم تا ترا بگیرم دست
By your new, pure invention formed	نیت نیک تست کامد پیش
I'll take you back to your own home.[15]	می‌رساند ترا به خانه خویش[16]

Neither the old man who owns the garden nor Khizr offers him advice and guidance about any specific path. Mahan promises himself to never, ever seek vice or commit bad deeds again. Upon that pledge, he is suddenly catapulted back to Egypt and finds his friends sitting sad and dressed in azure. He, too, is dressed in azure like his friends and he launches into tales of his adventures.

The remaining verses are about the color blue as in the shades of azure blue and turquoise blue to find the story's way back to the pavilion with Bahram, who having heard the story is excited and sleeps with Azargun, the marigold, and is pleased.

Before this last part, Mahan could see all the other characters walking toward him. However, Khizr appears to Mahan out of nowhere and more like an apparition that somewhat and somehow resembles Mahan. This indicates a transformative moment in which Mahan realizes a level of self-consciousness (thus the use here of the name Hushyar, observant).

As mentioned earlier, a myth often has a religious and ideological quality. Still, this reading shows that Nezami has manipulated whatever the original story had been to provide several subtexts and contexts. According to him, there is nothing wrong with wealth, talking to a couple, accepting a horse, beautiful girls, and sex. However, these are among the fertile areas in which grave mistakes and greed increase.

As for patterns, numbers, and colors (elements that are overused in mystic readings), all stories in *Haft Paykar* feature them. The entire book contains numbers and numerical patterns. The story begins when Bahram Gur (a Persian romantic king (421–438) and a renowned hunter) finds the portraits of seven princesses in a room and decides that he wants all the princess as his wives. To make his affairs easy, he orders a building erected for each, domed pavilions with a color that symbolizes the climates from which each of the girls comes. The pavilions are associated with a day of the week and the name of a planet. Afterward, he visits one building a day from the first of the week to the last. He asks each of the princesses to tell a sensual tale matching the mood of the color of the pavilion and the planet. This is the larger frame story that encompasses shorter stories based on the Indo-Iranian tradition of storytelling. It dichotomizes many aspects of life from day and night, black and light, and darkness to Paradise and Hell. It juxtaposes the natural, historical, fictional, Islamic, and Zoroastrian concepts and signs. It includes type, prototype, archetype, and specific characters.

The entire story might be seen as an allegory, starting with the description of the storytelling princess and colors to set the mood for fantasy. However, each one of the above episodes also has the characteristics of a pictorial allegory. In most of them, the first story uses colors, sounds, and descriptions of land before describing the event that occurs in that land. The episode in paradise's (*pardis* in the original Persian) fruit garden begins with the description of a lengthy list of fruits that cannot realistically grow in the same region. However, those descriptions foretell the next event, which involves beautiful women (however fake they might be), wine, and sex. *Shaftaloo* or *holu* (peach) connotes the cheek of a beautiful woman or a lover's kiss; jujube fruit refers to the color of the lip of a mistress, *shemshad* (boxwood or marjoram plants) always indicates the tall, elegant, figure of a beloved; pistachio refers to women's sex organ; and *anar* or *nar* (pomegranate), in Nezami's poetry, is rarely anything but women's breasts. The words ab-e *angur* (the water of grapes) always mean wine. Even the large, sweet apples contain wine. *Shekar khand* (sweet smile) is yet another reference to the smile of a female beloved, used in many other poems. Perhaps the writing about such an assortment or reciting them is the most voluptuous description to a king that could have had a sensual effect. Still, the lines containing them are part of the pictures which includes the spicy party with 17 lithe girls in the story of that night.

The trials or labors in the story of Mahan are about the difficulty of overcoming the common human flaws, the most consequential of which is naïveté, catalyzed by three deceivers Hayel, Hayla, and Ghayla as well as the old man. Khizr, in the end, might be a Nezamian metaphor for self-awareness, which he sees necessary for the arrival, finally, of good judgment. It should not be a surprise that Nezami might use such a metaphor. As Patrick Frank notices in the story of Khosrow and Shirin, Nezami "relates that one day when he came to his patron, the Seljuq sultan Toghrol Shah III, the ruler dismissed his cup-bearers and musicians saying: 'Since now Khizr has come, we should turn away from wine/in order to gain the Water of Life from Khizr.'"[17] Moreover, Frank offers a perceptive interpretation of the scene where Khizr appears to Mahan. He writes, "In this self-presentation, Khizr links his apparition with the mental change of the hero: he has come in his usual function as helper for those in distress, but also as the personification of the hero's 'good intention.'"[18]

Finally, if one can see a connection between the story of Mahan and Sufi ideology, one can think of other possible connections just as easily. The stories told by the seven princesses address Bahram directly or indirectly. Each of them targets a flaw in the king and tries to correct him by showing how the protagonist in the stories dealt with similar problems. In attempting to portray the education of a Zoroastrian king, Nezami could have naturally been inspired by another Zoroastrian and pre-Islamic concept. Mahan is reminiscent of a name in the book of Zoroastrian judicial, social, moral, civil, and criminal codes and laws entitled *Matigan-e Hezar Datistan* (*Book of a Thousand Judgements*).[19] Given that name and the subject of judgment, that book or knowledge of it generally could have been a source of Nezam's inspiration, as was the case with the concept of Kherad and the book of *Minuye Kherad*. Given this possibility, we might notice that the key concept amid flawed humanity common in all seven episodes is misperception. Mahan lacks judgment when he mistakes Hayel for a friend, Hayla and Ghayla for fellow wanderers, the rider for a benevolent fellow traveler, and the princess for a beautiful sex partner. In that regard, no one can for sure read the story as the description of a disciple who strives to pass through seven trials, or barriers, or stages of Sufism.

To extend this interpretation further, Khizr in this story functions very much like the divine Zoroastrian *Soroush*, which can also be written as *Sarosh, Sorush*, and in Avesta as Saravash. This name can mean angel, the 17th day of every solar month (which is also mentioned in the story, and it is not considered a good thing), intellect, and even Gabriel.[20] Of course, Soroush also played a prominent role in the stories of Ferdowsi's *Shahnameh*, and Nezami could have well taken his model from that book if not directly from Zoroastrian sources. One of Soroush's functions in Zoroastrian mythology was to make demons disappear. Ahmad Khorasani and Tayebeh Golestani, who provide a similar interpretation of this story, describe the Angel (or God as they call him) Soroush as the God of truth, promise, awareness, contentment, justice, and the enemy of the *divs* (demons/ghouls) and other traits. Accordingly, drunkenness, greed, breaking promises, laziness, and a few other flaws cause plagues and are represented by the *divs* (and the ghouls).[21] They believe that at the end of each of the four encounters with the divs, a rooster, Soroush's companion appears to counter the evil forces.[22] However, Nezami does not mention this God-like angel in this story even though he does so elsewhere frequently. Another possible explanation of the similarity of Khizr's apparition to Mahan is that at that moment of self-awareness, his anima emerges to guide him, very much the role that Beatrice played for Dante's character in his allegory.[23]

Therefore, there are similarities between Dante and Nezami in their influential use of a few themes and motifs. Dante and Nezami have used imageries regarding hell and Paradise in their fantastical allegories, albeit more elaborately in the former's works. Moreover, they were both highly influential. Dante changed the Italian literary language and helped to shape people's imagination of hell and Paradise. Nezami influenced the writing styles of poets in the Persianate world and beyond and set the criteria for romance poetry.

Nezami makes it easy for us and explains the nature of his book. The following verses are from a longer section in which he describes *Haft Paykar* as a literary and artistic product.

> A tale both fine and rare, a gift, / with supple bones and sweetest pith.
> That you may see its beauty clear, / with every art I've decked it fair
> My grace comes easy, costs me slight; / It decks with precious gems each point;
> Some untouched lovelies, virgins all, / like rose-buds 'neath a silken veil.[24]

The longer version presents the components of Nezamian allegory and the way he describes it, namely as poetry that includes his various arts, sources of knowledge, rhetoric and Sakhon. It explains what he means by secrets (dilemmas of *kherad*) and the key (painting and pointing them out) to facilitate understanding while enjoying them like the eternal water of life. The first two lines of the section[25] and its title, "On the Completion of the Book and Prayers for [king] Ala a-Din Karp Arsenal," further confirms another aspect of Nezami's matière, namely his connection with the court.

Thus, Dante and Nezami have used imageries regarding hell and paradise in their fantastical allegories, albeit more elaborately in the former's works. It requires extensive research and studies to find further connections and a possible common source. For example, were both authors familiar with the small Sasanian book of *Arda Viraf* (*Arda Viraz Nameh*) written in Middle Persian through its Arabic and Persian translation? The book narrates the dream journey of a pious Zoroastrian into the ether world. "Wīrāz was sent in order to verify (1) Zoroastrian belief about the invisible world, and (2) the efficacy of the rituals of the Zoroastrian community. This scene of piety troubled by religious uncertainty seems to be set some time after the fall of the Achaemenid Empire; but the final redaction of the text probably refers to the early Islamic period (see especially Ardā Wīrāz 1.23–27 for an explanation of the journey's purposes)."[26] Furthermore, its plots, events, and characters are like those of *Divine Comedy*: both depict (with various levels of focus and intensity) hell, purgatory, paradise, a woman representing faith, nature of meetings, and includes an episode like the story of ascension.[27]

Otherwise, Dante's allegory is more social and political, and Nezami's allegory, as explained, is to help his literary construct related to human nature, a part of *Haft Paykar*'s overall meaning. I also believe Dante and Nezami are different because of the historical and cultural settings in which they wrote their masterpieces but also in terms of their genre and function of their allegorical constructs. Nezami's "The Story of Mahan" comes close to the fantastical portrayals of supernatural phenomena in Dante's *Divine Comedy*. However different their messages might be, they both contain allegories highlighting human values. In the poems discussed here, both have used fantasy and surreal themes to contemplate rationality and reason.

Considering the studies of the stories of *Layli o Majnun*, various stories of ascension in previous chapters, and "The Story of Mahan" we might also revisit the questions of religion and mystic themes in Nezami's poetry. To show that "The Story of Mahan," as another fantasy and mythical type of portrayal is different from Dante's work in terms of religion, I will explain the appearance of religion and myth in Nezami's work in a little more detail here. Dante's religiosity is not generally disputed.

ISLAM, MYSTICISM, AND ZOROASTRIANISM FOR NEZAMI

There is no doubt that in *Makhzan al-Asrar* (*The Treasure House of Secrets*) and in many introductory segments of his romances, Nezami devotes a significant amount of space to poetry that revolves around religious motifs. These expressions have caused many scholars to read his work solely through a religious lens. These expressions, however, are not intrinsic to the stories. In writing them, he has a rather habitual professional purpose: writing poetry on various themes resulting in the division of his introduction into many preset topics. These topics might have universal appeal, but it is how Nezami tells them that keep them alive. Many of those passages reveal his notion of religion via creative writing rather than dogmatic religious doctrine. **As the discussion of the ascension story in that book showed, his form is his real treasure, his treasure box, treasure house, where he keeps the gems and pearls with which he weaves his poetry.** Another example of this is his ascension story that resembles fantasy (and even science fiction in its broader sense) more than religious verse. In them, his pictorial allegories use religious notions to move toward the goal of their versification. The following passage from *Layli o Majnun* exemplifies this notion well. He uses a religious allegorical/simile construct for the portrayal of the beloved.

My Ka'ba is the beauty of your face	ای کعبه من جمال رویت
My altar is your residing place.	محراب من آستان کویت[28]

Allegories of the *Ka'beh* toward which Muslims do their daily prayers and the allegory of *Mehrab* or altar give meanings to the description of the desire and love of the narrator for his beloved (Majnun and Layli) and at the same time refer to a prominent religious narrative. Sometimes a poet might reverse the process of such portrayal by using a personal narrative to portray a religious conviction, such as love for God. In both cases, the very act of allegorization is meant to be the center of attention, not real religious fervor. In *Layli o Majnun*, he writes:

Let me stay with you, that is my need	بگذار که از سر نیازی
Let me pray in your direction, I must indeed.	در قبله تو کنم نمازی
If I make a mistake in the number of prostrations	گر سهو شود به سجده راهم
I will seek pardon in my makeup prayers.	در سجده سهو عذر خواهم[29]

In these poems, all elements are allegorical, and all are derived from religion, and yet none has anything to do with religiosity. By such parallel imagery, the poet demonstrates that he not only understands the messages and daily rituals of different religions, but that he is also able to render them playfully, masterfully, and eloquently. By the way, Majnun's answer that "you and I do not contain in the same skin because I am killing myself and you are in love with yourself" has been used as an indication of the author's mysticism. Majnun is literarily dying because of his poor living condition and malnutrition. He is not saying that I have killed the self in me, allegedly a mystic creed. Yet, he also says that he can live without food or without the need to satisfy his other physical needs: love.

Again, Nezami draws on religious themes or even religious philosophy for his metaphorical and allegorical constructs. Here is another example of his neutrality vis-à-vis the content of the subject from a segment of *Layli o Majnun* when Layli's husband dies.

Whatever happens in the world possesses	هر نکه که بر نشان کارست
A necessary purpose it addresses,	دروی به ضرورت اختیارست
All that exists is subject to control,	در جنش هر چه هست موجود
Leading it on to its predestined goal.	درهی است ز درهمای مقصود
A piece of paper has two separate sides,	کاغذ ورق دو روی دارد
When one is visible, the other hides;	کماجگه از دو سوی دارد
On this side are the plans we contemplate,	زین سوی ورق شمار تدبیر
On that side are the reckonings of fate;	زانسوی دگر حساب تقدیر
Few writings on one side have any guide	کم باید کاتب قلم راست
To what is written on the other side-	آن هر دو حساب را به هم راست
You count so many roses, how they charm you,	بس گل که تو گل کی شمارش
But pick them and their hidden thorns will harm you;	بینی به گرد خویش خارش
Going by just their colors and their shapes,	بس خوشه حصرم از نمایش
Who can distinguish sweet from bitter grapes?	کانگور بود به آزمایش
Many are hungry, and they think that when	بس گرسنگی که مستی آرد
They eat a great deal they'll be well again,	در هاضمه تندرستی آرد
Although the opposite is also true	بر وفق چنین خلاف کاری
Since overeating can be bad for you,	تسلیم به از ستیزه کاری
And moderate fasting's often preferable	القصه، چو قصه این چنین است
To wolfing victuals down until you're full;	پندار که سر که انگبین است[31]
To sum up, then, just as the proverbs say,	
Appearances can lead us all astray.[30]	

His relativism is drawn from his poetics, and his poetics determines his position on the subject. Furthermore, in a section of *Layli o Majnun*, Nezami poses a philosophical or jurisprudential question to explain later the condition and mindset of his characters.[32] In this passage, Nezami presents an elegant way of circumventing the concept of determinism and free will (جبر و اختیار), which was contentiously debated among the different schools of Islamic thought. Nezami humanizes, materializes, and otherwise canonicalizes religious jurisprudence or at least philosophical questions in these lines. It is also interesting to note that Dastgerdi, Sarvatian, and Zanjani have offered slightly different translations by selecting options from the original manuscripts available to them and show slightly different tendencies as to how the passage should be read and interpreted. One last point about the passage is that here, too, Nezami's view on eating is more influenced by *Minuye Kherad*, which advises against overindulging, than the sources of his own time.

I should also add that some of these so-called religious references are not even necessarily Islamic. They passingly point to the tenants of the Abrahamic religions, the Mesopotamian myth of creation, and widely known Biblical tales such as the story of Joseph in the well and Egypt

(Genesis 37:12–36) and various early and late prophets Moses, Jesus, and Mohammad. As mentioned in Chap. 2 regarding Sakhon, Nezami sometimes seems to say that he is authoring a book as essential or eloquent as the *Koran*, perhaps an impressive and daring statement to make in his time. For Nezami, religion and history did not begin with Islam, which is significantly influenced by the previous ideological metaphorical paradigms. His description of religion and spirituality (which he uses as subjects and theme for his poetry) are gentle and general and can be applied to any religion, including Zoroastrianism. Many of his statements philosophically resemble the advice about religion in *Minuye Kherad*. To be sure, western poets, Christian or secular, also refer to and construct pieces upon the texts and stories of books of Ruth, Job, and Daniel, as well as the Psalms and the Song of Solomon, and the contemporary literary scholars read their works using a variety of literary approaches and do not always claim that because a poet involves a Biblical character or well-known tale that the poet is then being religious or writing with religious intentions.

All chapters of this book have, in one way or another, challenged the notion that Nezami promoted Islam or Sufism and that these ideologies inspired him. Since the allegation is a central subject of this book, I continue to provide a few more examples. The claim of Nezami's Sufism has not truly been substantiated either. No one has offered a thorough study of the social, religious, or political condition of the twelfth century to explain why and how a well-educated poet or a scientist (as the contemporary scholars like to portray Nezami) becomes part of a Sufi order or movement in which, a true believer follows a teacher or lead disciples, interacts with a likeminded community, considers an unknown reality behind known forms, longs for a mysterious beloved, constantly comments on annihilation of one or another sort, and advocates pantheism. Proving that Nezami held all or some of these characteristics is upon those who consider Nezami as an advocate and explain his poetry in terms of ideology. I believe Islamic mysticism or Sufism was initially about the rejection of the material aspects of life and about being alone or one with God. In that sense, it was an individual and personal path. Sufism needed an institution when it became a group and an ideology that conceptualized, regulated, and codified that path. Furthermore, with the appearance of the masters and disciples and their *Khaneqa* (their place of worship and study), they organized themselves accordingly. Soon after that, as is typical of all ideologies, there were competitions and divisions. Mysticism was no longer about the relationship between man and God; it was about an ideological path. There is no way one can explain a poet like Nezami, who had no affiliation with any of the Darvish groups and instead was financially connected with the court as part of that historical scheme. However, it is easy to see Nezami's prominent place, his unique status, and his influential style in the history of classical Persian literature.

Even if the messaging and thematic aspects of classical Persian literature morphed from the outwardly, social, and identity-focused poetry of Rudaki and Ferdowsi into an open expression of the inwardly preoccupation with the other world, perfected in the works of Rumi or Jami, still the transition was not a sudden radical shift or universal. If there were such a messaging change, it must have taken place over centuries and certainly after the Mongolian tribes' invasions in the thirteenth and fourteenth centuries, and as such, Nezami could not have been in the middle of this alleged transition. Nezami's view of death and life is nowhere near the confused conceptualization of the Sufi theorist or like the tender and poetic expression of life and death by Rumi. Nezami is still concerned with identity but mainly from a humanist perspective, which explains his return to Zoroastrian core philosophy when portraying human nature. His portrayals echo Hooshang's book of *Javidan Kherad*, emphasizing wisdom, education, health, bravery, good speech, and good deeds, all of which do not have a prominent presence in Sufism and which emphasizes the measures for the next world's salvation. Even if it were true, such transition would have too many anomalies explaining the history, invasions, and social discourses; the changing genres and subgenres also explain the diversity of classical Persian poetic outputs. Nezami's characterization, to be sure, is also not entirely loyal to the original stories. It is a modern imposition to read Nezami's stories of ascension as symbolic portrayal of a cosmos as divine for the purpose of conveying secret Sufi messages and teachings, because the poet is not part of the story, some version of the story had already existed, and at the end of the stories, he does disappear or annihilate. As mentioned repeatedly, he is present, a participant, before and after each story to boast about his craft and to ask for compensation, and yes to praise the God and the king. These points are a reminder of the need to analyze Nezami's poetry based on its merit and not an alleged missive. I also must point out another obvious fact. Many scholars including some Sufi interpreters of Nezami also passingly refer to Nezami as a *sha'er-e bazmi* (a poet of banquets and entertainment, a troubadour), and by doing so they contradict their interpretation of his poetry. This view reduces Nezami's allegorical romances and fantasies to a feast's side entertainment. I understand the need for categorization because it helps analysis. However, we must remember that categories of classical Persian poetry are complex and words such as *bazm* and Sufi cannot provide a sufficient analytical tool.

What twelfth-century mystical commentaries on the *Koran* match Nezami's references to that book? It is not sufficient to point out referencing the verses because, as mentioned before, even today's secular writers can be inspired by any religious book. Furthermore, we should remember that worldviews and ideologies do not appear without an institutional context and are not propagated by individuals living in isolation (as they also claim). Sohravardi (d. 1168) lived around the same time but nowhere near Nezami's region, and his life activities match his philosophy as a Sufi thinker. In addition, Sohravardi himself seems to have been highly influenced by Mazdeism. Khaqani (d. 1190) lived in the same region as Nezami, and his upbringing and background explain the Christian references in his poetry. To be sure, Iranian mystical activism grew as a systematic ideological movement only in the thirteenth century after the invasion of the Mongols, and for an explainable reason, as that invasion interrupted the revival processes that had begun with the Samanids' cultural movement and its literary reflection in the works of Rudaki and Ferdowsi. The Arab invasion brought Islam, and the Mongol invasion catalyzed mysticism. Nowhere in Nezami's poetry can we see systemic philosophizing or theologizing of such concepts as God's relation to man or God's unity. It is easy for students of Islam and Islamic studies to classify Sohravardi, Ibn al-Arabi (1240), and Nezami in the same or similar ideological categories, but it is not necessarily an illuminating categorization.

Ontologically, for Sohravardi, light, to give an example, was a metaphysical phenomenon and for Nezami, it was a supple metaphorical device. For Sohravardi, the *'aql* or intellect (as in his *'Aql-e Sorkh*) strives to teach how to ascend to the skies to meet with an angel. For Nezami, *kherad* or reason, helps to bring the skies to earth to enrich his poetry. Intellectually, for Sohravardi, these concepts were formed in the later centuries, and Nezami, in the twelfth century was still, as mentioned earlier, deep down influenced by the Zoroastrian notion of duality. We cannot find an Islamic mystic stage of growth that begins with the simple to divine love and a form of brotherly commitment anywhere, including science-fiction movies these days. Moreover, unfortunately, ideological readers of Nezami's work have not shown how Nezami's verses, even those on religion and its prophet, are similar to verses on the same subjects by Sana'i, Rumi, Attar, and Jami in describing Islam in mystical terms and in portraying Mohammad as the epitome of perfection. We should see such notions and realizations and the stages of attaining them, even in individual experiences of mysticism. How can we apply such ae process to Nezami's life? If a similar concept is apparent in his work, he used it for his *Sakhon*. He could not have been inspired by the prolific works of the Sufi authors who came after him. Suppose a comparison is needed for this purpose. In that case, he should be compared with his contemporaries mentioned above or the works of the philosophers and scientists who existed before his time, such as the *Minu-ye Kheraz* and other Pahlavi texts, and the writings of Borzouyeh, the Persian physician of the Sasanian period. There are many sources (including state-supported online sites in Iran) that continue to refer to Nezami as a pious Muslim and Aref. Technically, he cannot be both. For example, the role of wisdom is different according to each of these religious ideologies. In the first, wisdom is guided by God, and in the second, wisdom is the guide and can lead to God. Verses supporting both designations can be found somewhere in *Panj Ganj*, verses that Nezami has weaved to show his mastery of language in complicating already complex thoughts. Yet, Nezami sees the role of wisdom independent of God, as a natural human goal.

Naturally, Nezami's use and references to religion and the Prophet of Islam provide a wealth of evidence to Muslim scholars in their attempt to prove the poet's religiosity, mysticism, or both. However, these scholars use the methodology to prove Nezami's religiosity and mysticism by showing that his verses can be proved to be religious because there are similar verses and concepts in the *Koran*. As shown thus far, the reality is that Nezami applies the Koranic verses as raw materials to construct his allegories, the same way he has used the other sources.

Here is an example of rigorous use of this methodology in an article by Abbasali Vafa'i.[33] The author cites the following verse by Nezami and a verse from Koran to show that they are saying the same thing. Nezami's verses read:

| It is the human who, out of bravery, | آن آدمی است کز دلیری |
| Expresses blasphemy when he's half hungry. | کفر آرد وقت نیم سیری[34] |

The verse cited is from Hud chapter 11-9, which in English reads, "If We ever favor man with Our Mercy, and then take it away from him, he becomes utterly desperate, totally ungrateful."[35]

Let us assume that these Persian and Arabic statements are saying the same thing. Given all we now know about his extreme literary preoccupation, it is just more logical to think that Nezami has read the Arabic verse and has used it to create his Persian one (remember that he said that the poets are at the rank of prophets and that his poetry is at par with Koran?). It is illogical to think that Nezami has created a similar verse to Koran because he is a Sufi. Secondly, Nezami's line is from a section outside of the story of *Layli o Majnun*, a section entitled "Khorsandi va Qana'at" (satisfaction and contentment). The section is part of a larger segment (per other editions) entitled "Remembering those we lost." In it, Nezami speaks of numerous common senses and conventions on ethical issues and ways of conduct, as the subject of his wordplays, and each of the subsections ends with a beautiful verse about wind and how wine might provide a little rest and happiness. The segment can, in fact, be considered a *khamriat* of its own. Again, these are not part of the romance we read two pages later and admired.

Right above that quoted line in the article, the authors mention another line from Nezami, also without much elaboration. The line reads:

هرکه داد خرد نداند داد / آدمی صورتست و دیو نهاد³⁶

Like the previous example offered by Vafa'i, this one is also simply mentioned as evidence without discussion or context. The third line is one of the several verses in the larger passage that together form one of those Nezami's playful constructs around a word. That line and a few around it read:

Each person has a hidden friend,	هر کسی را نهفته یاری هست
A confidant, that help with lend:	دوستی هست و دوستداری هست
'Tis wisdom, from which succour comes;	خرد است آن کز او رسد یاری
He has all things who wisdom owns,	همه داری اگر خرد داری
Who gives not wisdom its just due,	هرکه داد خرد نداند داد
Though man in form, his nature true	آدمی صورتست و دیو نهاد
Is demon-like; angelic men	وان فرشته که آدمی لقب است
Are those with wisdom – Wonderous thing!³⁷	زیرکاند و زیرک عجب است³⁸

He is saying that everyone has a friend somewhere who might show up to be a confidant and even a lover. Therefore, people should think rationally because wisdom can help. You can consider yourself rich if you have wisdom. But alas, he who does not recognize righteousness of wisdom is a human in appearance but a demon inside. In addition to the meaning, even the symbols convey a Zoroastrian philosophical notion of wisdom.

Such scholarship is decontextualization and isolation for the sake of mystification. And by context and isolation, I mean ignoring the subsection, the section, and the general location of a single line. Let us start with the word *kherad*. It means intellect, reason, sagacity, sanity, sense, understanding, judgment, mind, wisdom, and knowledge. However, I believe the word should be understood as rationality or reason, particularly in its historical sense. The Pahlavi word *xratav* encompasses all these meanings, and Nezami seems to do so in his works where the word kherad (alone or in compound forms) has appeared more than a hundred times.[39] Here too, his verses remind of the *Minu Kherad*, Minu-ye Kherad, *Minuvi Khered*, or *Mēnōg-ī Khrad* (all versions of which refer to the book of reason, literally the spirit of reason). Reason or wisdom is of course a central concept in Zoroastrianism, that with which the world is managed by Ahura Mazda, who embodies that very Kherad. That book, too, provides advice and thoughts on ethics and way of conduct and common-sense wisdom. In the above case, the actions are formed around kherad, and Nezami considers rationality and common sense to be the best of friends. Many of the more miniature tales in *Haft Paykar* can be explained by Nezami's decision to use *kherad* as a subject of his pictorial allegories. He even named the second volume of his last book, *Kheradnameh* (book of Reason). To be sure, numerous lines in the entire section and on that same page are the versified version of the statements about rationality from *Minuye Kherad*. Many of them start with *harkeh*, meaning anybody, in Nezamian style.

Another source on this ancient concept that could have influenced classical poets such as Ferdowsi, Naser Khusrow, and Nezami is the book of *Dinkard V and Dinkard VI* (a significant source on pre-Islamic philosophy). In it, *kherad* is defined as the power to distinguish and to know the good from the bad. It is not only knowledge and wisdom but also a value system. Thus, *kherad* in this Dinkard is also the rationality required for man "to improve himself and others."[40]

Thus, I believe similar to the ways Nezami has rendered themes that refer to the Koran; he has also used, directly or indirectly, materials from Zoroastrian sources including the Pahlavi (Middle Persian) book of *Minuye Kherad* or *Menog-i Kherad* (translated as the Spirit of Wisdom) as he has used commonly understood elements of Islam or Mysticism. Without mentioning this source, Bürgel also points out the significance of *kherad* (wisdom) to Nezami, particularly in his *Iskandarnemeh*.[41] (I avoid saying Nezami advocated on behalf of Zoroastrianism or the book of *Minuye Kherad* for the same reason that I disagree with the notion that he advocated Sufism or Islam.)[42] As I will exemplify, this Zoroastrian book of *Minuye Kherad* (numinous/paradisiacal wisdom/reason) is relevant to the discussion of Nezami's other themes and subjects. The book features two central characters. Dana or the Wise poses 62 questions and the divine Minuye Kherad or Reason answers the questions. The embodiment, and personification, in the flesh, is a frame story in which the answers to the questions collectively convey a worldview, a path of conduct, a system of ethics, and above all, the ways of reason (four variations of it). The translation of Minuye Kherad's title to The Spirit of Wisdom is a good, simple rendition. However, it does not convey the depth, importance, and multitudes of the meaning of the word kherad in ancient and even contemporary Persian society. Kherad can be translated into English as wisdom, understanding, judgment, intellect, rationality, and reason.

On the other hand, wisdom would be the translation of the word *ʿaql* (as in the title of Sohravardi's famous treaties *ʿAql-e Sorkh*), which in its Arabic original can mean mind and stands as a narrow synonym for *kherad*. I slightly prefer "reason" or "reasoning" because the tone and tenor of the book convey a sense of rationalization and reasoning. *Kherad* could be a synonym for *manteq* (logic, reason) as well. To be sure, the antonyms of *kherad* such as bi *kherad*, *na kherad*, or the older form *tireh kherad* mean lacking and destitute of reason, intellect, judgment, and clear mind.[43] Moreover, the book is more than a book of advice because it often refers to the core philosophical, ethical, and moral bases of ancient Persia, some of which are emphatically echoed in Nezami's work in direct or allegorical ways. In *Khosrow o Shirin*, he even includes a segment on "reasoning toward a viewpoint and achieving knowledge," which has no relevance to the book's story but is a perspective through which one might understand God.[44] However, the approach is more Platonic and Greek rather than Sufi.

Another case is a verse from the *Koran* and then two "corresponding" lines from Nezami's work to show that Nezami promotes a Koranic verse/concept and that he is a mystic. The Koranic verse reads, "We have certainly created man into hardship."[45] The quoted Nezami's lines read.

The dust of your body is mixed with toils	خاک تو آمیخته رنجهاست
In the heart of this dust, there are many treasures. ...	در دل این خاک بسی گنجهاست
We have come to suffer	ما ز پی رخ پدید آمدم
Not for a conversation with each other.	نز جهت گفت و شنید آمدم[46]

A juxtaposition of lines (which are not next to each other) that hardly resemble each other does not prove Nezami's mysticism or Islamic advocacy either. Even if they were similar, it would not prove Nezami's mysticism. To be sure, there is a more similar line in a passage of *Minuye Kherad*, which presents a concept that is much closer to Nezami's line mentioned above. It reads:

"And this, too, one has to consider, that, in order to become a chooser in this matter, trouble is to be undergone; and it is necessary to become acquainted with this matter, because, in the end, the body is mingled with the dust, and reliance is on the soul. And everyone is to undergo trouble for the soul and is to become acquainted with duty and good works; because that good work which a man does unwittingly is little of a good work, and that sin which a man commits unwittingly amounts to a sin in its origin. And it is declared by the Avesta."[47]	برای تشخیص این امر باید رنج برد. و به این چیز آگاه باید بود. زیرا که در پایان کار تن به خاک آمیخته شود و اتکاء بر روان باشد. و هرکسی باید برای روان رنج برد و از کار نیک آگاه باشد. زیرا که آن کار نیکی که مردم نا آگاهانه کنند، کار نیک کمّری به شمار می آید. ولی آن گناهی که که نا آگاهانه کنند، آن گناه بر ذمه شان باشد. و از اوستا پیداست.[48]

Nezami's line and, in fact, the entire passage has one word (*ranj* meaning trouble or suffering) remotely in common with a word in the Koranic text (*kabad*, hardship and also a middle tract of sand and with a kasreh it could mean liver, and in either case, the only occurrence in the *Koran*). Then he asks each of the princesses to tell a sensual tale matching the mood of the color of the pavilion and the planet. In Nezami's context, the word means "to take pain," as in the poem/proverb "Na bordeh rang, ganj moyasar namishavd" meaning if you do not exert yourself, you will not gain a treasure (no pain, no gain). Nezami's line has nothing to do with God saying that he created man to face hardship. Besides, the focus of Nezami's verse is not the suffering but rather reason. Moreover, his passage has many more words and meanings in common with the Pahlavi text as quoted above. That Nezami's verses resemble *Minuye Kherad* better than it resembles the *Koran* does not justify any scholar to claim that Nezami was an advocate of Zoroastrianism either. As I have emphasized a few times, he simply versifies ideas from any useful resource available in the service of his literary creation. The similarities of viewpoints, ideas, and thoughtful guidance between Nezami's work and *Minuye Kherad* is obvious and not accidental; however, the connection could be direct (he read the text) or indirect (through the works of other writers). Either way, the ideas are from *Minuye Kherad*.[49] In fact, *Minuye Kherad* is itself an allegory. There is a remote formalistic resemblance between the Nezamian pictorial allegory and the one in *Minuye Kherad*; however, this does not prove that Nezami was a Zoroastrian. The resemblance could even be accidental.

In addition to a superficial comparison between Nezami's poetry and Koranic verses, many articles, including this one, also juxtapose Nezami's name with the names of renounced Sufi characters such as Hallaj to convey a sense of similarity between them, albeit without any analysis. There is not much information about the reception of his little work, which he wrote in Arabic. Even the famous sentence attributed to him ("I am the Truth") has been the subjection of contention.

As mentioned in various places, the first reason for the prevalence of ideological readings of Nezami's poetry is that historically western scholars saw all cultural output in Iran and the Middle East as Islamic. Second, the rise of Islam to the state ideology of Iran resulted in Iranian scholars implicating and inculcating Islam and the *Koran* into various fields. Third, there is a tendency in Iran to stress the meaning of a poem (here mystic messages) than on discussing the structure or form. These are related to an anticipation of a hidden meaning and an underappreciation of the nature of poetry, mainly classical narrative poetry, which is an amalgamation of stories, sources, ideas, verbal images, meanings, fluency with language, rhythm, rhyme, meter, and a myriad of techniques artistically and gloriously rendered to present an account of events and the description of deeds.

Once again, I do not deny the existence of spirituality in Nezami's poetry. Readers are entitled to find such an aspect in his verses and enjoy it as well. I do challenge the view that Nezami was an advocate of Islam, as a mystic and the views that see his poetry as Sufi poetry, and the views that see Nezami as a believer in secrets, the mirror of the unseen, or the existence of a key that could open the codes either in his mind or in the entire world. One of the ontological questions is that the religious interpreters of Nezami's poetry rarely agree on a comprehensive definition of Sufi poetry. Is poetry, since the eleventh century, solely Sufi poetry because of a shift to more introspective worldview, a shift to inward? Did such as change occur rather abruptly? Was Nezami a connecting ring between the previous social poetic discourse and the forthcoming mystic notion if it was a process? What definition of Sufi poetry can be exemplified in the works of both Nezami and Jami? Is an Islamic mystical poem a work containing any Islamic teachings, themes, or references? In what sense and aesthetic viewpoint are the ghazals of Hafez understood to be a development over Nezami's love poetry? Why are there no more "super-star" Persian poets after Jami? Unlike the contemporary era in which poets and readers are well connected through print and other media and a shift in social discourse could trigger a change in literary activities, the classical poets were separated by long distances and big spans of time. Kings, local rulers, local languages, wars, invasions, climate, cultures, religions, and perhaps genres and schools of poetry were all factors in poetic changes. In the west, contemporary and even Renaissance poets draw on Christian themes. However, contemporary poets have not experienced the same history and knowledge that formed the intellect of classical poets. Contemporary poets are undoubtedly more this-worldly and more materialistic even when they speak of spirituality. However, the significant differences among the past poets help us understand which ones operated entirely within a religious paradigm and which ones could operate in its proximity. Some poetry contains spiritual and mystical themes and references, but some promote and advocate them. These should not be conceptualized under the same category.

In challenging the religious and mystical readings of his poetry and the verdicts about Nezami's piety, I offered here a textual and literary analysis of his work and a few extra-textual points regarding the occasions in his poetry where he allegorizes astrology, wine, or *ka'ba*, all of which can be construed as blasphemy by official Islam. However, overall and in terms of methodology, I challenged those alleged mystic and religious aspects of Nezami's work by focusing on the diversity of his literary themes and subjects and his constant preoccupation with his Sakhon and pictorial allegories. This return to the discussion of religion, love, ancient philosophies, Dante's Divine Comedy hopefully helps liberate Nezami's literary works from the framework of faith so we can pay attention to the aesthetics of his poetry. In the story of Mahan, Nezami's primary effort is invested in the creation of a pictorial allegory. In an allegorical construct, the Sun travels east-west in the sky over the riverbank, Mahan moves from one side to another of the feast site, like a sunny figure adored by all. After they ate plenty of food and fruits at dawn and drank more sparkling red wine, the mood changed above in the sky and among the party participants. The Nile River and its bank are now covered by silver, getting darker. The allure of the twilight gradually eclipses the vitality and the sound of the songs and laughter. The dark creates a chasm between Mahan and the rest of the guests who admired him like the popular boy of a prom party.

Shakespeare portrayed this transformative moment in a memorable line of words when he wrote, "The bright day is done, and we are for the dark."[50] To summarize and reiterate, trying to find a Sufi message in all these depictions prevents us from seeing the elephant in the room: Nezami's description of nature and its connection to his characters' inner and outer conditions.

If it is necessary to characterize Nezami's literary output, instead of Sufi mystic or Islamic, there are more plausible labels including spirit-lifting, enlightening, or simply beautiful: a manifestation of the Persian culture of that era, which by the way, included influential concepts from several religions. I also believe that Nezami's voice and thoughts are present in his work (as is the case for most literary works). However, his voice is not concerned with ideology or teaching religious moralistic values. No single ideology can claim or explain such a vast literary output.

Of course, in a mythical and fantastical sense, unknown circumstances, magic, and metaphysics come to play to create a situation in which knowledge or reasoning can help. *Haft Paykar* offers other such stories. For example, "The Tale of Good and Evil" (Dastan-e Khayr o Shar) was told to King Bahram in the Sandal pavilion by the princess of the sixth climb on Thursday. There too, with a few lines playing with the word "sandal" in connection to natural elements, he presents the characters, one of which tells a story, and the other listens wholeheartedly. In the story, one friend deceives the other friend brutally only to be shocked by the unexpected consequence of his evil actions. As opposed to presenting this story as a mystical story in classrooms, one can read it as a manifestation of Zoroastrian dualism, which continued to influence intellectual and literary constructs well into the Islamic period. According to some estimates, even his meters were affected by the 12-syllable *Fahlaviat* genre of the pre-Islamic era.[51]

Having had this rather extended discussion of religion, I reemphasize that even in his most similar fantastic and mythical portrayal of hell, paradise, and love in "The Story of Mahan," or in "The Tale of Good and Evil," Nezami's portrayal of love is comprehensive and not an abstract concept. In terms of piety and advocacy too, while Dante focuses on religion and social issues, Nezami's message is more about *kherad* or the consequences of lacking *kherad*. This chart summarizes their different substance and forms resulting in their distinct allegories.

Divine comedy	Love: Specific	Imagery: Surrealist	Religion: Advocacy	Fantasy/myth: Biblical	Symbolism: Exterior meaning	Allegory: Major
Seven treasures	Love: Various	Imagery: Realistic/ surrealist	Religion: As a theme/ motif	Fantasy/myth: Koranic and ancient	Symbolism: Literary use	Allegory: Mini

Even, concerning the concept of *kherad*, we do not witness any ideo-logical advocacy or a commentary on his city's social and political events either. In addition to constant praise of *kherad*, many of Nezami's charac-ters escape predicaments independently without divine intervention or a piece of wise advice from a Sufi guide. Even in the case of Mahan, it is not clear what the specter of Khizr represents or what kind of intervention he offers. He certainly does not provide any advice to the man who has already promised himself to change. Are we to understand his transfer from his dreamlike journey back to his house as God's intervention? Indeed, given Charles Sanders Peirce's deliberation on semiotics, a reader might see this Khizr character as a prophet based on Islamic belief. However, giving further thought to Peirce's Semiotics and his notion of symbols, one can see that the Khizr image here cannot signify an imagi-nary, folkloric, immortal character because of the uncertain characteriza-tion and his similarities with Mahan. However, the image can signify a cause-and-effect relationship between Mahan's internal feelings and his transformation. Historically, scholars, particularly in Iran, have overem-phasized the hermeneutics of Nezami's poetry. This emphasis intensified with the rise of Islamic discourse to the state ideology in 1979. Now the new ruling elite were also invested in their desired hermeneutics. As a result, Nezami's signs and signification and their beauty have been sacri-ficed. Why can't we read Khizr as Mahan's subconscious? Lastly, Sufi read-ers take the color of the garment in the last scene as an indication of the formation of a Dervish circle. The designation of azraq, blue, turquoise, to Sufiism goes back to a vague statement by the tenth-century Muslim writer Kashefi Sabzevari, who, like other such mullahs, fabricated strange concepts and stories. He believed blue was the color of mature dervishes' garments because they look upward toward the blue sky. To be sure, in Nezami's case, this blue has an intertextual reference to the color of the castle where the story is told and the color of the river Nile by which the plot unfolds. The pre-Islamic concept of Jam-e Jam (used by Nezami) also had seven lines, the fourth of which was blue. Nezami is simply construing images based on cultural reminiscences. Thus, the tired argument that the death at the end of some of Nezami's stories indicates a sort of *fana*, unity, or Sufi ending does not apply here.

By noticing and analyzing the concept of *kherad* (reason) in many parts of every book Nezami wrote, we might think of reevaluating or think of exceptions regarding the modern convention that the medieval mind believed that human reason alone could not lead to salvation. This mindset about the necessity of God's intervention or the guidance of a wise man in showing the right path is powerful in Sufi discourse. Yet, contemporary fundamentalism also believes in the power of intervention. Finally, Nezami's poetry still does not fit the characteristics of the Sufi poetry not only because of his diversity of themes and subject or for his unique style of writing and pictorial allegories but also because he does not portray homoerotic tales or any allegorical love for a young man as became common in Sufi discourse. His poetry also excludes any political, homosexual, and even violent presentations of some mystic texts, particularly the later ones of the Safavid period.

NOTES

1. Dante Alighieri, *Divine Comedy* (Purgatory) by Mark Musa (Bloomington: Indiana UP, 1996), 17.94–96.
2. Christopher Kleinhenz "Dante and the Bible: Intertextual Approaches to the Divine Comedy" in *Italica*, Autumn, 1986, Vol. 63, No. 3 (Autumn, 1986), 225–236, 225.
3. Nezami uses the words hell and paradise but mostly as a metaphor or adjective. In his five versions of the story of ascension, Nezami does not describe "paradise" in detail. The word "purgatory" (barzakh) does not appear often.
4. See for example, Sakineh Abasi, "Barrasi Qeseh Mahan" in *Nameh Parsi*, 10, 4, 2005, 13–32 and Yusef Abasabad, "Ta'mol-e Erfan Shenakhti dar Dastan-e Mahan" in *Erfan-e Islami*, 13, 52, 2017, 109–124. Bürgel briefly refers to this story stating "Mahan encounters various uncanny people, which turn out to be demons. Finally, Mahan meets, or rather is met, by Khizr, who has taken Mahan's shape, thus leading him to self-knowledge. Khizr is present at several crucial moments as an inspirer of Nizami." But did Nezami really portray Khizr as an inspirer? See, Bürgel, J.C. "Nizami's World Order" in *A Key*, 41.
5. Attributes and titles such as Sufi, *rohani* (clergyman), *mard-e khoda* (man of God), *shaykh* (sheikh), *hakim* (philosopher, theosophist, medicine man, wise), *aref* (sagacious and holder of highest degree in mysticism) do not define Nezami as accurately as *sha'er-e dastansara* (the storytelling poet).

6. This concept continues to influence literary critics of contemporary poets including Forough Farrakhzad. See, Kamran Talattof, "Personal Rebellion and Social Revolt in the Works of Forugh Farrokhzad," in Nasrin Rahimieh and Dominic Brookshaw, *Forugh Farrokhzad, Poet of Modern Iran* (London: I.B. Tauris, 2010).

7. His last name in an early version of Dastgerdi's edition is Gushyar. In the more recent edition, the name is Hushyar. In other editions, including Sarvatiayn, it is mentioned as Kushyar. These variants might mean aided by ears, by intellect (observant), or by effort. I think Hushyar matches Mahan's (desired) trait better. His ears do not play a role in the story. He is not that active, except when he fights the dragon. However, his desire to reach inside to the inter intellect and become "observant" impacts all episodes and comes to fruition in his encounter with what he thinks is Khizr. The name Mahan is related to both the moon and months.

8. *Kolliyat*, 529.

9. Hayla is female, and Ghayla is the male ghoul.

10. This recalls the anecdote about the well/paradise in Jerusalem, which Christian Lange mentions at the beginning of his informative book, *Paradise and Hell in Islamic Traditions* (Cambridge: Cambridge UP, 2016), 1–2. However aware of that story Nezami might have been, he is not concerned with the Islamic principles as his character freely goes in the well and comes out from the other side.

11. *The Haft Paykar*, 186.

12. *Kolliyat*, 538–39.

13. To understand Nezami's favorable approach to women, compare his poems to the numerous anti women's verses by capable poet, ode writer, Anvari (1126–1189) who lived close to the time of Nezami (1141–1209). Without any reason or justification, he declares:

| To get (do) a wife (woman) in the time and day | کابین روزگار زن کردن |
| Serves no purpose but to pimp. | بجز از محض قلتبانی نیست |

The titles of a couple of Anvari's chapters/segments are simply misogynist. I should add that Anvari also wrote against the poets' métier and criticized them for wanting to get rich by writing poetry and getting compensation from the court. It might be too unlikely, but one cannot dismiss the possibility that Anvari was perhaps criticizing Nezami's two major passions.

14. For an informative article on the genre, see Julia Rubanovich "In the Mood of Love: Love Romances in Medieval Persian Poetry and their Sources" Carolina Cupane, Bettina Krönung, editors, *Fictional Storytelling in the Medieval Eastern Mediterranean and Beyond* (Leiden: Brill, 2016), 67–94. See also the perceptive article, Alyssa Gabbay, "Love Gone Wrong,

Then Right Again: Male/Female Dynamics in the Bahrām Gūr-Slave Girl Story" Iranian Studies, December 2009, Vol. 42, No. 5, Special Issue: Love and Desire in Pre-Modern Persian Poetry And Prose, pp. 677-692.

15. Nizami Ganjavi, *The Haft Paykar*, 196.
16. *Kolliyat-i Khamseh*, 542.
17. Patrick Frank, "Drinking from the Water of Life," in *A Key to the Treasure*, 111.
18. Ibid., 113. That Khizr becomes a Sufi feature in the later depictions of this imagined character is irrelevant to Nezami's twelfth-century work. Even Patrick's analysis of Khizr in Sharafnameh should not influence our reading of the story of Mahan.
19. See Maria Macuch, "MĀDAYĀN Ī HAZĀR DĀDESTĀN," *Encyclopædia Iranica* (accessed on 16 October 2017).
20. Several works of Ebrahim Purdavud and Mehrdad Bahar explain this God-angel entity.
21. Ahmad Khorasani and Golestani, "Tahlil va Naqd-e Dastan-e Mahan-e" in *Zaban va Adabiyat-e Farsi*, 33, summer 2014, 57–84.
22. A post-Islamic version of this notion appears in religious texts and Persian poetry; however, Nezami does not refer to the rooster in his ascension stories even though some Islamic sources on Me'raj do so.
23. Gwenyth Hood, *Dante's Dream: A Jungian Psychoanalytical Approach* (Kalamazoo: Medieval Institute, 2021), 77–86.
24. Nizami, *Haft Paykar*, trans. Meisami, 267–68.
25. The passage starts with:

چون فروزنده شد به عکس و عیار / نقد این گنجه خیز رومی کار

26. ARDĀ WĪRĀZ in *Encyclopedia Iranica*, Vol. II, Fasc. 4, pp. 356–357.
27. Peterson, Joseph H. "The Book of Arda Viraf." www.avesta.org.
28. *Kolliyat*, 392 (line 14).
29. In the conversation between Salam Baghdadi and Majnun. *Kolliyat*, 406 (51).
30. Davis, 208.
31. *Kolliyat-e Khamseh*, 408.
32. Ibid.
33. Abbasali Vafa'i "Simaye Payambar Akram beh Onvan-e Ensan-e Kamel dar Khamseh-e Nezami" *Matnshenasi Adab-e Farsi*, 6, 1, spring 2014, 1–24.
34. *Kolliyat*, 321. Sarvatiyan lists alternative words in other manuscripts including kofr, goft, kaf and choses *goft* (page 80).
35. See, "Towards Understanding the Quran" at https://www.islamicstudies.info/tafheem.php?sura=11&verse=9&to=14.
36. *Kolliyat*, 433.
37. Nizami Ganjavi, *The Haft Paykar*, 24.

38. *Kolliyat,* 433.
39. Of course, Ferdowsi uses this word throughout his magnificent *Shahnameh.*
40. Zhaleh Amuzgar, A. Tafazoli, (eds). *Dinkard Panjom* (Tehran: Moin, 2007).
41. Bürgel "Nizāmī's World Order" in *A Key to the Treasure,* 17–52.
42. Ahmad Tafazoli, trans. *Minuye Kherad* (Tehran: Bonyad-e Farhang-e Iran, 1975).
43. Ferdowsi and other Shahnameh writers before him expand on the concept of *kherad. Dehkhoda* offers an extensive list of the compound words made with *kherad,* the meanings of which confirm this complexity. Other texts on *kherad* were written in the pre-Islamic era, including *Javidan Kherad* (The Eternal Intellect) or, as might later have been named, *Pandnameh Hooshang* (Hooshang's Book of Advice).
44. *Kolliyat-e Hakim,* 81.
45. The phrase is (لَقَدْ خَلَقْنَا الْإِنْسَانَ فِي كَبَدٍ).
46. *Kolliyat,* 50.
47. The English rendition is from *Pahlavi Texts,* Part III (SBE24), E. W. West, tr. [1885], at sacred-texts.com, p. 3. The word *ranj* is used to translate the Koranic verse to match the same word in Nezami's line.
48. *Minu-ye Kharad,* Tehran, translated from Pahlavi by Ahmad Tafazoli (Tehran: Bonyad-e Farhang-e Iran, 1975), 3.
49. The dominant and reductive tendency is to categorize many Pahlavi texts under the advice genre: andarz nameh, or book of advice.
50. William Shakespeare, "Antony and Cleopatra," Act 5, Scene 2.
51. See for example Moin's studies on the effect of *Mazdayasna* on a few post-Islamic poets. Mohamad Moin, *Mazdayasna va Adab-e Farsi* (Tehran: Tehran UP, 2015).

CHAPTER 8

Sublime Métier: Nezami's Literary Techniques and His Pictorial Allegory

Previous chapters offered examples and content and thematic analyses of the variety of themes, subjects, and techniques which Nezami uses in constructing his narrative poems and his pictorial allegories. Remembering the poem which I quoted at the beginning and my arguments in Chap. 2, it should now be clear that what interests Nezami the most is a re-representation of the world through Sakhon writing.

When poets begin their eloquent writing	قافیه سنجان که سخن برکشند
they portray treasures of both worlds by rhyming.	گنج دو عالم به سخن درکشند

Several seminal subjects that he used to produce Sakhon were explored in previous chapters. However, this chapter offers examples of more subjects and themes Nezami uses in his work, hoping that their juxtaposition will further show the lack of any ideological or religious motivation except for the love of Sakhon. The occasional comparisons between the work of Nezami to other poets' work in previous chapters also showed that most of those subjects were popular poetic themes in the late eleventh and twelfth centuries.

In this concluding chapter, I focus more narrowly on Nezami's métier, sources of inspiration, and his literary techniques by analyzing a few more pertinent examples of pictorial allegories related to his literary forms. Moreover, I will expand on the notion of Nezamian pictorial allegory (as

© The Author(s), under exclusive license to Springer Nature Switzerland AG 2022
K. Talattof, *Nezami Ganjavi and Classical Persian Literature*,
Literatures and Cultures of the Islamic World,
https://doi.org/10.1007/978-3-030-97990-4_8

the core of his structural approach to Sakhon, poetry) by analyzing, explaining, and expanding on its components to better explicate the key techniques employed in constructing them even in works with religious materials. I will also argue that Nezami's ethics and, indeed, his morality are not derived from any metaethical notion or a structured ideology such as Islam or Sufism. I will interpret Nezami's system of ethics in terms of the situation he sets up in his highly allegorical works. All this will again show that neither religion nor ethics and morality can be considered the prime impetus or sole source of his creativity. These also constitute yet another reason to free Nezami's work from the constraints of religious or mystical readings.

As argued and illustrated, in his portrayal of characters and concepts, Nezami relies overwhelmingly on allegories (*tamsil*) that are short, comparisons (*tashbih*), and metonymy (*badi', degargui*). His style of allegory or his version of *tamsil* only shows a minor difference in comparison with metonymy. In his *tashbih*, the comparisons and similes are imagined or tacit. In his allegory, the comparison and similes are based on a picturesque and even visual harmony; the analogy is achieved by using two sets of elements that function in a comparable way. Nezami ignores this slight difference and combines the two, thus creating his own type of *balaghat* (eloquence) and *badi'* (rhetoric). This re-designation is word choice blending, the similarities of the compared elements. I conceptualize this process as *Nezamian pictorial allegory*, a mini allegory, if you will, in which an object or a concept is equated with the meanings that exist outside the narrative without a clear storyline on either side. His devotion and his ethics belong to words, playing with words, arranging words, alliteration, rhyme, rhythm, meter, music, making allegories defined by *Ebham* (ambiguity) *iham* (double meaning, polysemy),[1] *tada'i* (association), *jaygozini tasviri* (pictorial replacement), *mora'at-e nazir* (observing the parallel), coinage (creating new compound words), *est'areh* (metaphors and all of its type and varieties), and certainly *jenas* (play on words, or puns).[2] Nezami's *radif* (a word following the rhyme) also adds meaning and musicality to his verse in significant ways. This and previous chapters offer an ample example of verses that contain these features.

These devices provide Nezami's allegory with certain consistency and characteristics. These characteristics include sensibility through which he conveys significant meanings, an effect that makes readers enjoy and want to read more, aesthetics that impresses the readers for the coordination among the words in terms of sound, form, and relationship, and mood often conveyed through imagery.

Nezami creates his pictorial allegory around Sakhon as well. In a famous section in which he seems to be resenting the ruler Toghrol Arsalan for not compensating him, he speaks of Sakhon even though the segment is entitled Praising Arsalan.[3] A few mini allegories intersperse the segments. For example, one starts with these verses:

The realm of the Sun became prosperous	از آن شد خانه خورشید معمور
because it sought to light the world's darkness.	که تاریکان عالم را دهد نور
Clouds' magnanimity conquered the world entirely	جهای ابر از آن آمد جهانگیر
because it sought to feed baby plants so generously.	که در طفل گیاهی را دهد شیر[4]

These lines present a surface story about the obvious facts that the Sun provides light and prevents the world from being dark and the clouds that produce rain, which provides water (milk) for the plants and the greens. Through a sort of syllogism, the underlying story deduces the same condition that the kings who can succeed if they take care of their subjects (including the poet Nezami, as exemplified before) by nurturing or rewarding them. One verse in particular points to the second layer of meaning, which is, as usual, about the state of being of the characters or people. It reads:

Till when such as an orator must be isolated	چنین گوینده‌ای در گوشه تا کی
till when such an eloquent poet should be uncompensated.	سخندانی چنین بی‌توشه تا کی

Hamid Dabshi writes, "Persian literary humanism was formally courtly and politically accommodating, and yet the seeds of dissent, predicated on a tropically decentered, amorphous, and miasmatic subject was always evident in it—narratively in Ferdowsi's Shahnameh; romantically in Nezami's *Khamseh*; formally in Omar Khayyam's subversive quatrains; thematically in Naser Khusrow's politically defiant poetry; metaphysically in Sanai, Attar, and Rumi's mystical poetry; and indeed lyrically in Rumi, Sadi, and Hafez's ghazals." According to the verses above, the poet is sidelined and deprived of any sustenance or stipend. The word *gusheh* in the first half-line generally means cornered. Its occurrence in a couple of verses by Nezami has caused some scholars to portray him as a hermit or *goshehgir*.

In the line above, Nezami complains about being *sidelined* or *isolated* by which he meant unrecognized.[5] Historical facts about his overdue payments, expressed by Nezami himself elsewhere, support this reading.

THE ANATOMY OF NEZAMIAN PICTORIAL ALLEGORY

An allegory is described as a story, poem, or even a picture that lends itself to interpretation because it is believed that it contains a hidden meaning, often of a moral or political nature. In the exceptional case of Nezami, he conveys important ideas often directly and reserves his allegories for storytelling. The Nezamian pictorial allegory is also different from a parable or fable. Its surface story is only there to explain or foreshadow an even or the state of mind of a character with no specific hidden philosophical message or lesson about a broader issue. Instead, its purpose is to show (or boast about) the astonishing possibilities and pictures that words, when juxtaposed playfully, can offer on the surface while also describing people, places, animals, events, or thoughts at the same time. For example, the hidden story in a Nezamian pictorial allegory might be about a character's dealing with a death, while the surface story would be about an analogous situation involving autumn, the constellations, animals, or preexisting stories that include an analogous situation. In this first/surface part of the allegory, he employs symbolism not only to subliminally foretell the event and the status of his characters but also to create mood, atmosphere, and supports and draw on his theme. I should repeat that to Nezami, somewhat like Zoroastrians, the body, whether that of women, men, animals, stars, or plants, is an essential and respected feature. He does not understand the body from an Islamic jurisprudence or Sufi perspective. This belief makes the connection between the two layers of his pictorial allegory more plausible and natural.

The above allegories exemplify Nezami's method of coining metaphors by combining nouns and adjectives and all in the service of his allegorical construction, illustrated in the chart below.

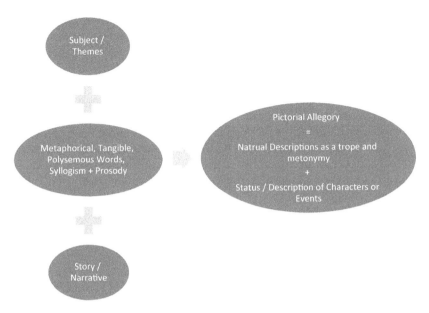

That is, the natural elements of the earth, space, stars, gardens, and nature in general (as tropes and metonymy) compositely and intensely cohabit in a rhyming, rhythmic verse or a passage to influence, foretell, or elucidate the expression of the literal and tangible mental or physical status of characters or events to produce a pictorial allegory.[6] Nezami's mastery of the Persian language, his impressive repertoire of vocabulary, and his bold use of his poetic options/authority in playing with the meters, shapes of letters, and length of syllabi enable him to perform this art of Sakhon brilliantly. These multiplex features reveal themselves when one begins to explain, interpret, or translate a passage. This description explains why many scholars refer to Nezami's poetry as complex or erroneously as "dur az zehn" (out of mind, elusive).

A few of these techniques are used in each of his allegorical constructs. As illustrated before, the Nezamian pictorial allegory consists of a short unit of tightly interconnected (in terms of meaning, goal, tone, sound, shape, attitude, and its extra-textual reference) verses, and it usually consists of 4 to 14 lines. It is a story within a story, a poem within a poem, or an image within an image. Its interpretation might be challenging not because it does or does not contain an intricate meaning or a philosophical message, but rather because its semiotic references might be from a variety of texts, sciences, or religions requiring an intertextual approach or even an interdisciplinary reading of the piece.

After the time of Abd al-Rahman Jorjani, the notion of the nature of literature became the subject of a series of debates that led to the establishment of well-defined literary techniques and theories. Nezami's Sakhon is profoundly informed by literary theories of the time as demonstrated not only in the quality of the verses, but also in the content of the verses that he wrote on the subject. Sakhon takes all the three literary branches mentioned above to a new level. That is, Nezami constantly experiments with *ma'ani* (studies of meaning and enunciation and their connection, close to rhetoric); *bayan* (studies and use of similes, metaphor, irony, ambiguity, polysemy, exaggeration, rhetorical and imaginative); and *badi'* (originality, novelty, creativity). In other words,

> He carefully, proportionally chooses his words, more carefully chooses its synonym.
> He selects a word that allows him to find multiple homonyms for it.
> He finds such adjectives for nouns that enable him to add a layer of meaning.
> He offers categories of flora and fauna in a way that enhances his meter.
> He offers incredible metaphors, and that alone is a sign of genius (in Aristotle's words).
> He includes countless similes, analogies, and terms with double meanings.
> He shows a mastery of symmetry, oxymoron, repetition, and rhyming riddles.
> He is careful in using hyperbole, paradox, euphemism, and the oxymoron.
> He does not use easy allusions, semantic opposition, and antonyms.
> He makes compound nouns frequently, particularly with the word Sakhon.
> He incorporates irony, epigram, and satire in his stories.
> He incorporates his alliteration, onomatopoeia, homophonic pun in a single line.
> He substitutes words thoughtfully, the recitation of which requires practice.
> He relentlessly offers balanced and associative pictorial passages.
> He has excelled beyond the reach of other poets in the play on words, additive pun.
> He knows how to feature colors, animals, stars, objects, flora, fauna, people, or objects.
> He can use all these techniques in his pictorial allegories.

I list Nezami's different abilities above because I want to find one single Nezamian pictorial allegory that best demonstrates all these techniques. It would be almost impossible to find such an allegory. However, I wonder how many of the above techniques have been used in this previously mentioned passage from *Layli o Majnun* when he describes Layli's condition.

Seas of tears welled up in her eyes	دریا کهر بر آهیخت
tears the size of ships poured from her eyes.	کشتی کشتی زدیده میریخت
She ate sorrow in secret with no breather	میخورد غمی به زیر پرده
the sorrow consumed her, and it did not bother.	غم خورده ورا و غم نخورده
Golden rings in her ear	در گوش نهاده حلقه زر
She listened at a ringing door to hear.	چون حلقه نهاده گوش بر در
Enduring the ring that enchained her	با حلقه گوش خویش میساخت
She never wished it on another.	وان حلقه به گوش کس نینداخت
Searching by light of the fountain, of moon spring	در جستن نور چشمه ماه
she wandered, gushing about like a water spring.	چون چشمه بمانده چشم بر راه[7]

Words repeatedly include *darya, dideh, kashti, khord, gham, gush, chun, halqeh,* and *cheshmeh.* These words have close affinity in terms of sound or meaning to zir, zar, dar, ra, rah. The combination creates the tale of a sad woman, alone and sobbing, always expecting to hear the news of her beloved as if she is a water spring coursing around the way hoping to meet the source of moonlight, which constantly shines above her path and yet cannot share her chagrin caused by her restricted society. *Cheshmeh mah, cheshmeh,* and *cheshm beh reah* are excellent wordplay. The goal is not simply to say that Layli is sad in her solitude. The goal is how to say it using the above literary techniques such that a reader is gripped by the story but also as much by beautifully crafted language, the Nezamian allegory. This formula applies to all subjects, whether the religious story of ascension, the praise of the heavens, or the description of a love scene such as in the Seven Beauties and *Khosrow and Shirin.* In most places, many of his pictorial allegories are constructed around the images of the sea (darya) and the ship (keshti) which mean slightly different things in each instance. Such images are curious for a man who, according to his biographers, did not travel much in his lifetime and perhaps spent no considerable time on the sea.

Now let us focus on just the first line in which the words *darya* (sea) and *keshti* (ship) are repeated and are used to measure Layli's tears in a spectacular exaggeration while creating an *Ebham* ambiguity. The two words are, in a sense, from the same pictorial family, replaced with another family of words in the following line. The obscure verb *bar-ahikht* (to pull up) invokes an image of pearl diving. One imagines the eye as sea and its tears, pearls.[8] Other pictorial allegories precede and follow this one, and the combination of them constitutes this poem's entire segment. His allegory here, too, has surface and under-surface intentions; the first demonstrates his rhetorical/Sakhon ability in constructing a, somewhat aquatic, pictorial story, and the second is the information and description of a character that helps push the narrative forward. His allegories or components of his allegories might also provide multi-level meanings or multiple pictorial presentations, all telling a story of their own yet as part of the larger story. I will illustrate this mechanization in examples of the themes that might deceptively seem to critics as Nezami's source of ethics, particularly those who limit their analysis to formalist or ideological readings. These explications will support my final contention that his métier explains his style of creativity, his ethics, and his incentives.

THEME AND SUBJECT, NOT BELIEF AND SUBJECTIVITY

Whether philosophical or scientific (in the medieval sense), the number of subjects is numerous, and many scholars have paid close attention to this about Nezami and have written about them.[9] Over the last four decades, an exponentially increasing number of scholars, mostly in Iran, have portrayed Nezami as a highly devout Muslim, a sheikh, a mullah, or a clergyman, and have concluded that the poet's thinking and naturally lofty ethical views stem from his religiosity. Through a comparative analysis of Nezami's portrayal of women and his concept of literature, I have challenged the notion that religion was the only source of inspiration for Nezami's literary output in my previous works on Nezami. Here, I continue this line of investigation regarding the highly anachronistic nature of Nezami's creative output to think about the source and nature of Nezami's ethics. Through textual analysis, I contend that Nezami's ethics and, indeed, morality are not derived from Islam, or religions, or in general any metaethical notion either. After all, Nezami's ethics were significantly different from those of Khaqani, a poet who lived around the same time, in the same area, and shared the same religion. The latter's treatment of Mo'tazeleh and scholastic topologists, for example, epitomizes a solid religious and ideological advocacy and belief system. Such prejudice or outright preachiness is absent in Nezami's work and his life story to the extent that it is known. His poems are primarily concerned with clear topics and specific situations, signaling, if anything, a general notion of applied ethics. A close reading of Nezami's relevant poems not only can prove that he was not an ideological advocate in any way but can also help us understand his morals and ethical system.

In other words, Nezami's system of ethics can be located more specifically in terms of the situation he sets up in his works, which in turn sheds further light on his choices of themes and motifs. This idea is based first on my understanding that the moral principles, which Nezami follows, seem to have stemmed from his sense of right and wrong (abundantly demonstrated in his verses related to *kherad*), perhaps gleaned from his understanding of history, education, and culture. Such notions are reflected in the conceptualization of his profession. Therefore, we can pay attention to what I think Nezami presents as a clue to his ethical principles, which might not have necessarily been following the prevalent social ethics of his time, thus explaining his anachronistic situation. Naturally, the point of departure for me has been the poet's work, his art of Sakhon, or if you will, his métier, of which he is proud.

Theories related to morality and ethics are diverse. The social contract theory of which David Gauthier is well known delineates our rights and obligations and considers emotional bonds between persons as non-essential and deliberate. Similar notions are held in the economic man model. However, the model is based on broader economic utilitarianism based on which decision-makers choose the options that are expected to be most beneficial: a combination of rationality and self-interest. Some feminists propose the paradigm of the mother-child relationship as a supplement to the model of individual self-interested agents. The two relationships, in their view, can presumably negotiate. Jane J. Mansbridge contends that people make choices by distinguishing three forms of motivation: duty, self-interest, and love.[10] I take comfort in reading Lawrence Kohlberg's work on ethics, where he sees social relationships as constitutive in the formation of ethics and morality. Kohlberg believed that human beings progress successively in their command of moral reasoning advancing through different levels and stages.[11] One of the final stages in this process is related to the social contract, which for an individual author would mean his commitment to his work. Alasdair MacIntyre also reinterprets Aristotle's ethics as a more effective way to renew moral agency and practical rationality, and that would be the source of virtue, which can lead to justice.[12] Even though Nezami wrote on common narratives and for commission or was rewarded for his books by rulers, patronage does not seem to have played a role in the ethics and morality of his poetry. If anything, he often encourages all to practice justice and peace, which can indicate his dismay with the social and power relations and conflicts in his time. The importance and relevance of patronage, however minor, clearly stops at the end of the introductory parts to his stories.

All these are further complicated if applied to a variety of ethics in terms of totality or applicability. Are we looking for an overarching and universal system of ethics in the poet's work? Yet, how do we conceptualize ethics in the middle ages? How did people then practice any ethical system? Were they concerned with their own morality or was everything based on religious practice? In particular, what was the driving force behind the highly held concept of ethics and morality for Persian authors such as Nezami Ganjavi? We perhaps find answers to these questions by finding an overarching concept or an organizing element that may weave throughout his literary output. If we do find such a key element, we will get close to answering the question about the source of his ethical system. However, we should keep in mind that ethics have meant different things to different philosophers. Even for the contemporary philosopher Emmanuel Levinas, ethics is not a rationalist assessment and calculation of self-legislation, freedom, happiness, or, more generally, the virtues.

Indeed, numerous thinkers of the classical period were influenced by or at least preoccupied with religion and the metaethical system it offered or inspired. To be well versed in the religious ethical codes was also an indicator of intellectualism. However, as religious authors' positions were significantly different on many social issues including gender, justice, and religiosity itself, there is a need for additional factors or in fact alternatives to explain variations in authors' attitudes toward ethics and morality. Ethics systems were not and could not be suddenly born out of an ideological paradigm; it was the individuals who extracted them. In addition, every ethics tradition develops over years and in response to historical, economic, and political exigencies, going through numerous changes to accommodate new realities.

Based on all this, there is no evidence that Nezami unequivocally believed in a religious metaethics system, nor is there any evidence that he tried to extract his ethics from religion. Many of those who believed in such systems often presented their ideas in casuistry verses. Nezami, as I have said, is preoccupied with Sakhon or the art of literature as elocutions or as perlocutionary acts. Here, I argue that Nezami was not a utilitarian, deontologist, or ethicist. I further argue that for Nezami, among other factors, it was his commitment, or if you will, his contract with his art, that shaped his principles and his ethical system. From there, he developed numerous progressive positions on a variety of social and literary issues, including such seminal concepts as love, the treatment of women, justice, peace, and a sort of religious tolerance. This contention is based on my readings of numerous verses in which Nezami contemplates the art of poetry, its comparison to prose, its untranslatability, and the poets' essential qualities, such as creativity and studiousness, promptness, honesty, and respect for others developed through contact in part with regal courts, in which he likely witnessed much of the good and bad of humanity. This argument developed from contemplating his subjects, which leads me to conclude that Nezami's ethics stem from his professionalism and commitment to the art of words. To be more precise, I surmise that the integrity with which he focused on his métier, which was also highly personal to him, contributed to a set of ethical and moral principles that reversely governed the way he conducted his literary activity and his relationship with people in his life and his audience. He applies his honor to the treatment of his theme and subjects as well. That is, his so-called contract is neither with others nor with family; neither with the economy nor with necessities, neither social nor psychological. His convention is shaped in relation to his work, his métier. And his craft to him does not hold any absolute truth either as he clearly states in *Layli o Majnun* that:

Do not try to figure out poetry and its arts because the best one is the one that lies.	در شعر مپیچ و در فنّ او چون اکذب اوست احسن او[13]

Clearly, the word *akzab*, lie, refers to the imaginative nature of poetry and its symbolic quality. Isn't then the presentation of all themes and subjects, including religion, the artful form of imagination? That is, the truth for Nezami or many other past poets might be in the very essence of their art or their work. It is nevertheless safe to assume that diligent poets had a great sense of what "hard work" entailed.

To explain the connection between Nezami's ethics and his profession and to conclude the connection between all aspects of his work and his life, I will juxtapose my findings under several headings. I start with the concepts that are more often considered the basis of the poet's drive in his activities. The answer might indeed be found in this juxtaposition and, more importantly, in how he dealt with words and ethical issues.

Before going further, however, I have to justify my use of verses in which a character and not the poet himself is speaking. After all, there are several places where a character is not saying something desirable or in accordance with the poet's overall belief system, an issue that, despite its simplicity, has not been resolved when it comes to judging the poet. I am aware of this problem, and my justification in using them is that when Nezami inserts his voice in those cases, he often sides with his protagonists and heroes, and when he is talking outside his narrative, he does not offer any contradiction.

The portrayal of lovemaking scenes, genitalia, wine drinking, good and evil dichotomy (as in the story of "khyr va sharr" in *Haft Paykar*) helps bring us to the conclusion that Nezami's expressions of the ethical issues are highly influenced by the literary exigencies, the needs of the logic of the narrative, the force behind his literary characterization. Such portrayals are frequent, and in the end, the practice itself becomes the source of his ethics system.

More importantly, in terms of literary creativity and his portrayal of characters and concepts, Nezami relies overwhelmingly on allegories (*tamsil*), comparison technic (*tashbih*), and metonymy (*badi'*, *degargui*). One may argue that many poets use these techniques. True. However, in Nezami's case, almost all utterances are brilliantly constructed through these devices or through a combination of several of them, often blurring their distinctions. He also uses lesser-known figures of speech such as a concept similar to salb and *ijab* (سلب و ایجاب). In jurisprudence, *salb* can mean negation or "to strip away" something, and *ijab* is to affirm something (or to render an act/edict obligatory or binding). In a poetic context, the poet/narrator might negate/reject a possibility from one perspective and then affirm/request it from another angle. In his *Layli o Majnun*, Nezami offers such constructs. In one of the verses of *Layli and Majnun*, Salam goes to Majnun and tries to befriend him. Majnun is not moved by what he hears from him; however, he moves physically from his spot to answer Salaam.[14]

| Nothing that he had heard moved him, | مجنون ز حدیث آن نکورای |
| but he moved to stand up (to say something). | از جای نشد ولی شد از جای |

Nezami's exaggerated play with colors and shapes and timing of the zodiac and constellations is also unique among the Persian poets. Sometimes he comes close to using Adynaton, a technique rooted in Greek tradition, denoting a rhetorical device, a form of hyperbole. In it, exaggeration is taken to a seemingly impossible extent. In those moments in Nezami's poetry, a reader might stop thinking about the meaning and appreciate the pictorial allegories. The broader point here is that his style of allegory or his version of *tamsil* only shows a minor difference compared to metonymy. In his *tashbih*, the comparisons and similes are imagined. For example, he compares the lips of a beloved or the words of a sage to sugar. Nezami ignores this subtle difference and combines the two, thus creating a particular type of *balaghat* (eloquence) and *badi'* (rhetoric). The reason for this re-designation is that often the words that indicate the similarity of the compared elements or the two levels of his allegory are chosen with care, almost certainly taking a substantial amount of time to select. These are the reasons and the features that allow the conceptualization of this poetic process as the creation of *Nezamian pictorial allegory* as a mini allegory, if you will, in which an object or a concept is equated with the meanings that exist outside the narrative, causing *Ebham* (ambiguity) and *iham* (double meaning, polysemy). In that sense, the Nezamian pictorial allegory is only somewhat longer and more extended than a simile, metaphor, or metonym. In that sense, I can expand on the definition of the pictorial allegory as a construct with two meanings, a figurative meaning and another or secondary figurative meaning, which together tell a little story as part of a bigger story. It was possible to see this mechanization in a textual and discursive review of the themes already discussed or in the subsequent samples. Some of these allegories might deceptively seem to critics as Nezami's source of ethics and religiosity, particularly to those who limit their analysis to a structuralist or ideological reading.

As shown in previous pages, Nezami is perhaps the only poet who has written extensively on literary terms, theory, and criticism, within his poetry. In addition, numerous verses describe or entertain the concepts such as *qasideh, ghazal, badi', tanz, bayt, she'r, sha'er, soften, naghz*, and even *zibanevesi* (writing beautifully): concepts that were discussed as elements of his Sakhon and allegorical constructions.

SELF-REPRESENTATION

Relevant to the topic of conduct is the issue of self-representation. Poets often talk about themselves in the introductory sections and the conclusions to their poems. As mentioned, Nezami writes a concise chronology of his life and the death of his wives in *Iskandarnameh*. (He discusses wives or just one?) Authoring stories, he says, is pleasurable, although sometimes difficult, and can ease his sorrow.[15] Self-representation is an aspect of his literary practice and is more than a mere reference, a *takalos*, or a nom de plume. His self-representation is also often part of the creative process and, as usual, also presented through allegory. In *Eqbalnameh* he writes:

Prancing, entered a jasmine chested	درآمد خرامان سمن سینه‌ای
she gave me in the mirror, a razor-blade.	به من داد تیغی در آینه‌ای
Don't be so worried about yourself	که آشفتهٔ خویش چندین مباش
see yourself but don't be selfish.	ببین خویشتن خویشتن بین مباش
As I looked close in the mirror	نظر چون در آینه انداختم
I recognized my face with no error.	در او صورت خویش بشناختم[16]

The metaphors of jasmine chested, blade, and mirror all allegorically serve the illustration of a moment of self-realization. Similarly, in *Khosrow o Shirin*, he writes:

When you read this book of poetry	نظامی نیز کاین منظومه خوانی
you will see Nezami in it clearly.	حضورش در سخن یابی عیانی
No secret to this art, just consummate splendor	نهان کی باشد از تو جلوه‌سازی
which tells you a hundred secrets in each line	که در هر بیت گوید با تو رازی[17]
In a hundred years, if you ask, he is where?	پس از صد سال اگر گوئی کجا او
each verse shouts back to you: he is there.	"زهر بیتی ندا خیزد که: "ها، او

As mentioned, Nezami constantly obliterates the separation between the poet (himself) and the poems (his work). Yet, behind the allegories, the expressions lead directly to a parallel, succinct autobiographical narrative that focuses on his practice. At times, he is open about this parallel: "It is profitable to utter speech, at that time--When, from the uttering of it, reputation becomes lofty."/"Of so many eloquent ones (ancient poets)—remember this (my) speech-- I am the remembrancer of (their) speech in the world."/"Save that, with speech, I should chant the rose (utter a modulated melody)-- Should express, over that rose, a (joyous) cry like a nightingale."[18] In brief, it suffices here to say that hardly anywhere else has anyone offered such a combination of allegory and similitude for self-representation. This area of his work thus conveys truths about his approach to life, work, and ethics.

DISCURSIVE FIELD: THE POET AND HIS POEMS

I maintain elsewhere that the term Sakhon in Nezami's work is synony-mous with "literature," "literary work," and "poetry."[19] Comparing the Nezamian concept of Sakhon with the use of the word in the works of Rumi (d. 1273), Sa'di (d. 1291), and Hafez (d. 1389/90), who have also used the word frequently, I find that for these latter poets, Sakhon is closer to its contemporary usage, meaning "parole," "speech," or "talk," or sim-ply *harf*. Here, I would like to think that Sakhon is indeed also directly tied to Nezami's ethics system. In Sakhon, all thoughts, ideas, motifs, advice, and principles come together for the sake of nothing but Sakhon itself. If the source of ethics were outside of his art, he would not have represented so many different themes, including scientific, philosophical, romantic, and religious motifs to different ends. Poets with a metaethical system are consistently focused on a specific theme and/or message.

Nezami's description of the literary field in which his works take shape illustrates his preoccupation with thematic varieties, with his messages, but ultimately with his profession. In *Haft Paykar*, he writes:

I sought books, hidden all over	بازجستم ز نامه‌های نهان
they were scattered around, the world over.	که پراکنده بود گرد جهان
From Arabic and Persian books	زان سخنها که تازی است و دری
in the Bukhara or Tabari areas	در سواد بخاری و طبری
Pages that I touched with my fingers	هر ورق کاوفتاد در دستم
were soon bundled in folders.	همه در خریطه‌ای بستم
When I penned my gathered knowledge	چون از آن جمله در سواد قلم
the best of my poems emerged.	گشت سر جمله ام گزیده، بهم [20]

This notion or commitment regarding thematic variations versified above is repeated throughout his collection.[21] Reading the related poems indicates an elevated level of self-consciousness about coherency between the theme, knowledge, and the poetic outcome, which he believes consti-tutes the desirability of the poem. He is indeed outspoken about how to write poetry and why, and I sense he would have been offended to see a reader dismissing his informed imagination by imposing a religious ideol-ogy on his output and intent.

LITERARY PRODUCTION, LITERARINESS OF WORK, AND CREATIVITY

This passion for Sakhon, for words, this adroitness in rhetoric, runs through Nezami's diverse poetic utterances like an ornamental chain, connecting them all intertextually and stylistically. No other ideological or social view plays such a constitutive role. This understanding of the role of the art of writing for the poet explains the appearance of so many compound and derivative forms of the word Sakhon such as *sakhundan* or *sakhunvar*, and *Sakhonsanj*, meaning a person who demonstrates an oratorical, eloquent, and poetic manner when writing or speaking and a person who can appreciate and judge such writings. Even here, we find evidence that his literary approach is only aesthetic or playful and only ethical in terms of the poet's responsibility vis-à-vis poetic output and its readers. Some of the lines below are expressed on behalf of his characters in the introduction or the text of his poetic narratives; however, they speak to the poet's specific view of his art in *Haft Paykar, Layli o Majnun, Sharafnameh*, and *Makhzan al-Asrar.*[22]

I endeavored to have in my composition	هم کردم که در چنین ترکیب
an extraordinary arrangement of depiction.	باشد آرایشی ز نقش غریب
I am a wordsmith, you know that	دانی که من از آن سخن شناسم
the old from new verse, I can tell that.	کهنات نو، از کهن، شناسم
The benefits of your poetry shall commence	سخن گفتن آنگه بود سودمند
if they bring you prominence.	که آن گفتن آوازه گردد بلند
From no one, have I borrowed	عاریت کس نپذیرفتهام
I have said only what my heart dictated.	آنچه دلم گفت بگو گفتهام
I erected a magic work as norm	شعبده تازه برانگیختم
I built a shape out of new form.	هیکلی از قالب نو ریختم

Thus, one message that stands out in the Nezami's themes on poetic activities is that "a poet must do hard work in order to produce fine work."[23] This contrasts with the mystic poetic efforts in which the emphasis is on hard work to understand the divine but where words of praise flow easily. Moreover, he often describes extensively the processes of choosing the themes and the rhymes for his work, which reveal an emphasis on form rather than content and message.[24] Even in talking about the "divine" narrative of creation, he does not fail to explore allegorical limits. *Makhzan al-Asrar* is a sublime example of how he expands imaginatively on a religious metaphorical construct.

MÉTIER AND ETHICS

Nezami explains how he engages in hard work and how he gets results, adding elements to the description of what might be considered his métier or his profession as a Sakhon writer and romancer. The description of his work habits brings some of the previous segments together in a systematic way. Let us see what the poems about Nezami's way of working tell us in some of his verses from *Kheradnameh*, *Makhzan al-Asrar*, *Khosrow o Shirin*, *Iqbalnameh*, and *Haft Paykar*.[25]

At dawn, when I was awoken	سحرگه که سربرگرفتم ز خواب
my face, like the sun beaming, vast open.	برافروختم چهره، چون آفتاب
If poetry is far from pleasantry	هر مخفی کرادیش دوری است
examine, revise, it is necessary.	دست بر او مال، که دستوری است
I would cross out and delete	آنچه به از علم بر آرد علم
that which of science is deplete.	گر منم آن حرف، در او کنش، رقم
From the nightly sleeplessness, I am drunk	من از ناخفتن شب، مست مانده
my pen like a sword in my hand, still drawn.	چو شمشیر قلم در دست مانده
As thoughts overcame me, like a storm thunder	چو طوفان اندیشه رام گرفت
night fell on the threshold of my chamber.	شب آمد، در خوابگاهم گرفت
That night, sleepless, hungry, feeling exhausted	من آن شب تهی مانده از خواب و خورد
In that azure sky, I felt fallen and floated.	شناور در این برکه لاجورد
Enough! oh magician, word weaver, poet	بس کن ای جادوی سخن پیوند
why repeat the same old, same old, so frequent?	سخن رفته چند گویی، چند
As far as I can tell, just like the spring breeze	تا توام، چو باد نوروزی
I will avoid repeating old creeds.	نکم دعوی کهن دوزی

These lines indicate a strong sense of self-awareness regarding the poetic process. The constitutive motif and theme offered in these lines also surface in Nezami's other poems. Conversely, such a theme, such deliberate literary mindfulness, does not appear with such frequency and intensity in the works of other classical or, for that matter, even contemporary poets. That in itself is telling. This self-awareness turned into self-consciousness in his introduction to *Layli o Majnun*. It was the only book Nezami crafted on command/request (from Shervanshah), and he was worried that the lack of a rich context and the simplicity of the story of an Arab boy in a distant desert area would prevent him from creating a readable poem.[26] Thanks to his son's encouragement, he started the work, and it is safe to say that he must have worked hard to be able to produce his masterpiece narrative poem of nearly 4700 lines in just four months. The anecdote, the product, and the process all speak to the poet's main preoccupation, namely his métier.

Also telling is that on one of the occasions where Hafez talks about his artistic ability in poetry, he measures himself against Nezami.[27]

My poems resemble pearls woven in string	چو سلک در خوشاب است شعر نغز تو حافظ
in tenderness, they surpass Nezami's poetry.	که گاه لطف سبق می برد ز نظم نظامی

Assuming that Hafez is correct in his boasting, we should also assume that there is no one better than Hafez to acknowledge Nezami's passionate, poetic professionalism.

NEZAMI'S MÉTIER AND HIS READERS

The reason for Nezami's remarkable preoccupation with quality is also related to his apprehension about the reception of his work. Through numerous utterances, in works such as *Sharafnameh* and *Haft Paykar*, the poet enters a literary, aesthetic, and professional covenant with his readers, be they patrons, peers, or the assumed ordinary readers.[28]

I possess many valuable wares	متاع گران مایه، دارم بسی
I hide them unless someone cares.	نیارم برون، تا نخواهد کسی
A pearl buyer seeing a closed case	خریدار در چون صدف دیده دوخت
will not buy anything in such dull state.	بدین کاسدی در نشاید فروخت
With such endeared pearl which I have	مرا با چنین گوهری ارجمند
a pearl admirer is what I need to have.	همی حاجت آید به گوهر پسند
If you ought by virtue of a new dictation	وگر بایدت تا به حکم نوی
to hear from me a new insinuation.	دگرگونه رمزی ز من بشنوی
Remove obstacles, open your ear	بر آن کن پنبه ها را ز گوش
so hear new garments renew the threadbare.	که دیبای نو را کند ژنده پوش
I wrote accounts worthy of tribute	گفتش گفتنی که پسندند
not for percipient readers to ridicule.	به که خود زیرکان بر او خندند

Indeed, Nezami's consciousness of his readers provides an opportunity for contemplating the classical understanding of such concepts as reader response, the role of the author, and the continuity of textual life. In the above lines, Nezami is concerned with his readers and his critics. Who were they in his eyes? Like many other poets, Khaqani, his contemporary, praises Nezami in one of his *Manshe'at* books. Did Nezami think about

Khaqani while writing? Yes, both talked about each other. However, whether Nezami gave much thought to Khaqani or not, many of his poems indicate that he was concerned with the future, with the broader issue of the imperishability of his work among the work or past, present, and future wordsmiths.

More on Nezami's Literary Discourse and Devices

The juxtaposition of these fundamental elements of Nezami's dictions, as illustrated in his various thematic diversity, including romance, religion, and philosophy, is expressed from his characters' mouths or on his behalf. This leads us to imagine his character as coherent and conscious and follows a systematic approach to literature and his work. Nezami's approach to aesthetics and his views of the characteristics of good poetry are all related to the qualities necessary to be a responsible poet, be aware of his peers' works, and finally be sensitive to social matters. The awareness about these qualities allows him to refer to himself, albeit in other people's tongue, as a mirror or a seer:[29]

In the magic of poetry, I am so complete and invincible	در سحر سخن چنان تمام
that I have been named the mirror of the invisible.	کاینه غیب گشت نام

This couplet and many more render the notion of his métier and do not feature philosophical thoughts or the essentiality or particularity of any single worldview. If he did preoccupy himself with religion, he would have belonged to a different discourse, such as the one presented by poets like Khaqani or Sana'i. On the contrary, he often takes pride in the authenticity and nobility of his woven words regardless of the message. He composed each of his narrative poems in a distinctive style. His *Divan* too shows similar literary concerns.

To connect all these argumentations and thoughts about the nature of Nezami's poetry and the source of his ethics, I categorize his frequent or significant thematic concepts into three general groups indicating the techniques with which he presents them.

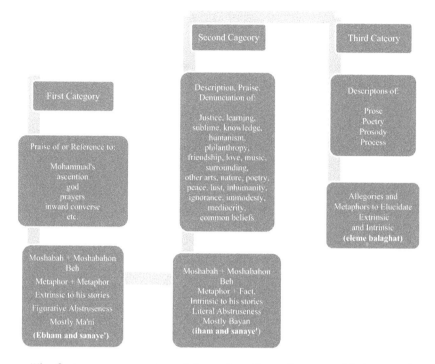

The first category consists of the praise of or reference to Mohammad's ascension, God's prayers, inward conversation, and similar themes. This category is often based on the model of *Moshabah* plus *Moshabahon Beh* (metaphor + metaphor) and is often extrinsic to his stories and present figurative abstruseness. They are mostly *ma'ni* and *bayan* (*Ebham* and *sanaye'*).

The second category consists of descriptions or praise of justice, learning, sublime, knowledge, humanism, philanthropy, friendship, love, music, surroundings, other arts, nature, poetry, peace, or in some cases the denunciation of lust, inhumanity, ignorance, immodesty, mediocrity, and shared beliefs. These parts are often based on *Moshabah* plus *Moshabahon Beh* constructs. They include metaphor plus facts, intrinsic to his stories and literal abstruseness.

The third category consists of descriptions of prose, poetry, prosody, and literary processes. These are written in allegories and metaphors to elucidate extrinsic and intrinsic rhetoric elements (*elem-e balaghat*).

All of Nezami's themes and motifs can be divided into three categories that are distinguished by their predominant features: *Ebham* (ambiguity, imprecision), *iham* (multiplicity of meanings), and *balaghat* (rhetoric, eloquence).[30] Some of the motifs (the first category) are not intrinsic to his narrative even though stories are at the core of the bulk of his output; those motifs appear in the introductions and consist of metaphors and metonyms about allegorical concepts. They include *moshabehon beh* and only occasionally *moshabeh* but hardly any *vajeheh tashbih*, for example because there is no reasoning or logic for the comparison or simile. The second category is often located in the core of his stories and consists of metaphors and concrete, descriptive terminology about real or tangible human issues. Here we see *moshabehon beh, moshabah*, as well as *vajhe tashbih*. Here, there is a tangible reason and logic behind the construct.

In the third category, Nezami talks about himself as a poet, his poetry, his views of literary activities, and his literary theory. These are not intrinsic to the stories, but they have an intrinsic effect on his art, his Sakhon writing, his romancing, and his métier. That is, he writes his poetry according to his system of rhetoric, his *elem-e belaghat*. His commitment to the latter category, which also affects the first two categories, constitutes his integrity and ethical approach to his work based on which he feels responsible primarily to the literary communities of his time and beyond.

If we take a step further and look at the topics and subject matter from another perspective, we can illustrate the third category as an overarching and organizing factor, thus indicating the source of the poet's work ethics and morality system. Moreover, Nezami's professional approach to literature, his métier, and not his religious beliefs can explain his creativity and his manipulation of historical and religious sources.

Motifs	Themes	Genres	Devotion/E thics
•Symbolic •Natural •Unlikely •Cosmic •Mental •Mystical •Scientific •Superstition •Etc.	•Peace •Love •Sentiments •Devotion •Goodness •Admonitory •Relationship •Etc.	•Religion •Romance •Philosophy •Epic •Subgenres •Etc.	•Iham •Ebham •balaghat • Allegory •Sublime Métier

Such catalogues of motifs are used by many poets and the way they decide how to juxtapose their metaphorical items is based on what is called *tanasob* (suitable and proportional matching of two consecutive words/ metaphors paired in one verse) or *mora'at-e nazir* (suitable and proportional matching three or more juxtaposed words/metaphors in a verse). His motifs include the symbolic, natural, unlikely, cosmic, mental, mystical, scientific, superstition cases, and concepts that come together sometimes in highly unlikely depictions. For example, compare Sa'di's famous verse (ابر و باد و مه و خورشید و فلک در کارند), in which the words cloud, moon, and sky from the same category are used in a tangible sense with Nezami's use of same words in an extremely imaginative style in a verse from *Layli o Majnun* and another from *Khosrow o Shirin*:

از کوی زمین چو بگذری باز / ابر و فلک است در یک و تاز

چو ابر از پیش روی ماه برخاست / شکیب شاه نیز از راه برخاست

Prominent themes are peace, love, sentiments, devotion, goodness, admonitory, relationship, and so on. The genres include religion, romance, philosophy, epic, and subgenres. Again, literary devices such as his type of *Ebham* (ambiguity) and *iham* (double meaning, polysemy), and most of all *jenas* (play on words, pun), mentioned above are indicative of his genuine devotion. Nezamian pictorial allegory is only somewhat longer and more extended than a simile, metaphor, or metonym and is often an expression with two meanings, literal and figurative, and with only a hint to an absent story.

Thus, his books have a somewhat similar structure. Each consists of introductory parts and the main text/story divided into segments and parts, and each segment or part includes several pictorial allegories. Each includes all the elements of classic narrative poetry stories, sources, ideas, verbal images, meanings, fluency of language, rhythm, rhyme, meter, and many techniques to represent as artistically and gloriously as possible the account or the celebration of events and deeds.

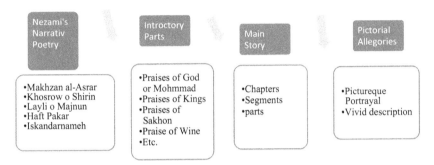

Again, Nezami compacts all these features within the framework of the preset classical prosody, which at one point were organized in a brief statement known as "the five Ms" by Shams Qays Razi in his book *Al-Mu'jam fi Ma'a'ir Ash'ar alAjam.*[31] He is nevertheless a pioneer in the use of the various Persian poetic meters, such as the one below, which indicates the juxtaposition of short and long syllables.

$$ \_ | \_ | u | u | \_ | u | \_ | u | \_ | \_ / \quad \_ | \_ | u | u | \_ | u | \_ | u | \_ | \_ $$

No matter what meter he uses, he often adds three musical sounds to his verse: one by the internal sound of the words, one by the association and combination of the words, and one created by the rhyming words. This study of this aspect of Nezami's poetry has a long history going back to just a century after the poet; however, few contemporary analyses exist.[32] This and previous chapters offered ample examples of verses that contain features of rhyme, rhythm, and musicality, but there is a need for further studies of Nezami's versification and use of prosody and his laborious, creative word choice that match the music, the mood, and the mentality of characters, as we all read the description of the main event. For example, he might use the alliteration sound of sh in words such as *Shab* (night), *Shir* (lion), *Sharab* (wine), *Shabdiz* (dark), *Shaban* (shepherd), *Roshan* (bright), or a compound form of some these words such as,

Shabikhun (raid), *Shabafruz* (floodlight used for stars and the moon) as well as the names of stars and planets such as *Moshtari*, *Khorshid*, to find the best rhyming word or series of words that not only can fit the prosody pattern of the piece, but also can help construct the pictorial allegory. At the same time, he might use any word with two or more meanings or replace another concept. *Shab*, for example, might be the actual *shab* in the first half of a verse and disappointment and sadness in the second. This musicality and tone in Nezami's versification encourages reading, and the joy of reading his work comes close to the sensation and expectation one might experience reading the extraordinary, august *Shahnameh*.

Except for the length of his verses (and the obvious references to the pre-Islamic concepts and philosophy), I do not see any evidence that Nezami was inspired by the form of pre-Islamic Persian syllabic poem. In his poetry, the classical rhyme tradition developed during the Islamic period plays an essential and influential role in his rhyming scheme both phonetically and semantically. Nevertheless, the music, rhyme, and rhythm match the characters' descriptions and activities, which are often based on a pre-Islamic understanding of social norms and divisions. In addition to the SH sound, he also uses R and M sounds often. In terms of verbs, he plays with those that end with an R and AND. The point here is that he looks at the masnavi prosody style simply as a form, and he intends to perfect it. However, for some reason (perhaps because Rumi wrote a renowned masnavi), the couplet form has also become associated with mysticism (and yes, there are articles about *erfan* in the *Shahnameh*).[33]

There are no other credible documents besides these poems discussing or listing Nezami's ethical practices or morality. In the above and other poems of his *Five Treasures*, he promotes what might be a universal set of ethical and moral practices then and now: do not hurt others; do not give into rage, respect others; be independent; seek knowledge; face the consequences of your actions; be beneficial to your community; get along with your fellow humans; and be friendly. He frequently features his notion of justice, but the metaphors and similes for the concept become an allegorical theme in some sections. Many religions have tried to promote these qualities. All this is perhaps well summarized in the Avestan phrase, "Humata, Hukhta, Hvarshta," or the popular "good thoughts, good words and good deeds" dictum. The approach behind the advice and ethical edicts in *Minuye Kherad* (and a few relatively rare similar texts), which seems to have directly or indirectly informed Nezami's poems, emphasizes integrity, justice, and all sorts of good things and good deeds, all collectively conveying a system of ethics and morality. Dana, who travels the world searching for the truth, meeting all sorts of people, and experiencing all sorts of situations, comes to fruition when he finds *kherad* (reason, wisdom, and rationality). Nezami's literary journey from his *Makhzan al-Asrar* to *Kheradnameh* (the Book of Wisdom or Reason) also goes through numerous domains of humanity.[34]

A FEW FINAL THOUGHTS

Simply put, the essence and nobility of Nezami's literary endeavors are aesthetical and not ideological, and, therefore, the source of his ethics system and drive should be sought in his work and not his any type of advocacy. That is, as a man of letters who pursues a sublime métier, Nezami ends up with Sakhon as one of the most fundamental fixations of his life. I conceptualize this aspect of Nezami's character as his literary ethics or his artistic morality system and see them indeed as rooted in Nezami's commitment to his métier. To be sure, it is based on such ethics that he encourages poets, readers, and people, in general, to be highly responsible for their actions, activities, and expressions, and worries at the same time about his work as to whether or not he would be received by them. He encourages moderation in drinking, caution in making conclusions, and fairness in making a judgment. These qualities are more common among the literati than ideological advocates. This sense of responsibility and this aspiration for an affable response appear where he allegorically describes the metaphorical Buraq (the imaginary horse) when he encourages "peaceful speech," when he describes a beautiful lover, depicts the arrival of autumn, or when he constructs his Sakhon on wisdom, discourse, and madness to also stories with the meanings of such images. The source of information for him can be science, history, nature, or the religions of Islam and Zoroastrianism. In all this, he is indeed perfecting his métier, his preoccupation par excellence, that which requires professionalism, a system of ethics, and a systemic approach to art and life. Other famous poets might have adopted such a code of ethics around the high profession, but Nezami remains one of the few who conceptualized it inside their literary output. This complexity is part of his notion of Sakhon, which according to what was discussed, has a complex construct. To understand Nezam, his poetics, profession, and ethics, one has to traverse the limits of the structuralist and ideological readings, which often seek to find *the* hidden purpose, codes, and keys.

Finally, to recap everything, Nezamian pictorial allegories (many examples of which we saw in the chapters on Layli and Majnun, Story of Ascension, and Sublime Métier), like the *tamsils* in the works of other Persian poets, seem to rely heavily on metaphors, thus making the name of this literary device to some extent a misnomer. This ambiguity in the definitions created a long debate among medieval literary scholars (Mahshari, Ibn Asir, Jorjani). However, the allegories of poets such as Rumi, Hafez, and Sa'di, who employ ambiguity, often contain an underlying meaning and message. Hafez's allegory is short and concise; whereas the other two weave longer tales. Furthermore, *Kalil O Demneh* and *Manteq al-Tayr* are filled with allegorical parables serving a variety of functions. All this is somewhat different from the western medieval literature in which allegories often buttressed the genre of dream and apparition. The fluidity, flexibility, and diversity of the definition of the literary device of allegory allow me to conceptualize Nezami's metaphorical construct in terms of allegory with his unmissable use of literary devices as a means of rhetorical craft and as a wordsmith. Again, this conceptualization makes reading Nezamian pictorial allegory as religious or even philosophical parables impossible. Philosophical parables are best exemplified in the Biblical and the Koranic verses and speeches or in the case of Plato's presentation of the cave, all of which beg philosophical reading. In Nezamian pictorial allegory, the first layer requires interpretation to figure out his extra-textual references, the multiple meanings of words, the particular sound of specific terms. The more picturesque first layer or surface story can be distinguished by the subject and thematic materials and be categorized as astrological, astronomical, geological, natural, seasonal, philosophical, fictional, mystical, or verbal types (the last in cases the goal is to play with words and sounds). The second layer of meaning is obvious and always a "garden of eloquence" about the event, the people, the fundamental elements of the story.

For two reasons, his peculiar allegories do not call for an allegorical interpretation in traditional sense (allegoresis) or in a way we might approach Attar's *Elahi Nameh* or his metaphysics.[35] First, it is never clear how Nezami thought of his strategy of the allegorical composition to make assumptions about his personal belief. His work is only allegorical because of its unique form and not for hidden messages. Nezami's deliberate juxtaposition of images and complex and double-meaning expressions results in complex verses which at times requires the reader to pause and re-read. This complexity has encouraged critics to think that the poet has hidden a message in every problematic verse. To exemplify this quality one last time, I refer to the story of the war between Dara and Alexander in Iskandarnameh. The description of the context of the conflict, the miscalculations which lead to war, and the description of the battles all include natural elements and natural imagery. The allusions, similes, and metaphors are selected with care to convey specific meanings and effects. Here is one scene in which the war intensifies:

The two armies attacked, pismires and locusts collide	دو لشگر چو مور و ملخ تاختند
They waged war, a world size army on each side	نبردی جهان در جهان ساختند
With steel swords, solid arrows, and gore	به شمشیر پولاد و تیر خدنگ
They created a passage out of a narrow path	گذرگاه کردند بر مور تنگ
They began to sting like yellow bees	چو زنبور گیلی کشیدند نیش
They used arrowheads to wound the bees	به زنبوره زنبور کردند ریش

Again, these few lines require some thought and deliberation because words such as mur, zanbur, jahan have been used to imply different meanings and mental images, and terms such as *gili* or khadag convey different connotations. The challenge is however not related to a hidden message requiring hermeneutic interpretation. At the same time, Nezami's approach to the source, the history of Alexander and the Achaemenid kings, might very well indicate the change in the poet's thinking and approach to literature and aesthetic philosophy.

Second, the definition of allegory and function of allegorical interpretation should not indeed be conceived as a universal formula. Classical Persian poetry's content, context, and concerns have been varied. For Nezami, the Zoroastrian underlying logic, the portrayal of carnal love, the fictional construction of history all can be explained in literary terms and not because of a so-called Nezamian *ainos*.

Therefore, his literary allegory is based on his vision of the literary garden, both metaphorical and physical. This is despite the number of layers of meanings. The tropes of morality, justice, mystics, ethics, and religion are elements he uses to construct his Persian gardens, which are his allegories. These elements could be dominant as the trope of figurative representation, making some of the Nezamian utterances resemble what we understand as a contemporary tropism—the elements of his encompassing garden function as simile and metaphors for the earthly life. As an example, we learn plenty about Layli's hair and eyebrows by describing gardens and what it contains. However, the words *mu* (hair) and *abru* (eyebrows) are hardly used (and in some of those rare occasions where they are used, they convey other literal meanings).

As I mentioned in Chap. 2 on Sakhon, Nezami holds a higher status for poetry over prose. All the techniques mentioned above and devices serve poetry better. Nezami does not write prose, and his writing does not have any prose features; "poetry for the sake of poetry" is his guiding principle. It is taking a risk to say, but nowhere in his large amount of work has he ever mentioned any affiliation with any Sufi or mystic orders while many other Sufi poets did.

None of this should be surprising to students of Nezami's poetry. If we can but break away from the frameworks of the prevalent ideological readings, all these arguments will make clear sense. In a field as vast as classical Persian studies, analysts risk encountering counterexamples for every assumption they make about the metaphorical referencing. With this in mind, I included in my analysis numerous verses and passages that render religious themes as data that could have challenged my findings. Nevertheless, I acknowledge that for every religious/mystical designation that critics adduce, one can find exceptions and vice versa. In the mountain of loosely connected scholarship, which designates the classical text as the products of religious advocation, there lies a set of facts that point in other directions: facts related to principles of the field of literary theory, comparative literature studies, and facts from within the texts. In some cases, the opposite might be true.

The data and analyses in this book allow a broader conclusion. Form, genre, and discourse are more reliable analytical categories than Sufi sentiments for appreciating the sophistication of classical Persian poetry and understanding the shifts that have occurred in its more than a millennium history. We also need to think of classical literary history as the formation of dialogic genres influenced by a variety of shifting national and transnational discourses rather than a linear evolutionary process or, more imposing, as the product of a religious paradigm. Such an approach explains better the aspirational similarities of the early twentieth-century Persianist literary movement with what poets such as Rudaki and Ferdowsi and others aspired in the ninth and tenth centuries.

Aside from all the factual, textual, and historical analysis presented in the above pages, I want to add a more personal note here at the end of the book. I hear phrases such as "the joy of reading," "independence of the text," or "the changing meaning of texts" regularly. I frequently come across references to Roland Barthes' notion of the "Death of the Author," a concept that holds that an author's intentions, politics, and religion, should be the significant factors in interpreting their writing. Many scholars do not hesitate to apply such notions to analyzing highly ideological and political contemporary fictions. So, it is flabbergasting to see that the poetry of Nezami, who, compared to numerous other classical poets, has shown rationality and open mindedness is so extensively deprived of a modern, inspiring, and thought-provoking interpretation the way reading, reinventing (and cinematic production) of the works of western classical poets such as Shakespeare, Dante, and Homer have resulted in the expansion of our imagination and our horizon. What prevents the production of modern plays and films to be made based on the story of Khosrow and Shirin or Layli and Majnun? What is the reason that obscures the fact that writing poetry was an act of faith for Nezami? That writing faith was not the act of poetry? Can we all agree that as a poet, Nezami's job was to create beauty, whether by rendering beautiful subjects or creating new forms?

Thus, I strive for another broad conclusion. Contemporary literature, also referred to as modern, has the tendency or a large capacity to become inept and thus ephemeral. Writing in free verse or short and long prose forms aims at saying something socially significant, something extrinsic to the literature, requiring a minimal formalism but extensive social and discursive reading. Some classical masters also used their sophisticated forms to draw attention to extrinsic matters. To be accurate, some classical masters such as Rudaki or Jami with careful forms embedded external references; however, others such as Nezami or even Rumi and Hafez strove to present their forms as the mark of their achievement, references notwithstanding. For Nezami in particular, fitting sign and referent into one form was the challenge, the job. Going back to the distinction between two conceptual sets of religion and religious symbolism versus knowledge and literary metaphors that constitute the signs and references in one or another literary work as well as the hermeneutics versus semantic focuses that inform one or another reading of literary works, we can see that Nezami's form best reconciles with the internal meaning of his allegories, and not a metaphysical system. The fact that he seized lexicons and notions that were even unusual for his own time and the difficulty of dealing with this formalist complexity should not push us to the comfort of a reductive, ideological reading.

As we continue our studies to know better this incredibly talented and impactful Nezami, let us be open to his demonstrated strength in metaphor, allegory, and allusion to things both lighter and more profound than the subject that rests upon the surface. That is the way to acknowledge his sublime métier and to acknowledge his status as a Persian wordsmith living around writing above the limitations of religious moralizing and didacticism.

NOTES

1. Some of these classical literary devices and techniques are common in many languages, and the formalists paid a great deal of attention to them.
2. An interesting example of Jenas, which has several types, is this couplet:

آن قوم کیانی از کیانند / بر جای کیان نگر کیانند

The word *kian* (kings and who) is repeated four times, each time with different meanings or usage. The verse was used as an example in an article that discusses comparable topics. See Abdolreza Sayf and Sayed M. Reza Ghaybi "Bar-rasi va Tahlil Sakhtari She'r-e Nezami" in *Adab-e Farsi*, Spring 2009, 81–102. It presents an idea about Nezami's language that has been widely refuted.

3. This of course comes as a little surprise because as Aruzi Samarqani states, "Saljuq family were all poetry lovers." Nizami Samarqandi, *Chahar Maqaleh*, ed. M. Qazvini.

4. *Kolliayt* 85.

5. Scholars have described Nezami with similar adjective to *gushehgir*, such as *ozlat neshin* or *khaneq neshin*. See for example, the introduction in *Kolliyat*, Introduction by Sa'id Qanei, 126–127.

6. Similar constructs existed in the pre-Islamic poetry of Iranian languages in which the second layer was also personal. In the committed literature of the 1960s and 1970s, the second layers were political with a revolutionary message and thus had to remain somewhat ambiguous and deeply metaphorical.

7. *Kolliayt* 343.

8. Rumi has a single verse in a ghazal in his *Divan-e Shams*, which reads: My eyes look like River Jeyhun for crying/I wonder where my beloved is gone in this sea. It offers similar similes, but the sea is a river that is sometimes referred to with the word *darya (that river is also called Amu Darya)*, and the precious stone does not stand for the tears but rather for the beloved.

9. A league number of Nezami's scholars to the *A Key to the Treasure*: Priscilla Soucek and Muhammad Isa Waley, Ziva Vesel, Renate Würsch, Leili Anvar, Gabrielle van den Berg, Mario Casari, Patrick Franke, Angelo Michele Piemontese, Carlo Saccone, and Kamran Talattof. Many other authors have contributed to *The Interpretation of Nizami's Cultural Heritage in the Contemporary Period: Shared Past and Cultural Legacy*, ed. Rahilya Geybullayeva and Christine van Ruymbeke (NY: P.L., 2020).

10. See, Jane Mansbridge, *Beyond Self-Interest* (Chicago, UCP, 1990).

11. Lawrence Kohlberg, *The Meaning and Measurement of Moral Development* (Worcester: Clark UP, 1981).

12. Alasdair MacIntyre, *A Short History of Ethics* (New York: Routledge, 1998).

13. *Kolliyat*, 316 (14–15).

14. Elsewhere in the book, he directly uses the word *salb*, writes:

دستی سلب خلل ندیده / برد از پی آن سلب دریده

15. "Nizami's Unlikely Heroines: A Study of The Characterizations of Women in Classical Persian Literature," in The Poetry of Nizami Ganjavi:

Knowledge, Love, and Rhetoric, ed. K. Talattof and J. Clinton (New York: Palgrave Macmillan, 2000), 51–81, 63.
16. *Kolliyat*, 892 (lines 6–8).
17. *Kolliyat*, 286 (66–67).
18. Based on a translation by H. W. Clarke from Nizami (1881), 801–5. The lines begin with:

مض گفتن آنکه بود سودمند / کز آن گفتن آوازه گردد بلند

19. See, Kamran Talattof, "Nizāmī Ganjavi, the Wordsmith," in *A Key to the Treasure*. The Persian word for literature, *adabiyat*, comes from the word *adab*, which also connotes culture, proper behavior, politeness, pleasant demeanor. This is indeed how Persian literature has maintained a close affinity with Persian ethics. However, for Nezami, the concept of Sakhon also conveyed all those affinities. Through the Sakhon, the intended or unintended literary encounters could have focused on ethical self-ramification.
20. *Kolliyat*, 425–6 (27–32).
21. We can read many such verses in *Haft Paykar*. For example,

وز دگر نسخها پراکنده / هر دری در دفینی اکنده

22. *Kolliyat*, 425 (26); 306 (31); 602 (8); 15 (3–4). There is a debate about one of the lines from *Makhzan al-Asrar* that best illustrates my point about Nezami's play with words. He writes:

| Eat and wear those like lion and leopard | آن خور و آن پوش چو شیر و پلنگ |
| Those which you can grab every year. | کاوری آنرا همه ساله به چنگ |

The above translation might elucidate its meaning. Understanding or translating the poem in such a way is the appearance of the names of the two animals together, even though the word *shir* has multiple meanings. However, this literal translation or interpretation does not make sense. It gives rise to too many questions, and it remains vague. However, I believe it was B. Sarvatiyan who accidentally came across another meaning for the word *palang*; it is also a carpet or cloth made of the leaves of the bamboo plant. This meaning makes perfect sense.
23. We saw examples from *Makhzan al-Asrar* before. A related passage from *Layli o Majnun, Haft Paykar, and Sharafnameh* starts with:

خواهم که به یاد عشق مجنون / رائی سخنی چون درمکنون

24. Regarding the thought process that leads to the selection of themes, he pens a passage starting with:

مرا چون هاتف دل دید دمساز / بر آورد از روای همت آواز

And the passage about his own life and love experiences starts with:

مرا طالعی طرفه هست از سخن / که چون نو کنم داستان کنی

About the rhythm and prosody in *Layli o Majnun*, he begins with:

نخریست سبک ولی رونده / ماهیش نه مرده بلکه زنده

25. *Kolliyat*, 892 (1); 77 (10–11); 85 (9); 826–27 (23, 43); 454 (1, 6).
26. As he expresses these literary concerns, he shows concern in a thoughtful passage that begins with:

میدان سخن فراخ باید / تا طبع سواری نماید

27. *Divan-i Hafiz: Tashih-e P. N. Khanlari* (Tehran: Kharazmi, 1980), 469.
28. *Kolliyat*, 602 (13–15); 426 (32).
29. *Kolliyat*, 314 (6).
30. *Ebham* means unclear, double meaning, and is synonymous with *na roshani, zehan azad mikhahad*, Iham, do *pahlu*, and *yek lafz ba chand mani*.
31. The traits starting with letter *mim* include: *moratab* (organized), *ma'navi* (meaningful, moral, spiritual), *mozun* (rhythmic, musical), *motekarer* (frequent, numerous), *motesavi* (equal, referring to the meter), and *be-ham-manandeh* (rhymed).
32. For an article on the study of rhyme in Nezami's *Khosrow o Shirin* see, M. H. Sardaghi and Nahid Nasr Azadani, "Ghenaye Qafieh dar *Khosrow o Shirin*" in *Fonun-e Adabi*, 8, 1, 14, spring 2016, 119–132. However, Nezami has written about his careful process of allegorization in several places, including in his last book, where he says:

سحرگه که سربرگرفتم ز خواب / برافروختم چهره چون آفتاب
سرِ سخن برکشیدم بلند / پراکندم از دل بر آتش سپند

33. For another short study of symbolism in *Khosrow o Shirin*, see Jabbar Nasiri, "Namadshenasi-e Mafahim-e Shir va Anar dar Khosrow va Shirin-e Nezami" in *Fonun-e Adabi*, 12, 1, 30, Spring 2020, 105–116.
34. Ahmad Tafazoli, trans. *Minuye Kherad* (Tehran: Bonyad-e Farhang, 1975), 64–92.
35. For a discussion of this terminology, see M. Domaradzki, "The beginnings of Greek Allegoresis." *Classical World* 110, 3, 2017: 299–321.

REFERENCES

Abasabad, Yusef Ali. "Ta'mol-e Erfan Shenakhti dar Dastan-e Mahan," *Erfan-e Islami*, 13, 52, 2017, 109-124.

Abasi, Sakineh. "Barrasi Qeseh Mahan az *Haft Paykar*," *Nameh Parsi*, 10, 4, 2005.

Ahmed, Shahab, *What is Islam?: The Importance of Being Islamic* (Princeton: Princeton KUP, 2016).

Alaqih, Fatamah. "Sima-ye zan az didgah-i Nezami" in *Farhang* 10 (Fall 1992), 317-30.

Alighieri, Dante. *Divine Comedy* by Mark Musa (Bloomington: Indiana UP, 1996).

Allen, Terry. *Timurid Heart* (Wiesbaden: LRV, 1983).

Amuzgar, Zhaleh and A. Tafazoli, (eds). *Dinkard Panjom* (Tehran: Moin, 2007).

Ansari, Z. *Life, Times and Works of Amir Khusrau Dehlavi*, (New Delhi: Amir Khusrau Society, 1975).

Anvar, Leili. "The Hidden Pearls of Wisdom: Desire and Initiation in Laylī u Majnūn" in *A Key to the Treasure of Hakim Nizami*, ed. Johan Christoph Bürgel and Christine van Ruymbeke (Leiden: Leiden UP, 2011).

ARDA WIRAZ in *Encyclopedia Iranica*, Vol. II, Fasc. 4, 356-357.

Asefi, Tajmah. *Asman va Khak: Elahiyat-e She'r-e Farsi az Rudaki ta Attar* (Tehran: Nashr-Daneshgahi, 1997).

Ayati, Majid. *Dastane Khosrow va Shirin* (Tehran: Jibi, 1974).

Azadeh, R. *Zendegi va Hunar-e Nezami Ganja-i* (Baku, Baku Science Academy, 1979).

Azar, Amir. and Mahnaz Najafi "An Investigation of Nezami's Works Translated in the West," in *Journal of Natural and Social Sciences*, 2015; www.european-science.com, 4, 2, 260-272.

© The Author(s), under exclusive license to Springer Nature Switzerland AG 2022
K. Talattof, *Nezami Ganjavi and Classical Persian Literature*, Literatures and Cultures of the Islamic World, https://doi.org/10.1007/978-3-030-97990-4

Bacher, Wilhelm. *Nezami's Leben und Werke und der zweite Theil des Nezamishcen Alexanderbuches, mit persischen Texten als Anhang,* (Leipzig 1871).

Bakhtin, Mikkail. *The Dialogic Imagination,* ed. Michael Holquist, trans. Caryl Emerson and Michael Holquist (Austin: UTP, 1981).

Bakhtiyar, Pizhman. (ed.), *Makhzan al-Asrar-e Nezami,* (Tehran: Peygah, 1988).

Bashiri, Iraj. "A Brief Note on the Life of Manuchehri," http://www.angelfire.com/rnb/bashiri/Poets/Manuch.html.

Beelaert, Anna Livia. "Khaqani Shervani" in *Encyclopedia Iranica,* vol. XV, 5, 523-529.

Behruz, Zabihollah. "Taqvim va Tarish: Az Rasad Khaneh Zartosht ta Rasad-e Khayyam" in *Iran Kode,* 15.

Bekhrad, Joobin. "Ramblings of an Iranian Wino," *Reorient: Middle Eastern Arts and Culture Magazine* (September 13, 2016), file:///C:/ Users/talattof/ Desktop/ Ramblings%20of%20an%20Iranian%20Wino.html.

Bertel's, Evgenii Eduardovich. *Nizami i Fuzuli* (Nizami and Fuzuli). Vol. 4 of *Izbrannye Trudy.* (Moscow: Izd-vo vostochnoi literatury, 1962).

Bertel's, Evgenii. *Nizami: Tvorcheskii put' poeta* (The Creative Path of the Poet). (Moscow: Izd-vo Akademii nauk SSR, 1956).

Bouhdiba, Abdelwahab. *Sexuality in Islam* (London: Saqi, 1998).

Bowra, C. M. *Heroic Poetry* (London: St. Martin's Press, 1961).

Brookshaw, Dominic Parviz. "Lascivious Vines, Corrupted Virgins, and Crimes of Honor: Variations on the Wine Production Myth as Narrated in Early Persian Poetry," *Iranian Studies,* 47:1 (2013), 87–129.

Browne, E.G. *Literary History of Persia* (Cambridge: The UP, 1951-1956).

Balaÿ, Christophe, C. Kappler, and Z. Vesel. *Mélanges offerts à Charles-Henri de Fouchécour,* ed. (Tehran 1995).

Bürgel, Christoph. "Nizāmī's World Order" in *A Key to the Treasure of Hakim Nizami,* ed. Bürgel, Johan Christoph and Christine van Ruymbeke (Leiden: Leiden UP, 2011a), 17-52.

Bürgel, Christoph. "The Contest of the Two Philosophers in Nezamis First and Last Epics," *Yad-Nama* (Rome, 1991), 1:109-17.

Bürgel, Christoph. "The Idea of Non-Violence in the Epic Poetry of Nezami," *Edebiyat,* 9, 1 (1998): 61-84.

Bürgel, Christoph "The Romance" in E. Yarshater, *Persian Literature* (NY: Bibliotheca Persica, 1988), 161-79.

Bürgel, Christoph. "Nizāmī's World Order" in *A Key to the Treasure of Hakim Nizami,* ed. Johan Christoph Bürgel and Christine van Ruymbeke. (Leiden: Leiden University, 2011b).

Burgel, Christoph. "Occult Sciences in The Shahnameh;" in *The Poetry of Nizami Ganjavi: Knowledge, Love, and Rhetoric,* (New York: Palgrave Macmillan, 2000).

Casari, Mario. "Nizami's Cosmographic Vision and Alexander in Search of the Fountain of Life" in *A Key to the Treasure of Hakim Nizami,* ed. Johan Christoph Bürgel and Christine van Ruymbeke (Leiden: Leiden UP, 2011).

Chelkowski, Peter J. "Aya upra-yi turmdut-i Puchini Bar Asas-i Kushk-i Surkh-i Haft Paykar-i Nizami Ast?," in *Iran-Shinasi* 3, 4 (Winter 1991), 714-22.

Chelkowski, Peter J. ed. *Reza Ali Khazeni Memorial Lectures in Iranian Studies, V. 2,* (Salt Lake City: University of Utah, 2013).

Chelkowski, Peter. "Nizami: Master Dramatist," in E. Yarshater, *Persian Literature* (New York: Bibliotheca Persica, 1987), 190-213.

Clinton, Jerome W. *The Divan of Manuchihri Damghani: A Critical Study* (Minneapolis: Bibliotheca Islamica, 1972).

Clinton, Jerome. "A Comparison of Nizami's *Layli and Majnun* and Shakespeare's *Romeo and Juliet*" in *The Poetry of Nizami Ganjavi: Knowledge, Love, and Rhetoric,* edited, introduction, by K. Talattof and J. Clinton (New York: Palgrave Macmillan, 2000).

Cross, Cameron. "The Many Colors of Love in Niẓāmī's Haft Paykar: Beyond the Spectrum" in Interfaces 2, 2016, 52–96.

Dabashi, Hamid. "Harf-i Nakhostin: Mafhum-i Sokhan dar Nazd-i Hakim Nezami Ganjavi" *Iranshenasi* III, 4, (Winter 1992), 723-40.

Dabashi, Hamid. *The World of Persian Literary Humanism.* (Cambridge: Harvard University, 2012).

Daniel, Elton. *The Political and Social History of Khurasan Under Abbasid Rule* (Minneapolis: Bibliotheca Islamica, 1979).

Davidson, Olga M. *Poet and Hero in the Persian Book of Kings,* (Ithaca: Cornell UP, 1994).

Davis, Dick. *Borrowed Ware: Medieval Persian Epigrams* (Washington: Mage, 1997).

Davis, Dick. "On Not Translating Hafez," *New England Review,* 25 (2004), 1–2.

Davis, Dick. *Epic and Sedition: The Case of Ferdowsi's Shahnameh* (Fayetteville: University of Arkansas, 1992).

Davis, Hadland F. *Wisdom of the East: The Persian Mystics, Jami.* (London: John Murry, 1908).

de Blois, François. *Persian Literature: A Bio-bibliographical Survey Begun by the Late C. A. Storey,* (London: Royal Asiatic Society, 1994-1997).

de Bruijn, J. T. P. *Pearls of Meanings: Studies on Persian Art, Poetry, Sufism and History of Iranian Studies in Europe* (Leiden: Leiden UP, 2020).

Dehlavi, Amir Khosrow. *Layli o Majnun* (Tehran: Ketabchin, 1969).

d'Hubert, Thibaut and Alexandre Papas (ed.), *Jāmī in Regional Contexts: The Reception of ʿAbd al-Raḥmān Jāmī's Works in the Islamicate World* (Leiden: Brill, 2018).

Dustkhah, Jalil. *Avesta* (Tehran: Murvarid, 1983).

Ebtehaj, Hooshang. (Sayeh), "Saqinameh" in *Masnavi,* at Chekameh (https://xakameh.com/).

Elwell-Sutton, L.P. *The Persian Meters* (Cambridge: Cambridge UP, 1976).

Ferdowsi, Abolqasem, "Rostam va Sohrab," *Shahnameh,* edited by M. A. Furughi. (Tehran: Javidan, 19--.), 83-98.

Ferdowsi, Abolqasem. *The Tragedy of Sohrab and Rostam,* trans. Jerome Clinton, (Seattle: University of Washington Press, 1996).

Fragner, Bert G., Ralph Kauz, and Florian Schwarz (eds), *Wine Culture in Iran and Beyond* (Vienna: Austrian Academy of Sciences, 2014).

Franke, Patrick. "Drinking from the Water of Life -- Nizami, Khizr and the Symbolism of Poetical Inspiration in Later Persianate Literature" in *A Key to the Treasure of Hakim Nizami*, ed. Johan Christoph Bürgel and Christine van Ruymbeke (Leiden: Leiden UP, 2011).

Frye, Richard, "The New Persian Renaissance in Western Iran," in *Islamic Iran and Central Asia (7th-12th Centuries)* (London: Variorum Reprints, 1979).

Gabbay, Alyssa "Love Gone Wrong, Then Right Again: Male/Female Dynamics in the Bahrām Gūr-Slave Girl Story" Iranian Studies, December 2009, Vol. 42, No. 5, Special Issue: Love and Desire in Pre-Modern Persian Poetry And, pp. 677-692.

Geybullayeva, Rahilya and Christine van Ruymbeke *The Interpretation of Nizami's Cultural Heritage in the Contemporary Period*, ed. (Frankfurt: P. L., 2020).

Hafez, *The Divan of Hafez* by Reza Saberi (Oxford: UP of America, 2002)

Hafez, Divan-e Hafez, by Rahim Zulnur (Tehran: Zafar, 2006)

Halperin, David M. *How to Do the History of Homosexuality* (Chicago: UPS, 2002).

Hanaway, William. "Blood and Wine: Sacrifice and Celebration in Manuchihri's Wine Poetry," *Iran*, 26 (1988), 69–80.

Hood, Gwenyth. *Dante's Dream: A Jungian Psychoanalytical Approach* (Kalamazoo: Medieval Institute, 2021).

Idarechi, Ahmad. *Sha'iran-i Ham'asr-e Rudaki* (Tehran: Bunyad-e Afshar, 1992).

Islami-Nodushan, M. "Mardan va Zanan-i Shahnamah" in Nasir Hariri, ed. *Ferdowsi, Zan, va Terazhedi* (Babol: Kitabsara, 1986).

Jackson, Peter. (ed.). *The Cambridge History of Iran,* volume 6, *The Timurid and Safavid Periods* (Cambridge: Cambridge UP, 1986).

Jafari, Mohammad. *Hikmat, Irfan, va Akhlaq dar Shir-I Nezami Ganjavi* (Tehran: Kayhan, 1991).

Jami, Abd al-Rahman, *Masnavi-i Haft Awrang* (Tehran: Sa'di, 1972).

Jami, Abd al-Rahman. *Salaman va Absal,* trans. By Fitzgerald, (Tehran: Asatir, 1994).

Jokar, Manuchehr. "Molahezati dar Sakhtar-e Saqinameh," *Faslnameh Pazhuheshhay-e Adabi* (no. 12 and 13 summer and fall 2006), 99-121.

Khadivar, Hadi and Fatemeh Sharifi, "Eshterakate *Layli o Majnun*-e Jami va Nezami va Amir Khosrow Dehlavi" in *Majaleh-e Zaban va Adabiyat-e Farsi, Daneshgah-e Azad-e Fasa*, 1, 2, (2010), 37-56.

Khorasani, Ahmad and Tayebeh Golestani, "Tahlil va Naqd-e Dastan-e Mahan-e" in *Zaban va Adabiyat-e Farsi*, 33, summer 2014, 57-84.

Khoshkhu, Mansureh and Malek Farrokhzad, "Eshterakat-e *Layli o Majnun*-e Nezami va Jami" in *Andishe-ha-ye Adabi*, 4, 2013, 11, 164-175.

Kleinhenz, Christopher. "Dante and the Bible: Intertextual Approaches to the *Divine Comedy*" in *Italica*, Autumn, 1986, Vol. 63, No. 3 (Autumn, 1986), 225-236.

Kohlberg, Lawrence, *The Meaning and Measurement of Moral Development* (Worcester: Clark UP, 1981).

Korangy, Alireza. *Development of the Ghazal and Khāqānī's Contribution* (Wiesbaden: Harrassowitz Verlag, 2013).

Krotkoff, Georg. "Colour and Number in the *Haft Paykar*" in *Logos Islamikos: Studia Islamica*, ed. Roger M. Savory and Dionisius A. Agius (Toronto, Canada: Pontifical Institute of Mediaeval Studies, 1984).

Landau, Justine, Nasir al-Din Tusi and Poetic Imagination in the Arabic and Persian Philosophical Tradition," in A.A. Seyed-Gohrab, ed., *Metaphor and Imagery in Persian Poetry*, Brill (2011): 15-65.

Lange, Christian. *Paradise and Hell in Islamic Traditions* (Cambridge: Cambridge UP, 2016).

Lazard, G. "The Rise of the New Persian Language," in *Cambridge History of Iran*, vol. 4 (Cambridge: Cambridge UP, 1975), 595–632.

Le Goff, Jacque. *The Medieval Imagination*, trans. Arthur Goldhammer (Chicago: University of Chicago Press, 1988).

Lornejad, Siavash and Ali Doostzadeh, *On the Modern Politicization of the Persian Poet Nezami Ganjavi* (Yerevan: Caucasian Centre for Iranian Studies, 2012)

Losensky, Paul. "Saqi Nama," *Encyclopædia Iranica*, online edition, 2016, available at http://www.iranicaonline.org/articles/saqi-nama-book.

MacIntyre, Alasdair. *A Short History of Ethics* (NY: Routledge, 1998).

Macuch, Maria. "MĀDAYĀN Ī HAZĀR DĀDESTĀN," *Encyclopædia Iranica*, online edition, 2017, http://www.iranicaonline.org/articles/madayan-i-hazar-dadestan.

Maddi, Arjang. "Bar rasi-i suvar-i khiyal," *Farhang*, 10 (Fall 1992), 331-408.

Mahdavi Dameghani, Ahmad. "Aqayed-e Nezami dar Tohid va Safat-e Barita'ala" in *Iran Shenasi*, 3, 3, (fall 1991), 458-468.

Mahjouri, Mahmoud, Ebrahim Estaji, Abdollah Gholami, Zahra Mirnezhad "Andarzha-ye Minu-ye Kherad va Ta'sir-e an bar *Shahnameh*" in *Matn Shenasi*. 10, 3, 39, (Autumn 2018), 147-164.

Mansbridge, Jane J. *Beyond Self-Interest* (Chicago, UCP, 1990).

Manuchehri Damghani, *Divan-e Manuchehri*, (Tehran: Zavvar, 1968).

Mashhadi, M. and Esfandiari. "Tahlil-e Bonmayeh-haye Erfani Khosrow o Shirn" in *Pazhuheshnameh Erfan* 19, 2018, 162-183.

Matini, Jalal. "Azadigi va Tasahul-e Nezami Ganjavi," in *Iran-Shinasi*, 4, 1 (Spring 1992), 1-20.

McGovern, Patrick. "Iranian Wine at the 'Dawn of Viniculture,'" in *Wine Culture in Iran and Beyond*, eds. Bert G. Fragner, Ralph Kauz, Florian Schwarz (Vienna: Austrian Academy of Sciences, 2014), 11–12.

Meisami, Julie Scott. "Fitnah or Azadah? Nezami's Ethical Poetic," *Edebiyat*, N. S. volume 1, no. 2, 1989, 41-77.

Meisami, Julie Scott. "Kings and Lovers: Ethical Dimensions of Medieval Persian Romance," in *Edebiyat*. 1, 1, 1987a, 1–27.

Meisami, Julie Scott. "Poetic Microcosms: The Persian Qasida to the End of the Twelfth Century," eds. Stefan Sperl, Christopher Shackle, *Qasida Poetry in Islamic Asia and Africa* (Leiden: Brill, 1996),137–82.

Meisami, Julie Scott. "The Theme of the Journey in Nezami's *Haft Paykar*," *Edebiyat*, 4, 2 (1993)155-72.

Meisami, Julie Scott. *Medieval Persian Court Poetry* (Princeton, N.J.: Princeton UP, 1987b).

Meisami, Julie Scott. *Structure and Meaning in Medieval Arabic and Persian Poetry* (London: Routledge, 2003).

Merguerian, Gayane Karen and Afsaneh Najmabadi, "Zolaykha and Yusof: Whose Best Story?" *IJMES*, 29, 4 (November 1997), 485-508.

Minu-ye Kharad, translated from Pahlavi by Ahmad Tafazoli (Tehran: Bonyad-Farhang, 1975).

Moayyad, Heshmat. "Dar Medar-e Nezami: Naqdi bar Layli o Majnun" in *Iranshenani*, Fall 1992, no. 15, 548-522.

Moin, Mohammad. *Mazdyasna va Adab-e Farsi* (Tehran: Tehran UP, reprinted 2015) Moscati, Sabatino. *The Face of the Ancient Orient* (Chicago: Quadrangle Books, 1951)

Molé, Marijan. *Culte, mythe et cosmologie dans l'Iran ancien* (Paris: Presses universitaires de France, 1963).

Nafisi, Said. *Mohit-e zendegi va ahval va ash'ar-e Rudaki* (Tehran: Ibn-e Sina, 1962); 309–10.

Nasiri, Jabbar. "Namadshenasi-e Mafahim-e Shir va Anar dar Khosrow va Shirin-e Nezami" in *Fonun-e Adabi*, 12, 1, 30, (Spring 2020), 105-116.

Nezami Aruzi, *Chahar Maqaleh* (Four Discourses), translated by E.G. Browne in *Journal of The Royal Asiatic Society*, (July, October 1899).

Nezami Ganjavi, J. *Haft Paykar*, ed. Dastgirdi (Tehran: Ibn-Sina, 1955).

Nezami Ganjavi, J. *Kolliyat-e Hakim Nezami Ganjavi*, ed. Vahid Dastgerdi, Introduction by Sa'id Qanei (Tehran: Behzad, 1999).

Nezami Ganjavi, J. *Kolliyat-e Khamseh-i Hakim Nezami-i Ganjah-i*, ed. Dastgirdi, 4th ed. (Tehran: Amir Kabir, 1987).

Nezami Ganjavi, J. *Layli and Majnun* by Nezami Ganjavi, Dick Davis, trans. (Odenton, MD: Mage Publishers, 2020a).

Nezami Ganjavi, J. *Layli and Majnun*, trans., Dick Davis (Odenton, MD: Mage Publishers, 2020b).

Nezami Ganjavi, J. *Layli o Majnun*, ed. Behruz Sarvatiyan (Tehran: Tus, 1984a).

Nezami Ganjavi, J. *Makhzad al-Asrar*, ed. Behruz Sarvatiyan (Tehran: Tus, 1984b).

Nezami Ganjavi, *Khosrow va Shirin-e Nezami* edited by Barat Zanjani (Tehran: Daneshgah Tehran, 1997).

Nezami Ganjavi, *Laili va Majnun-e Nezami Ganjavi* ed. Barat Zanjani (Tehran: Danishga-e Tehran, 1990)

Nizami Ganjavi, *Laili and Majnun*: A Poem translated by James Atkinson (Allahabad: Panini office, 1915).

Nizami Ganjavi, *The Haft Paykar: A Medieval Persian Romance*, translated with an Introduction and Notes by Julie Scott Meisami (Oxford: Oxford UP, 1995).

Noorani, Yaseen. "Heterotopia and the Wine Poem in Early Islamic Culture," *IJMES*, 36:3 (August 2004), 345–66.

Orsatti, Paola. "Nationalistic Distortions and Modern Nationalisms," *Iranian Studies*, 48:4, (2015) 611-627.

Peterson, Joseph H. "The Book of Arda Viraf." www.avesta.org.

Plato, *The Laws* (London: Penguin Books, 2004), 649a.

Porshekuh, Said and Abasali Vafai, Barrasi Tatbiqi Me'rajih-haye Khamseh Nezami, *Pazhuhesh-haye Adabiyat*, 1, 2, 139, 23-51.

Purjavadi, Nasrollah. "Badeh," in *Encylopædia Islamica* at http://www.encyclo-paediaislamica. com/madkhal2.php?sid=122.

Qomshe'i, Sayed M. "Tasvir-e Me'raj dar Ash'ar-e Sana'i, Khaqani, va Nezami" in *Kayhan-e Farhangi*, (Isfand 2006), 245.

Radfar, Abol Qasem. *Ketab Shenasi Nezami Ganjavi* (Tehran: Motale'at Farhangi, 1992).

Rashid, Muhammad. "Eshq va Etiqad dar *Makhzan al-Asrar*," *Danishkadih-e Adabiyat-e Ferdowsi*, no. 88-9, (Spring 1990), 87.

Ritter, Helmut. Über *die Bildersprache Nezamis* (Berlin: De Gruyter, 2013).

Rubanovich, Julia. "In the Mood of Love: Love Romances in Medieval Persian Poetry and their Sources" in *Fictional Storytelling in the Medieval Eastern Mediterranean and Beyond* (Leiden: Brill, 2016), 67-94.

Rudaki, A. Jafar, *Divan-e Rudaki* (Tehran: Javan, 2001).

Rypka, Jan and Karl Jahn. *History of Iranian Literature* (Dordrecht: Reidel, 1968).

Safa, Zabihollah. *Tarikh-e Adabiyat dar Iran* (Tehran: Amir-Kabir, 1977).

Sai'idi Sirjani, Ali. *Sima-ye do zan*. (Tehran: NoAvaran, 1991).

Sanai, Abu-al-Majd. *Hadiqatu' l-haqiqat*, (enclosed garden of the truth) (Tehran: Hirmand, 1996).

Sarvat, Mansur. ed., *Majmu'ah-e Maqalat-e Kungreh Hakim Nizami* (Tabriz: 1993).

Sarvatiyan, Behruz. "Falak joz Eshq Mehrabi Nadarad," in *Adabestan* 18 (1991), 34-39.

Sarvatiyan, Behruz. *Aineh-ye Ghayb-e Nezami Ganjavi dar Masnavi-ye Makhzad al-Asrar* (Tehran: Sabzan, 2006).

Sarvatiyan, Behruz. ed. *Makhzan al-Asrar-e Nezami* (Tehran: Tus, 1984).

Sarvatiyan, Bihruz. *Sharafnamah-e Ganjah'i* (Tehran: Tus, 1989).

Sattari, Jalal. *Halat-e 'Eshq-e Majnun* (Tehran, 1988)

Seyed-Gohrab, Asghar A. "A Mystical Reading of Nizami's Use of Nature in the Haft Paykar" by in in *A Key to the Treasure of Hakim Nizami*, ed. Johan Christoph Bürgel and Christine van Ruymbeke (Leiden: Leiden UP, 2011).

Seyed-Gohrab, Asghar A. "Longing for Love: The Romance of Layla and Majnun" in *A Companion to World Literature*, ed. Ken Seigneurie (NY: John Wiley & Sons, Ltd. Published 2020), 861-872.

Seyed-Gohrab, Asghar A. "The Rose and the Wine: Dispute as a Literary Device in Classical Persian Literature," *Iranian Studies*, 47: 1 (2013), 69–85.

Seyed-Gohrab, Asghar A. in "Majnun's Image as a Serpent," in *The Poetry of Nizami Ganjavi: Knowledge, Love, and Rhetoric*, edited, introduction, and significant contributions by K. Talattof and J. Clinton (New York: Palgrave Macmillan, 2000).

Seyed-Gohrab, Asghar A. *Layli and Majnun: Love, Madness and Mystic Longing in Nizami's Epic Romance* (Leiden: Brill, 2003).

Seyed-Gohrab, Asghar A., "Corrections and Elaborations: A One-Night Stand in Narrations of Ferdowsi's Rostam and Sohrāb," in *Iranian Studies*, Vol. 48, No. 3, (2015).

Sprachman, Paul. "Le beau garcon sans merci: The Homoerotic Tale in Arabic and Persian" in J. W. Wright Jr. and Everett K. Rowson, *Homoeroticism in Classical Arabic Literature*. 192-209.

Sprachman, Paul. *Suppressed Persian: An Anthology of Forbidden Literature* (Costa Mesa: Mazda, 1995).

Stack, Shannon. *Heart: A Political and Social Study*, Ph.D. Dissertation, ULC, 1975.

Tabatabai, Sassan. "Rudaki, the Father of Persian Poetry: A Critical Translation, the Poetry of Rudaki," (PhD thesis, Boston University, 2000), 318–19.

Tafazzoli, Ahmad. "Dadestan-i Menog-i Xrad" in *Encyclopædia Iranica*, Vol. VI, Fasc. 5, 554-555.

Talattof, Kamran and J. Clinton *The Poetry of Nizami Ganjavi: Knowledge, Love, and Rhetoric*, (NY: Palgrave Macmillan, 2000).

Talattof, Kamran. "Nezami Ganjavi, the Wordsmith: The Concept of Sakhon in Classical Persian Poetry," in *A Key to the Treasure of Hakim Nizami*, ed. Johan Christoph Bürgel and Christine van Ruymbeke (Leiden: Leiden UP, 2011a).

Talattof, Kamran. "What Kind of Wine did Rudaki Desire?: Samanids' Search for Cultural and National Identity" In *Layered Heart: Essays on Persian Poetry*, ed. A.A. Seyed-Gohrab (Washington: Mage, 2018), 127-171.

Talattof, Kamran. *Modernity, Sexuality, and Ideology in Iran: The Life and Legacy of a Popular Female Artist* (Syracuse: Syracuse UP, 2011b).

Vafa'i, Abbasali. "Simaye Payambar Akram beh Onvan-e Ensan-e Kamel va Kamal-e Ensani dar Khamseh-e Nezami" *Matnshenasi Adab-e Farsi*, 6, 1, (Spring 2014), 1-24.

Vahid Dastgirdi, *Ganjinah-e Ganjavi*. (Tehran: Iran Sokhan, 1317).

van den Berg, Gabrielle. "Descriptions and Images -- Remarks on Gog and Magog in Nizāmī's Iskandar Nāma, Firdawsī's Shāh Nāma and Amīr Khusraw's Aʾīna-yi Iskandarī" in *A Key to the Treasure of Hakim Nizami*, ed. Johan Christoph Bürgel and Christine van Ruymbeke (Leiden: Leiden UP, 2011).

van Ruymbeke, Christine. "Nizami's Poetry versus Scientific Knowledge: The Case of the Pomegranate," in *The Poetry of Nizami Ganjavi*.

van Ruymbeke, Christine. "What is it that Khosrow learns from the Kalīla-Dimna stories?" in *A Key to the Treasure of Hakim Nizami*, ed. Johan Christoph Bürgel and Christine van Ruymbeke (Leiden: Leiden UP, 2011).

Vesel, Ziva. "Teucros in Nizāmī's *Haft Paykar*" by in *A Key to the Treasure of Hakim Nizami*, ed. Johan Christoph Bürgel and Christine van Ruymbeke (Leiden: Leiden UP, 2011).

Wilson, G. E. *The Haft Paykar* (The Seven Beauties) (London: Late Probsthain and Company, 1924).

Yarshater, Ehsan. "The Theme of Wine-Drinking and the Concept of the Beloved in Early Persian Poetry," *Studia Islamica*, 13 (1960), 43–53.

Yarshater, Ehsan. (ed.), *Persian Literature* (Albany: Biblio- theca Persica, 1988).

Yusufi, G.H. *Chishmih-yi rowshan* (Tehran: Ilmi, 1970).

Zarghani, Mehdi. *Tarikh-e Adabiyat-e Iran va Qalamrov-e Zaban-e Farsi* (Tehran: Fatemi, 2019a).

Zarghani, Mehdi, *Tarikh-e Badan dar Adabiyat* (Tehran: Sokhan, 2019b)

Zarrinkub, A. H. *Pir-e Ganjeh* (Tehran: Sokhn, 2001).

Zipoli, Riccardo. *Irreverent Persia: Invective, Satirical and Burlesque Poetry from the Origins to the Timurid Period (10th to 15th Centuries)* (Leiden UP, 2015).

Zolfaqari, Hasan. "Moqayeseh Chahar Ravayat-e *Layli o Majnun*," *Pazhuhesh-ha-ye Zaban va Adabiayt*, 1, (Spring 2009), 59-81.

INDEX[1]

[1] Note: Page numbers followed by 'n' refer to notes.

Brookshaw, Dominic Parviz, 138
Browne, E. G., 4, 7, 14n21, 50n97
Bürgel, Johan Christoph, 6, 10, 53,
    67, 71, 91, 98n11, 108, 117,
    226, 233n4

C
Casari, Mario, 133n2, 266n9
Chelkowski, Peter, 98n17,
    98n25, 101n70
Clinton, Jerome, 138
Cosmology, 117
Cross, Cameron, 98n24

D
Dabashi, Hamid, 13n8, 18,
    49n53, 72
Dabir-Siyaqi, M., 102n85
Damghani, Manuchehri, 168n3
Daniel, Elton, 221
Dastgerdi, H. V., ix, 9, 12n1, 14n15,
    101n69, 196, 198n9,
    199–200n41, 220, 234n7
Davidson, Olga M., 102n89
Davis, Dick, ix, 7, 50n102,
    100n46, 100n49, 136n52, 157,
    168n4, 198n7, 198n9,
    199n20, 199n34
Davis, Hadland F., 92
de Blois, François, 13n6
De Fouchécour, C.-H., 108, 112,
    117, 134n11
Dehlavi, Amir Khosrow, 40, 47n12,
    98n11, 126, 193–195
d'Hubert, Thibaut, 103n97
Dinkard VI, 226
Domaradzki, M., 268n35
Doostzadeh, Ali, 12n3
Dustkhah, Jalil, 73

E
Ebtehaj, Hooshang. (Sayeh), 140
Elwell-Sutton, L.P., 154
Epigram, 242

F
Farrokhzad, M. M., 99n31, 102n91
Ferdowsi, Abu al-Qasim, viii, 2, 3, 9,
    10, 13n8, 19, 39, 45, 47n12,
    53–97, 131, 150, 164, 171n46,
    216, 222, 223, 226, 236n39,
    236n43, 239, 264
    Shahnameh, 3, 6, 19, 56, 58, 59,
    78, 83, 84, 100n56, 102n85,
    102n91, 150, 164, 210, 216,
    236n39, 239, 260
Fitzgerald, Edward,
    103n103, 103n105
Fragner, Bert G., 169n14
Franke, Patrick, 266n9
Frye, Richard, 169n16

G
Genre, role of, vii
Geybullayeva, Rahilya, 266n9
Ghasemipour, Ghodrat, 98n16
Goethe, Johann Wolfgang, 6
Golestani, Tayebeh, 216
Gregory, Andrew, 134n6

H
Hafez, 13n8, 18, 20, 22, 23, 25–27,
    46, 47n12, 53, 60, 141, 142,
    146, 147, 149–152, 166,
    170n25, 172n61, 172n62,
    173n81, 229, 239, 251, 254,
    262, 265
    Divan, 38, 150, 255

Printed in the USA
CPSIA information can be obtained
at www.ICGtesting.com
LVHW011640161123
764105LV00006B/347